COMPETING KINGDOMS

Women, Mission, Nation,
and the American Protestant Empire, 1812–1960

Edited by
Barbara Reeves-Ellington, Kathryn Kish Sklar, and Connie A. Shemo

DUKE UNIVERSITY PRESS *Durham & London 2010*

Library of Congress Cataloging-in-Publication Data
appear on the last printed page of this book.

Duke University Press gratefully acknowledges the
support of the Dean of the School of Liberal Arts of Siena College for
providing funds toward the production of this book.

Competing Kingdoms

AMERICAN ENCOUNTERS/GLOBAL INTERACTIONS

A series edited by Gilbert M. Joseph and Emily S. Rosenberg

To our partners:
Richard Reeves-Ellington, Thomas Dublin, and William Fischer

This series aims to stimulate critical perspectives and fresh interpretive frameworks for scholarship on the history of the imposing global presence of the United States. Its primary concerns include the deployment and contestation of power, the construction and deconstruction of cultural and political borders, the fluid meanings of intercultural encounters, and the complex interplay between the global and the local. American Encounters seeks to strengthen dialogue and collaboration between historians of U.S. international relations and area studies specialists.

The series encourages scholarship based on multiarchival historical research. At the same time, it supports a recognition of the representational character of all stories about the past and promotes critical inquiry into issues of subjectivity and narrative. In the process, American Encounters strives to understand the context in which meanings related to nations, cultures, and political economy are continually produced, challenged, and reshaped.

CONTENTS

ACKNOWLEDGMENTS

This book evolved from the conversations of an international group of historians who gathered in April 2006 at a conference at the Rothermere American Institute, University of Oxford, to discuss the work of American women missionaries in American cultural expansion. Our purpose was to go beyond an examination of women's experiences to contextualize and historicize their achievements across cultural and political systems. To accomplish this, we invited historians of the United States together with historians of the Middle East, Africa, Japan, China, and India to join us. These historians' fields crossed the boundaries of women's history, religious studies, and foreign relations. Their essays, published here for the first time, bring an interdisciplinary, transnational perspective to the study of American women and the expansion of American culture beyond the borders of the United States.

The conference was sponsored by the University of Oxford; the State University of New York, Binghamton; the American Philosophical Society, Philadelphia; the Huntington Library, San Marino, California; the American Studies Foundation of Japan; and the Institute for Women's Studies at Tokyo Woman's Christian University. We thank these generous sponsors. In Oxford our gracious host, Dr. Richard Carwardine, made us feel at home. The conference benefited enormously from the contributions of our session chairs, Maria Jaschok, Mary Renda, Jay Sexton, and Daniel Walker Howe. We are grateful to those who attended the conference and sparked stimulating discussion. Those discussions have done much to shape this volume. For this we thank in particular Dorothy Akubue-Brice, R. Bryan Bademan, Shiela Bora, Anne L. Foster, Carol Scally-Grigas, Loretta Long, Mary Beth Norton, Julyana Peard, Anne Pullen, Johanna Seles, Regina Sullivan, and Cristina Zaccarini.

We thank our editor at Duke University Press, Valerie Millholland, for her wise counsel, Miriam Angress and Leigh Barnwell for their patience, Mark Mastromarino for expertly shepherding the book through the production process, and Lawrence Kenney for copyediting. This book was made sharper, tighter (and, perhaps most important, shorter) thanks to the comments of our two anonymous readers.

INTRODUCTION

Barbara Reeves-Ellington, Kathryn Kish Sklar,
and Connie A. Shemo

The project to internationalize American history has made considerable progress since an international group of scholars led by Thomas Bender demonstrated the effectiveness of transnational perspectives in *Rethinking American History in a Global Age.*[1] Yet much remains to be done. Most historians of the United States continue to work exclusively in English, and important archival sources for the internationalization of U.S. history remain unexploited. Although the intersection of gender and foreign relations has offered important contributions to U.S. history, the efforts to internationalize the field through the lens of U.S. women's history have barely begun.[2] The contributors to this book utilize one of the largest collections of archival sources in the United States about American women abroad—those associated with Protestant missionaries—and they examine evidence from the perspectives of the local environments that missionaries inhabited. They take up Emily Rosenberg's challenge to historians to make gender central to the study of foreign relations.[3] Seeking to showcase female agency and locate non-American actors, while not focusing on separate spheres of activity or excluding male missionaries, the authors strive to recognize "all the players in the game."[4] By presenting multiple cultural perspectives, the essays in this book expand the field of U.S. women's history into international arenas, reveal the global spread of American culture, and broaden the scope of analysis of the history of the American empire.

The notion of competing kingdoms offers a framework for exploring how women's different allegiances and identities shaped and were shaped by missionary projects that were grounded in American values and influenced by other national entities. The essays presented here encourage scholars and students of U.S. history to see women missionaries not as a homogeneous group of cultural imperialists but as people who reinvented the meanings of American nationalism and imperialism as they negotiated competing nationalisms and imperialisms in varying colonial settings. Frequently working across the boundaries of gender and race, these women reached beyond the limits of their home cultures. The consequences of their actions cannot be easily categorized. They were invariably obliged to work with people who often reconfigured their projects, and the outcomes of their work varied in different parts of the world. Even in the comfortable confines of an American colonial state—the Philippines—women missionaries still navigated between the power of that state and the nationalisms of local communities. They were neither pawns of nor apologists for the state.

In grappling with the history of American empire, we examine neither formal military occupation and political control nor informal economic control.[5] Instead, building on recent scholarship that emphasizes the cultural dimensions of American imperial expansion, we trace the dynamic spread of American religious culture abroad by a global network of American Protestant women who, in an era when the United States was emerging onto the world stage as a global power, worked to advance a universal kingdom of God.[6] In the twenty-first century, as people in almost every region of the world contend in one form or another with the pervasive reach of American culture, a gendered analysis of the scope of American soft imperialism is essential if scholars are to explore how American empire is perceived, experienced, and negotiated around the world. American Protestant women missionaries were central to the connections between domestic and global events that shaped American imperial culture from 1812 to 1960.

Domestic social changes transformed American women's lives during the first half of the nineteenth century and provided a solid foundation for their global activism. By 1880, one in three students in higher education was a woman; by 1890, two out of three missionaries were women; by 1915, women's mission societies formed the largest American women's social movement.[7] In that era the missionary movement attracted educated, talented people who hailed from social strata that exercised considerable political leadership.[8] Abroad, women missionaries represented mainstream processes in American life, particularly in the fields of education, health-care, and the diverse arenas of women's social activism.

Scholars of contemporary American society have viewed religion as basic to domestic culture and foreign relations.[9] Yet religious history is infrequently included in current efforts to internationalize American history.[10] Despite the increase in scholarship on women missionaries stimulated by Jane Hunter's *Gospel of Gentility* (1984), the analysis of religion in the intersection of women's history and American foreign relations has not developed robustly since Hunter's work.[11] This book presents a fresh perspective on that history.

Because evangelical Protestantism gave urgently needed coherence to the nation's internal political, social, and economic structures in the era between 1780 and 1950, it also did much to configure its external interactions with the world. Carrying the Protestant Reformation of the sixteenth century forward into modern times, evangelical Protestantism shaped American society, the growth of the American nation-state, and the development of American empire.

One key to the power of evangelical Protestantism in the United States was its successful growth as an entrepreneurial business. The separation of church and state, achieved through state constitutions, required Protestant denominations to find sources of support other than the taxes that sustained state-established churches elsewhere in the Western world. Evangelical denominations like the Congregational, Presbyterian, Methodist, and Baptist, among others excelled at competing for the loyalty and financial support of average people because, thanks to ideas generated in the Second Great Awakening (1798–1857), they stressed the good news that individuals could achieve their own salvation—could personally control and improve their life circumstances in ways that accorded with God's will. Envisioning themselves as the agents of this good news, some laypeople, women as well as men, carried it abroad to India, the Sandwich Islands, and the Ottoman empire at the same time that others took it over the Appalachian Mountains into the Ohio River Valley.

Women benefited generally from the empowerment of the laity within evangelical Protestantism, but the opportunity to carry the good news abroad offered them extra benefits that addressed their gendered location in American society, namely, an alternative to marriage, meaningful work, and emancipation from at least some of the gendered constraints of their culture. Excluded from the work of preaching, which was with rare exceptions a male preserve, women missionaries engaged in the kinds of work most subject to accusations of cultural imperialism. Education, moral reform, social work, and medical work aimed to transform the cultures of host countries around the world where American women lived and worked. Across denominations women missionaries engaged in projects to "save" women and children.[12]

Missionary women anchored their work in a belief system that considered other religions inferior and perceived non-Protestant women as degraded others who needed rescuing. Their positive regard for women in Protestant Christianity was a crucial component of their assumptions about the superiority of the Anglo-Saxon race.[13] Our analysis of missionary constructions of race is therefore an integral part of our effort to link women, mission, nation, and empire. As this book demonstrates, many missionaries wrestled with the contradictions between ideologies of racial hierarchy and ideas of an essential equality among all peoples within a Christian brotherhood and sisterhood. Demonstrating the complexity of American missionary attitudes toward race, the essays place the construction of racial categories by Americans in a broader transnational context.[14]

We use the term *American Protestant empire* to accomplish three objectives: to capture the Protestant character of American expansion; to highlight the denominational diversity of Protestant expansion; and to acknowledge the anti-Catholic dynamic of American cultural expansion during this era. The tensions between teaching "nothing but Christ" (imposed by missionary boards as an ideal in the 1840s) and achieving religious conversion through cultural institutions (usually the norm regardless of board edicts) generated constant conflict in the American missionary endeavor, particularly for women missionaries who were heavily involved in cultural work.[15] Women missionaries shared the view of most evangelical Christians that all people deserved the triple advantages of Protestant Christianity, American civilization, and American forms of government. This perspective was most evident in the American colonization of the Philippines, where American missionaries followed the flag. Yet even when American missionaries operated in environments in which overt American political power was absent, as was typically the case, missionary goals usually supported U.S. political goals.

The American Protestant empire carried American evangelical religion, national identity, and political goals overseas in an unstable mixture that interacted with local environments in unpredictable ways. The separation of church and state could be politically subversive in some colonial contexts, especially in those that challenged the power of state-affiliated churches, such as the Catholic Church in the Philippines and the Greek Orthodox Church in the Ottoman empire. The American Protestant empire was decidedly anti-Catholic and anti-Orthodox.

Anti-Catholicism motivated early nineteenth-century mission boards as well as the individual Americans who ventured into the world to spread the Protestant Reformation.[16] The Roman Catholic Church, which had long promoted international missionary programs, was expanding its reach in the United States at that time. European nuns established convents and schools in North America as early as the 1730s.[17] American Protestant women missionaries set out for foreign lands at the same time that European nuns worked to counter Protestant attempts to convert Catholic immigrants in the United States.[18] Protestant women sought to advance Protestantism in Catholic as well as in non-Christian countries. The term *American* became synonymous with *Protestant* in the Philippines and elsewhere. Though American Catholic missionary activity remains an important aspect of American religious and cultural expansion, our focus on Protestant missionaries explores that hegemonic thrust and its internal diversity.[19]

Denominational differences figure prominently in these pages. Early in the nineteenth century, women missionaries, almost always wives, came from the financially powerful mainline evangelical Protestant denominations: Congregational, Presbyterian, Methodist, and Baptist. After the American Civil War, women missionaries came increasingly from the denominational and ecumenical women's boards that emerged in the 1860s and 1870s. Toward the end of the century, women from independent and more marginal denominations that were influenced by revised mission theories of premillennialism (for example, Assemblies of God, Brethren in Christ, Bethany Indian Mission) volunteered.[20] By paying attention to denominational diversity the essays in our book challenge the standard periodization of American women in mission and offer insights into the diverse ways in which women of different denominations adapted to their host environments.

Scholars have generally accepted the idea of a decline in women's missionary work in the mainline Protestant denominations after the 1920s; yet the work of independent missionaries continued to grow thereafter. Women missionaries in independent missions lacked the financial backing of missionaries in mainline denominations and relied more heavily on their host governments. Even women missionaries from economically powerful denominations had to work more closely with local reformers after the 1930s, as American support for missions declined rapidly with the coming of the Great Depression. By extending our time frame beyond the heyday of women's foreign missionary work, we offer a more complete narrative of change over time and explore a broader range of the work done by American women missionaries in diverse cultural contexts.

Although scholarship in the 1980s and 1990s pointed to the importance of the work of American women missionaries in American cultural expansion, it nonetheless constructed an image of women supported by strong mission boards who spread American culture with little regard for host cultures. Influenced by recent critiques of the concept of cultural imperialism as a unidirectional exercise of power, the essays in this book view missions as sites of encounter and exchange where individuals met, interacted, and triggered change.[21] They analyze the extent to which local actors put missionary ideas to new uses and highlight the process by which Americans who joined in projects of social transformation struggled to meet the demands of their host cultures. Missionary goals rarely competed with American political goals, but they frequently collided with the cultural, religious, and political goals of the local environments in which missionaries worked. By examining American missionaries in various colonial settings and incorporating the multiple perspectives of rival players and contesting ideas, the essays complicate the framework of metropole and colony.[22]

Our attention to geographic context includes examples of American women missionaries who worked within the United States. We take seriously Amy Kaplan's call for historians to challenge the "central geographic bifurcation between continental expansion and overseas empire."[23] We therefore include essays on the work of women missionaries among people who were, in various ways, constructed as foreign in the United States, such as women's home missions among African Americans and Chinese immigrants and immigrant missions among Native Americans. These essays raise important questions about the meaning of *foreign* within the United States. American women missionaries offer a valuable opportunity to view more completely the range of social forces that made the United States a powerful agent of change at home and abroad. Their experience challenges historians to create new definitions of empire and see new links among gender, mission, nation, and American empire.

This book is organized in four parts and a conclusion. Part I showcases reflections on women and empire by two contributors, Jane H. Hunter and Ian Tyrrell, whose scholarship has done much to shape efforts to internationalize U.S. women's history. In parts II, III, and IV, the contributors address, respectively, our three major categories of analysis: women, mission, and nation. We recognize the interconnections and interdependence of these categories and separate them chiefly for the purposes of emphasis and analysis as we explore American cultural expansion. In a conclusion Mary A. Renda traces the book's themes of imperialism and anti-imperialism, which defy easy categorization but illuminate the centrality of American Protestant missionary women in the construction of American empire before 1960.

In part I, two chapters review earlier groundbreaking scholarship on women and mission. Jane Hunter, whose *Gospel of Gentility* influenced the work of many of the contributors to this book, revisits previous research to emphasize the strength and breadth of evangelical American women's embrace of the moral reformation of the world. Her essay, "Women's Mission in Historical Perspective: American Identity and Christian Internationalism," charts the strains of imperialism and internationalism in the work of American missions and discusses new patterns that have emerged in the decades since her work appeared. If nineteenth-century missionary discourses that heralded Christ's dominion on earth resembled the promotion of a new world order that moderns recognize as racialized and imperial, they also advanced a new understanding of Christian internationalism that evolved from missionary encounters and became progressively more inclusive of other cultures and religions.

In "Woman, Missions, and Empire: New Approaches to American Cultural Expansion," Ian Tyrrell reviews the concept of empire to show how the idea of American empire fits into concepts both classical and modern but also diverges from historical models. He rejects an American exceptionalism that would posit American empire as somehow unique but nonetheless finds that transnational networks of moral expansion are a distinctive feature of American empire. Revisiting his earlier book *Woman's World/Woman's Empire*, Tyrrell explores the often uneasy relationship missionaries of the World's Woman's Christian Temperance Union had with the idea of empire. He shows how their work in the Philippines put them in a position to work against formal colonial policy and examines the multiple ways in which, in alliance with their male supporters, they attempted to use American power abroad to implement their vision of a moral empire at home.

The essays in part II substantially revise the larger narrative of American religious history by revealing the centrality of women and gender to the origins of the American global missionary endeavor and to imperialist and anti-imperialist strains in American national culture. The contributors address a wide range of questions: How are gender identities and relationships constructed? How do they shape women's engagement in mission and their power relationships with men? How do they define missionaries' relationships with people of different cultures?

The early nineteenth-century evangelical press highlights women's position at the center of the foreign mission movement. Mary Kupiec Cayton's essay, "Canonizing Harriet Newell: Women, the Evangelical Press, and the Foreign Mission Movement in New England, 1800–1840," illuminates the extraordinary impact on women's financial and organizational contributions to the global missionary endeavor of the death in India in 1813 of the missionary Harriet Newell. Cayton argues that widely read female memoirs brought together traditional forms of female piety with an expansionist missionary impulse that enabled women to see themselves in new forms of social activism and fueled the growth of missions before the American Civil War.

In "An Unwomanly Woman and Her Sons in Christ: Faith, Empire, and Gender in Colonial Rhodesia, 1899–1906," Wendy Urban-Mead explores the gendered and racial tensions inherent in missionary work in the settler colony of Rhodesia (present-day Zimbabwe). Her essay shows that frontier conditions could expand the scope of women's missionary work and open a space that promoted native leadership, thereby challenging, although not erasing, racial boundaries between missionaries and their converts. Yet these changes could be short-lived as areas ceased to be frontiers. Urban-Mead complicates our understanding of the sphere in which women missionaries operated by showing how much their sphere changed over time in response to changes in local conditions and church leadership.

Connie A. Shemo's essay, " 'So Thoroughly American': Gertrude Howe, Kang Cheng, and Cultural Imperialism in the Woman's Foreign Missionary Society, 1872–1931," analyzes the relationship between the prominent American missionary Gertrude Howe and her adopted Chinese daughter, the missionary physician Kang Cheng, to complicate the idea that American women missionaries were agents of cultural imperialism. Shemo argues that ideologies of race inherent in the policies of American mission boards worked to limit the culturally expansive potential of unmarried American women missionaries. At its broadest level, the essay draws on the relationship between Howe and Kang to explore the tensions between missionary ideas of a spiritual equality between all believers and the pervasive influence of theories of racial hierarchy that enforced traditions of racial segregation.

Susan Haskell Khan emphasizes anticolonial possibilities as she explores Indian nationalism and a nascent women's movement in India as they influenced the impact of American women missionaries at home. In her essay, "From Redeemers to Partners: American Women Missionaries and the 'Woman Question' in India," Khan acknowledges that women missionaries in India contributed to discourses that stoked racist impulses in the United States. Yet reform movements in India informed the ways in which American women sought to undermine the racism prevalent in American missions and led them to new understandings about international cooperation after the First World War.

The essays in part III view missions as sites of encounter, places where diverse cultures met and engaged. They emphasize the relationships women missionaries had with the states of their host countries. The contributors utilize local sources to expose conflicts inherent in missionary endeavors between American objectives and local expectations. Their essays emphasize the marginality of American missions in local environments.

In "Settler Colonists, 'Christian Citizenship,' and the Women's Missionary Federation at the Bethany Indian Mission in Wittenberg, Wisconsin,

1884–1934," Betty Ann Bergland argues that the Women's Missionary Federation, in part because of its marginal status as a church of immigrants and a women's society, mediated between the American state and the tribes it endeavored to serve, affording a space from which Indian converts could combat the racist ideologies that worked to their detriment. Bringing the insights of Norwegian immigrant settlers and their Indian converts to her essay, Bergland problematizes definitions of *American* and *foreign* within the United States and complicates older narratives that present missionaries as instruments of cultural destruction.

Sue Gronewold examines competing visions of womanhood at an American mission in Shanghai in the 1920s and 1930s. In "New Life, New Faith, New Nation, New Women: Competing Models at the Door of Hope Mission in Shanghai," Gronewold traces the changing fashions of dolls sewn by young Chinese women at the mission. She examines these changes to show how American women missionaries of the China Inland Mission and Chinese supporters of the New Life Movement campaign promoted by Chiang Kai-shek's Nationalist government fashioned mutually supportive views of New Women for evangelical Christianity and Chinese nationalism.

In " 'No Nation Can Rise Higher than Its Women': The Women's Ecumenical Missionary Movement and Tokyo Woman's Christian College," Rui Kohiyama analyzes the example of a strong state able to dominate the missionary enterprise. By the 1920s, Japan had become a colonizing power in its own right. Kohiyama points out that none of the Japanese associated with the Tokyo college adopted the American women's motives for promoting Christianity and female leadership. Using the insights of prominent Japanese Christians, she shows that the college's Japanese leaders intended to shape a national Japanese institution that reflected the ideals of an increasingly imperial Japan and effectively thwarted the intentions of American Baptist women.

Beth Baron also underscores the complex negotiations among missionaries, local communities, and government officials in colonial and postcolonial Egypt. In "Nile Mother: Lillian Trasher and the Orphans of Egypt," Baron explains why the Assembly of God missionary Lillian Trasher was able to find a niche for her missionary work and build an orphanage where eight thousand children were cared for until her death in 1961. Baron shows that Trasher's independent mission was successful because Egyptians supported her venture at a time when colonial and postcolonial states provided limited services and private persons were unable or unwilling to care for orphaned and abandoned infants and children with disabilities.

Part IV consists of essays that illuminate the connections between home missions and foreign missions and highlight their contested identities. Many values central to American nationhood became vehicles for programs of reform at home and abroad for women missionaries as they sought to shape new Protestant nations. The essays here engage with scholarship on the language of domesticity to reveal the complex ways in which understandings of womanhood, home life, national affiliation, and racial typing informed responses to missionary projects in local communities.

The ability of people targeted by missionaries to use missionary messages for their own ends is emphasized in Barbara Reeves-Ellington's essay, "Embracing Domesticity: Women, Mission, and Nation Building in Ottoman Europe, 1832–1872." Reeves-Ellington traces the avenues through which American missionaries promoted an American discourse of domesticity to Bulgarian Orthodox Christians in the Ottoman empire and examines its reception and reconfiguration by Bulgarian women and men. Anglo-American ideas about women's domestic responsibilities, female education, and national progress appealed to educated urban Bulgarians, who rearticulated a language of domesticity to serve anticolonial ends as they challenged Ottoman reforms during a period of increasing Bulgarian nationalism.

In "Imperial Encounters at Home: Women, Empire, and the Home Mission Project in Late Nineteenth-Century America," Derek Chang shows that, by constructing African Americans and Chinese immigrants as foreign, white Baptist women in the United States contributed to shaping American discourses on race and national belonging that depended on gendered ideas of domestic respectability. Yet, as Chang argues, African American and Chinese clients were able to counter missionaries' notions of difference by rearticulating their ideas about belonging. They reconceptualized the idea of the nation and carved out their own space as missionaries drawing on their understanding of their transnational identities.

Sylvia M. Jacobs highlights the complex transnational sentiments of African American women missionaries who worked among black Africans of the Congo Free State at the height of European imperial expansion in

Africa. In "Three African American Women Missionaries in the Congo, 1887–1899: The Confluence of Race, Culture, Identity, and Nationality," Jacobs shows how black women missionaries negotiated racial and national identities in their encounters with African women and children, white missionaries, and European colonial administrators. American culture shaped their perceptions of Africa. Although they recognized commonalities with their African clients, their experiences in Africa confirmed that they were Americans first and foremost. Ultimately they rejected the idea of transnational belonging.

Missionaries of the Woman's Board of Missions came late to the U.S. colony of the Philippines, where American women already worked as army nurses, colonial administrators, and teachers. As Laura R. Prieto explains in " 'Stepmother America': The Woman's Board of Missions in the Philippines, 1902–1930," the mission project to Christianize both paralleled and meshed with the colonial state project to civilize. However, just as the federal government failed to extend rights like woman's suffrage to its new territories overseas, so women missionaries ultimately failed to assimilate Filipinas into their ideals of modern Christian womanhood. The gradual assumption of control of the mission by Filipinos accompanied the collapse of women's separate institutions and anticipated not only an independent Philippine nation but also the end of America's experiment with colonialism.

In the conclusion, Mary A. Renda reveals the commonalities that thread through these essays and connects them to earlier scholarship. She emphasizes the religious faith and sense of duty that inspired and supported American women in their missionary work, affirms the usefulness of their projects to many people at home and abroad, and underscores the diversity of missionary encounters that defy easy classification. Tracing the ways in which women challenged gendered restrictions to expand their realm of influence, she nonetheless illuminates two linked and omnipresent themes in women's expanding agency. The "language of domesticity" and the "racial dimension" of "woman's work for woman" form the double helix of race and empire that underpinned nineteenth- and twentieth-century international women's activism.

The essays offered here highlight the shifting and contested terrain of the larger global arena in which Protestant Christianity vied for influence from the early nineteenth century to the mid-twentieth. Women missionaries shaped fundamental aspects of that story as they struggled with the construction of their gendered identity, with the goals of their missionary agendas, and with the spirit of their own nationalism as it fostered and competed with local nationalisms. Profoundly transnational, their history reveals America as *"inherently* an international phenomenon."[24] They did much to create a distinctively American form of empire—and opposition to empire—that was based on cultural institutions rather than on military and economic might. The authors of these essays illustrate the advantages of viewing global patterns through the lens of local encounters. They offer a rich, new historiographic turn for future efforts to conceptualize American empire and for future studies of American women internationally considered. Above all, they support a growing consensus that American women's history is intrinsically transnational.

NOTES

1 Thomas Bender, *Rethinking American History in a Global Age* (Berkeley: University of California Press, 2002). Over the past two decades, several issues of the *Journal of American History* have included forums in which scholars have discussed transnational approaches to the study of United States history. See, for example, issues from October 1991, September 1992, September 1999, December 1999.

2 On the intersection of gender and foreign relations, see Kristin L Hoganson, *Fighting for American Manhood: How Gender Politics Provoked the Spanish-American and Philippine-American Wars* (New Haven: Yale University Press, 1998); Mary Renda, *Taking Haiti: Military Occupation and the Culture of U.S. Imperialism, 1915–1940* (Chapel Hill: University of North Carolina Press, 2001). On the intersection of women's history and international history, see Leila J. Rupp, *Worlds of Women: The Making of an International Women's Movement* (Princeton: Princeton University Press, 1997); Ian Tyrrell, *Woman's World, Woman's Empire: The Woman's Christian Temperance Union in International Perspective, 1880–1930* (Chapel Hill: University of North Carolina Press, 1991). For an example of U.S. women's history as international history, see Kathryn Kish Sklar, Anja Schüler, and Susan Strasser, eds., *Social Justice Feminists in the United States and Germany: A Dialogue in Documents, 1885–1933* (Ithaca: Cornell University Press, 1998). On the importance of transnational history to women's history, see the roundtable discussion, "The Future of Women's History: Considering the State of U.S. Women's History" in the *Journal of Women's History* (spring 2003).

3 Emily S. Rosenberg, "Gender," *Journal of American History* 77, no. 1 (1990), 116–24.

4 Jean Comaroff and John Comaroff, *Of Revelation and Revolution: Christianity, Colonialism, and Consciousness in South Africa* (Chicago: University of Chicago Press, 1991), 9–10.

5 For some of the many interpretations of American empire, see Andrew J. Bacevich, *American Empire The Realities and Consequences of U.S. Diplomacy* (Cambridge, Mass.: Harvard University Press, 2002); Michael Hardt and Antonio Negri, *Empire* (Cambridge, Mass.: Harvard University Press, 2000); Amy Kaplan, *The Anarchy of Empire in the Making of U.S. Culture* (Cambridge, Mass.: Harvard University Press, 2002); Amy Kaplan and Donald E. Pease, eds, *Cultures of United States Imperialism* (Durham: Duke University Press, 1993); Walter LaFeber, *The New Empire: An Interpretation of American Expansion, 1860–1898* (Ithaca: Cornell University Press, 1963); Charles S. Maier, *Among Empires: American Ascendancy and Its Predecessors* (Cambridge, Mass.: Harvard University Press, 2006); Richard Van Alstyne, *The Rising American Empire* (New York: Oxford Universty Press, 1960); William A. Williams, *Empire as a Way of Life: An Essay on the Causes and Character of America's Present Predicament, along with a Few Thoughts about an Alternative* (New York: Oxford University Press, 1980); William Nugent, *Habits of Empire: A History of American Expansion* (New York: Knopf, 2008).

6 For an example of the cultural dimensions of empire, see Kaplan and Pease, *Cultures of United States Imperialism*.

7 Patricia R. Hill, *The World Their Household: The American Woman's Foreign Mission Movement and Cultural Transformation, 1870–1920* (Ann Arbor: University of Michigan Press, 1985); Kathryn Kish Sklar, *Florence Kelley and the Nation's Work* (New Haven: Yale University Press, 1995).

8 Richard J. Carwardine, *Evangelicals and Politics in Antebellum America* (New Haven: Yale University Press, 1993); Daniel Walker Howe, "The Evangelical Movement and Political Culture in the North during the Second Party System," *Journal of American History* 77, no. 4 (1991), 1216–39.

9 Seth Jacobs, *America's Miracle Man in Vietnam: Ngo Dinh Diem, Religion, Race, and U.S. Intervention in Southeast Asia, 1950–1957* (Durham: Duke University Press, 2004); Melani McAlister, *Epic Encounters: Culture, Media, and U.S. Interests in the Middle East, 1945–2000* (Berkeley: University of California Press, 2001; Andrew Preston, "Bridging the Gap between the Sacred and the Secular in the History of American Foreign Relations," *Diplomatic History* 30, no. 5 (2006): 783–812.

10 Religion as a category of analysis was largely absent from Bender, *Rethinking American History*, and Kaplan and Pease, *Cultures of United States Imperialism*.

11 Jane Hunter, *The Gospel of Gentility: American Women Missionaries in Turn-of-the-Century China* (New Haven: Yale University Press, 1984); Patricia Grimshaw, *Paths of Duty: American Missionary Wives in Nineteenth-Century Hawaii* (Honolulu: University of Hawaii Press, 1989); Amanda Porterfield, *Mary Lyon and the Mount Holyoke Missionaries* (New York: Oxford University Press, 1997); Lisa Joy

Pruitt, *A Looking-Glass for Ladies: American Protestant Women and the Orient in the Nineteenth Century* (Macon, Ga.: Mercer University Press, 2005); Dana Robert, *American Women in Mission: A Social History of Their Thought and Practice* (Macon, Ga.: Mercer University Press, 1996); Mary Zwiep, *Pilgrim Path: The First Company of Women Missionaries to Hawaii* (Madison: University of Wisconsin Press, 1991).

12 Mary Taylor Huber and Nancy C. Lutkehaus, eds., *Gendered Missions: Women and Men in Missionary Discourse and Practice* (Ann Arbor: University of Michigan Press, 1999); Hunter, *The Gospel of Gentility*; Tyrrell, *Woman's World*; Laura Wexler, *Tender Violence: Domestic Visions in an Age of U.S. Imperialism* (Chapel Hill: University of North Carolina Press, 2000).

13 Joan Jacobs Brumberg, "Zenanas and Girlless Villages: The Ethnology of American Evangelical Women, 1870–1910," *Journal of American History* 69, no. 2 (1982), 347–71. For reflections on the importance of race in the work of British women missionaries, see Jane Haggis, "White Women and Colonialism: Towards a Non-Recuperative History," *Gender and Imperialism*, ed. Clare Midgely, 45–75 (Manchester: Manchester University Press, 1998).

14 For an argument on the importance of this project, see Paul A. Kramer, "Empires, Exceptions, and Anglo-Saxons: Race and Rule between the British and United States Empires, 1880–1910," *Journal of American History* 88, no. 4 (2002), 1315–53.

15 Paul William Harris, *Nothing But Christ: Rufus Anderson and the Ideology of Protestant Foreign Missions* (New York: Oxford University Press, 1999); William R. Hutchison, *Errand to the World: American Protestant Thought and Foreign Missions* (Chicago: University of Chicago Press, 1987); Webb Keane, *Christian Moderns: Freedom and Fetish in the Mission Encounter* (Berkeley: University of California Press, 2007).

16 For the motivating forces behind the first American interdenominational mission board, see Clifton Jackson Phillips, *Protestant America and the Pagan World: The First Half Century of the American Board of Commissioner of Foreign Missions, 1810–1860* (Cambridge: East Asian Research Center, Harvard University: 1969).

17 Emily Clark, *Masterless Mistresses: The New Orleans Ursulines and the Development of a New World Society, 1727–1834* (Chapel Hill: University of North Carolina Press, 2007).

18 Carol K Coburn and Martha Smith, *Spirited Lives: How Nuns Shaped Catholic Culture and American Life, 1836–1920* (Chapel Hill: University of North Carolina Press, 1999).

19 For recent scholarship on American Catholic missionary thought and experiences, see *U.S. Catholic Historian* (Summer 2006).

20 Dana Robert, "'The Crisis of Missions': Premillennial Mission Theory and the Origins of Independent Evangelical Missions," *Earthen Vessels: American Evangelicals and Foreign Missions, 1880–1980*, ed. Joel A. Carpenter and Wilbert R. Shenk, 29–46 (Grand Rapids, Michigan: William B. Eerdmans, 1990).

21 Ryan Dunch, "Beyond Cultural Imperialism: Cultural Theory Christian Mis-

sions, and Global Modernity," *History and Theory* 41 (2002), 301–25; Jessica C. E. Gienow-Hecht, "Shame on US? Academics, Cultural Transfer, and the Cold War—A Critical Review," *Diplomatic History* 24, no. 3 (2000), 465–94; Gilbert M. Joseph, Catherine C. LeGrand, and Ricardo C. Salvatore, *Close Encounters of Empire: Writing the Cultural History of U.S.–Latin American Relations* (Durham: Duke University Press, 1998); Rob Kroes, "American Empire and Cultural Imperialism: A View from the Receiving End," *Rethinking American History in a Global Age*, ed. Thomas Bender, 295–313 (Berkeley: University of California Press, 2002); Mary Louise Pratt, *Imperial Eyes: Travel Writing and Transculturation* (London: Routledge, 1992). Padma Angol, "Indian Christian Women and Indigenous Feminism, c. 1850–1920" *Gender and Imperialism*, ed. Clare Midgely, 79–103 (Manchester: Manchester University Press, 1998).

22 Antoinette Burton, *Burdens of History: British Feminists, Indian Women, and Imperial Culture, 1865–1915* (Chapel Hill: University of North Carolina, 1994); Catherine Hall, *Civilising Subjects: Colony and Metropole in the English Imagination, 1830–1867* (Chicago: University of Chicago Press, 2003); Ann Laura Stoler and Frederick Cooper, "Between Metropole and Colony: Rethinking a Research Agenda," *Tensions of Empire: Colonial Cultures in a Bourgeois World*, ed. Frederick Cooper and Ann Laura Stoler, 1–56 (Berkeley: University of California Press, 1997); Peter Van der Veer, *Conversion to Modernities: The Globalization of Christianity* (New York: Routledge, 1996).

23 Kaplan, *The Anarchy of Empire*, 17.

24 Kroes, "American Empire," 295–313.

I RE-VISIONING AMERICAN WOMEN IN THE WORLD

American Identity and Christian Internationalism

Jane H. Hunter

The events of the early twenty-first century present a challenge to historians of the United States as well as to scholars in political science, international relations, and the history of the Middle East. While the world history movement has swept up our colleagues in European, Asian, and African history, Americanists have too often remained stuck within the stories of the American continent, content to take advantage of the oceans on the east and west to disregard the global context which has governed American history, just as it has the histories of other nations around the world. Though most American historians today would disavow any notion of American exceptionalism—any notion that the nation's founding political documents have somehow sanitized American national projects—the failure of American historians to engage with larger international frameworks has allowed their students and readers to retain naive notions about the unique righteousness of the American role in the world. American historians now confront an urgent responsibility to insert American power, both hard and soft, back in the national story so that all Americans can develop a fuller understanding of its global consequences.

The erasure of the history of American foreign relations from the stories historians tell is an unfortunate and paradoxical result of the new American history. During the late twentieth century, the historical study of the American people was revolutionized, illuminated by the penetrating insights of social history and, more recently, by the creativity of a new group of cultural historians. The social historical turn, then the linguistic turn and the new cultural history have been enormously fruitful, but they have often restricted their focus to Americans' national land mass, indeed the site of ample drama and conflict. This golden age of American history has come at a cost. With the exception of continued attention to the century's wars, including the Cold War, American history textbooks have cut back their attention to what has been considered old-fashioned diplomatic history to showcase the dramatic insights of social history. The events of 9/11 and thereafter have shown American historians, along with other academics, the cost of Americans' ignorance about their country's global presence.

One exception to American ignorance has been the ongoing obsession of Americans with the Vietnam legacy—a scab that American writers, filmmakers, and politicians continue to pick at, even as the Vietnamese people themselves move on. The question of what Americans should have learned from the Vietnam War remains contested terrain, especially salient for a nation confronting the agonies and errors of Iraq. Certainly it influenced historians who came of age during the years of the Vietnam War. A generation of Vietnam scholars reflected on the ways in which the framework of the Cold War distorted the vision of American policy-makers, who misinterpreted the nationalist desires of a people subjected to a series of colonial masters. David Halberstam's *The Best and the Brightest* (1972) summarized the puzzlement of my parents' generation upon discovering that the best minds in the United States were inadequate to the task of understanding the ongoing conflict in Southeast Asia.[1]

This was the context in which I wrote my decades-old missionary book, *Gospel of Gentility: American Women Missionaries in Turn-of-the-Century China* (1984).[2] In part it emerged from my experience in the British colony of Hong Kong in the early 1970s, refracted through the emerging field of women's history. It was also preeminently a Vietnam-era book, a work of cultural self-scrutiny. Its focus was on American women missionaries themselves, and although the book sympathized with the courage and the eloquence of many of its subjects, it argued against the blinding arrogance of their worldview. Martin Marty, the historian of religion at the University of Chicago, noted that it shared in the late twentieth-century "horror" of cultural imperialism, and I concur.

I would not dispute that analysis now, but I consider it both too easy

and incomplete. For in judging the intent of missionary work to dominate and transform, I did not adequately assess indigenous uses. Lacking
sources and access to China itself, I told only one part of the missionary
story. In the post-Vietnam era, too, I was in a small group writing about
religious expansionism. Although the story of the United States in Buddhist Vietnam had religious resonances, religion played a minor role in
historians' reflections on Vietnam's Cold War legacy.

In the twenty-first century, though, the nation has been mired in a
different conflict, one that has its most proximate origins in radical Wahabi
Islam and in the astonishing events of September 11, 2001. This book
contributes to the process of telling a history for this new age. Armed with
language skills and the predilections of social historians, these scholars
attend to the role of religion at home and abroad. They examine both the
sending and the receiving end of the missionary exchange. They resist the
temptation to simplify, acknowledging that American religious expansionism interacted with the forces of modernization and nationalism around
the world to create a rich cultural milieu not susceptible to easy interpretation. The arrival of American missionaries in the Middle East and in South
and East Asia in the nineteenth century inspired curiosity and encouraged
modernizers in those parts of the world, but also contributed to stories
and lessons disseminated throughout the United States by a vast missionary publishing enterprise.

The history represented here attempts to be multiarchival, history told
not just from one side but from several. These essays look at missionary
actors, but in addition they address the richly varied ways in which local
elites, congregations, Bible women, college students, and political oppor-
tunists responded to the missionary message, skillfully deploying it for
local ends which might or might not bear resemblance to the original
intents. They open a swirling force field composed of competing loyalties
to nation, God, class, and self. They suggest that one would do well
neither to simplify these relationships between unequals nor to exaggerate
the power of missionary proselytizers in this cultural exchange. These
complex, nuanced portraits offer insights into the past and present alike.

The essays share another theme. They focus on gender, looking especially at the interaction between religious and political culture and American women. American women were the majority of churchgoers from the
late colonial period through the rest of American history, but only since

1920 have they been welcome at the ballot box. American religious history can lay more claim than political history to representing the agency of American women. Despite their limited personal wealth, women were extraordinarily successful fundraisers in the church because of their important role in congregations around the country. Often considered a subordinate, dependent class within their societies, American women were only indirectly represented in the actions of the American government during the nineteenth century and early twentieth, the time focus of these essays. Yet, paradoxically, when women's political right to direct influence on American foreign policy was at its most limited, their symbolic meaning in the culture was perhaps at its highest. When Alexis de Tocqueville contemplated the reasons for the success of the upstart new republic in the 1830s, he concluded that much of it could be explained by "the superiority of their women," by which he meant the extreme virtue and selflessness attributed to mothers and wives in the culture of the time.[3] The essays address the relationship between that ideology (promoted by men and women) and the expansionism which extended the American Republic to the Pacific Ocean and took American missionaries around the globe. How did that distinct culture built on professions of selflessness interact with American imperial projects?

Historians have referred to women's culture as the ideology of women's separate sphere, or of domesticity, and initially empire and home seemed to exist at opposite cultural poles. Recent work, including much represented here, has suggested otherwise, arguing in fact that imperialism was dependent on domesticity as a way of inspiring, legitimating, and redeeming its projects. I concur with that analysis but consider it too simple. For in a constantly recalibrating system, American women's culture and its expression in American missionary projects were not static. Women's foreign missionary experience fed back into American culture and ideology in the interwar years and ultimately represented a source of *challenge* to the dominant nationalist culture. This fluidity in the past is suggestive for those who might see gendered activism as a source of hope in a divided present.

One of the earliest insights in U.S. women's history appears frequently in the work offered here: the importance of a sentimentalized Christian domesticity in defining nineteenth-century women's desired field of action. For a long time, historians have known that domesticity was important to women's sense of their mission. More recent work, however, has suggested how important that sentimentalized domesticity was to the American imperial project writ large. So-called Manifest Destiny saw American expansionism as a divine force of history, introducing progress and civilization as it went. Recent work, including a number of essays in this volume, reference an article by the literary studies scholar Amy Kaplan entitled "Manifest Domesticity," in which the author suggests how the sentimental press used the purity of women's sphere to strengthen and clarify American imperial projects.⁴ The elastic stretching of national boundaries westward across the continent did not exist apart from the American hearth and parlor but instead transported it and indeed used it as *justification* for military conquest.

Kaplan begins her essay by focusing on an article from 1847 in the influential women's magazine *Godey's Lady's Book*. Illustrating "Life on the Rio Grande" is an engraving of an idealized American family gathered in a clearing, their campfire creating a small locus of domestic life in the midst of a forest of towering trees.⁵ Kaplan points out that it was not only the towering trees that were looming over the tiny family group. When the piece was published, the Mexican–American War was raging, and the Rio Grande itself was at issue in a newly imposed and more encompassing border. Yet that context does not appear in the story or in the engraving accompanying it. Kaplan nonetheless argues the significance of that family group to the goals of the war. As the accompanying text suggests, the domestication of the wilderness and the superior claims of Anglo-American civilization helped to justify the conflict. It is important to the virtue of this endeavor that the small American family be oblivious to it. Picnicking as they are, in all innocence, this family group with its women and children preferred not to see the violence just beyond the picture's frame. Indeed it is that insistence on seeing no evil—that resolute fixation on the ideal at the end—that justifies and sanctions empire.

Clearly sentimental literature helped to script the midcentury social imagination that united domestic culture with the bigger themes of empire. Its interweaving of ideas of empire and domesticity was born out in the broader culture, the culture *Godey's* represented and encapsulated. Those themes were not always entirely divorced from each other. One such midcentury example appears in a newspaper written by students at the graduation of North Granville Ladies' Seminary in New York State in

Life on the Rio Grande, engraving by W. H. Ellis for *Godey's Lady's Book*, 1847.
Courtesy of the Sophia Smith Collection, Smith College, Northampton, Massachusetts.

1866. In their student newspaper, the Granville graduates initiated a ritual which by late century would become part of the common culture of school graduations around the country: the class prophecy. What did this group of religious young ladies imagine lay in their future? They envisioned themselves reuniting twenty years hence and reported on their heroic if careworn lives, nearly all married and operating within precisely the sphere of manifest domesticity described by Kaplan. Virtually all had married, they assumed, but they had married an expanding American empire along with their husbands. One's husband was a minister to France and had recently returned to Washington, where he was secretary of state. Another, after teaching in the West, lived "in the City of Mexico," where her husband was the governor of "this new American possession." Yet another appeared "dignified and matronly." ("She was so sure she would never marry.") In fact, she had married a missionary and lived in Australia. Her house was humble—just a log cabin, "but the vines and roses climbing over the verandah about it make it a beautiful home." What is extraordinary is the geographical and indeed imperial reach of these domestic fantasies from one group of ordinary young girls in New York State just after the Civil War.[6]

This piece of adolescent prophecy drew clear lines that are also important in mapping women's relationship to empire in midcentury. It was important that women provide succor and support in these imperial adventures—and not manifest unvarnished pride or ambition themselves. The power of woman's sphere to redeem expansionism depended on woman's innocence and ignorance of aggressive intent. The balance of the spheres assumed contrary male and female principles. Among this group of schoolmates, one was held up for disapproval. This self-important pariah, revealing that she is an advocate of woman's rights, spurns her husband and has left him at home with the children. She has recently published "a long essay on Woman's Superiority." Her classmates rush to censure her. The moral of the tale is common in nineteenth-century writing: "In the exerting of pure home influence is woman's truest work. . . . If we are Christian women we need not fear for rights."[7]

The cause of women's rights violated the tenet of self-sacrifice that was a necessary part of the sentimental woman's sphere. In midcentury and beyond, mainstream women drew their strength and their identity from an ideal of Christian womanhood that gained its highest glory from its ability to exercise power indirectly through suasion and influence. And of course the casualties of the early mission field, as we learn from one of the essays below, guaranteed the disinterestedness of the benevolence exerted by women in their sphere.

As a nineteenth-century concept, domesticity depended on boundaries, the ability to separate hearth from world. Domesticity was expansive, but it succeeded only when it had successfully converted savage to homebody. Homes required walls and doors. The cozy nourishment of domesticity resulted from its ability to keep the forces of disorder and confusion at bay, beyond the walls, outside the house. Readers of *Godey's* in 1847 might know that the Mexican–American War was raging just beyond the frame of that tale, but for those of virtuous mind that war was immaterial. The beauty of the cozy family scene was sufficient—pure, true, and good enough to redeem any violence and death. The boundaries that domesticity constructed around itself ordered and contained the pure savagery that might otherwise accompany unbridled empire.

When that sphere accompanied missionary families in journeys to outposts in foreign lands, the contrast between an idealized form of domestic nurture and the savagery beyond constructed a highly charged

Sarah Judson, missionary wife
in Burma, who died at sea.

racial narrative as well. (For example, see the depiction above of the missionary Sarah Judson nursing her babe, oblivious to the savagery just beyond her bed curtain.)[8] Like the walls of a home, compound walls, as much of the work here describes, kept out foreign influences, attractions, customs, cultures. The resoluteness of home customs and ritual resulted from the surrounding challenges. Within a colonial social world which depended on the domestic service of indigenous servants, the "disembodied shades" referred to by Kaplan are constant reminders of the insufficiency of domestic efforts. Kaplan's work provides theory to help one understand the racial exclusiveness that was often missionary practice, especially in established expatriate and colonial communities pulled between the contracting and expansive notions of female culture.

By the end of the nineteenth century, the kind of sublimated ambition-through-domesticity described in sentimental literature yielded to another model for female aspiration, a model that featured female accomplishment in the world rather than suasion and nurture through the home. One can track this change in aspiration in the dreams of educated girls. In high school prophecies from the 1890s, girls joined boys in having destinies and vocations of their own. In a range of class prophecies from the Northeast, high school newspapers projected individualized professions for each of their graduates, male and female, not simply a role as wife, with ambition described merely by proxy. By the end of the century, girls deemed champions of women's rights were no longer pariahs, as in 1865, but successful political leaders—named the governors of "Dakota," Massachusetts, and New York. Other female graduates had become great novelists, lawyers, sheriffs, captains of baseball nines.[9] Important changes in American culture at home translated into new ways of organizing and conceptualizing woman's work on the missionary field.

These changes emerged in the nature of the volunteers and in the gender ideology they espoused. Increasingly, educated girls came to imagine themselves to have, at least fleetingly, a self detached from the home that might make a contribution to the world. The mission field both attracted and trained New Women, women defined not by their domestic subordination, but by their confidence that they had something of their own to offer their fellows.

The social construct of the New Woman took form as a discursive category and as an image from popular literature, just as the ideology of domesticity had. At least some of its roots extended into the very notions of women's separate sphere and gifts. Yet it differed substantially from the model offered by *Godey's Lady's Book* and the domestic subordination of the graduates of North Granville Ladies' Seminary. For the New Woman was encouraged to take her own counsel, assert her own self, in the service of transcendent goals. Advisers from the liberal and Christian reform communities argued that national culture needed more than women's moral sensibilities. The world and the nation also needed their *agency*. The Christian reformer Reverend Francis E. Clark, the founder and guiding spirit of the popular evangelical youth organization Christian Endeavor, for instance, in 1886 spoke on the topic "A Young Woman's Rights." He observed that today's young woman "always seems to be afraid of her own individuality." He was clear he did not want to encourage anything "odd and bizarre or pert and perverse" (in itself an interesting gloss on the negative associations of individuality for girls). He did urge on girls their God-given right to "be yourself." Worth more than anything, he opined, was "your right to *be self-reliant, and in the best sense of the term, independent.*"[10] Clark saw his counsel to self-sufficiency not as a challenge to his admonitions to follow the Lord, but as a *freeing* of young women to follow the higher good. As a Christian reformer, he felt his enemy was not a girl's independence but the shallowness of her domestic life.

Another champion of female self-sovereignty was Frances Willard, founder of the Woman's Christian Temperance Union (WCTU) who early in life had confronted the limitations on a girl's life within the constraints of midcentury domesticity. As she left school and became eligible for marriage, a difficult time for many, she felt she had lost her "occupation," an apt title for the active life she pursued as a girl. Despite the extraordinary life she in fact crafted for herself, she reflected critically on the constraints imposed on a maturing girl: "I always believed that if I had been left alone and allowed as a woman what I had as a girl, a free life in the country, where a human being might grow, body and soul, as a tree grows, I would have been ten times more of a person in every way." For girls confronting life thereafter, in 1888, Willard urged action: "Yes, the world wants the best thing; *your best*, and she will smite you stealthily if you do not hand over your gift." She modeled her book for girls, entitled *How to Win*, on a book for boys and advocated an activist agenda. Rather than adopting the passive "reverie" considered becoming for girls, she demanded focus and commitment. She asked her readers to take "resolute aim" beyond the household to apply their special gifts to the world at large.[11] The discourse of self-reliance acknowledged girls' rights and responsibilities to consider themselves as individuals with their own responsibility to larger causes.

Willard's and Clark's interest in girls' autonomy was not in enabling young women to run off with traveling salesmen or join the circus. As Christian reformers, Willard and Clark believed that the evangelical cause they cared about, the moral reformation of the world, was woman's true interest. They believed that, in gaining their freedom, women would be free to join an army of Christian soldiers. When the illustrator Charles Dana Gibson drew, satirically, this New Woman, he went so far as to put her in the pulpit, a logical extension of the ideas Clark and Willard were promoting. Gibson was also attracted to military metaphors suggesting the association between the war of the sexes (a constant theme) and turn-of-the-century imperialism itself.[12] Although New Women did not fight in the Spanish–American War, they did found cadet corps in the high schools and demonstrate their equal abilities in marching and drilling to their male classmates. One can read some of the claims for newly vigorous and public women as a claim for women as well as men to recognize their responsibilities to the state—and to the empire. The gender type of the New Woman, like the gender type of the domestic helpmate, also interacted with imperial ideology to foster imperial expansion. And indeed, one can even argue, as Kristin Hoganson does in *Fighting for American Manhood*, that the crisis in masculinity which accompanied the rise of the New Woman helped to create the nationalist momentum for empire.[13] Gender has certainly been a creative force in the making of the American national culture of empire.

But the ideology of gender has been notoriously unstable. If sphere-based thinking sanctioned and sanctified mid-nineteenth-century imperial projects, gender, as embodied in the women's missionary enterprise, was critical to beginning the process of the unmaking of a national culture based on racial and imperial hierarchy.[14] Domesticity, like manliness and civilization, constituted an elastic conceptual category which could be stretched to fit an array of apparently contradictory projects.[15] Sphere-based ideology, especially when invigorated by the organizational efforts of the turn-of-the-century woman's missionary societies, proved critical in attempting to check nationalist and imperialist scripts. Many women missionaries, home boards, and churchwomen supporters might have allied their Christian cause with the "spread Eagle" nationalism of the moment, but the separate women's culture emerging from domesticity was responsible for some critical challenges to that dominant culture. The point is not whether or not most women espoused a domesticity that was congenial to a hypernationalist imperial culture; undoubtedly most women did. More important is the question of *where* challenges to that culture came from. Certainly in the early part of the twentieth century, anarchists and socialists, many from the immigrant working classes, were the strongest voices challenging dominant orthodoxies. They were also persecuted and largely silenced during the Red Scare in 1919–20. One other set of voices came from a less easily marginalized group. Middle-class reform women, sometimes unmarried, in concert with reform-minded men from the Christian lobby, provided another coherent voice, explicitly allying their voice and cause with peace.

Critical to these developments was the single woman missionary, settlement worker, or reformer, who may have taken on the emotional coloring of woman's sphere but who needed to take an expansive view of her

New Woman in the Pulpit by Charles Dana Gibson
(detail from "In Days to Come the Churches May Be Fuller").

home in order to populate it. In contrast to earlier visions of domesticity, which located woman's sphere within strong, protective walls, turn-of-the-century female activists hypothesized more flexible and porous walls which welcomed in the world and its children. As Progressive reformers founded settlement houses, went to medical school, and organized social work, separate women's missionary boards grew up in increasing numbers both to serve the needs of women and children in the mission field and to respond to the declining availability of ordained men who could address the suffering perceived all over the globe. The deaths of men in the Civil War and the draw of the frontier had created a class of so-called superfluous women who could avail themselves of freedom from marriage. The late-century preaching of the Social Gospel as well suggested the important roles which could be played by such women as lay workers—teachers and doctors—in tending to needs in the field. If married women found themselves ensnared in the bonds of domesticity, including maternity and

New Woman as Soldier by Charles Dana
Gibson (detail from "In Days to Come Who
Will Look After This Boy?").

the ordering of homes, single women had fewer interfaces between them
and the benevolent empire that was their missionary calling. They looked
out at the society which surrounded them and had a better chance of
seeing what was there. (In the group portrait below, Flora Heebner's
direct gaze suggests the single woman's greater ability to focus on the
world around her in contrast with the contained families of the American
Board of Commissioners for Foreign Missions station in Shanxi, China.)[16]

Several forces then conjoined to form a distinct kind of gendered,
Christian internationalism. Women missionaries combined the gendered
obligation to love and nurture with the organizational discipline of the
Progressive era. Single women chose as their "children" the peoples in
need both at home and in mission fields around the world. This too was
domesticity, but it was something quite different from the midcentury
domesticity described by Kaplan. Most especially it was not always the
story of the American nation.

Flora Heebner, with Willoughby and Mary Hemingway, Shanxi, China, 1904. By permission of the Houghton Library, Harvard University ABC 78.1, box 20, and Wider Church Ministries, United Church of Christ.

The historian Ian Tyrrell has discussed the ways in which organized women's voices from the end of the nineteenth century sought to tell stories that differed from the tales of American nationalism. While white male historians and American political leaders were working to construct and legitimate the story of the American nation, Tyrrell argues, some women and some African Americans considered other affiliations primary —as Christians, as women, as members of a Pan-African alliance.[17] His study of history writing in the nineteenth century suggests that women's interpretations of the story of temperance and suffrage internationalism served to check national excesses. These narratives were marginalized in the writing of academic history and in the nationalist mainstream at the time but have left their testaments for readers today.

Similarly, Tyrell's earlier work on the World's WCTU foregrounded the work of female temperance reformers who sought a global women's alliance, uniting women from all continents to challenge the actions of temporal nation-states. Willard wanted her organization to "go everywhere" as well as "do everything," and in 1893 the World's WCTU sent out an "around-the-world missionary" to promote its cause. One can argue that Willard threw her energies into transforming national culture and law in the name of a Christian morality, thus performing the important role of trying to sanctify or improve American imperial projects. But she worked from both sides. Her King was always celestial, and her means to the kingdom threw her in league with temperance advocates elsewhere.[18] Branches of the World's WCTU took on expatriate vices as well as indigenous ones, attacking the dens of iniquity in foreign concessions and lamenting the terrible examples of their countrymen.

Indeed the association of the values endorsed by the WCTU with women's activism in general was sufficient that Progressive women were among the keenest critics of American participation in the First World War. As people in the American West all know, the Montana native Jeanette Rankin, the first woman member of the House of Representatives, cast the sole negative vote opposing the declaration of the First World War, and this at a time before the United States as a whole had passed a woman suffrage amendment. In this she was remaining true to a substantial body of Progressive women's ideology. Jane Addams, the Hull House settlement worker, previously a saint in Progressive America, was vilified after she refused to support American participation in the war. In 1920, despite the acquiescence of the major women's suffrage organization in the war effort, the Methodist Woman's Foreign Missionary Society (WFMS) allied its enthusiasm for the passage of the Nineteenth Amendment enfranchising women to a global antimilitarist standard. That year, the society's periodical told Methodist women that since they "had learned through bitter and bloody experience that women must do their part in making a warless world," their votes and voices should "register their unequivocal opposition to the futility and insanity of war" and seek to further "world peace and world friendship." The Methodist WFMS told its readers that "every missionary and every supporter of missions is an internationalizing agency and an active factor in the creation of the will to peace."[19]

Similarly, as the historian Karen Seat demonstrates in new work, some Methodist missionary women championed an enlightened racial ideology in missionary periodicals at a time of increasing racial stratification in American society at large. The evolution of the title of the periodical of the woman's board itself reflected movement from a sensationalist marketing of allegedly primitive customs to an endorsement of the full humanity of peoples of different cultures and nations. At its founding in 1869 and thereafter, the WFMS periodical was known as the *Heathen Woman's Friend*, a name which its defenders claimed "expresses so much." However, in the 1890s, missionaries in Japan requested a name change. They argued that the name *Heathen Woman's Friend* was a "misnomer" and a "hindrance to their work." After conducting a survey, the board found that indeed many missionaries did find the word *heathen* objectionable, and in a close vote the board changed the name to *Woman's Missionary Friend*. This marker of the growing enlightenment of the Methodist WFMS was especially significant at a time when racial hierarchies were under scientific construction and Jim Crow laws were being passed and upheld throughout the American South. In 1905, the editors of the WFMS publication worked to educate their membership: "Sympathetic mission study is never helped by making our 'little brown brother' ridiculous. . . . In all discussion emphasize the similarities rather than the differences of character between yourself and them. By this method of approach, manners and customs will not seem 'queer,' for that would be evidence of anything but a cosmopolitan spirit."[20] The language of cosmopolitanism in this decade was not always favorable. (George Bernard Shaw so intimated in 1907 in his ironic equating of "cosmopolitan riffraff" with "hypocrites, humbugs, Germans, Jews, Yankees, foreigners.")[21] A WFMS missionary even asked her readers to support the anti-imperial struggles of the Congo in 1906, arguing the identity of feeling which should unite "our happy homes" with the suffering of the black people in the Congo: "If God has made 'of one blood all nations to dwell on the earth,' he has also made their nerves of the one material and their hearts to beat with the same joy or sorrow as ours." Seat argues convincingly that the WFMS and its writers promoted a message of liberal Christian universalism which regularly challenged American racism.

The advocacy of Christian transnationalism was not limited to Methodists. The author Helen Barrett Montgomery, a woman's rights activist and later a supporter of Baptist women's missions, challenged head-on any idea that the dominant Eastern religions were pagan, arguing that "to describe Buddhism as paganism merely shows a lamentable amount of ignorance."[22] Woman's rights advocacy did not always extend to support for racial equality, as the late-century history of the woman suffrage movement lamentably demonstrated. The contributions of the extended women's missionary circle are therefore especially significant.

Of course, missionaries in major imperial cities tended to live within the expatriate societies which grew up around them at the turn of the century, as suggested by Frederick Cooper and Ann Stoler in *Tensions of Empire*.[23] Colonial cultures increasingly existed in a bourgeois world which could ally missionary projects with home-based life habits, including the habits of race. Here, sometimes, single women's involvements with so-called native peoples as companions, partners, or adoptive parents challenged the hierarchies of expatriates. It would be hard to call these affiliations normative. If single women adopted native children, in some parts of the world such adoptions were primarily financial arrangements which were compatible with de facto segregation. Yet in those instances when missionary women adopted in fact and brought their children to live with them, racial orders were substantively challenged both abroad and at home.

One of the prime contributions of Seat's study is her discussion of the adoption of a Japanese child by the missionary Elizabeth Russell and the impact it had on her thinking about race. Seat writes, "Through raising May [Russell's adoptive daughter] she experienced the reality of racial discrimination as a personal wound" and describes how her experience with her adoptive daughter politicized Russell. Russell was not alone in her advocacy and joined a broader Christian lobbying movement in the United States that directly targeted anti-Japanese sentiment and discriminatory immigration law. Anti-Japanese sentiment on the West Coast had gained force during the early twentieth century, especially targeting the same taboo racial mixing which had been used to enact lynch laws in the American South. When virulent racism won the day in 1924, with the passage of the racially discriminatory National Origins Act, humiliating the Japanese as "aliens ineligible for citizenship," the WFMS protested, beginning their annual report of 1924 with a "Plea for Understanding." Both the general mission board of the Methodist Episcopal Church and the WFMS took their outrage to President Calvin Coolidge. In a letter the WFMS stated that they represented more than six hundred thousand American women who requested a "reconsideration of this Exclusion Act with a view to eliminating race discrimination and to re-establishing the bonds of friendship that will make possible cooperation in works of peace throughout the world." The Japanese nation responded to the National Origins Act with a day of mourning and anger, and the prescient Secretary of State Charles Evans Hughes predicted that the humiliation of Japan would bear bitter fruit in the future. Following this dismal moment, the women's liberal reform community met at Vassar College. It was a broad group that included the League of Women Voters, Federation of Women's Clubs, the Young Women's Christian Association (YWCA), the WCTU, Council of Women for Home Missions, and the Federation of Women's Boards of Foreign Missions. The mission-affiliated women constituted the largest group at the conference, and together they discussed action, listened to the recommendations of nonwhite women, and apologized to them for Western, white arrogance. The meeting was reported in the Methodist publication, and it was noted that "prominent Negro women were members of the institute and valued participants in discussions." The group together sent a cable of apology to the women of Japan, pledging a "united effort to promote . . . the principles of justice."[24] This substantial lobby originated from within the liberal wing of the missionary community.

Missionary activists confronted other challenges to their message of sisterhood (and brotherhood) in Christ. As the essays in this book suggest, the forces of anti-imperialist nationalism around the world made few distinctions between American businessmen, diplomats, and missionaries. In the 1920s, nationalists in China, Egypt, and India lashed out at missionaries, among others, when it became clear that the Western powers were not interested in hearing their protests of their subject status. In many parts of the world, women who had felt their mission redeemed by their selfless service found themselves targeted with businessmen and diplomats as objects of the anti-imperialist furies of the moment.

In response, Christian organizations regrouped. At the forefront in these efforts to reconceptualize and internationalize their mission in the United States was the YWCA. YWCA workers in China especially seem to have taken to heart the message of Chinese nationalist May 4 protesters, which roiled college campuses and the circles of modernists against the decision made at Versailles to allocate German assets in Shandong to the Japanese. Many YWCA workers saw their lives change as a result. One such

worker is described in Karen Garner's study of the life and work of the
YWCA secretary Maud Russell, who began her service as a Christian
socialist and was profoundly and personally transformed by her experiences in China in the 1920s. Anger at the mission community sent YWCA
workers to study the laws of extraterritoriality, contributing to new understandings of their role as beneficiaries of empire.[25] In an interview later in
her life, Russell credited the parent board of the YWCA as well as field
secretaries with forward thinking about the situation in China. The New
York YWCA office sent her to Moscow for six months, telling her, "You
know China is going Communist, and we need to understand what it
means." Russell became a lifelong champion of Maoism and the revolutionary generation in China, a spokesperson for the Fellowship for Reconciliation, and a target of the Federal Bureau of Investigation and Mc-
Carthyism. She cited the YWCA as the original sponsor of her political
education.[26]

Like the WFMS, as Garner has argued in different work, the YWCA
joined with other women's organizations in common cause for the advancement of international understanding and advocacy for women of the
world. With seven other women's organizations, the YWCA formed the
Liaison Committee of International Women's Organizations in 1925 and
took aim at such issues as trafficking in women and children. Garner
argues that the YWCA's goals could be summarized as "Christian internationalism, civilization and women's liberation" and quotes Margaret
Jeffrys Hobart of the American YWCA in 1919 excitedly endorsing the
potential of woman's vote: "No politician . . . who has thrown his influence
on the side of the liquor interests or of the underworld, or who has favored
the powerful. Who opposes the greedy who fleece the poor; no statesman
who has espoused the cause of the strong nations against the weak or who
has fostered a spirit of national arrogance, should expect to receive her
vote. If we really mean what we say, if we want Christ's Kingdom and his
Lordship on earth, the way to do it is to bring that Kingdom into every
nook and corner of our lives." Another Christian internationalist wrote,
"Citizenship must not be localized, must not be selfish, else women will
fail in the high task set before them. Women must see their civic responsibilities in the light of a world that is needy and suffering." Two decades
later as Europe prepared for war, a World YWCA secretary decried "selfish

nationalism" and "sinful aggression" that "opposed God's will and destroyed world peace."[27] If, as Kaplan has argued, the doctrine of domesticity undergirded and enabled racism and imperial expansionism in the nineteenth century, by the twentieth century one strain of Christian moral domesticity had evolved as a consistently vocal and articulate voice against racism and nationalism and for international understanding and human kinship in the American political landscape.

The story of this book is ongoing; the intensity and the political stakes of that struggle are as high today as at any time in the past. All around the world, the American and British missionary presence is robust. Even in China, like the former Soviet Union a historical enemy of the West and its religions, American and British missionaries are abundant and active, often officially described as English teachers but propelled by missionary commitments and training. What does this new missionary wave mean? At the least, in China it means the adoption of a "don't ask, don't tell policy," which must be the official position of the Chinese Communist Party. (When explaining their affiliations, English teachers in China sometimes refer to the "humanitarian organizations" responsible for their presence.) The supply of evangelical speakers of English who will work in distant outposts for modest salaries is solving a pressing immediate need for China: the dissemination of English proficiency through all parts of the country. In the twenty-first century China is replicating the strategic use of Western missionaries for self-strengthening, just as it did at the turn of the nineteenth century. Missionaries, on their side, have been building up warm contacts with students and colleagues whom they can invite to Christmas celebrations, which double as cultural and religious events, and gradually introduce to Christianity, which is currently of interest all over China. The history of missionaries in the contemporary world is increasingly the history of nonmainstream, evangelical, and fundamentalist denominations, often downplayed in the official missionary narrative, though restored to their proper importance in this volume. The Assembly of God, the Brethren, even the China Inland Missions were conservative denominations rooted firmly on the antimodernist side of Anglo-American religious history. In the past, historians have set fundamentalist religious affiliation in sharp contrast to the modernizing impact of political and commercial culture, but in our era the matter is more complex. Much of the world does not distinguish between evangelical and mainstream Protestant denominations, seeing them both as representatives of American culture writ large.

Certainly that is the case when one asks about the impact of American (and British too) evangelical missionaries on gender relations in the developing world. It is true that in some ways today's evangelical missionary program dates back to the late nineteenth century. A surfing of the Web for images of China missionaries in 2003 revealed the card of a young missionary couple affiliated with the Fundamental Baptist Missions International. An image of a missionary proselytizer outlined against a map of China indicated that missionaries were "Shining the Light of the Gospel in a Land of Darkness."[28] The rhetoric of darkness and light in this image is not contemporary, cosmopolitan gospel, but the gospel of salvation and redemption of a simple, bimodal world. Religious fundamentalism is matched with moral fundamentalism. American efforts to limit family planning initiatives and launch AIDS prevention programs which encourage African men to "just say no" to extramarital sex emerged from this simple moral world. In the United States, too, many evangelical religious groups have been attempting to turn back the clock on the movement toward gender equality. Such groups as the Promise Keepers and Focus on the Family have been committed to restoring the traditional family in which men will commit to reliable breadwinning, faithfulness, and family headship and women to domestic and reproductive labor and subordination.

Yet these are not the total messages or perhaps even the dominant message evangelical Americans actually bring to the developing world. Of interest here is an article from 2006 that appeared in the *New York Times Magazine*. Entitled "Post Colonial Missionaries: What in God's Name Are Missionaries Doing in Africa?," it tells the story of an evangelical family who traveled to rural Africa to bring the message of Jesus Christ to the Samburu people of Kenya with none of the educational, public health, or economic programs of some liberal missions. But for this family there was no ambiguity when it came to the local Kenyan custom of female genital cutting. Rick Maples, the father of the family, explained, "It's a spiritual issue, it's a public health issue, it's a human rights issue. The body is God's temple, and to mar it a sin." Part of his distress had to do with the denial of the pleasures of sex implicit in the practice. He called the notion that evangelicals were antisex a misapprehension deriving from their disapproval of premarital sex. In fact, the issue of genital cutting was one way for the Maples to focus their own sense that the Samburu *needed* Jesus. They had a clear campaign plan: "Once people have accepted the Lord, we'll talk about how God created sex and ordained sex, and that sex is to be enjoyed." Women's status in Samburu society presented similar problems for Carrie Maples, Rick's wife. She noted her dismay that one man did not know the name of his bride and that young girls were given to old men to settle family debts. She concluded, "The woman is not a doormat." Whatever chasms have existed within American society on the appropriate status of women and relations between the sexes, in contrast to indigenous Samburu culture Americans have discovered some surprising commonality. The *New York Times* reporter agreed, concluding, "Amid the Samburu culture, the Mapleses could seem to be not only Christian crusaders but also bold and progressive social activists, champions of female emancipation and sexual fulfillment."[29] American feminists, anthropologists, and nongovernmental organizations have attempted to frame their responses to African gender systems in more nuanced terms, acknowledging the ways in which sensationalist responses to genital cutting mirror an earlier era's simultaneous fascination with and revulsion at foot binding.[30] One can argue that both approaches are reductive, imperialist ways of understanding complex cultures. Yet these scruples are likely to be lost on Africans themselves, who rightly ascertain the similarities between the visceral responses of Americans of vastly different initial ideological agendas.

What influence will this century's evangelical missionaries have on American domestic affairs? What impact will this generation's missionary lobby have on American international politics? There have been some indications—the insistence of President George W. Bush's administration on freedom of religion, for instance. The Mormon Church in the United States sends many of its youth to missions around the world, a fact which might argue that the State of Utah should be among the most internationalist and progressive in the nation. Indeed, the Obama administration's appointment of a former Mormon missionary as the U.S. ambassador to China suggests the surprising alliances that international missions might bring to domestic American politics.

Yet it seems certain that the impact of this new evangelical missionary outpouring will confound the intents of its initiators. The historian Jonathan Spence, in an early book entitled *To Change China*, noted that those who were most changed by the efforts of early Western missionaries were the missionaries themselves.[31] It is perhaps too soon to know whether missionaries like the Maples will be the rule or the exception, but questions about the impact of global exchange on gender roles undoubtedly have relevance well beyond the interwar years. The example of the American evangelical coalition against global warming and in stewardship of the earth suggests some of the mysterious ways in which history can sometimes work. And the savage crises of the contemporary world provide fresh opportunities to apply the message and vision of Christian women's interwar internationalism.

NOTES

1 David Halberstam, *The Best and the Brightest* (New York: Random House, 1972).

2 Jane Hunter, *Gospel of Gentility: American Women Missionaries in Turn-of-the-Century China* (New Haven: Yale University Press, 1984).

3 Alexis de Tocqueville, *Democracy in America*, vol. 2, chap. XII, section 3.

4 Amy Kaplan, *The Anarchy of Empire in the Making of U.S. Culture* (Cambridge, Mass.: Harvard University Press, 2002).

5 *Godey's Lady's Book*, April 1847, 177.

6 Jane H. Hunter, *How Young Ladies Became Girls: The Victorian Origins of American Girlhood* (New Haven: Yale University Press, 2002), 377.

7 Ibid., 378.

8 Thanks to Joan Jacobs Brumberg's work for drawing my attention to this illustration in *Women of Worth: A Book for Girls* (New York: W. A. Townsend, 1860).

9 Hunter, *How Young Ladies Became Girls*, 381–82.

10 Rev. F. E. Clark, "A Young Woman's Rights," *Ladies Home Journal*, November 1886, as quoted in Hunter, *How Young Ladies Became Girls*, 403.

11 Frances Willard, *How to Win: A Book for Girls* (New York: Funk and Wagnalls, 1886), 26–27, 33, as quoted in Hunter, *How Young Ladies Became Girls*, 403.

12 Charles Dana Gibson, details from "In Days to Come the Churches May Be Fuller," "In Days to Come Who Will Look After This Boy?," *Pictures of People* (New York: C. Scribner's Sons, 1896).

13 Kristin L. Hoganson, *Fighting for American Manhood: How Gender Politics Provoked the Spanish–American and Philippine–American Wars* (New Haven: Yale University Press, 1998).

14 Kaplan's book addresses both the making and unmaking of a coherent national culture.

15 Gail Bederman, *Manliness and Civilization: A Cultural History of Gender and Race in the United States, 1880–1917* (Chicago: University of Chicago Press, 1995) has demonstrated the ways in which the concept of manliness and civilization could be used both by proponents of Jim Crow racism and by its opponents.

16 Flora Heebner, with Willoughby and Mary Hemingway, Shanxi, China, c. 1904, ABCFM Papers, Houghton Library, Harvard University ABC 78.1, box 20. (Also used in Hunter, *Gospel of Gentility*, 54.)

17 Ian Tyrrell, "Making Nations/Making States: American Historians in the Context of Empire," *Journal of American History* 86, no. 3 (December 1999), 1015–44.

18 Ian R. Tyrrell, *Woman's World/Woman's Empire: The Woman's Christian Temperance Union in International Perspective, 1800–1930* (Chapel Hill: University of North Carolina Press, 1991).

19 As quoted in Karen K. Seat, *"Providence Has Freed Our Hands:" Women's Missions and the American Encounter with Japan"* (Syracuse: Syracuse University Press, 2008), 152.

20 As quoted ibid., 123–25.

21 *The Oxford English Dictionary.*

22 As quoted in Seat, *"Providence Has Freed Our Hands,"* 126–29.

23 Frederick Cooper and Ann Laura Stoler, eds., *Tensions of Empire: Colonial Cultures in a Bourgeois World* (Berkeley: University of California Press, 1997).

24 Seat, *"Providence Has Freed Our Hands,"* 114, 153–56.

25 Karen Garner, *Precious Fire: Maud Russell and the Chinese Revolution* (Amherst: University of Massachusetts Press, 2003).

26 Maud Russell, personal interview (New York, 1983).

27 Karen Garner, "Global Feminism and Postwar Reconstruction: The World YWCA Visitation to Occupied Japan, 1947," *Journal of World History* 15, no. 3 (June 2004), 191–227.

28 [Name removed], located in 2003, search terms "China missionaries."

29 Daniel Bergner, "The Call," *New York Times Magazine*, January 29, 2006.

30 For instance, see Stanlie M. James and Claire C. Robertson, eds., *Genital Cutting and Transnational Sisterhood: Disputing U.S. Polemics* (Urbana: University of Illinois Press, 2002).

31 Jonathan D. Spence, *To Change China: Western Advisers in China, 1620–1960* (Boston: Little, Brown, 1969).

New Approaches to American Cultural Expansion

Ian Tyrrell

I t is hard to recall in these post–Iraq war days just how recently a dis-course on U.S. empire became explicit and acknowledgment of American imperial roles commonplace. A resurgence of interest, however, began about a decade earlier, around the time my book *Woman's World / Woman's Empire: The Woman's Christian Temperance Union in International Perspective* was published. The shift was partly spurred by the rise of postcolonial studies, with an important collection of articles edited by Amy Kaplan and Donald Pease appearing just two years later in 1993. In many ways, *Woman's World / Woman's Empire* spoke hesitantly to the origins of a new con-juncture, one concerning a "new kind of empire." That empire was charac-terized by a set of transnational networks of cultural communication, exchange, and power. The WCTU's work was consistent with this larger and highly contemporary theme of an American cultural and economic expan-sionism that knew no borders. The World's WCTU provided an early blueprint for a deterritorialized form of American empire, centered around the networks of nongovernmental organizations conveying American val-ues. Though implicated in European racial hierarchies and dependent on the power and material connections of European economic and political imperialism, the WCTU did not wholeheartedly endorse classical imperial-ism, formal or otherwise; its gender consciousness cut across race at times, and its efforts at reform and conversion targeted not only colonial peoples but also Europeans (and others) who fell short of WCTU standards on drug abuse or the equal treatment of women. In this sense the WCTU promoted an American evangelical outreach of global, messianic, and universalistic dimensions rather than being tied to any particular territorial power.[1]

Though organizationally distinctive, the WCTU did not exist in isolation. Understanding its contribution to women, empire, and missions requires setting the movement in the context of a transnational and cross-organizational study of American cultural expansion in the late nineteenth century and early twentieth. In this essay, I first outline the nature of empire and comparative imperialism, showing how the WCTU worked within American colonialism and cultural expansionism while remaining quite critical of formal imperialism. The WCTU was not an orthodox missionary group. Though its domestic history began in 1874 as the National Woman's Christian Temperance Union, after the founding of the World's Woman's Christian Temperance Union in 1884 the American organization cooperated with a growing list of affiliated unions around the globe. It sent its own women's temperance missionaries abroad and also interacted with regular missionaries and their committees at home. Three key issues are examined in which the relationship of the WCTU as a conduit between metropolitan and colonial forces developed: the military canteen, the supply of alcohol to so-called native races, and the regulation of prostitution. Little attention has been given to these aspects of WCTU history, and even less is known about the effectiveness of these campaigns in domestic American debates. In order to assess the impact upon American policies, however, a salient truth must be recognized: the WCTU operated as part of a cross-gender reform coalition, despite its pedigree of sisterhood and the strong, cross-national gender bonds it forged with missionaries and indigenous peoples in many countries.

As Fernand Braudel stated, "Imperialism is not a word to be uttered lightly." It is usually taken to mean the political domination of geographically separate territories and their peoples, a definition that superficially does not fit U.S. experience.[2] Yet evaluating the American example is complicated by the problem of exceptionalism. There is a tendency to assume a European model based upon formal acquisition of territory, seized from tribal societies or sovereign states—and the peoples in the lands so acquired are subject peoples, not citizens or even potential citizens. But one can easily identify many gradations within this rather rigid framework in and between European empires: there are crucial distinctions between commercial seaborne empires and land-based ones; between white settlement colonies and others; and between formal acquisition of territory and informal control. One can also find a bewildering combination of these forms. For this reason, an American empire must be set comparatively against a range of historical empires, not against an American idea of what an empire ought to be.[3] The American experience has some features in common with the British empire, to which it has been closely related, and some differences. The United States was no exception in regard to empire, but a variation on a larger theme.

Many of that empire's characteristics were not unique to American expansion. These characteristics cover such classic themes as informal rule, cooptation and collaboration between colonials and imperialists, and the mixed picture of continental territorial acquisition, trading posts, and strategic steppingstones for the acquisition of markets. Alongside similarities to a range of empires, however, one can detect contributions that are, while not entirely unprecedented, perhaps disproportionately American: these have included an ideological distaste for formal colonialism and a tendency to deploy hegemonic transnational organizations and institutions rooted, nonetheless, in American cultural experience.[4] This strategy of cultural hegemony was pioneered in the expansion undertaken by Protestant reformers and missions in the late nineteenth century. It is arguable whether this social formation ought to be described as an empire. Yet to understand the global position of the United States in the twentieth century one needs innovative ways of evaluating the meaning of the entire web of cultural as well as economic relationships contributing to the extension of European power and dependent upon that power. At the same time, one must also take into account contradictory elements within the thinking of Western Christian missionaries and not merely typecast them as cultural imperialists.[5] That would be too simplistic a label. Perhaps the element of anti-imperialism and ambivalent relationships with empire within women's missionary experience stems from the competing kingdom of transnational religious affiliation. Yet anti-imperialism also stemmed from experience, from the practices of confronting the contradictory messages implicit in reformers' cultural expansion abroad.

Despite American innovations within the practices of cultural expansionism, the United States did have a continental empire decidedly territorial in the nineteenth century. To be sure, the area of the Louisiana

Purchase was soon broken into territories able to be admitted to the Union. It is this process upon which the U.S. vision of itself as a Jeffersonian empire of liberty rests. Therein the inhabitants of new territories would in due course become the citizens of new American states. Partly this self-conception is a matter of judgment about the role of formal sovereignty and citizenship. It masks the realities of naked aggression in the taking of territories and the suppression of their Native American populations. But even within the accepted framework, anomalies existed. The Arizona and New Mexico territories acquired in the Mexican–American War of 1846–48 were held as quasi-colonies until 1912, long after they had surpassed the usual population bar for admission as states. The acquisition of Alaska from Russia in 1867 left the native residents as wards of the government, not potential or actual citizens. Mission activities among the Amerindians within the continental United States, like military activity, could be seen as a training ground for empire and as part of an imperial process. But most of the work done on missions and empire concerns overseas American expansion, where a different pattern prevailed. Acquisition of the Philippines has traditionally been seen as a "great aberration."[6] It does, however, together with the simultaneous acquisition of Puerto Rico and Guam from the Spanish, the protectorate over Cuba at the end of the Spanish–American War, and the annexation of American Samoa and Hawaii, fit elements of the classic seaborne, commercial empire strategy beloved of the Dutch and to some extent the British.

Yet the dominant (though not the only) form of American empire concerned neither continental territory nor the colonies gained after 1898. Rather, it involved cultural expansion in the period of great missionary activity of the late nineteenth century and early twentieth, expansion that is consistent with the networks of communication thesis outlined above. Although William Appleman Williams and his disciples studied the open door policy of economic expansion in the 1960s, cultural expansion has not received the attention it deserves—despite the pioneering work of Emily Rosenberg.[7] It is often assumed that this projection of global cultural influence began in the 1920s, but American cultural hegemony has a longer history.[8] Missions fit broadly into this earlier cultural expansion. Economic and cultural interests were intertwined in American muscle flexing from the 1890s. When the United States engaged from 1905 onward in a series of quasi-colonial occupations of, and temporary interventions in, a number of Caribbean countries, especially Haiti and the Dominican Republic, all in the interest of American finances and property rights, the actions also had cultural and political impacts upon the occupied peoples.[9]

It was not just cultural expansion but specific forms of Protestant Christian moral expansionism that characterized the new American empire. American imperialism had a strong tone of evangelical moral reform, even officially as seen in the pious reflections on the acquisition of the Philippines by President William McKinley. There is a strong case for historians to investigate the importance of evangelical religion in the ideas of American policy-makers in the late nineteenth century.[10] Theodore Roosevelt and other architects of American empire such as Alfred Thayer Mahan were tough realists, but they had a thoroughly religious as much as a strategic view of empire. It is little known that Mahan served ten years on the Board of Missions of the Protestant Episcopal Church and told Roosevelt in 1901 that it was important for the European powers to gain in Asia "simple, entire liberty of entrance for European thought, as well as European commerce." Both Mahan and Roosevelt justified the use of force in international relations in terms of the spread of Christian civilization.[11]

The morality issue was closely connected with the way Americans needed to distance themselves from European empires—there was a felt need to assimilate American empire to exceptionalism.[12] Other nations also claimed moral objectives as rationales for imperial acquisitions and believed in their own exceptionalism, as in, for example, the French sense of *mission civilisatrice* and the British creed of the rule of law and a Pax Britannica. But this negates neither the importance of exceptionalist ideas in the way Americans marketed their own empire to themselves, nor the specific cluster of ideas projected abroad. It was not just some abstract, generalized notion of exceptionalism driving policy on this score. The issue of morality was closely connected with the role of women and missions, and the role of women, in turn, was one of the distinctive elements that contributed to notions of American exceptionalism. Women's role in cultural expansion brought Protestant evangelism, imperialism, and American exceptionalism together via transnational moral reform.

Until the 1990s, the topic of women was a neglected theme in American empire, yet the role of women is one of the areas in which one can detect gender differences vis-à-vis many European empires. In the classic literature on American exceptionalism, much of the debate has been focused on social class, but the theme of women is a crucial one. Belief in exceptionalism appeared in the influential early work of Catherine Beecher. In *A Treatise on Domestic Economy*, Beecher proclaimed, "The democratic institutions of this Country . . . have secured to American women a lofty and fortunate position which, as yet, has been attained by the women of no other nation." In Beecher's mind democratic institutions had placed women "in [their] true position in society, as having equal rights with the other sex."[13] To be sure, American women themselves were not sure whether they really were exceptional in practice; issues of gender subordination they seemed to share with less fortunate peoples. These themes nagged at them; they also shared Christianity across national boundaries. But American women reformers considered that only in the United States was evangelical Protestantism fully developed. The WCTU, like its co-workers in cultural expansion abroad, developed a hierarchy of religious beliefs in which evangelical Christianity stood at the summit, above other Protestants, then Orthodox and Catholic Christians, as the table of spiritual achievement descended toward Islam and other allegedly heathen faiths. This gave Protestants the right, as they would see it, to proselytize Catholics, including in the colonial realm of the Philippines.[14]

Evangelical religion and belief in exceptionalism shaped the outward thrust of cultural expansion in which women were implicated as architects and emissaries. Many American evangelicals espoused a widespread belief that the United States was part of a providential plan to prepare for the coming of Christ. Beecher had stressed that the American Republic was the means by which the Messiah of the nations would make "effectual" the "regeneration of the Earth."[15] American women could aid this millennial purpose. By strengthening the home and, through it, American morality, women would build a glorious future for the United States. Frances Willard and the WCTU elaborated on this interpretation and exported this evangelical domesticity in a global crusade against intemperance and for women's emancipation.[16]

Protestant evangelicalism aspired to remake the world so that men and women could demonstrate their moral worthiness. This was an aggressively expansionist position, one which imparted great energy to the missionary crusades of the nineteenth century. To this enterprise temperance women made distinctive contributions. It was the innovative nondenomi-

national, transnational organizations bridging the gap between the religious and the secular, between the moral and the political, and between
the domestic and the foreign that were the most significant for American
empire understood as a set of cultural, transnational networks of communication. This work entailed not the usual sedentary, often denominational, and nationally bound types of many missionary endeavors, but
rather transnational, peripatetic, and interdenominational ones. Women
from both the British empire and Scandinavia were prominent in the
World's WCTU, though they did not tend to be the architects of cultural
and moral expansion.

The WCTU's transnational format was highly innovative, drawing on
officials such as missionaries and other functionaries from a variety of
countries, holding World's conventions, and duplicating its bureaucratic
structures across the globe. Its culturally expansionist, millenarian, and
other characteristics were extended to and imitated by some other equally
significant transnational organizations, including mixed sex and male-
dominated societies. The WCTU's Do Everything program was directly
copied by Christian Endeavor, as its president, Reverend Francis Clark,
admitted.[17] The WCTU also predated the Student Volunteer Movement
for Foreign Missions. One of the most significant organizations for stimulating missionary activity, the volunteers also adopted a nondenominational approach, and the frequent world tours of its leader, John Mott,
bore more than a passing resemblance to the WCTU's round-the-world
missionary work.[18] The highly evangelistic World League against Alcoholism also drew on the WCTU example and benefited from its direct input
from 1919 to 1933.[19]

Among WCTU themes that became characteristic of American cultural
expansion in the 1890–1930 period was cooperation with local groups to
gain access to indigenous cultures and to expand the depth and range of
WCTU membership. In the process, the WCTU exploited de facto discontent with colonial rulers. The World's WCTU missionaries tapped into local
missionary networks, particularly in India, establishing themselves as a
conduit between missionaries and domestic audiences for moral reform in
the United States. The WCTU attracted, as regular missionaries did, indigenous support, particularly from Eurasian and low-caste groups and others
who were discontented with the hierarchies of their own society. Indigenous converts became roving temperance lecturers and reformers, break-

ing through conventional gender barriers. A celebrated example was Pandita Ramabai, the "high-caste Hindu widow" and author of *The Peoples of the United States* (1889). Much less known than Alexis de Tocqueville's *Democracy in America* as an example of how others saw the nineteenth-century United States, Ramabai's work is nevertheless instructive of complex colonial-metropolitan relations. She elicited "generous support" from the WCTU and the Ramabai Circles formed in American cities as a result of her protracted visit in 1886–88.[20]

Collaboration is always an important theme in empires, and people like Ramabai became collaborators in a form of empire by supporting and helping to refashion the WCTU in a multicultural direction; they helped make the WCTU work one of intercultural mediation, interpreting Western messages to the indigenous and offering criticisms as well as comfort to the organization's quasi-imperial project.[21] The wider missionary enterprise also had to function in this way if it was to be successful, particularly by being translated into the vernacular cultures, spoken idioms, and written languages. Missionary processes both secular and religious relied on collaboration, but the collaborators often modified the meaning of the message.[22] This was true in the WCTU too, but its transnational and domestic American purposes were well served by the way the mediation occurred. Whereas there was often tension between missionaries and empire conventionally conceived, the WCTU did not stand for formal empire and could more easily present an alternative form of cultural hegemony. Ramabai demonstrated how the WCTU could profit from its image as the representative of the United States—a "nonimperialist Western power." She "juxtaposed a staunch anti-British stance with an equally strong pro-American one, as a consciously employed strategy of resistance" to colonialism. Consequently, however, Ramabai saw "liberation only through a Western model for India's progress." She came close to endorsing American modernism and cultural hegemony over stereotypical European empires.[23]

The nondenominational nature of WCTU work gave it economies of scale and, being less bound by older institutions, it was able to exploit new groups and advocate new tactics. This nondenominationalism, which Ramabai highlighted, also contributed to the reformist nature of its institutions and gave it more than a hint of a different kind of relationship between Europeans and subject colonial peoples than was present in

British rule. According to Ramabai, "Out of all the many unions that exist in the developed countries, this union [the WCTU] is the best and the greatest." She compared it favorably to the numerous women's mission societies that "do not have the unity among themselves that they should and do not accomplish as many good things as the temperance union has taken upon itself to do." She praised "its extraordinary and outstanding organization."[24]

Another advantage was the ability of the WCTU to connect with a powerful domestic political lobby in order to bring about change in the United States and in its new colonial administrations as well as to influence the wider conduct of foreign affairs. In undertaking this task, the WCTU compared empires, trying to distinguish the American version from others, in order to show that the American could be different—more moral and even anticolonial in spirit. The translation of missionary and reform experience in the wider world into American imperial and domestic policy through the WCTU came in many forms, but none so important or prominent as the military canteen, the export of alcohol to underdeveloped peoples, and army regulation of prostitution.

A vital spur to convert imperial attitudes and practices on the use of alcohol into domestic policy came from the Spanish–American War and its aftermath, especially the insurrectionary war in the Philippines. The American occupation meant more military forces and more conspicuous action by the military. This action seemed to conflict with the civilizing mission proclaimed by American policy-makers. The WCTU's *Union Signal* for December 12, 1901, has a very contemporary ring to it. Despite all the talk about trade possibilities and the white man's burden, the exports of American culture had mainly been soldiers and the imports from the Philippines mainly the dead and their coffins, according to the *Union Signal*. These "insular possessions," as the American government euphemistically called them, had proven already to be very troublesome; the big question for the *Union Signal* was "how to . . . turn war into peace" as well as loss into profit, and "to do them good morally and religiously by self-sacrificing teachers and missionaries, instead of harm by the importation of whiskey."[25]

By 1900 the United States had indeed shouldered the white man's burden. A central cause of concern for the WCTU's version of this imperial civilizing program was the canteen system. In 1890 Congress had tried to ban intoxicating beverages at military canteen posts located in prohibition states or territories. Yet the army still allowed beer and wine sales at the discretion of post commanders. There the position stood until 1898. The wctu lobbied for a law to make the canteens dry immediately after the Spanish–American War began. They were quickly successful in 1899, but the law was poorly written, and the McKinley administration declared that prohibition was not enforceable. This position outraged the wctu. The U.S. Army was, in the opinion of temperance groups, a poor example for the Filipinos.

Two issues got mixed up in subsequent debates. One was the actual canteen system, and the other was the larger question of the licensing of saloons by the new American administration in the Philippines. While the prohibition of all saloons in Manila was the hope, the wctu and its allies argued that the canteens were a bad example for both soldiers and locals. The National wctu sought to discover what reformers could do "toward righting the atrocious conditions in the Philippines," where, "under super-vision and sanction of American authorities," liquor interests "flourish."[26] Bessie Scovell, the president of the Minnesota wctu, emphasized that "again and again has my blood boiled at the reports from missionaries and others of the hundreds of American saloons being established throughout our new possessions."[27] The wctu publicized throughout the United States information gathered by its own visiting campaigners and by the missionaries of the church societies whose members were affiliated with the wctu.[28] An American missionary and wctu member, Cornelia Moots, a sister of Carrie C. Faxon, a wctu campaigner sent to investigate the saloons in the American possessions, stated that "liquor sold in the canteens has the same effect as liquor sold from the regular saloon"; the practice increased the number of saloons rather than decreased them.[29] The effects on the young soldiers concerned temperance women as much as the effects on the Filipinos. The wctu's national convention reported that a quarter of the cases of soldiers confined in Philippine hospitals were related to drink.[30]

The canteen issue had repercussions back home in changing the strat-egies of temperance reformers toward alcohol control policies. By this time the wctu had, like most other American temperance organizations, begun to rally around the issue of national prohibition. This was not an inevitable result, despite the view expressed by historians that the temperance movement had fixed upon this goal by the 1880s.[31] In fact temperance forces had divided over the issue in the 1890s and considered both high license and disinterested management solutions to the alcohol problem. The campaign against the military canteen in the Philippines became a covert way to experiment legislatively with incremental forms of prohibition. Increasingly this is what the Anti-Saloon League of America (ASL) and its allies did, but the WCTU had shown the way. In "all great battles," explained the WCTU legislative tactician Margaret Dye Ellis, there existed a "central point of attack."[32] In the case of prohibition, it was, according to Ellis, the campaign against the liquor canteen in the Philippines. It was significant that this turn toward prohibition accompanied American imperial expansion. Anxieties about expansionism stimulated the shift to national prohibition. This shift was not the product purely of changing tactics and strategies within the American temperance movement domestically.

The canteen touched upon empire in two other ways: first, the canteen implicated the U.S. government in the Philippines directly in the liquor trade and thus stained the reputation of the nation internationally and especially among the Filipino people at a time when the government was attempting to quell rebellion and justify its territorial acquisition. A second way was protecting the nation's borders from the possible contagion that exposure to the ideas and practices of foreign nations might bring. Prohibitionists were alarmed at the expansion of the army made necessary by the imperial adventure and hence of the numbers of canteens and the number of army personnel exposed to drinking. Moreover, there was the supposed impact of other bad habits young men caught up in drinking at the canteens would learn. Soldiers who acquired a taste for alcohol in the Philippines would, it was argued, move on to frequent saloons off the army bases, and there they would not only add to the supply of drinkers, but also pick up nasty habits such as a fondness for gambling and prostitution, practices considered equally evil by prohibitionist forces. Since one-half of the American army was stationed in colonial outposts as late as 1907, the impact on practice at home was obvious, with a considerable number of soldiers returning annually to the mainland camps and spreading their supposed licentiousness.[33] Making the canteens dry would help protect the army's youth from temptations everywhere. The domestic and foreign imperatives were inseparable.

The struggle over the canteen showed the central role of the WCTU in political lobbying. The ASL was becoming powerful after 1900, but it lacked international presence, and its role in the canteen issue should not be exaggerated. There was no ASL equivalent to the World's WCTU until the formation of the World League Against Alcoholism in 1919.[34] Despite the emergence of the ASL, lobbying of Congress by the WCTU was exceptionally heavy at the turn of the century in the aftermath of the war in the Philippines.[35] WCTU missionaries such as Katharine L. Stevenson and the former missionary Margaret W. Leitch testified before Senate committees and other bodies. Though the Committee on Military Affairs recommended against total prohibition, the Senate voted in favor of abolishing the supply of liquor at the military canteens, and the new, enforceable law was enacted on February 2, 1901. Some opposing congressmen credited the WCTU with the victory, claiming, in the language of Shakespeare, that temperance women "doth make cowards of us all."[36]

Missionaries (and the WCTU) also wanted the Philippine government to abolish American-style saloons freely operating in Manila and vicinity after 1898, though in this demand they had only partial success. They succeeded in getting a massive reduction in the number of saloons, but the appointed Philippine government, named the Philippine Commission, had its powers on this issue delegated by Congress and, being under the control of unelected, proto-imperialist officials was not as susceptible to threats of electoral reprisals. The Philippine Commission pursued a policy of high license to limit so-called native access to European-style alcohol and restricted the places and times at which European liquors could be sold.[37] Lobbying by missionaries was more effective when channeled through transnational organizations to the imperial center, where the Congress could directly pass legislation to change the regulation of morality, as in the case of military appropriations. The WCTU was an ideal vehicle for that approach.

The abolition of the army's involvement in the sale of alcohol helped to discharge evangelical reform concerns about the imperial adventure—to cleanse it and give it a good moral purpose. The WCTU thus helped, inadvertently, to make empire legitimate. The controversy contained all of the overtones of the correct example to be set internationally and the need to develop a morally superior position to other empires in order to provide world leadership. The WCTU developed thereby an alliance (partly unconscious) with the military occupiers. Though reluctant to endorse U.S. policy openly because the temperance ranks contained a good many people who were opposed to imperialism and war, the *Union Signal* now effectively endorsed the administration, but only insofar as it could turn "barbarism into civilization." The paper also praised the work of the American army's commanding general, Nelson A. Miles, who supported the canteen legislation and in 1902 inspected conditions in the Philippines.[38]

However, the WCTU continued to be uncertain about the morality of empire and enough in tune with the marginalized anti-imperialists of the United States to rule out any wholehearted endorsement of American colonial policy. Lillian Stevens, the national president of the WCTU, remained uneasy about the spread of empire, urging the United States to avoid a permanent occupation of Cuba and charging that special economic interests were likely to subvert humanitarian endeavors there and in the Philippines. "To resist all these temptations will require the most sterling honesty," proclaimed the *Union Signal*.[39] In fact the WCTU's sympathies with Miles were equally indicative of their "in-between" political position—somewhere uneasily between support of formal empire and opposition to it. The WCTU had not backed a winner in supporting Miles. He had fallen afoul of the American administration in the Philippines and the military establishment in the United States and was relieved of his position as commander of the army at the earliest possible moment. As the example of Miles indicates, the WCTU's allies were not necessarily the dominant political groups in the U.S. government, and they faced hostility from wide sections of the army. Moreover, though the WCTU got the canteen law enacted, the army maintained its officers' clubs, where liquor could be sold, and violations of the law at the post exchanges for the enlisted men occurred.[40]

The new sense of moral obligation gained from the acquisition of colonies not only extended inward, toward defense of the United States through the canteen law as a trial run for national prohibition; it also extended outward to affect the nation's participation in the transnational discourse of imperialism over alcohol and drugs. The WCTU took advice from missionaries, including non-American ones outside the American colonies, who agitated for protecting the peoples of the underdeveloped world from the deleterious impacts of European expansion. These effects included economic dislocation, but the missionaries generally distinguished between good and bad European commerce. Bad European commerce was "not only not a profit but a hindrance to normal trade" and included the provision of alcohol and drugs to colonized peoples and other indigenous groups.[41] This European discourse was a highly paternalistic one in which the "darkness of heathenism" did not know what was best for itself. The WCTU joined this transnational lobbying for an international regime hostile to the export of alcohol to the colonial world. Ellis spoke to Secretary of State John Hay "for the women of the world" and on behalf of the Scottish missionary to the New Hebrides John G. Paton. She coordinated missionary petitions condemning the supplying of alcohol by American traders in the South Pacific.[42] WCTU lobbying helped gain passage in 1902 of the Gillett-Lodge bill banning American trade in alcohol with the New Hebrides and surrounding islands.

Later, the WCTU successfully lobbied the U.S. government to support stronger international conventions on the prohibition of the export of certain types of alcohol to Africa. The American government called for a more moral policy to be adopted at the international treaty negotiations at The Hague in 1906, though the treaty on the question never fully satisfied the WCTU and contained many loopholes that kept the organizations involved in a constant state of agitation over the issue.[43] Coordinated by Wilbur Crafts, the secretary of the International Reform Bureau, and his wife, WCTU Sunday School Superintendent Sara Timanus Crafts, the campaigns of the WCTU and other missionary groups intensified in the years before the First World War, focusing not only on alcohol but also on the prohibition of opium to colonial peoples.[44]

The WCTU also took a central part in the crusade against the official inspections of prostitutes carried out in the Philippines by military doctors for the health and safety of the American army in the field. The issue here had already been confronted by the World's WCTU in a controversial way in the case of the British Army in India, when the WCTU missionaries Kate Bushnell and Elizabeth Wheeler Andrew had in 1897 castigated the World's WCTU president, Lady Isobel Somerset, for her endorsement of the system sanctioning licensed prostitution in brothels established for the benefit of the British army in the Indian military cantonments. Willard had initially supported her friend Somerset, thus causing huge controversy within the American WCTU and abroad, where the English purity campaigner Josephine Butler threw her considerable weight behind efforts to unseat Somerset and denounce Willard. Somerset was eventually forced to repudiate her stance, an action interpreted by the abolitionist forces as a triumph against regulation. As this embarrassing experience concluded just prior to the acquisition of the Philippines, the WCTU was concerned that the U.S. version of empire should not be morally stained, as the British Raj was. The WCTU stressed the need to remove the sanction of vice from the American flag—to make it, as Stevenson later observed, "stand in the Far East as the symbol of righteousness."[45] As in the canteen issue, Ellis, the WCTU's Washington representative, led the campaign, lobbying even Roosevelt himself. She obtained in 1902 an official army book of medical inspection documenting the existence of a child prostitute and her examination by U.S. Army surgeons. Ellis circulated this information among the missionary communities at home and abroad and used it to great effect in embarrassing the U.S. military. She threatened electoral reprisals against the Republican party. Secretary of War Elihu Root, other officials, and ten departmental clerks were inundated with hostile petitions, letters, and personal callers, forcing Root to reverse U.S. policy and ban inspections.[46] Yet here, too, as in the issue of the canteen, success was only partial. The inspection of prostitutes was stopped, but informally doctors continued to report to the military on the condition of suspect women.

Reformers were likewise unable to stop the selling of sex by Filipinos. Resistance to U.S. colonialism consisted not only in well-recognized armed conflict, but also in Filipinos' maintenance of social practices that predated the American occupation. The U.S. administration had tried to develop a type of moral regulation similar to that used by Spanish colonial authorities. The Americans were reluctant to interfere in such practices as prostitution and cockfighting, precisely because the Philippines was already a source of military and political conflict that would be further inflamed by a thoroughgoing effort to transform the moral landscape.[47] But to focus on moral reform's impact in the Philippines would be to miss the point. The WCTU was victorious in preventing the stain of legalized prostitution upon the American flag and able to trumpet the superiority of the American type of empire amid the growing competition among European powers for supremacy in the Far East, where regulation of prostitution was still common.[48] Moreover, reformers' antiprostitution campaigns were intended to undermine any possibility that sexual regulation as practiced in the Philippines would become a model for the American mainland.[49]

Temperance women and other reformers joining an informal evangelical Christian coalition in Washington could not dominate the strategies and practices of American empire. Diplomats, politicians, opinion makers in the media, foreign governments—and the objections of colonials to moral regulation too—stood in the way. Compromises were always necessary, as in the canteen and prostitution issues. But the point remains that the style and the agenda of American policy were influenced by the activities of reform women. They were active agents, though not autonomous and far from all-powerful ones.

The WCTU's Ellis was, said the *Union Signal*, deliberately based in Washington in order to carry on these struggles.[50] Since most American women could not vote, Ellis had to remind those she lobbied that seven-eighths of the members of the WCTU outside the South had husbands or sons in the Republican Party.[51] This indirect influence partially compensated for the frustration these women felt at their exclusion from the franchise. Nevertheless, the point highlighted the necessity to work within a coalition of evangelical groups whose objectives were in turn profoundly shaped by the views of women and their missionary advisers.

To the extent that it was influential, the effective lobbying of the WCTU came from its networks—which meant not only drawing upon the missionaries but also knowing how to deploy missionary letters and petitions in the nation's capital. The lobbying over the canteen saw the WCTU cooperating with a host of organizations. On one occasion in December 1901, Ellis represented the WCTU at a Washington meeting with the Secretary of State alongside Charles Lyman, president of the International Reform Bureau, to support the prohibition of the traffic in alcohol and other drugs with the so-called native races in the Pacific. The ASL's Howard Russell spoke briefly, and Reverend Stephen Baldwin, secretary of the Foreign Methodist Episcopal Missionary Society, expanded on the role of opium in China. Wilbur Crafts emphasized at the same meeting the need to "protect the child races," and the president of Christian Endeavor, Francis Clark, focused on the "effects of strong drink" observed in his travels around the world, "especially among those in the dark corners of the earth."[52] The WCTU needed the support of these influential reformers. It was part of a coalition aimed ultimately at transforming the United States and instituting what reformers regarded as a moral government, but in addition it aimed at using foreign policy as a vehicle for the evangelical regeneration of the world.

The pattern of interorganizational cooperation rested crucially upon partnerships of women and men. Women's influence was not always or even principally exerted by women alone. The WCTU had male support and males as affiliate members. The WCTU was not just a sisterhood, although that term was widely used. It was also very much concerned with brotherly relations and companionate marriage. Willard always praised the role of the Christian brother as well as that of the sister—she called the ideal men her "knights" of "the new chivalry."[53] Men and women were in fact intimately connected in the shaping of American empire. Among the examples of husband-and-wife teams working for American cultural expansion and moral reform, none was more prominent than Wilbur Crafts and his wife, Sara.[54] They toured the eastern Mediterranean together in 1904, and in 1907 they traveled in the Far East "to arouse interest" in promoting "the great treaty which will unite sixteen civilized nations in a plan to suppress intoxicants and opium in all uncivilized countries."[55] Similarly portrayed was the family of Margaret Ellis at her home away from home in the nation's capital. John Ellis, in fact, was the perfect WCTU husband: he aided Margaret's research by cutting news clippings and was literally by her side during her forays in Washington.

Such couples represented the ideal in terms of Protestant family values. The Ellises had grown children but referred to each other as mother and father in terms of endearment. In reporting an interview with Margaret Ellis, the WCTU official Elizabeth Gordon described these terms "the dearest names on earth."[56] The WCTU's male allies deferred toward mothers rather than sisters in Christ. Crafts conceded, "We men folks who have been in the fight must give the first place in influence to the organized motherhood of the W. C. T. U."[57] This conception of an "organized motherhood" did not weaken the WCTU in males' estimations because it mixed Victorian domestic sentiment, filial veneration, and experience. Ellis was commonly described as a tough woman, quiet yet resolute and convincing, and she reportedly struck fear into the hearts of some legislators.

Reporting on the role of Ellis, Crafts commented, "Wherever a good thing is done in [morals] legislation, we may be sure 'there is a woman in the case.'"[58] Ellis's motherly role as the mender of buttons on her husband's coat was combined with her formidable political reputation. A "stateswoman who is skilled in light housekeeping," Ellis had to rush her interview with Gordon so as to get back to the task of calling on the president's personal secretary to obtain one of many personal meetings.[59]

Because of the need to utilize male power structures, the women of the WCTU were not uniquely influential in the building of either American versions of empire abroad or in the lobbying to implement concomitant moral reform changes at home. Moreover, their organizational links were mainly to the Methodist, Baptist, and other evangelical churches, whereas there is some evidence that it would have helped to have, in addition, stronger links with the Protestant Episcopal Church. Though nominally Dutch Reformed in affiliation, Theodore Roosevelt worshiped in an Episcopal parish church and worked closely with the Episcopal bishop Charles Brent of the Philippines on the issue of anti-opium diplomacy. But while Roosevelt's successor, William Howard Taft, was a Unitarian and wary of sectarian religion, he was a politician who recognized from his time as governor-general in the Philippines the importance of missionaries as de facto agents of the Philippine colonial state. "I found Methodist brethren and missionaries at my back ready to furnish all the assistance I needed," he recalled.[60] Evangelicals had better access to the Methodist McKinley. In fact he met the WCTU leadership after their annual convention in 1900.[61] His death was much lamented by the WCTU, and with good reason, but the point remains that the WCTU's political clout was part of a much wider network of church and missionary groups. (This is why there is a need for a broader investigation of transnational voluntaristic societies in comparative perspective, and of the men's as well as of mixed sex societies.)

The WCTU and similar organizations such as Christian Endeavor highlight another neglected theme in American empire. That empire took shape within the confines of Pax Britannica. The WCTU and Christian Endeavor both looked principally toward the Australian, New Zealand, South African, and Canadian connections as vital to the global extension of their work. It is no accident that W. T. Stead, a friend of the WCTU, in his *The Americanization of the World* pointed to this phenomenon of boring within the white empire as the essence of the American imperial challenge to British dominance and as a source of competitive advantage. Stead used the WCTU as an example of the coming American style of moral hegemony.[62] More generally, Britain's empire served for American reformers not only as a comforting foundation of racial identity as Anglo-Saxons, but also as the facilitator of the sinews of power and knowledge on which Americans relied to convey their rather different and sometimes subversively anticolonial messages. WCTU missionaries took advantage of the British empire linguistically by focusing much of their travel in places where English was the dominant European language spoken; they also availed themselves of the communications networks of British cable lines and steamship services, and of the physical protection that Britain's gunboat diplomacy could provide in places beyond European colonial authority. Architects of American reform would by the 1920s self-consciously posit the moral superiority of the American way over other empires. They depicted the export of American moral values through prohibition and other moral and religious policies as a form of new internationalism.[63] This sentiment was manifest in the activities of the World League against Alcoholism. Yet this policy had its roots in the mission experience of the 1890s working within the British empire and in the reaction to the American acquisition of its own formal empire.

The role of the British empire as an arena for American cultural expansion leads to the question of cross-national influences in colonialism's histories. The global agenda and practice of American moral reform organizations went beyond a metropole/colony dialectic. Rather than colony and metropole alone, there were also the ties between different metropoles and their different colonial systems. In her study of the evangelical ties between Jamaica and the Baptist missionaries of Birmingham, the English historian Catherine Hall deftly charts how ideas of manly English citizens—"with their dependents in place" both "at home" and "in the empire in their various stages of being 'civilised' "—replaced those of the brotherhood of man.[64] She shows that empire is a reciprocal process, and her approach ought to be heeded now, if it has not been before. But Hall has been criticized for ignoring U.S. influence on Jamaica and neglecting cross-national reform and multilateral missionary networks.[65]

Whatever the merits of such a study and its thesis concerning the essence of imperialism and national identity, the American case cannot be essentialized in relations between, say, the United States and the Philippines alone. The U.S. empire was—and is—everywhere. The model of transnational organizations is a better one, as in the case of the World's WCTU, wherein missionaries circled the global, connecting with and translating a variety of experiences across European empires. In studying missions and American empire, a critical problem is that the export of American moral reform abroad was not a simple matter of white imperialists versus colonial peoples of other faiths and races, but one of the attempted imposition of American standards on other Anglo-Saxons and other Europeans as well. These included Greek Orthodox, Catholics, Coptics, and Armenians, not to mention Islamic and other non-Christian people. Thus WCTU work was not simply directed to the "dark peoples" of the earth.

These are just some of the myriad of questions raised by the study of the WCTU as a transnational missionary organization. The WCTU developed cross-national networks of influence and lobbied along with a coalition of Christian groups, consolidating, mediating, and translating missionary observations and agitation into domestic American practice on social purity and temperance. The WCTU campaigned against drugs in the colonial world; opposed compromise with American moral reformers' standards of social purity; and showed surprising clout in leading the movement to prohibit alcohol in the army canteen system. It was uneasy about American empire, seeking after 1902 to improve the moral standards in the American colonial possessions and thus reforming the system from within. Though its victories were largely in terms of symbolic politics, its ideological approach and organizational achievements presaged forms of networked imperial influences that came to be associated more generally with American informal empire in the twentieth century. Only by grasping the originality of the WCTU project will one see the lineaments of the American approach to empire, whose origins lie not in twentieth-century power politics and ideological struggle, or in late nineteenth-century economic motives and the desire for the Open Door policy alone, but in the cluster of Protestant moral values, the culturally expansionist ethic behind these, and the distinctive twist upon gender relations and the role of women displayed in nineteenth-century American reform movements abroad.

NOTES

1 Ian Tyrrell, *Woman's World / Woman's Empire: The Woman's Christian Temperance Union in International Perspective, 1880–1930* (Chapel Hill: University of North Carolina Press, 1991), 220 (quote), 287; Amy Kaplan and Donald Pease, eds., *Cultures of United States Imperialism* (Durham: Duke University Press, 1993). Michael Hardt and Antonio Negri raised this new problematic in *Empire* (Cambridge, Mass.: Harvard University Press, 2000). See also Amy Kaplan, "Violent Belongings and the Question of Empire Today," *American Quarterly* 56 (March 2004), 1–18.

2 Fernand Braudel, *The Mediterranean in the Ancient World* (London: Allen Lane, 2001), 307.

3 The study of comparative imperialism still sometimes suffers from political formalism. See, for example, David Abernethy, *The Dynamics of Global Dominance: European Overseas Empires, 1415–1980* (New Haven: Yale University Press, 2000), 19–20. He argues that informal empire ought to be totally excluded from the idea of imperialism. Abernethy is critical of Jack Robinson's and Ronald Gallagher's idea of a British free trade empire backed by strategic possessions. "The Imperialism of Free Trade," *Economic History Review* 6, no. 1 (1953), 1–15. By Abernethy's definition, much of what the British did does not qualify as imperialism, even though naval and other strategic actions globally were perceived by contemporaries as critical to the survival of the territorial empire.

4 Giovanni Arrighi, "The Three Hegemonies of Historical Capitalism," *Review* 8 (summer 1990), 365–408.

5 Ryan Dunch, "Beyond Cultural Imperialism: Cultural Theory, Christian Missions, and Global Modernity," *History and Theory* 41 (October 2002), 301–25.

6 Samuel Flagg Bemis, *A Diplomatic History of the United States* (New York: Henry Holt, 1936), 467.

7 Emily Rosenberg, *Spreading the American Dream: American Economic and Cultural Expansion, 1890–1945* (New York: Hill and Wang, 1982).

8 Ian Tyrrell, "Prohibition, American Cultural Expansion, and the New Hegemony in the 1920s: An Interpretation," *Histoire Sociale / Social History* 27 (November 1994), 413–45.

9 See Mary A. Renda, *Taking Haiti: Military Occupation and the Culture of U.S. Imperialism, 1915–1940* (Chapel Hill: University of North Carolina Press, 2001); Melvin M. Knight, *The Americans in Santo Domingo* (New York: Vanguard Press, 1928); Emily S. Rosenberg, *Financial Missionaries to the World: The Politics and Culture of Dollar Diplomacy, 1900–1930* (Cambridge, Mass.: Harvard University Press, 2003).

10 But see Andrew Preston, "Bridging the Gap between the Sacred and the Secular in the History of American Foreign Relations," *Diplomatic History* 30 (November 2006), 783–812.

11 Mahan, quoted in R. N. Leslie, Jr., "Christianity and the Evangelist for Sea Power: The Religion of A. T. Mahan," *The Influence of History on Mahan: The Proceedings of a Conference Marking the Centenary of Alfred Thayer Mahan's "The Influence of Sea Power Upon History, 1660–1783,"* ed. John B. Hattendorf (Newport, R.I.: Naval War College Press, 1991), 138; Brian Stanley, "Church, State and the Hierarchy of 'Civilization': The Making of the 'Missions and Government' Conference, Edinburgh, 1910," *The Imperial Horizons of British Protestant Missions, 1880–1914,* ed. Andrew Porter (Grand Rapids: Eerdmans, 2003), 61; Edward H. Cotton, *The Ideals of Theodore Roosevelt* (New York: D. Appleton, 1923), 39–60, 137–76.

12 Paul Kramer, "Empires and Exceptions: Race and Rule between the British and United States Empires, 1880–1910," *Journal of American History* 88 (March 2002), 1314–53.

13 Catherine Beecher, *A Treatise on Domestic Economy for the Use of Young Ladies at Home,* rev. ed. (1841; Boston: Thomas H. Webb, 1843), 33–34.

14 Tyrrell, *Woman's World,* 102–4.

15 Beecher, *A Treatise on Domestic Economy,* 37.

16 Ruth Bordin, *Frances Willard: A Biography* (Chapel Hill: University of North Carolina Press, 1986), 23.

17 Francis Clark, *Christian Endeavor in All Lands* (Boston: United Society of Christian Endeavor, 1906), 266.

18 Cf. Michael Parker, *The Kingdom of Character: The Student Volunteer Movement for Foreign Missions, 1886–1926* (Lanham, Md.: University Press of America and American Society of Missiology, 1998).

19 Ian Tyrrell, "World League against Alcoholism," *Alcohol and Temperance in Modern History,* ed. J. Blocker, D. Fahey, and I. Tyrrell, 2 vols. (Santa Barbara: ABC-CLIO, 2003), 691–92.

20 Meera Kosambi, "Introduction: Returning the American Gaze: Situating Pandita Ramabai's American Encounter," in Pandita Ramabai, *Pandita Ramabai's American Encounter: The Peoples of the United States (1889),* trans. and ed. Meera Kosambi (Bloomington: Indiana University Press, 2003), 23.

21 Ramabai Sarasvati, *The High-Caste Hindu Woman* (New York: F. H. Revell, 1901); Antoinette Burton, *At the Heart of the Empire: Indians and the Colonial Encounter in Late-Victorian Britain* (Berkeley: University of California Press, 1998), 89, 93, 105; *Pandita Ramabai's America: Conditions of Life in the United States,* ed. Robert E. Frykenberg (Grand Rapids: Eerdmans, 2003).

22 Dunch, "Beyond Cultural Imperialism," 322.

23 Kosambi, "Introduction: Returning the American Gaze," 38.

24 *Pandita Ramabai's America,* 273.

25 *Union Signal,* December 12, 1901, 8.

26 *Annual Report of the National Woman's Christian Temperance Union, 1900* (Chicago: WCTU, 1900), 94.

27 Bessie Laythe Scovell, "President's Address," *Minutes of the Twenty-Fourth Annual*

Meeting of the W.C.T.U. of the State of Minnesota (St. Paul, Minn.: W. J. Woodbury, 1900), cited in Kathleen Kerr, "How Did the Reform Agenda of the Minnesota Woman's Christian Temperance Union Change, 1878–1917?," *Women and Social Movements in the United States, 1600–2000*, Web site of Alexander Street Press.

28 *Union Signal*, November 7, 1901, 3.

29 WCTU, *Annual Report, 1900*, 95.

30 Ibid., 94.

31 Cf. Gaines M. Foster, *Moral Reconstruction: Christian Lobbyists and the Federal Legislation of Morality, 1865–1920* (Chapel Hill: University of North Carolina Press, 2002), 166.

32 *Annual Report of the National Woman's Christian Temperance Union . . . , 1901* (Chicago: WCTU, 1901), 318; Richard Hamm, *Shaping the Eighteenth Amendment: Temperance Reform, Legal Culture, and the Polity, 1880–1920* (Chapel Hill: University of North Carolina Press, 1995).

33 *Union Signal*, September 5, 1901, 4; October 17, 1901, 9; February 5, 1903, 4; Brian M. Linn, "The Long Twilight of the Frontier Army," *Western Historical Quarterly* 27 (summer 1996), 143.

34 Tyrrell, "World League," 691–92.

35 WCTU, *Annual Report, 1901*, 318.

36 E.g., Senator William J. Sewell, February 22, 1901, cited in *Union Signal*, March 7, 1901, 9; Foster, *Moral Reconstruction*, 169.

37 A. J. Brown, *The New Era in the Philippines* (New York: Fleming H. Revell, 1903), 111; *Fourth Annual Report of the Philippine Commission, 1903*, part 1 (Washington: Government Printing Office, 1904), 49.

38 *Union Signal*, March 7, 1901, 9; December 12, 1901, 8 (quote); April 24, 1902, 8.

39 *Union Signal*, December 12, 1901, 8.

40 "U.S. Army 'Prohibition,' 1890–1953," *Schaffer Library of Drug Policy* http://www.druglibrary.org/schaffer/alcohol/prohibit.htm, December 1, 2004.

41 Arthur J. Brown to Secretary of State, March 8, 1907, with Resolution of the Board of Foreign Missions of the Presbyterian Church in the U.S.A. file 721–15, RG 59, Numerical and Minor Files of the Department of State, 1906–10, National Archives, Washington.

42 *Union Signal*, December 12, 1901, 5.

43 Alvey Adee to Marie C. Brehm, October 15, 1906, file 721–5; Robert Bacon to Henry L. Wilson, November 13, 1906; Memorandum, Alvey Adee to Robert Bacon, November 27, 1906, file 721/9–10, RG 59, Numerical and Minor Files of the Department of State, 1906–10, National Archives, Washington.

44 Gaines M. Foster, "Conservative Social Christianity, the Law, and Personal Morality: Wilbur F. Crafts in Washington," *Church History* 71 (December 2004), 799–819; Dr. [Wilbur] and Mrs [Sara] Crafts and Mary and Margaret Leitch, *Intoxicating Drinks and Drugs in All Lands and Times*, 10th rev. ed. (Washington: International Reform Bureau, 1909), 230–34, 247–49, 250, 271, 272–76; Tyrrell, *Woman's World*, 161–62.

45 *Union Signal*, October 7, 1909, 3.

46 Tyrrell, *Woman's World*, 213–17.

47 Paul Kramer, "The Darkness that Enters the Home: The Politics of Prostitution during the Philippine–American War," *Haunted by Empire: Geographies of Intimacy on North American History*, ed. Ann Laura Stoler (Durham: Duke University Press, 2006), 371–72. On cockfighting policies, see, for example, the correspondence Henty Ide to Mercer Johnston, May 15, 1906, box 38, Mercer Green Johnston Papers, Library of Congress.

48 *Union Signal*, May 1, 1902, 8; October 7, 1909, 3; Elihu Root to Acting Governor of the Philippines, February 18, 1902 (2039/18.5), box 246, Record Group 350, Bureau of Insular Affairs Records, National Archives, Washington.

49 See calendar of petitions in Adjutant General's Office Files, index, roll 936, microfilm series 698, for example, Wilbur Crafts, January 21, 1902, National Archives, Washington; "State Regulation of Vice at Manila," (Boston) *Woman's Journal*, September 1, 1900 (2039/1), box 246, Bureau of Insular Affairs; Tyrrell, *Woman's World*, 213–17.

50 *Union Signal*, January 2, 1902, 8.

51 Ellis to Clarence Edwards, Chief of the Division of Insular Affairs, February 18, 1902, cited in Tyrrell, *Woman's World*, 216.

52 *Union Signal*, December 12, 1901, 5; Stephen L. Baldwin, *Foreign Missions of the Protestant Churches* (New York: Eaton and Mains, 1900).

53 Willard, *Glimpses of Fifty Years* (Chicago: Woman's Temperance Publishing Association, 1889), 574, 576, 588.

54 Foster, *Moral Reconstruction*, 110–13.

55 *Union Signal*, April 11, 1907, 9; *White Ribbon Signal* (Sydney), August 9, 1907, 6.

56 *Union Signal*, January 22, 1903, 5.

57 Ibid., January 17, 1901, 8.

58 Ibid.

59 *Union Signal*, January 22, 1903, 5.

60 *New York Times*, April 28, 1911, 3.

61 WCTU, *Annual Report*, 1900, 328; *Union Signal*, December 12, 1901, 5.

62 William T. Stead, *The Americanization of the World, or The Trend of the Twentieth Century* (1901; New York: Garland Publishing, 1972), 103–04.

63 Tyrrell, "New Hegemony in the 1920s," 413–45.

64 Catherine Hall, *Civilising Subjects: Metropole and Colony in the English Imagination, 1830–1867* (London: Polity Press, 2002), 9, 432.

65 Simon Gikandi, Thomas C. Holt, Philippa Levine, and reply by Catherine Hall, "Roundtable on Catherine Hall's *Civilising Subjects: Metropole and Colony in the English Imagination, 1830–1867*," *Journal of British Studies* 42, no. 4 (2003), 505–38.

II   WOMEN

Women, the Evangelical Press, and the Foreign Mission Movement in New England, 1800–1840

Mary Kupiec Cayton

> The highest excellence, exhibited in the life of a female, usually receives,
> after her death, no other tribute than the remembrance and the tears of the grateful
> circle, which she adorned and blessed. . . . But Providence has called some females
> to more public duties, and connected their names with events of general interest.
> The history of the hearts and lives of such, is the just property of all.
> *The Life and Writings of Mrs. Harriet Newell*

In 1812, Harriet Atwood Newell set sail from Salem, Massachusetts, bound for India. She was eighteen years old. The bride of the missionary Samuel Newell, Newell believed she had been called to educate and civilize a benighted people, bringing their souls to Christ. Newell never reached her Asian mission. Though she never witnessed her faith to the heathen she sought to save, she became saint, martyr, and heroine for generations of evangelical women. "The death of Mrs. Newell, instead of overcasting our prospects," prophesied Reverend Leonard Woods in a memorial sermon, "will certainly turn to the advantage of missions. . . . *Her* character will be identified with that holy cause. Henceforth, every one, who remembers Harriet Newell, will remember the Foreign Mission from America."[1] By 1840, the first comprehensive history of American foreign missionary work as much as canonized her. "Perhaps, no early missionary," the chronicler of early missions wrote, "even by a long life of faithful labors, has accomplished more for the heathen, than she accomplished by consecrating herself to their causes, and dying for them before the mission had found a resting place."[2]

How Harriet Newell became an iconic figure in evangelical Christianity in the first half of the nineteenth century involves much more than the details of her life. The story of the rise to cultural prominence of Newell and women like her involves a host of convergent cultural factors: the emergence of an evangelical culture that had missionary endeavor at its

Harriett Newell, ca. 1812. By permission
of The Library Company of Philadelphia.

heart and was developed discursively through print; the role of that evangelical print culture in capturing the imaginations of women who thereby
could envision women as cultural heroines; and the development of a
genre of missionary memoir that positioned women as important players
on a world stage. Newell's story came to symbolize for many women
evangelicals the central role they had been called to play in world history.
Heroines of a new culture, an "imagined community" galvanized through
the publication and dissemination of missionary narratives, they helped to
create a new place for middle-class women as influential actors in the
public realm.[3]

THE CONTEXT: NEW ENGLAND
EVANGELICALISM'S FOREIGN EXPANSION

Harriet Newell's rise to the status of cultural icon begins not with Harriet
herself, but with the emergence of the culture for which she would become
the emblem of womanhood. In New England in the 1790s, where Congregationalism was the mainstay of the standing religious order, two camps
had begun to take shape, divided with respect to their positions on the
appropriate relation among reason, sentiment, and religious forms and

practices. Unitarians, influenced by secular rationalism, emphasized the continuity between reason and revelation. In contrast, the orthodox, as they called themselves, underscored the importance of visceral experience of conversion and of the disjunction between themselves and a secular order in need of redemption. Later called simply Congregationalists, they provided a critique of secularism which, though local in nature, also participated in the transatlantic, interdenominational evangelical movement of the era. Evangelicalism obligated those who had heard the good news to make it available to those who had not. To this way of thinking, conversion to Christianity represented not only a spiritual good for pagans but a temporal improvement of condition as well, since their cultures were seen as repositories of cruelty and superstition and degrading to those under their sway.[4]

Missionary efforts were not new, either to British or to American evangelicalism, in the 1790s. In New England, the Society for the Propagation of the Gospel, established in 1649, and a variety of domestic missionary societies dating from the 1770s had sponsored missionary ventures and published accounts of them in order to raise money.[5] What was new was the large-scale use of print—specifically, magazines—to create mass audiences. Harriet Atwood Newell might have lived and died in obscurity but for the role these expanding networks of communication played in affirming the common identity and interests of evangelicals living thousands of miles from one another.

Noting the increasing importance of periodical publication, the editors of the first such magazine of its type, the *Evangelical Magazine* (1793), based in London, included "Biography, Memoirs, Diaries, Authentic Anecdotes, Striking Providences, and the Expressions of Dying Christians" intended as antidotes to the frivolous tendencies of secular print. The magazine furnished its readers with "a species of information entirely new, and very important," news "which relates to the Progress of the Gospel throughout the kingdom." The *Evangelical Magazine* became the template for a host of American evangelical and missionary magazines for half a century. Providing a new reading public with pleasurable and moral matter, it built identification among a far-flung community of like-minded readers, stoking the fires of evangelical benevolence while raising money for missionary endeavors.[6]

At about the same time the *Evangelical Magazine* began publication,

William Carey, a British Baptist, came up with a design to evangelize the world. Inspired by his reading of Jonathan Edwards's life of the American missionary David Brainerd as well as by Captain James Cook's journals of exploration, Carey wrote an appeal for interdenominational evangelization to convert the world, *An Enquiry into the Obligations of Christians to Use Means for Conversion of the Heathen* (1792). The book resonated widely among the new evangelical audience. Three Scottish clergymen inspired by Carey used the *Evangelical Magazine* to call for the establishment of a society to convert pagans. Their London Missionary Society, founded in 1795, caught the attention of hundreds of British evangelicals with its call to prayer for world conversion and its planned mission to Tahiti. The Connecticut Congregationalist establishment, in correspondence with the Calvinist-based society, began to publicize British foreign missionary efforts to an American public shortly after their inception.[7]

Congregationalist New Englanders gradually absorbed evangelical periodicals and foreign missionary efforts into their own culture. A renewal of interest in revivals led to a resolution by the Connecticut General Association in 1795 to encourage "extraordinary prayer for the revival of religion and the advancement of Christ's Kingdom upon the earth."[8] The ministerial association sent a circular letter to its members, to nearby Presbyterian ministers, and to Congregational ministers in Massachusetts. Prayer groups met, sharing news of the London society's work. Five years later (and seven after the *Evangelical Journal's* appearance), evangelicals in Connecticut founded their own magazine, the *Connecticut Evangelical Magazine*. Like that of its London-based counterpart, its goal was to confirm the faithful in their identity as evangelical Christians by providing news of God's remarkable providences in sending awakenings of the spirit. Society memberships and contributions from the faithful funded the magazine; missionaries also urged subscriptions on the newly awakened. The magazine spread through much of New England and upstate New York. It published accounts of revivals and conversions, mainly in New England; narratives of missionary endeavors sponsored locally and by the London Missionary Society; devotional reading; and memoirs of the godly. In 1803, another evangelical Congregationalist group, the Massachusetts Missionary Society, followed with its own magazine, the *Massachusetts Missionary Magazine*. Both periodicals acknowledged the importance of prayer for world conversions, but in fact the missionary and evangelical efforts reported were mainly those made at home.[9]

These two periodicals became American prototypes for numerous evangelical Congregationalist publications that came to dominate magazine print culture in New England between 1800 and 1820. Eight evangelical Congregationalist magazines (and two evangelical newspapers) sprang up. Other denominations added fifteen more religious periodicals. Though a far greater number of secular titles were published in New England during this period, most were short-lived, half having publication runs confined to a calendar year and a quarter more confined to two.[10] Only eight had consistent runs of more than four years. In contrast, the series begun by the *Connecticut Evangelical Magazine* ran for 38 years, and the *Massachusetts Missionary Magazine* 132. Evangelical subscriptions also far outnumbered those of secular competitors. *The Monthly Anthology*, for example, a highly influential magazine among the intelligentsia and one much discussed by scholars, had a print run of nine years, with 440 subscribers in 1805. In contrast, *The Panoplist and Missionary Magazine United* claimed 6,000–7,000 subscribers in 1809.[11] In a print market in which evanescence was the rule, New England Congregationalists learned how to make magazines an important form of communication by connecting them with organizations to secure a stable base of financial support and a guaranteed readership.[12] Each new magazine number became a source of excerpts to be read at prayer meetings and gatherings of the pious, thereby linking godliness, benevolence, and missionary activity for communities of readers.

As domestic conversion and global evangelization became staples of regional evangelical discourse, the step to local involvement in foreign missions was short. Impressed by Carey's work and led by Samuel J. Mills, the son of the editor of the *Connecticut Evangelical Magazine*, a group of students from Williams College, a newly founded evangelical institution, met to pray for the world's future and devote their lives to foreign missions. They later formed the nucleus of a group at Andover Seminary which in 1812 became the American Board of Commissioners for Foreign Missions (ABCFM). The ABCFM (or the American Board, as it was sometimes called), dedicated itself to the conversion of "heathen" in foreign lands. As part of that effort, the organization founded its own evangelical magazine, *The Panoplist*. Begun as the mouthpiece of conservative Congregationalism in Massachusetts, it became the journal of record for missionary work within evangelical Congregationalism when it merged with the *Massachusetts Missionary Magazine* in 1809. The first foreign missionaries commissioned by the American Board included four of the initial six from the Williams College "Haystack Revival"—Adoniram Judson, Samuel Nott, Luther Rice, and Samuel Newell. This Samuel Newell was the man whom Harriet Atwood married in 1812 and with whom she set sail for India, intending to extend Carey's missionary work.

THE HEROINE:
HARRIET NEWELL, WOMAN MISSIONARY

Fame always involves being in the right place at the right time, and Harriet Atwood was. Sixteen years old in 1809 and the daughter of a merchant of Haverhill, Massachusetts, she was a student at Bradford Academy. The school had been founded three years earlier by evangelicals anxious for the "mental and moral culture" of their daughters.[13] Religious awakening spread from local churches to academy students. "A large number of the young ladies were anxiously inquiring what they should do to inherit eternal life," Harriet wrote in a letter to a friend that eventually became part of her published memoir.[14] Her own inquiry involved both an examination of her interior state and questions about her potential sphere of usefulness in the world. She was part of a culture that typically positioned women as recipients of evangelical efforts or, if agents, as contributors of sons and money to the cause. Believing herself called to works of benevolence and piety she could not as yet describe, Harriet sought a path for realizing a special calling.

Fate intervened the next year in the form of a meeting of the ministers of the General Association of Massachusetts, held at Bradford Academy.[15] There the Andover seminarians petitioned the ministers to sponsor their new foreign missionary society, and the new American Board commissioned them as its first missionaries. As spiritual awakenings spread, so too did mission fever. Ann (Nancy) Hasseltine, Harriet's classmate, had experienced awakening at the same time as Harriet. The mission advocate Adoniram Judson boarded with the Hasseltine family during the General Association meeting and had a dramatic impact on Nancy, who called on

Harriet in October to inform her "of her determination, to quit her native land, to endure the sufferings of a Christian amongst heathen nations—to spend her days in India's sultry clime." Harriet was moved by her friend's self-sacrificing determination, which involved not only leaving friends and family, but also marrying a missionary she barely knew. "How did this news affect my heart!" Harriet reflected. "Is she willing to do all this for God; and shall I refuse to lend my little aid?"[16]

Three days later, Harriet met Samuel Newell. Like several of the other newly commissioned missionaries, Newell was actively seeking a suitable wife. Carey directed prospective missionaries to venture forth with comrades or, even better, with wives.[17] Wives offered missionaries companionship and domestic support for their labors and would prevent vulnerable young men from entering into relationships with pagan women and going native. Women were also thought to be better equipped to work with heathen women and children as so-called missionary assistants. Harriet consulted head and heart, read works about missions, including newly reprinted American volumes by the British missionaries Melvill Horne and Claudius Buchanan, and sometime in 1811 decided to entrust herself to Newell and accompany him to India.[18] They married on February 9, 1812, and ten days later sailed for Calcutta on the brig *Caravan* with their fellow missionaries Adoniram and Nancy Judson. Samuel Nott Jr. and his new wife, Roxana Peck Nott, as well as Gordon Hall and Luther Rice, departed for India from Philadelphia, where the men had been studying medicine to prepare for missionary work.[19] In the summer of 1813, the party arrived in Calcutta, where the British East India Company, fearing civil violence and rebellion as a result of missionary activity, threatened them with deportation.[20] They thereupon set sail for the Isle of France (present-day Mauritius) to seek a place outside British authority to begin their missionary work. En route Harriet gave birth to a daughter, who lived for five days. On November 30, 1813, Harriet Atwood Newel's life ended. She was nineteen years old.

The Judsons eventually reached Burma and lived missionary lives filled with illness, narrow escapes, persecution, and imprisonment. Ann Judson's life, as well as her death in 1826, became as much the stuff of legend as Harriet's. Adoniram Judson went on to have three wives and conduct missionary work for four decades before dying on a return voyage to the United States in 1850. Luther Rice, like the Judsons, became a Baptist upon his arrival in South Asia and returned to the United States in August 1813 for a short mission promotion tour. He never went back, devoting the rest of his life to fundraising until his death in 1836. In 1815, the Notts returned to the United States when Samuel developed health problems. They lived to old age, their lives too given over to mission promotion. When the British East India Company reopened the field to missionaries in 1813, Gordon Hall made his way to Bombay. Samuel Newell, who had been laboring in Ceylon following his wife's death, joined him there in 1817. Both died of cholera, Newell in 1821 and Gordon in 1826.

Harriet Atwood Newell, the first of this group to die, never actually labored in the Lord's vineyard. But she was a woman, and she lived at a time when women had become a major American audience for missionary news. That fact was not lost on missionary promoters.

THE AUDIENCE: WOMEN AND THE EVANGELICAL PRESS

New England Calvinist women showed particular interest in missions and in the evangelical magazines that publicized and underwrote mission activity.[21] Alongside the new male-managed missionary organizations, women organized societies of their own, the first in 1802.[22] Cent societies, in which members typically contributed a penny a week to support missions, also flourished across New England. While these women's mission groups did not themselves publish magazines, women contributed heavily to organizations that did. Evidence tends to understate their role, often attributing female contributions to "anonymous" or to groups, generally not to named individuals.[23] The treasurer's reports of the Massachusetts Missionary Society for 1803 provide a good example of the ways the early financing of missionary activity may have obscured women's roles.[24] Anonymous contributors as well as contributors to the collective gifts of parish societies, meeting houses, women's auxiliaries, and cent societies and sponsors of organization membership for the local minister included many women whose names were never published as benefactors. When women did appear as named donors, it was usually through bequests made after their deaths. In 1805, the society began to note separately contributions received from female cent societies, along with women's contributions of books for frontier settlements. Magazines increasingly emphasized women's financial role in evangelical efforts in stories about the accomplishments and organizational structures of cent societies. "From the time of our Lord's crucifixion to the present day, probably from the patriarchal ages," the governors of the American Board wrote in 1813, "the larger proportion of his most faithful and devoted followers, have been found in the female sex. Here is a scene of action, in which women may take a lively interest without overstepping the limits, which a sense of propriety has imposed on female exertion."[25]

Women also became invested in the evangelical periodical press as it publicized and promoted evangelical work. Male managers and editors regularly praised "worthy and pious females in our country, who have associated to contribute to the funds of this Board." Women gradually began to appear in the magazine as subjects as well as contributors, although in ways that downplayed the agency and individuality of particular women in favor of their representation as types. After their deaths, women received the encomiums of (male) memorialists, who recounted lives of piety and benevolence. Young, inquiring women, identified pseudonymously, voiced questions in print, answered by older brothers, fathers, and ministers. Ministers recounted stories of female conversion, sometimes including the words of the women themselves. On occasion, women even wrote without editorial mediation in letters to the editor, in poetry, and in occasional articles. But memoir most of all made women visible as subjects in evangelical periodicals.

Derived from the funeral sermon, a genre long preached by New England ministers to recall and honor the lives of wives of prominent men, life stories provided women listeners and readers with models of holiness.[26] In death as in life, women's stories made their way into the public realm by way of male intermediaries—with ministers possessing final authorship over the version of the life story presented to the public. Over time, women's own voices made their way into the printed memorials, as some ministers began to quote from the journals or correspondence of their subjects. Stories featuring women of social prominence began to give way to eulogies about ordinary women of piety whose distinction lay not in their social standing but in their godliness. First identified only by first name, pseudonym, or native town, in time they became subjects of full obituaries, as the pages of magazines opened up to descriptions of "persons of every age, and from every grade in society, who have remarkably exhibited the power of religion." "The death bed of a youth, or even of a child, whose heart has been sanctified by divine grace," the editors of the *Panoplist* wrote, "is often the scene of much heavenly instruction."[27] Dying adolescent girls in particular spoke to the audience of young women who comprised the majority of the newly converted.

Women's authorial voices figured more directly in other pieces, often as they found themselves in the throes of inquiry and conversion. By convention, women never directly volunteered accounts of these experiences. Rather, they told their stories by request, often in epistolary mode, to male interlocutors. In 1800, for example, the *Connecticut Evangelical Magazine* printed an account of the conversion of Amelia. "I give you some particular account of myself," she wrote to the pastor who submitted her letter to the periodical for inclusion, only "according to your request."[28] An issue from 1802 underlined the inclusion of work by pious females in a letter from an unnamed correspondent, "observing that copies of letters on religious subjects written by females as well as others, are inserted in your Magazine, and perused with entertainment and instruction by your pious readers."[29] Prefaces to female stories generally attributed agency to male intermediaries, who shared letters that female correspondents would never think to impart of their own accord. Yet increasingly many of the published letters did indeed come from women. Other contributions, often parables or short stories of anonymous authorship, featured dialogues between sisters, stories of young women's conversions, pious letters of counsel to female friends and companions, and pseudo memoirs of female figures identified only by classical aliases. The *Massachusetts Missionary Magazine* even printed without introduction or comment occasional first-person narratives and poetry by women.[30]

As female readership grew, women began to address the evangelical public directly in letters to the editors, although in ways that transparently forwarded the ministry's agenda. Matilda, complaining of sermons from which she had not profited, lamented the dangers of an unconverted clergy: "I must express my own disbelief in his scheme of faith," she wrote of her minister: "A professional of religion without sincerity, will save no man" (or woman either, one presumes). A second woman, Jerusha P————D, sought the editor's help in dealing with pernicious gossip. Melisa, an even bolder female correspondent of the *Massachusetts Missionary Magazine*, offered advice about the magazine's editorial content, noting that "for one of our sex to address you relative to the theological complexion of the Magazine, may be thought rather assuming." She nevertheless made the case that the magazine ought to be "a family repository, rather than a system of metaphysics" and hinted that its profits depended on the editors' responsiveness to the concerns of a female audience. "It is the opinion of our female circle," she wrote, "that if the Editors will only reserve their strong meat which is sufficiently salted for polemic productions, and will devoutly feed us with the milk and honey of the gospel, that the Magazine will have an extensive and useful circulation, and furnish the Missionary Fund with considerable and needful profits."[31]

As Harriet Atwood came of age, this new public sphere with appeal to women was taking shape.[32] The evangelical press invoked women, courted them, printed their work, and relied on them for support. Admonished from pulpit and press that the only good literature was moral literature, evangelical women were not to waste time reading frivolous novels or idle memoirs. But the story of a pious young woman who dies young in willing sacrifice for the sake of the kingdom of God? That was a different story.

Women like Harriet Atwood were ready for a tale like Harriet Newell's. They had been prepared by a decade's worth of content that figured them as both appropriate subjects for evangelical writing and appropriate readers of it. Newell's story presented them with a new archetype of female evangelism that included sentiment, drama, pathos, heroism, and an exotic setting—and all in the name of God. Newell, although not by her own agency, became the first to entice legions of young evangelical women to find a way to relate to the far-off work of missions and to think about their role in the wide world beyond New England. She would not be the last.

THE PROMOTERS:
MISSIONARY HAGIOGRAPHY AND
EVANGELICAL MISSION

By 1812 the *Panoplist and Missionary Magazine* was a thriving concern with a monthly print run of thirty-five hundred copies.[33] Its readers included not only subscribers, but also those who borrowed subscribers' copies and those largely female audiences who heard excerpts read aloud during meetings of religious, charitable, and benevolent societies. "Never before were so many persons, in regions so remote from each other, and with views so enlarged and benevolent, engaged to make the gospel known in all the world," the magazine's editors boasted.[34] Noting interest in all things missionary, the magazine pledged to carry "proceedings of Bible Societies, and of other associations for the purpose of promoting Christianity, especially of Missionary Societies at home and abroad," with assurance to readers that these would be "procured and inserted as seasonably as possible."[35]

Missionary promotional literature was not a new genre, and the *Panoplist* editors would have been familiar with a tradition that used printed versions of missionaries' personal letters and journals to promote their work. Most often these were compiled by an editor and published in freestanding form after the missionary's death. They focused on the pity and compassion for the spiritually disadvantaged that the missionary's life affirmed. Two missionary memoirs in particular would have been well known among evangelicals: Jonathan Edwards's life of his son-in-law, the missionary David Brainerd, published in 1749 and reprinted in Edinburgh in 1765, and Samuel Hopkins's of John Sergeant, published in 1753, established templates for missionary hagiography. Brilliant young men full of benevolence and compassion for the miserable condition of others, each abandoned the home of his youth to bring the Gospel to heathen peoples and died young. Relying heavily on excerpts from the two missionaries' diaries and correspondence, these accounts gave rise to later advertisements by British evangelicals of their efforts in Asia, also conveyed in the form of epistolary news from missionaries—accounts which Harriet Newell herself read when mulling over her future lifework.[36]

With the organization of the American Board, the *Panoplist* dramatically increased its own coverage of Asian missionary activity, looking to tested modes of publicity to raise money. In February 1812, the magazine reported the ordination of the American Board missionaries, heralding "a new and important era in the annals of the American churches, the era of foreign missions," and their sailing for the orient "with their wives." Included also, however, was a poem "written in durable ink on a cambric work-bag presented to the wife of one of the young Missionaries, by her sister." Its sentimental, familial-based piety as well as its physical location on a domestic object rather than as a text that speaks directly to the public marked it as a text by and for women:

May He, whose word the winds and waves obey,
Convey you safe o'er ocean's dang'rous way,
From ev'ry danger, ev'ry ill defend,
Be your Support, your Father, and your Friend.
On the Other Side
The Christian's God in heathen India reigns,
Whose grace divine the feeblest heart sustains:
That thou may'st prove his constant guardian care,
Shall be thy sister's ardent daily prayer.
Be thine the joy to hear thy Savior's praise
Resound from pagan fanes in Christian lays;
And when this varying scene of life is o'er,
O may we meet thee on that blissful shore,
Where friends shall never part, farewells be heard no more.[37]

Like the report it accompanies, the poem makes no mention of the women by name—or even of the author of the poem (likely one of Nancy Judson's sisters). The poem conveys the pathos of any daughter, any sister, removing to a strange and distant place, never to be seen again in this life by those who love her. In its lack of direct reference to any public or commissioned work for the women, the poem typifies the positioning of women missionaries in the context of the private, interpersonal spaces they had always inhabited—a characteristic strategy of early American Board publications. Readers access women's experiences by "overhearing" communications meant for mothers, sisters, and female friends. By inserting their accounts of their experience into mission promotional literature, the American Board opened the door for women to be seen as public figures in the way male missionaries such as Brainerd, Sergeant, and Carey had been.

News of the missionaries appeared monthly in the magazine, most often in the form of excerpts from their shipboard letters. Letters written by males were attributed to the author by name, those by females simply to "the wife of one of the missionaries." American Board publications positioned male missionary correspondence within a public realm, presenting it as official reportage from commissioned agents to the organization. Women's correspondence, in contrast, took the form of letters to family and friends, their transformation into print making the reader party to an intimate exchange. While the men reported on the logistics of the mission and the formal progress of the party, the women focused mainly on feelings about departure for a strange land and longings for home and family.[38]

Communication from the missionaries became sporadic. In December 1812, only the letters of "two young ladies, now the wives of American Missionaries in India," were published. Written in language common to the conversion narratives of young women, these letters resembled exhortatory domestic sermons. They emphasized the dangers and loneliness of the missionary endeavor in order to improve the reader, to teach her about benevolence and self-denial in service of the spiritual needs of others. Willingly surrendering the comforts of home, of parents, of sisters, the authors suffered "those painful sensations of which a separation of our friends will be productive." Yet the seeds of spiritual self-abnegation promised to produce a new crop of intimate, sacred relationships, as this passage from one letter suggests: "If our sisters and our social friends must be forsaken, may we not find sisters in *each other*, and erect the social female altar in a land of pagans? Perhaps we may induce some of the wretched, degraded females of India, to join with us in worshipping our heavenly Father. Perhaps we shall be the first to teach some listening, attentive child to lisp the praises of Jesus. O my dear sister, thoughts like these, are sufficient to excite in our hearts a *wish* to spend our days in a heathen land." Another letter from one of the women encouraged a correspondent to "be made the favored of instruments, of leading many wretched female Indians, to the Lamb of God."[39] Heathen women awaited the gentle religious influences of women who would coach them in forming domestic circles of female piety, benevolence, and godliness such as the ones left at home. These communications transferred the language of female benevolent influence from the family circle to the world. Women's mission, in fact, increasingly became delineated through letters as distinct from that of the men and no less noble.

Roxana Nott, the first of the women missionaries to be identified by name, was forced by her husband's illness to assume the "deputy husband" role and to serve as correspondent for the family.[40] Harriet Newell was named for the first time (as "Mrs. Newell") in a letter by her husband and published in the same series as Nott's. In April, the *Panoplist*'s section entitled "Religious Intelligence" featured a substantial segment from Newell published under her own name. It included a long, descriptive letter about her travels and life in India, followed by extracts from her journal and letters to family and friends. With their publication, the missionary families became fleshed out, recurring characters in a serialized adventure with an exotic setting and a cast of characters whose interrelationships increasingly became a part of the story. (The heretofore unnamed "Mrs. Judson," for example, became the familiar and comfortable "Nancy.")[41]

Harriet Newell's journal finally provided readers with a public world in which women existed and acted beyond the household, in scenes of unimaginable exoticism. The women missionaries also had a clear and important calling that included domestic virtues but transcended the household. Harriet Atwood Newell, a practiced writer who had spent her schoolgirl years composing in a private journal, became a published author despite cultural conventions that discouraged female authorship. Male editors with female readerships to satisfy printed her work because of its potential utility in furthering the work of evangelization and fundraising.

Had she lived, Newell would likely have seen very little of her writing make its way into print, given the understandings about the place of women's writing in evangelical culture. But dead women's stories were different. Properly told through the eyes of male memorialists, they could become the object of public veneration in ways that those of living women could not. Although neither editors nor readers knew it, Newell had died a month before her journal extracts were published. By August 1813, readers did know it. A reprinted letter from her husband to her mother disclosed the intelligence to magazine readers. The account was complete with the deathbed details readers now expected in women's memoirs: final trials and tribulations, suffering, resignation, emotional final words to family and friends about heavenly reunions, exhortations to conversion for loved ones whose spiritual state might be precarious, peaceful resignation to the will of God. It was accompanied by new excerpts from her journal as well as by fragments of letters to loved ones and a formal obituary.[42] Soon Newell's death would give mission promoters the opportunity to translate her life story into the hagiographic dead missionary genre previously populated only by men. In death, her story could provide an Ur-narrative for benevolent women seeking a larger sphere of influence while never straying beyond the decent bounds of domesticity in aspiration or behavior. Over the next several decades, a number of women's missionary memoirs in the Newell mold captured the imaginations of generations of young evangelical women, heralding a new public for literature produced by and for women.

LEGACY: HARRIET NEWELL,
MISSIONARY SAINT

Harriet Newell's fame depended on the promotion of her tale by American Board officials, who decided to use it to publicize the efforts of foreign mission. The editors of the *Panoplist* noted in April 1814, a time when information was in short supply as New England found its overseas communications disrupted by war, that an evangelical public with an appetite for mission-related texts was "anxious to hear from the missionaries in Asia." Eleazar Lord of Andover Theological Seminary affirmed the same in his preface to the two-volume *A Compendious History of the Principal Protestant Missions to the Heathen*: "The attention of the religious public in this country, has been directed of late in an unusual degree to the subject of Missions to the Heathen." "The rapidity with which this attention has increased particularly in New England, and the effects which it has produced" meant that people wanted more information on the subject of missions, a fact "evident from the avidity with which every work relating to the subject of Missions, has been seized and read." In May, in an effort to supply the public with mission-related information, a letter of Newell's from 1811 was reprinted, accompanied by a long memorial poem about her. The letter, editors explained, had been "forwarded sometime ago for publication, but was deferred on account of the more urgent claims of other communications." More significantly perhaps, in the months between the revelation of Newell's death in August 1813 and her reappearance in the *Panoplist* in 1814, her story had been reprinted in a 250-page, free-standing memoir.[43]

Following evangelical custom, the memoir appeared under someone else's name. To this day, Newell's memoir is officially attributed to Reverend Leonard Woods, one of the founders of the American Board.[44] Samuel T. Armstrong, printer to many evangelical organizations during this period, included on the back cover of his edition of Newell's memoir a list of other materials he had on hand that he thought potentially appealing to the readers of Woods's sermon and Newell's memoir: Lord's history of missions to the heathen, Buchanan's work on Asia, two works by Horne on missions, a reprinted Edwards's life of Brainerd (identified as "*A Missionary*"), Woods's sermon on the ordination of the missionaries at Salem, a sermon by Theodore Dwight before the American Board, and "a few copies of the Likeness of Mrs. Newell, printed on fine paper, fit for frames."[45] The likenesses, which portrayed Newell as attractive, demure, and very young, were priced at seventy-five cents apiece, or three times as much as a cent society member would ordinarily contribute to the missions in the course of a year.

Between 1814 and 1840, Newell's memoir was reprinted in at least twelve cities and fifty editions. Seven editions issued from Armstrong's Boston presses before 1817. American editions also appeared in New York, Philadelphia, Baltimore, Utica, Lexington, and Andover; printers and publishers in London, Edinburgh, and Glasgow also conveyed her story to British audiences. By the 1820s, Newell's story circulated as a tract, and in Ireland as a chapbook. It inspired poems and the naming of ships. Memoirs of women missionaries followed, making frequent reference to Newell, their stories often closely resembling hers: a young, pious woman dies too young after becoming a wife and missionary in order to spread the kingdom of God and minister to heathen women and children. Her narrative, communicated through her journals and correspondence with intimates, creates a cast of missionary characters, describes the exotic culture to which she ministers, and moves inexorably toward her death, always beautiful and inspirational.[46]

How strong was the commitment to foreign missionary effort among women after Newell's lionization? The list of contributions to the American Board for 1818 shows average per capita and per society contributions from men continuing to exceed those from women. Women's gifts still came more often through organizations and anonymous donations than men's. Women, however, now formed the majority of contributors. In Massachusetts alone, they accounted for most of the ninefold increase in the number of contributing individuals and organizations between 1803 and 1818. Female gifts were important in providing the capital to support schools for heathen children, precisely the sort of work that fell to women missionaries like Newell. Donations attributed to women's societies skyrocketed, and schoolchildren (in schools run by women) became a new class of contributors. Women's reading and prayer circles, cent societies,

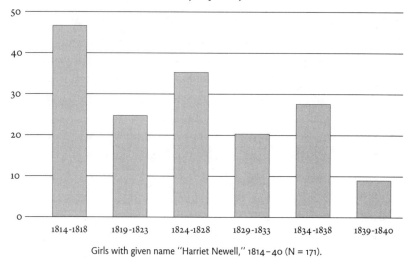

Girls with given name "Harriet Newell," 1814–40 (N = 171).

and societies gave for the welfare of heathen children. Women's contributions included not only direct contributions but also bequests, sales of jewelry and cloth, the proceeds of mite boxes, and money saved by forgoing the use of sugar for a year.[47]

One of the greatest measures of Newell's influence comes from an unorthodox source. If one types Harriet Newell's name into an Internet search engine surprisingly little about the woman herself emerges. Her name appears most often in sites associated with contemporary evangelical efforts, where she is still hailed as the first American foreign missionary to die in spreading God's kingdom. While those hits are not especially numerous, hundreds of "Harriet Newells" become visible in the work of people tracing family genealogies. If one searches the online genealogies and local history records in which the name appears and extracts as much identifying information as possible about the first 250 who appear to have been born between 1814 (the year after the story of Newell's life and death first became public property) and 1840 (and keeping in mind that these instances represent the tip of the iceberg) the numbers will approximate those that appear in the accompanying graph.

In my nonscientific sample of 250, I was able to find 171 Harriet Newells for whom I could identify an exact or almost exact year of birth. (The remainder of the cohort consists of individuals for whom circumstantial indicators point to a birth date in the target period: marriage after 1830 but before 1860, marriage to husbands born between about 1805 and 1840, childbirth between about 1830 and 1865.) I counted only individuals with the given name Harriet Newell followed by surname. That is, I did not count Harriet N.s, just plain Harriets, or Harriet Newells whose names were spelled in variant versions. The result: the given name Harriet Newell does not appear in genealogies prior to 1814 but shows up suddenly in 1814 and continues to be a notable choice for daughters for some time thereafter.

Of the 217 Harriet Newells I found with geographic locations associated with them—mostly places of birth, but sometimes places associated with marriage or childbirth—most turn up in New England, where foreign missionary effort originated in conjunction with evangelical Congregationalism and Presbyterianism; in the New England diaspora issuing from these states, mainly New York and Ohio; and in locations where the Calvinist traditions of Congregationalism and Presbyterianism were strong. That is to say, Harriet Newells covered the countryside in the places that gave rise to and sustained benevolent empire reform activities.[48]

The many Harriet Newells—prose and verse versions, engraved images, flesh-and-blood namesakes, would-be missionaries, the schooner that wrecked off the coast of New Brunswick in the same storm that killed Margaret Fuller Ossoli off Fire Island in 1851—testify to the power of her story. For many during the era of benevolent empire expansion and reform, she epitomized women's heroic mission to transform the world. No wonder, then, the proliferation of Harriet Newells and of women missionaries. It is no overstatement to say that the foreign mission cause in the United States became in large part a women's cause, popularized by an evangelical press in which women's stories came to play a large role.

In its first fifty years, the historian Marilyn Westerkamp writes, the American Board went on to establish missions in Gabon, South Africa, Greece, Cyprus, Armenia, Palestine, Syria, Persia, Turkey, India, Ceylon, China, Siam, Singapore, Borneo, Hawaii, and Micronesia as well as missions to the Cherokees, the Choctaws, the Chickasaws, the Creeks, the Pawnees, the Dakotas, the Ojibwas, the Osages, the Maumees, the Mackinaws, and to peoples in Oregon and New York. Of the 1,250 missionaries sent, more than half—691—were women.[49] Harriet Newell became the human face of a new breed of evangelical woman who looked to use domestic piety to make a difference—not only in her household but in the world. Piety, domesticity, benevolence, and sentimentalism may seem a far cry from the impulse to empire and cultural expansion. But though the connection at first seems counterintuitive, Harriet Newell's story shows how a new evangelical literature by and for women constructed a social imaginary in which saving the world was not only woman's work, but her truest, best, and most heroic role.

NOTES

Epigraph: *The Life and Writings of Mrs. Harriet Newell*, rev. ed. (Philadelphia: American Sunday School Union, 1831), 5.

1 Leonard Woods, *A Sermon, Preached at Haverhill, (Mass.) in Remembrance of Mrs. Harriet Newell, Wife of the Rev. Samuel Newell, Missionary to India. Who Died at the Isle of France, Nov. 30, 1812, Aged 19 Years. To Which Are Added Memoirs of Her Life.* 2d ed. (Boston: Samuel T. Armstrong, 1814), 32–33.

2 Joseph Tracy, "History of the American Board of Commissioners for Foreign Missions," *History of American Missions to the Present Time* (Worcester, Mass.: Spooner and Howland, 1840), 40.

3 The notion of "imagined communities" as creations of mass communication, especially print, is Benedict Anderson's, *Imagined Communities: Reflections on the Origin and Spread of Nationalism* (London: Verso Editions/NLB, 1983). Scholarly literature on women missionaries in this era includes works that position the topic in the context of the American religious—and especially evangelical—history and those that view the topic mainly through the lens of women's empowerment and agency. In the first category, see R. Pierce Beaver, *All Loves Excelling: American Protest Women in World Mission* (Grand Rapids: Eerdmans, 1968); in the second, Dana L. Robert, *American Women in Mission: A Social History of Their Thought and Practice* (Macon, Ga.: Mercer University Press, 1997), Amanda Porterfield, *Mary Lyon and the Mount Holyoke Missionaries* (New York: Oxford University Press, 1997), Patricia Grimshaw, *Paths of Duty: American Missionary Wives in Nineteenth-Century Hawaii* (Honolulu: University of Hawaii Press, 1989), and Marilyn J. Westerkamp, *Women and Religion in Early America, 1600–1850: The Puritan and Evangelical Traditions* (London: Routledge, 1999), 131–54. Joan Jacobs Brumberg's *Mission for Life: The Judson Family and American Evangelical Culture* (New York: New York University Press, 1984) discusses early foreign missionary efforts in the context of evangelical culture.

4 On the divergence of Unitarianism from orthodox Congregationalism in New England, see Mary Kupiec Cayton, "The Connecticut Culture of Revivalism," *Perspectives on American Religion and Culture*, ed. Peter W. Williams, 353–65 (Malden, Mass.: Blackwell, 1999); and "Who Were the Evangelicals? Conservative and Liberal Identity in the Unitarian Controversy in Boston, 1804–1833," *Journal of Social History* 31 (September 1997), 85–107. On transatlantic evan-

gelicalism in Britain and America, see Mark A. Noll, *The Rise of Evangelicalism: The Age of Edwards, Whitefield, and the Wesleys* (Downer's Grove, Ill.: InterVarsity Press, 2003); and Boyd Stanley Schluther, "Religious Faith and Commercial Empire," *Oxford History of the British Empire*, vol. 2, *The Eighteenth Century*, ed. P. J. Marshall (New York: Oxford University Press, 1998), 128–50.

5 See Laura M. Stevens, *The Poor Indians: British Missionaries, Native Americans, and Colonial Sensibility* (Philadelphia: University of Pennsylvania Press, 2004).

6 "The Preface," *Evangelical Magazine for 1793*, vol. 1 (London, 1793), 1–5.

7 On Edwards and British evangelicals, see D. Bruce Hindmarsh, "The Reception of Jonathan Edwards by Early Evangelicals in England," *Jonathan Edwards at Home and Abroad: Historical Memories, Cultural Movements, Global Horizons*, ed. David W. Kling and Douglas A. Sweeney, 201–21 (Columbia: University of South Carolina Press, 2003); on Edwards and the foreign missionary movement, see Andrew F. Walls, "Missions and Historical Memory: Jonathan Edwards and David Brainerd," 248–65, and Stuart Piggin, "The Expanding Knowledge of God: Jonathan Edwards's Influence on Missionary Thinking and Promotion," 266–96, in the same volume. See also Clifton Jackson Phillips, *Protestant American and the Pagan World: The First Half Century of the American Board of Commissioners for Foreign Missions, 1810–1860* (Cambridge, Mass.: East Asian Research Center, Harvard University, 1969), 12–20.

8 Quotation cited in Richard Douglas Shields, "The Connecticut Clergy in the Second Great Awakening" (Ph.D. diss., Boston University, 1976), 21. Initiated by Jonathan Edwards in 1748, the Concert of Prayer for world conversion was picked up as a theme by Scottish evangelicals, who circulated the theme back to New England evangelicals in the 1790s.

9 James R. Rohrer, *Keepers of the Covenant: Frontier Missions and the Decline of Congregationalism, 1774–1818* (New York: Oxford University Press, 1995), 56–69, 166n46; John A. Andrew III, *Rebuilding the Christian Commonwealth: New England Congregationalists and Foreign Missions, 1800–1830* (Lexington: University Press of Kentucky, 1976), 20. See also Mary Kupiec Cayton, "Jacob Norton's Reading: Print and the Making of a New England Evangelical Minister, 1787–1804," *Journal of the Early Republic* 26, no. 2 (summer 2006), 221–48.

10 By my count, Massachusetts produced forty-two secular periodical titles and Connecticut ten, with other New England states responsible for eight. Inventory sources include World Cat Online Catalogue; American Periodical Series; Benjamin M. Lewis, *An Introduction to American Magazines, 1800–1810* (University of Michigan Department of Library Science Studies, 5, 1961), 68–72; Frank Luther Mott, *A History of American Magazines, 1741–1850*, vol. 1 (New York: D. Appleton, 1930), 789–800. Mott, 131–39, notes the growth of religious magazines during this period but devotes comparatively little space to them, preferring instead to treat periodicals whose duration and circulation were much smaller but whose content fits better with a narrative celebrating the growth of secular literature.

John Tebbel and Mary Ellen Zuckerman, in *The Magazine in America, 1741–1990* (New York: Oxford University Press, 1991), barely mention the religious press, beginning their discussion of magazines with political and cultural influence with the antislavery movement (14–15). Candy Gunther Brown, *The Word in the World: Evangelical Writing, Publishing, and Reading in America, 1789–1880* (Chapel Hill: University of North Carolina Press, 2004), deals at length with the evangelical press but focuses on the period after it was already established.

11 Mott, *A History of American Magazines*, 200, 264.

12 See David Paul Nord, "The Evangelical Origins of Mass Media in America, 1815–1835," *Journalism Monographs* 88 (May 1984), and "Systematic Benevolence: Religious Publishing and the Marketplace in Early Nineteenth-Century America," *Communication and Change in American Religious History*, ed. Leonard I. Sweet, 239–69 (Grand Rapids: Eerdmans, 1993).

13 [Mrs. William Barrows], *A Memorial of Bradford Academy* (Boston: Congregational S. S. and Publishing Society, 1870), 3.

14 Newell, August 27, 1809, quoted from "her private papers," *Memorials of Rufus Anderson, D.D., Mrs. Harriet Newell, and Mrs. Ann H. Judson* (Lawrence, Mass.: American Printing House, 1885), 9.

15 The group, despite its name, included only the orthodox, largely evangelical ministry of Massachusetts, not the entire Massachusetts establishment.

16 Newell, in Woods, *A Sermon*, 96. See Robert, *American Women in Mission*, 6–7.

17 William Carey, *An Enquiry into the Obligations of Christians, to Use Means for the Conversion of the Heathens* (Leicester, 1792), 73. Ironically, Carey's first wife, Dorothy, at first refused to accompany him to India. In light of her subsequent mental deterioration and death, her initial decision not to go may have been the right one.

18 *A Collection of Letters Relative to Foreign Missions: Containing Several of Melvill Horne's Letters on Missions, and Interesting Communications from Foreign Missionaries: Interspersed with Other Extracts* (Andover, Mass.: Printed by Galen Ware, 1810); Claudius Buchanan, *Two discourses preached before the University of Cambridge, on commencement Sunday, July 10, 1810: and a sermon preached before the Society for Missions to Africa and the East, at their tenth anniversary, July 12, 1810: to which are added Christian Researches in Asia* (Boston: Samuel T. Armstrong, 1811).

19 Although printed literature on the missionary wives Harriet Atwood Newell and Ann Hasseltine Judson is substantial, there is perplexingly little on Roxana Peck Nott—or, for that matter, on her husband, who, as noted, returned from the Asian missions for health reasons in 1815 and lived until the age of eighty-one (James L. Hill, *The Immortal Seven: Judson and His Associates* [Philadelphia: American Baptist Publication Society, 1913], 78–79). Robert describes her career and explores some of the possible reasons for its absence in the evangelical literature on missions (*American Women in Mission*, 47–48). My best guess is that female missionary hagiography developed in a way that required its sub-

ject to be dead—and Roxana Nott lived to the age of ninety-one and died in Hartford, Connecticut.

20 See Karen Chancey, "The Star in the East: The Controversy over Christian Missions to India, 1805–1813," *Historian* 60 (March 1998), 507–22.

21 Scholars of magazine and periodical history during this period usually distinguish religious periodicals from so-called ladies magazines (see, for example, Mott, *A History of American Magazines*, 131–44, and Tebbel and Zuckerman, *The Magazine in America*, 27–38). Although ladies magazines certainly deserve treatment as a separate and distinct genre, current discussions of the growth of periodicals seem to imply that women first became heavily involved with the periodical press through publications directed only toward them.

22 Beaver, *All Loves Excelling*, 13–34.

23 Stevens, *The Poor Indians*, 95.

24 *Massachusetts Missionary Magazine* (hereafter *MassMiss*) 1 (June 1803), 73–77.

25 *Report of the American Board of Commissioners for Foreign Missions; Compiled from Documents Laid Before the Board, at the Fourth Annual Meeting* (Boston, 1813), 37.

26 See Laurel Thacher Ulrich, *Good Wives: Image and Reality in the Lives of Women in Northern New England, 1650–1750* (New York: Knopf, 1982).

27 "Address to the Public," *Panoplist and Missionary Magazine United* (hereafter, including minor title variations, *Panoplist*) 3, no. 1 (June 1810), 6.

28 "A Letter from a Young Woman to Her Pastor, Giving Some Account of the Exercises of Her Mind," *Connecticut Evangelical Journal* (hereafter, including minor title variations, *CtEvan*) 2, no. 1 (July 1801), 32.

29 "Letters from Fidelia," *CtEvan*, 2, no. 9 (March 1802), 337.

30 See, for example, the poem labeled "Communicated as an original Female Production," *MassMiss* 2, no. 5 (October 1804), 208.

31 *CtEvan* 1, no. 2 (February 1808), 67, 70; *CtEvan* 2, no. 4 (April 1809), 152–54; "Letter from a Lady," *MassMiss* 3, no. 12 (June 1803), 52–53.

32 The notion of the public sphere comes from the work of Jürgen Habermas, especially his *The Structural Transformation of the Public Sphere: An Inquiry into a Category of Bourgeois Society*, trans. Thomas Burger (Cambridge: MIT Press, 1991). The emergence of an evangelical press early in the national history of the United States suggests that at least initially evangelicals may have envisioned the religious press as an alternative, rather than a supplement, to public rational-critical realms of discourse developing at the same time.

33 Contract between the *Panoplist* and Samuel T. Armstrong, June 6, 1812. Evarts Family Papers, Manuscripts and Archives, Sterling Memorial Library, Yale University, Group no. 200, series no. I, box no. 4, folder No. 143.

34 *Panoplist* 9, no. 1 (June 1813), quoted in Mott, *A History of American Magazines*, 134.

35 "Address to the Public," *Panoplist* 3, no. 1 (June 1810), 2, 5.

36 Stevens, *The Poor Indians*, 1–33, 138–59.

37 This (so far as I can tell) is the first published reference in the New England evangelical literature to Harriet Newell—or to any other woman missionary. *Panoplist* 4, no. 9 (February 1812), 425–27.

38 *Panoplist* 4, no. 11 (April 1812), 522–23.

39 *Panoplist* 5, no. 7 (December 1812), 316–20.

40 See Ulrich, *Good Wives*, 35–50.

41 *Panoplist* 5, no. 10 (March 1813), 467–70, 471; id. 5, no. 11 (April 1813), 515–23.

42 *Panoplist* 9, no. 3 (August 1813, part I), 130–35, 140.

43 *Panoplist* 9, no. 11 (April 1814), 181–83; Eleazar Lord, "Preface," *A Compendious History of the Principal Protestant Missions to the Heathen, Selected and Compiled by the Best Authorities*, vol. 1 (Boston: Samuel T. Armstrong, 1813), iii; *Panoplist* 9, no. 12 (May 1814), 223–24, 230–31. See Leonard Woods, "Introduction," *Memoirs of American Missionaries, Formerly Connected with the Society of Inquiry Respecting Missions, in the Andover Theological Seminary: Embracing a History of the Society, etc.* (Boston: Peirce and Parker, 1833), 17–23. I am not certain of the actual publication date of the memoir, but evidence suggests it appeared in 1814. See "To the Public," *Panoplist* 10, no. 6 (June 1814); Benjamin B. Wisner, *Memoirs of the Late Mrs. Susan Huntington, of Boston, Mass., Consisting Principally of Extracts from her Journal and Letters: With the Sermon Occasioned by her Death*, 2d edn. (Boston: Cricker and Brewster, 1826), 96; and Ethan Smith, *A Sermon Preached to the Ladies of the Cent Institution, in Hopkinton, New-Hampshire, August 18, 1814* (Concord: George Hough, 1814), 19.

44 Woods, *A Sermon*.

45 Advertisement, "Samuel T. Armstrong, Woods, *A Sermon*," back cover.

46 American female missionary memoirs published in the decades following Newell's death and fitting the same generic mode include James D. Knowles, *Memoir of Mrs. Ann H. Judson, Late Missionary to Burmah: Including a History of the American Baptist Mission in the Burman Empire* (Boston: Lincoln and Edmands, 1829–32, 5 edns.; Philadelphia: American Sunday School Union, 1830 and 1838; Boston: Gould, Kendall and Lincoln, 1846), excerpted as Lady of New Hampshire [Ann H. Judson], *Conversations on the Burman Mission* (Boston: Massachusetts Sabbath School Union, 1830); Rev. William Ellis, *Memoir of Mrs. Mercy Ellis, Wife of Rev. William Ellis, Missionary in the South Seas, and Foreign Secretary of the London Missionary Society* (Boston: Crockett and Brewster; New York: Leavitt, Lord, 1836); Rev. John A. Clark, "The Character and Life of Mrs. S——," *Christian Keepsake and Missionary Annual* (Philadelphia: W. Marshall, 1837), 232–38, and "The Pawnee Missionaries," in *Christian Keepsake, 1839* (Philadelphia: W. Marshall, 1838), 25–59; *The Unpublished Letters and Correspondence of Mrs. Isabella Graham, From the Year 1767 to 1814: Exhibiting Her Religious Character in the Different Relations of Life* [ed. Joanna Bethune] (New York: J. S. Taylor, 1838); Edward W. Hooker, *Memoir of Mrs. Sarah Smith, Late of the Mission in Syria, Under the Direction of the American Board of Commissioners for Foreign*

Missions (Boston: Perkins and Marvin; Philadelphia: Henry Perkins, 1839); Rev. Miron Winslow, *Memoir of Mrs. Harriet L. Winslow; Thirteen Years a Member of the American Mission in Ceylon* (New York: American Tract Society, [1840?]; [Mrs. Joel Hawes], *Memoir of Mrs. Mary E. Van Lennep: Only Daughter of the Rev. Joel Hawes, D.D., and Wife of the Rev. Henry V. Van Lennep, Missionary in Turkey* (Hartford: Belknap and Hammersley, 1847); Fanny Forrester [pseud.], *Memoir of Sarah B. Judson, Member of the American Mission to Burmah* (New York: L. Colby, 1849). See also Daniel C. Eddy, *Heroines of the Missionary Enterprise: or, Sketches of Prominent Female Missionaries* (Boston: Ticknor, Reed, and Fields, 1850).

47 See American Board of Commissioners for Foreign Missions, *Report of the American Board of Commissioners for Foreign Missions, 9th Annual Meeting* (Boston: Samuel T. Armstrong, 1818).

48 My 217 Harriet Newells are distributed geographically as follows: New England, 50 percent (108); New York, 16 percent (34); Ohio, 6 percent (14); other U.S. states, 24 percent (mid-Atlantic, 14; South, 24; Midwest, 10; other, 4); Canada 2 percent (2); other (Jamaica, England), 2 percent (4).

49 Westerkamp, *Women and Religion in Early America*, 142.

Faith, Empire, and Gender in Colonial Rhodesia, 1899–1906

Wendy Urban-Mead

M ission work in colonial Africa was a gender-making enterprise, as this case study of the American missionary H. Frances Davidson (1860–1935) and two of her Ndebele-speaking African male students in colonial Rhodesia demonstrates. Present-day Zimbabwe was known as Southern Rhodesia when it was a British colony from 1896 to 1965. Davidson was a founding member of the group that brought the Brethren in Christ Church (BICC) to what is now Zimbabwe, and her vision, stamina, and skills as a "gifted linguist and formidable organizer" between 1897 and 1922 were key to the successful planting of BIC churches that continue to thrive in southern Africa.[1] Her students David (Ndhlalambi) Moyo and Matshuba Ndlovu took on a Christian identity as members and then leaders of the BICC, an act which led to their isolation from other Ndebele men. Later, as Davidson's principal assistant at the BICC mission in Zambia, Moyo also suffered when BICC male leaders moved to isolate Davidson.

Apparently aware of the gendered dimensions of mission, Davidson wrote the following in her diary in 1909: "My training before coming to the field was more of a man than of a woman. . . . I believe the Lord called me because I had more experience along some lines than many of our people. He wanted some one who was not afraid of obstacles and would be a help in a new country, and so quite unexpectedly to myself He laid hands on me. No doubt because he saw I would listen. Had He wanted *a nice modest womanly woman*, He no doubt would have chosen such."[2] By implication, Davidson called herself an unwomanly woman, noting her awareness that her situation was untypical even for most other female missionaries. In this essay I show how the BICC mission's initial position at this particular place and time allowed for an unmarried woman missionary to function as an honorary man and a spiritual mother to young African men.

The claiming of fictive kin relationships among Christians as a mode of interaction was possible at this earlier stage of the mission's encounter with Africans; Ndlovu and Moyo likened themselves to sons of their spiritual mother, Davidson.[3] Davidson took seriously her church's teaching "God is no respecter of persons" and extended this logic to the young African men in her charge, with whom she developed, for a time, a working relationship that contained elements of collegiality. The colonial government became more systematized, however, and the sending church in North America developed more bureaucratic and professionalized notions of mission work. By the 1920s this trend led to Davidson's forced retirement from the mission field, to the firing of her assistant Moyo, and to the embittered exit of Ndlovu from his position as pastor and church schoolteacher. The earlier years of fruitful collaboration between Davidson and these two men thus represent an unusual convergence at an institutional, temporal, and geographic periphery of both church and empire.

In her work on European women in the history of imperialism, Margaret Strobel has noted the need to investigate the "gendered nature of early cross-cultural contact" in the colonies.[4] Although Davidson was an American, she served in a European imperial context. Her case allows for exploration of the peculiar resonances among American identity, gender, Christian missions, and empire as the nineteenth century came to an end and the twentieth began. Davidson's praise for Cecil Rhodes, the founder of Rhodesia, and her ultimately maternal approach to the Africans with whom she worked stimulate analysis of her career in light of her presence as a white woman on an imperial frontier.

Another area of analysis looks at Davidson's relationship with dominant men of the BICC mission, revealing another important element in the dynamic of opening, then closing leadership opportunities. Informal conditions at the periphery gave Davidson more authority and allowed, for a time, if not real racial and gender equality, at least a serious application of

H. Frances Davidson, ca. 1900.
By permission of Brethren in Christ
Historical Library and Archives,
Grantham, Pennsylvania.

the idea that Africans and white women could in fact be brothers and
sisters in Christ and candidates for leadership.

THE BICC ESTABLISHED IN
THE MATOPO HILLS OF RHODESIA

In spite of Davidson's supposed unwomanly qualities, in many ways her
profile as an American female Protestant missionary of the late nineteenth
century is not unusual. The idea of a religious calling to foreign mission
work was common among male and female missionaries. Davidson's age,
single status, and rural midwestern, middle-class, evangelical origins place
her with the majority of other American women missionaries of that
period.[5] Like many Christians, Davidson shrank from seeing herself as an
achiever in her own right, attributing her accomplishments to God's use of
her as God's agent.[6] She wrote, "The Lord has laid upon me the burden of
pushing on his work . . . [and] he had to take what He could get even
though it was a weak unworthy woman."[7]

Many female missionaries found their lives in far-flung mission stations
afforded them a greater opportunity to exercise their talents than they had

at home, and Davidson's career vividly demonstrates the range of leadership options a capable, energetic woman could exercise at empire's periphery. Davidson taught German and Greek at MacPherson College in Kansas before she became a missionary. Very few in the church had been educated beyond the eighth grade, and none besides Davidson, including men, had earned a master's degree. She had already pressed the boundaries of acceptable female agency and leadership as far as she could in her North American environment. Her desire to go to a site as yet untouched by other mission efforts, where the "natives" were "raw," suggests on some level an awareness on her part that working far away from established institutions was the most likely place her energy and strength of will would find scope for application.[8]

However, Davidson belonged to a sect that stood, to some degree, separate from other Protestant denominations.[9] The Brethren in Christ were Anabaptists, a sect that stressed a nonworldly lifestyle and obedience to communitarian authority, and Pietists, who emphasized the need for a heartfelt, individual conversion experience.[10] Originating in the late eighteenth century in Lancaster County, Pennsylvania, by the 1890s the BICC had expanded to the Midwest, California, and Canada.[11] Brethren in Christ members practiced a trine-immersion baptism, foot-washing ceremonies in conjunction with the commemoration of the Lord's Supper, or "love feast," and a "holy kiss" of greeting extended only to fellow Brethren in Christ Christians.[12] When male members of the church greeted other male members of the church, or when female members greeted other females, a holy kiss on the lips marked their kinship in the Lord. The founding of the BICC's Matopo Mission in colonial Rhodesia in 1898 created conditions that temporarily led to the undermining of the church's insistence on female subjection to male leadership. Women were not allowed to preach, to speak publicly, or to serve as regional church leaders (bishops). However, the needs of the mission on the colonial frontier of Rhodesia led the married head of the mission, Jesse Engle, to rely heavily on the three women who accompanied him, especially H. Frances Davidson.[13]

The newness and remoteness of the mission's setting combined with Engle's willingness to use her allowed Davidson to preach and play a leading role.[14] Her vigor and organizational skills encouraged Engle to delegate to her the task of arranging the travel details, such as booking the overseas passages and cashing checks in London.[15] While the group was en route, the decision as to where to settle and build a mission was made in favor of Davidson's first choice. While Davidson recognized that "as the man and the leader of the group Engle had to be allowed to make the decision," she successfully convinced the others that Matabeleland in Rhodesia was the best option and should be favored over Engle's suggestion that they settle among the Africans in South Africa.[16] She argued that the "raw natives" of Matabeleland were the people who needed them most, not the Africans in the South African Republic, who had been in contact with missionaries and settlers since the 1830s.

When the group arrived in Cape Town, Davidson, eager to acquire the language, did not hesitate to acquire a Zulu grammar and Bible, since the Ndebele (or Matabele) people spoke a language similar to Zulu. In the meantime, Elder Engle arranged a meeting with Rhodes at his home near Cape Town to ask for a grant of land on which to begin mission work. Rhodes saw to it that the BICC missionaries received a three-thousand-acre tract of land outside of Bulawayo.[17] It was little more than a year since the Ndebele people had been defeated in the war of conquest of 1896. Rhodes regarded missionaries as "better than policemen and cheaper" at fostering African cooperation with colonial rule.[18] Engle wrote that, by way of returning the kindness, the missionaries would do their best at "civilizing and Christianizing the natives."[19] Davidson wrote of their arrival in the Matopos soon after the end of the Rising of 1896, a time when the inhabitants were "still seething" over their loss.

The early years at Matopo Mission, 1898–1902, were characterized by the missionaries' struggle to build structures in which to live, worship, and teach, by their sorrow over the deaths of several of the first workers, and by their first interactions with the Africans in the vicinity of the mission. The missionaries depended greatly on the local expertise, labor, and hospitality of the Africans. Davidson and Alice Heise started the first school at Matopo Mission, where Davidson was the head and main teacher. The school emphasized industrial and domestic skills as well as Christian education, basic literacy in Zulu, and arithmetic. The Christian Gospels, in Zulu, remained the reading primers as late as 1909.[20]

The BICC mission in Rhodesia admired Rhodes. H. P. Steigerwald, who succeeded Engle as head of Matopo Mission, referred to him in 1903 as "one of the great ones of earth" and praised Rhodes's accomplishment in turning a large section of the Matopo hills from wilderness into a park.[21] Davidson likewise praised Rhodes for his role as the generous benefactor of the mission and extolled him as the great "Empire builder, who perhaps more than anyone else had the welfare of the country at heart."[22]

While the nearly all-white BIC membership was not free of racism, the church's doctrine emphasizing that God "is no respecter of persons" led the missionaries in the early years at Matopo to enact the holy kiss with the first African brothers and sisters when they were baptized in 1899 and received into fellowship. Writing to the *Evangelical Visitor*, the missionary Sara Cress acknowledged that some folks at home might find it shocking to think of white missionaries kissing black converts: "One by one the candidates entered the water and were baptized by Elder Engle, the service being nearly all in the Zulu language. We suppose those poor people in the church at home who think it would be a dreadful thing to mix with these natives would have been shocked beyond measure had they seen us greet our new brethren and sister with the Holy Kiss. Of course we observed that command the same as at home."[23] Cress is self-conscious of the transgressive nature of the kiss when she indicates that folks at home would be "shocked beyond measure." Amy Kaplan discusses W. E. B. DuBois's observation that American racism should be seen as part of an "international network of imperial relations."[24] For a time in this as-yet-informal setting the missionaries at Matopo attempted to disregard the internationally recognized color line in their relationships with their new African brothers and sisters in Christ, while nonetheless remaining conscious of it.

However, the BICC as a mission society in colonial Rhodesia gradually compromised on this early sign of adherence to spiritual equality. The neighboring mission societies, with whom the BICC missionaries consulted, practiced segregation in their relations with converts. By 1916, the mission's deepening intermeshing with Rhodesian colonial values and the power structure there was evident when the missionaries in Africa petitioned the Foreign Mission Board at home for permission to discontinue the interracial holy kiss—not explicitly on grounds of race but rather of hygiene, that is, because of the many "loathsome" diseases that the native converts were prone to carry.[25] Nayan Shah's study of Chinese immigrants and epidemics in San Francisco has highlighted how "the entanglement of race in modern science, governance, and morality" reveals the paradoxical elements of modernity, which professes universal benefits for all while highlighting racial difference.[26] Shah's point suggests that the missionaries' decision in 1913 to discontinue the holy kiss on grounds of fear of contamination with the diseases of the native converts can also be understood in terms of the inexorably modernizing impact of being a mission church in a settler colony—the more worldly they became, the more modern, and thus the more scientifically and bureaucratically concerned with such matters as contamination from these racially different members of the church.

UNDERSTANDING DAVIDSON'S ROLE
IN REGIONAL CONTEXT

Contrasting Davidson's work with that of other energetic, talented women missionaries leads one to see the importance of geographic location and place on the timeline of colonial rule for understanding gender roles in Christian missions in Africa. In certain circumstances, even the most independent of women missionaries was limited to acting in a prescribed feminine sphere.[27] While Davidson supervised the sewing classes held for the African women, sewed clothing for her students, and untiringly served as nurse to her ill and dying colleagues, many of Davidson's other duties were those normally reserved for a male. In addition to arranging travel details and preaching, she conducted, under Elder Engle's official headship of the mission, administrative business with colonial officials and taught the young men.

Davidson's physical stamina and attendant role as nurse figured prominently in her continued place as a leader—almost by default—of the mission station; she never fell sick and was frequently called on to care for the others while she maintained the work of the station, making visits to homesteads, nursing Africans in the infirmary, and teaching in the school. Davidson kept the station running virtually single-handedly after Engle's death in April 1901. Davidson and Isaac Lehman, the other male missionary on site besides Engle, faced a challenge to their right to occupy the land. After a year of "much writing, surveying, and making trips to town" the mission was permitted to stay with a ninety-nine-year lease, and the other claimant received a different piece of land in exchange.[28] During the dispute, Davidson was the mission's contact with Native Commissioner H. M. G. Jackson, and the Foreign Mission Board gave her control over the mission's finances.

contrast
bio

Mary Edwards's career with the American Board of Commissioners for
Foreign Missions (ABCFM), a Congregational mission based out of Boston, serves as a good point of contrast with Davidson's. The ABCFM in
South Africa was active in Natal on a large scale, in an area heavily
influenced by British and Afrikaner presence since 1830. They ran the
regionally well-known Adams' College, a secondary school for African
boys, and Inanda Seminary for girls. Edwards was head of the Inanda
Seminary. She found that her male missionary superiors would not permit
her to undertake a cooperative teaching arrangement with a black male
teacher, John Dube. When she asked to be allowed to sit in on Dube's
classes in order to improve her Zulu, Edwards's superior, Daniel Lindley,
refused. It was not fitting that women missionaries, white or black, have
professional contacts with African men. Edwards's case seems to have
been typical of female missionaries serving at well-established missions.
Other strong single or widowed female missionaries similarly found themselves curbed by the male missionary leadership.[29]

Davidson, by contrast, took great pleasure in getting to know the
African men who lived near Matopo Mission.[30] She enthusiastically recounted an evening spent with the nearest headman, Mapita Ndiweni.
Ndiweni, like many of the elder generation of Ndebele at this time, was
himself not a Christian convert but encouraged his children to attend the
mission school. An entry in Davidson's diary reveals condescension mixed
with an unmistakable zest for Mapita Ndiweni's inquisitiveness: "Mapita
was here quite a while, and we had such a nice talk together. Poor man he
has such aspirations for something better. He said he thought he would
come over and have a talk and one can talk so much like talking to a white
man. He seems to realize so thoroughly just where he stands on religious
questions. . . . Today he wanted to go over the story of creation to see
whether he had it all right."[31] Significantly, the measure of a good conver-
sationalist, in Davidson's view, was someone who could converse like a
white man. All those whom she had to that point in her diary considered
worthy of her intellectual attention had been white men: the men on
shipboard and the men she met at Native Commissioner Jackson's. Now
Mapita became an honorary white man.

Davidson regarded the medium of Ndebele language as the heart of her
work (and her authority), for it enabled her to "talk, interpret, explain, as
well as to have heart-to-heart talks with the people."[32] She wrote that

somehow "the school room and out among the people are about the only places I feel at home here in Africa."[33] As was her pattern, she viewed her commitment and ability to learn Ndebele as having come from the Lord: "I should feel ashamed if I did not do better than those who have had so much less opportunity of an education than I and I feel that the Lord has given me the opportunity for some purpose of his own, and shall I neglect to improve the talents He has given me[?]"[34] Justifying her use of the language in the interest of the mission led her to conclude that failing to exercise her talents constituted neglect of God's gifts.

Davidson had enjoyed an unusual level of congeniality with her male colleagues at McPherson College. McPherson's location in the American Midwest, where women had opportunities that would have been barred to them in the East, is an important parallel. In both situations, it was Davidson's superior preparation, vigor, and command of language that made it possible for her to take advantage of the opportunities in both frontier settings. The timing and extent of institutionalization of the mission within its particular colonial context is important because Davidson also found herself increasingly hemmed in over time.

Eventually Davidson left Matopo Station. Changed relations with authoritative men played a crucial role at this point. In November 1901, Elder Steigerwald was installed as the official head of the Matopo Mission. Engle's replacement by the vigorous and stronger-willed Steigerwald diminished the scope of Davidson's initiative there. Engle held a place in Davidson's affections. He was a kindhearted man greatly beloved by his colleagues, including Davidson, who often referred to him as Father.[35] It soon became clear that she and Steigerwald, age-mates and both with quite forceful personalities, were not compatible. Davidson was accustomed to greater latitude than Steigerwald felt appropriate for a single female under his supervision.

DAVIDSON AND THE FIRST
AFRICAN CHRISTIANS

Davidson's diary contains many references to her conversations with the young African men who were the focus of her evangelizing efforts. She repeatedly gives expression to her hopes and fears for them. Some of the first Africans to come to Matopo Mission were the sons of chiefs and other families of importance. Matshuba Ndlovu, for example, was the son of a prominent man who had served as *isangoma* (medicine man) to the last Ndebele king, Lobhengula.[36] Ndlovu and Ndhlalambi Moyo proved to be Davidson's prize students at Matopo.

Davidson enjoyed many confidential evening chats with local male village leaders and the boys from her school, who would come to her hut to discuss a wide range of concerns, mostly religious ones.[37] While Davidson did not hesitate to exercise authority over her promising African students, she mentored them closely in her hopes to turn them into colleagues, indicating her yearning for some measure of partnership in the work. In a letter she wrote to the *Evangelical Visitor*, in 1905 from Mapane Mission, Davidson said, "At one kraal [homestead] two miles from here we saw 15 fine looking boys, and as we sat there and told them about Jesus, those bright eyes and sharp ears seemed to take in everything. *How we did covet them for God and his service*! but we could not prevail upon them to come to school."[38]

Conversion to Christianity, particularly the variety taught by the BIC, required a level of change that affected every aspect of the convert's life. Everything from sowing seed to giving birth was touched by indigenous ritual practice. For instance, people in Matabeleland took their seeds for a ritual treatment by the regionally powerful deity, Mwari, before planting their food crops. Christian converts were expected to use undoctored seed.[39] The BICC missionaries were imbued with supreme confidence in their own correctness, an attitude commonly found among the mission societies of the colonial period. They simply declared many elements of Ndebele daily life to be sinful and therefore forbidden.[40] Ngwabi Bhebe described the first generation of converts associated with the mission societies of early twentieth-century Rhodesia as belonging to a "quarantine" phase.[41] Davidson herself was aware, at least superficially, of the extreme demands conversion placed upon individuals. In 1900 she wrote in a letter to the *Evangelical Visitor*, "Only those who are willing to forsake friends and home can stand, and very few are willing to do this. We rejoice that a few are willing to take the Lord's way and we ask for your prayers for these as well for the rest."[42]

In spite of the compelling social dangers, some of the first pupils at Matopo took up the challenge earnestly. A group of youths came to Davidson on Christmas Eve in 1901 to confess their sins and ask that the other missionaries be summoned to hear their testimony. According to Davidson, the boys said, "We desire to confess everything and have all wiped away, and we do not want to repeat our wrongdoings, for we want to be ready when Jesus comes." At the end of this session, the missionaries and the boys kneeled together and "besought the Lord that they might be set completely free from their past life."[43] Davidson expressed her desire that they be done "forever with their heathen past."[44]

NDHLALAMBI MOYO

What did it mean for Ndebele men, as men, to become Christian in these early years after the arrival of the BICC in 1898? Some of the young men who went to the school at Matopo Mission did so on the urging of their fathers, who wanted them to learn English. Some fell away from church membership under the pressure to live up to Ndebele ideals of manhood that were at odds with a strict, alien Christian moral code. For some converts, opportunities for status provided an instrumental explanation for the decision to align oneself with missionaries. For example, Ndhla-lambi Moyo did enjoy certain markers of status unavailable to him in the era of the precolonial kingdom. Moyo's case also illustrates that social isolation and dangers could follow upon conversion, however, and renders a strictly instrumental motivation inadequate to explain some African men's motivations for remaining in the church.

Moyo first came to Davidson around 1899 after having worked at the mines for some time. He must have been exposed to Christianity some-where because he arrived at Davidson's door stating, "I became convicted of my wrongdoings," and he wanted to give his heart to Jesus.[45] He was baptized in 1902 and helped to build the African church membership at the newly established Mapane Mission when it opened in 1904.[46] The thirteen people baptized around 1907 by Levi Doner at Mapane had been under Moyo's tutelage.[47]

In September 1905 Davidson and Adda Engle, Jesse Engle's niece, visited Mapane while it was under Moyo's leadership. A man of the lowest-ranked group during the nineteenth-century kingdom, Moyo was of low status.[48] As an unmarried youth, he was not considered fully adult. Yet the people in the Mapane area listened to him "with great respect" and addressed him as Baba (father), a title reserved for married men of standing.[49]

Moyo's close association with Davidson and the other missionaries, while winning him stature, resulted in his losing an important point of connection both with his family and with other Ndebele men and even endangered his life. Moyo was required to give up beer as one aspect of assuming BIC Christian identity, and this isolated him from the mainstream of Ndebele manhood. If he did not drink beer, he could not participate in certain ceremonies necessary to the life of his family, many of which required offering beer to deceased ancestors and drinking beer on the occasion of weddings and funerals of family members. Moyo decided not to accept the inheritance of cattle left to him by his uncle because to do so would entail ritual offerings of beer to the uncle's deceased spirit. In spite of the central importance of cattle to the economy, established kinship ties, and the family's connectedness to deceased relatives, Moyo told Davidson, "I love the Lord more than I love the cattle."[50] In addition, Moyo encountered serious trouble with his relatives around 1905 when he and another convert, Sitshokupi Sibanda, helped Davidson find and enter one of the cave shrines dedicated to Mwari. Because he led the white missionary to the cave of the rain shrine, Moyo was blamed for the ensuing drought and lived through a period of death threats.[51]

Moyo accompanied Davidson when she left for the north, eventually establishing Macha Mission among the Tonga people of Northern Rhodesia (present-day Zambia). Davidson wrote that Moyo "had felt called some time before to carry the Gospel beyond the Zambezi": "As Ndhlalambi, who *took the name of David*, had felt the call definitely to give the Gospel to these people, and had had experience in evangelistic work, both at Mapani and at Matopo Mission, he was able in a comparatively short time to give the Gospel intelligently to the people, and also to assist us in acquiring the language."[52] Adopting the name David, he presumably honored Davidson's spiritual parenthood.[53]

DAVIDSON'S FURLOUGH, 1904-5

Davidson took a furlough from 1904 to 1905, which turned into a triumphal tour of the North American BIC congregations. Her speeches raised unprecedented sums of money, fulfilling her colleagues' belief that "the Lord will use Sister Davidson very much to stir up the interest there [in North America] for mission work."[54] The donations were used to support Matopo Mission, to build a new girls' school, and to fund her dream of going beyond the Zambezi River, where she could build a new station. While she was on furlough, her every move was closely reported in the *Evangelical Visitor*. She went to Pennsylvania, Ontario, Kansas, Indiana, and Ohio and attended the annual General Conference in the summer of 1904, when, "Under the spell of Sister Davidson's earnest plea, the attendants at Conference quickly contributed five hundred dollars."[55]

Davidson set up a fund for Moyo and Ndlovu, demonstrating her commitment to their acceptance as coworkers in the building of the BICC in Rhodesia. She and Steigerwald cowrote a Matopo Mission report for the *Evangelical Visitor* in which they described how "two of our boys" were particularly steadfast in the teaching at the mission school. Their hope was that people in North America would make contributions specifically to allow Ndlovu and Moyo to devote their full energy "to teaching and evangelizing among their people." They assured their readers that "you will be supporting worthy objects."[56] The *Visitor's* editors noted, "We hope this fund will be liberally supported."[57] By May 1905, supporters had sent fifty-six dollars earmarked for the support of "our native brethren."[58]

Davidson skillfully brought the members of the North American Brotherhood into a direct relationship with Moyo and Ndlovu by having the *Visitor* publish their letters. Both men gave detailed reports on events at Matopo since her departure. Ndlovu's and Moyo's letters indicate how they were handling duties she had previously held. Ndlovu, for example, served as head teacher while Davidson was away, while Moyo mentored the new Christians at Mapane Mission. Their work speaks both to her supervisory role and to her capacity to delegate and regard these young men as coworkers. When Ndlovu wrote, "I almost said that it is not I who teaches, it is Jesus. I try to teach all things that I am able to help them with," he was distinctly producing a style of self-abasement that was typical of Davidson's references to herself as an unworthy, if willing, servant of the Lord.[59] Ndlovu and Moyo offered greetings to the members of the church in America in terms of kinship, both making sure to greet the "brethren." Moyo, for example, wrote, "Tell me about the other brethren. I desire to write to them because they are brethren. Will you read these few words to them? Ngi ya tanda bonke abazalwane. Aku be kubo unmsa nokutula okuvela eNkosini yetu Jesu Kristu. Ba ngi kulekele ngi fumene amandhla okuhamba ngokufaneleyo endhleleni ye Nkosi. (Translation: I love all the brethren. May there be to them mercy and peace which comes from the Lord Jesus Christ. Pray for me that I may find strength to walk worthily in the way of the Lord)."[60] Moyo wrote, "Ngi ya tanda bonke abazalwane," which Davidson translated for her readers as "I love all the brethren." *Abazalwane* means "kin." Ndlovu also sent greetings, saying, "I desire to write to them because they are brethren." Aside from an obvious potential discussion of the gendered nature of these words (*brethren* is male-based in its etymology, whereas *abazalwane* means not "brothers" but "kin") there is the fact that these young, unmarried African men, of very low status in every official legal sense of the British colonial system, were claiming kinship with a host of white Christians in a place very far away that they had never seen and never would see. They did so on two grounds: first, because of the Christian habit of referring to fellow believers as brothers and sisters in Christ; second, because of the fact that they both regarded Davidson as something of a mother figure, and she regarded them as "her boys."[61] Davidson being forty-two years old, Ndlovu around twenty, and Moyo a bit older, this was not solely an adoption of the colonial demasculinization of African men by calling them boys. There was in addition the indigenous pattern of naming, whereby fictive kin relationships were and are often adopted. The long-held Christian pattern of kinship expressions among believers made a bridge between these worlds. The two young men could cross that bridge to America in their imaginations in a way that was not bound by colonial hierarchies of race and class.

This type of communication also created a bridge whereby the many readers of the *Evangelical Visitor* could claim and feel a connection with the two young men and, by extension, with the others at the mission, whom they also would never see. The *Evangelical Visitor* categorized the money collected on behalf of Ndlovu and Moyo as the fund "For Support of Native Brethren." Significantly, it was not for the "native boys." The fellowship in North America at this juncture seemingly accepted Ndlovu and Moyo as Davidson urged them to: as partners in the great work of evangelization.

After her return to Africa from furlough in 1906 Davidson realized her dream of founding her own mission station. With her American aide, Adda Engle, and two male converts, Gomo Sibanda and Ndhlalambi (now David) Moyo, Davidson founded the mission institution at Macha in

Northern Rhodesia, including a school, church, residence buildings, and a productive farm.[62] At Macha Mission, if only for a time, Davidson realized her dream of going out "*alone* in some remote corner of this country where Christ had not been named and work to the saving of souls and not caring whether any one ever heard of me again only so that *I might work unhindered*."[63] One must question what Davidson meant when she imagined herself going to a new mission site alone, in light of the fact that she was not unaccompanied on her trip to Macha. Her averment is not unlike the claims of missionaries who took credit for translating the Bible into various indigenous languages without noting the irreplaceable intellectual work of their African assistants.[64] The ambiguities of her position as a white missionary in the British African empire come to the fore as she highlights her aloneness in this venture even though there was a very real element of collegiality in her relationships with African coworkers like Moyo.

By 1909, church authorities were increasingly uncomfortable with the fact that a woman was in charge of Macha Mission. Her female missionary partner, Adda Engle, had recently married BICC missionary Myron Taylor. It was acceptable to have a single woman leader of a mission station if there was no suitable married male around, but now it was time for Davidson to step aside. The board pressed Davidson to accept Taylor's leadership. Bishop Steigerwald, in a letter from his base at Matopo Station in Southern Rhodesia, sent a directive to Davidson. He stated that "they thought [she] had taken the place of man long enough and time had come for [her] to be in subjection."[65] Davidson finally understood in clear terms a feeling that she had been unable to name but that had puzzled her and caused her agony. The men in authority over her were opposing her *because* she was a woman performing a man's tasks. Yet she reiterated that her transgression of gender boundaries was not of her own doing. In fact it was initiated and legitimated by the Lord himself, who had "laid hands" upon her. The Taylors helped to resolve the tensions. Davidson remained at her post at Macha after all, and the Taylors established a new mission some distance away at Sikalongo.

Finally Davidson was forced out of her position at Macha. By 1922, the Foreign Mission Board, no longer made up of her supporters, did not come to her defense when the same issues that caused the crisis in 1909 came to a head again.[66] The mission enterprise was institutionally and financially far more robust than it had been in earlier years; the Messiah

Training Home in Pennsylvania was producing a new generation of professionalized young men. In 1909 the board had had the financial success
of her furlough in 1904 relatively fresh in their minds. This time, the board
had no close ties to Davidson; her claims to exceptionality and indispen-
sability had eroded. The previously peripheral location of Macha Mission
from the formalizing efforts of the home church was no longer so distant.
The Foreign Mission Board cited advancing age as the ostensible reason
for their request that she retire. Knowing herself to be in excellent health at
sixty-two and wishing to live and be buried in Africa, Davidson was angry
and brokenhearted. Yet she agreed to step down. In her diary she acknowledged that the issue of her sex was again at the root of her troubles.
Fatalistic in accepting the board's authority, she returned to the United
States. She taught at Messiah College until she retired and moved to live
with her sister in Kansas, where she died in 1935.

Moyo remained a core worker and teacher at Macha until Davidson resigned. Davidson's successor at Macha Mission adopted a colonial rather
than a collegial approach to the contributions of African church workers.
Moyo was regarded as Davidson's pet and too far above his station. Moyo
was certainly not prepared to relate to the new male leader of the mission
with unceasing deference.[67] Within six years of Davidson's departure from
Macha and twenty-two years after his arrival there, Moyo was dismissed
from his position as lead teacher at the Macha School.[68] In the 1920s, the
leading men of Mayezane village (near Mapane), including their teacher
and pastor, Matshuba Ndlovu, clashed with the mission over the Africans'
desire to add higher grades to the village school. Ndlovu quit his teaching
post, took a job nearby working for a white farmer, and, by his own
testimony, "backslid" and abandoned himself to the "ways of Satan." By
1926 Ndlovu had repented and returned as pastor at Mayezane, but he
never again taught for the BICC.[69]

CONCLUSION

As a founding member of the BIC's Africa mission, Davidson proved
herself to be a knowledgeable, capable, and loyal missionary.[70] Yet from
the very beginning Davidson struggled with increasingly unbearable tensions between herself and male church authorities that ultimately led to
her premature resignation from mission work. As early as 1893, Davidson's

diary shows how she sought to submit to what she saw as God's will that she *was* a woman and to accept what she perceived were the limitations on acting out her sense of adventure because of her sex: "Would that I were a man then I could brave the dangers but what can a defenseless woman do? Forgive the thought. Thou madest me as I am and therewith I am content."[71] The issues surrounding gender and leadership that Davidson faced were not limited to her as an individual; but neither can they be understood solely from a gender-based interpretive framework. Her experiences as an educated, midwestern woman who became a founding missionary to Rhodesia were shaped by, and in turn helped to shape, the dynamics of change in the BICC. From its origins as a relatively closed sect that emphasized obedience to community ordinances as worked out by the church elders, the BICC experienced major changes as a result of its increasing openness to the mainstream of American evangelicalism and of its undertaking of foreign missions.

Davidson's continuously evolving individual, heartfelt response to a sense of divine authority led her, first, to a periphery of the British colonial empire and then, to test—but not defy—the limits of obedience to patriarchal church authority. In the spaces opened up by these imperial and ecclesiastical frontiers, Davidson exercised her linguistic and organizational talents, nurturing a growing conviction in the legitimacy of her calling.

Antoinette Burton's work on Josephine Butler, a British reforming feminist active in the same period as Davidson, highlights a dynamic in which Anglo-Saxon women of the British empire felt a special responsibility to the women under British colonial rule, claiming racial responsibility as part of their strategy to legitimize themselves as responsible and important imperial citizens. Colonized women were enslaved, degraded, and in need of salvation by their British feminist sisters. Burton called this a kind of maternal imperialism.[72] In the case of Frances Davidson, however, lie some interesting points of convergence and divergence with Butler's depiction of British imperial women. Davidson, as an American member of an Anabaptist-Pietist sect from the United States, did not identify her connection with either American national or British imperial citizenship as the key to her lifework. As white Americans, however, Davidson and her group of self-consciously unworldly Pietists–who as Anabaptists were suspicious of governmental associations—found the door to the evangelistic work they craved opened by the imperial prototype, Cecil Rhodes himself. Their mission station at Matopo, placed at the center of the recently quashed Ndebele rising against Rhodes's British South Africa Company, offered Davidson her first opportunity to interact with Africans in a leadership capacity.

The BIC's pacifist, politically disengaged, and antimaterialist values proved to be remarkably compatible with Rhodes's imperial project in Rhodesia. Davidson's friendship with Native Commissioner Jackson, her use of his help when she had to defend the mission's claim to its land, her venture to Northern Rhodesia as the head of a mission party aided by a white woman and two male black protégés are a few of many examples of her prominence in the mission's leadership and in its interface with British colonial authorities.

In her interactions with Africans, unlike British imperial feminists like Butler and her efforts on behalf of Indian women, Davidson concentrated on building up a core of male African converts who could join her as coworkers in evangelism: Africans would be both partners and intellectual companions, yet subordinate to her leadership. Her relationships with Matshuba Ndlovu and Ndhlalambi (David) Moyo exemplify the complex elements of imperiousness, mentorship, fellowship, partnership, and kinship in Christ that were all present in their interactions. Davidson's naming of the two as "her boys" shows how one childless, unmarried woman could gain spiritual progeny in the foreign mission field.

Kaplan's study suggests that an analysis of Davidson's work might be conducted in terms of the explicit expression of the connectedness between racial and imperial ideology and domesticity. The connectedness of these things was somewhat hidden at home, but on the imperial frontier of Rhodesia it was obvious. Davidson sewed garments for African pupils, nursed her ill coworkers, and cleared tables while male missionaries sat and talked, yet she also preached, headed the school, intellectually and spiritually mentored the prize category of male converts, and headed the founding of a new mission station in Macha, partnering with another single female missionary and two African men.

Davidson had reached the limit of opportunities for exercising her energies and talents in her youth at the western edge of American white settlement in Kansas. From her appreciation for the wide streets of Bulawayo that reminded her of a Kansas cattle town, to her ready capacity to take charge of opportunities to build institutions in a newly conquered territory now wide open for white, European agency, on the periphery of the economic and political power base that supported her, Davidson was an American of the late nineteenth-century Midwest. Her understanding of the Pietist teachings of her church gave her latitude to see where she might act contra to the male leadership that stood de jure over her, while remaining in good standing in the church. Davidson's internalized religious struggles kept her on the edge, but always just inside, of the boundaries established by the BICC, using evangelism as her shield when male missionary authority came too near. Together these imperial, ecclesiastical, geographical, and gendered dynamics converged in the calling of this unwomanly leader of a new church in Rhodesia.

NOTES

Thanks to Gloria Stonge and Adam J. Tarantino at the BICC Archives, Grantham, Pennsylvania. This essay was inspired by E. Morris Sider, "Hannah Frances Davidson," *Nine Portraits: Brethren in Christ Biographical Sketches* (Nappanee, Ind.: Evangel Press, 1978), 159–212.

1 Fiona Bowie, "Introduction," *Women and Missions Past and Present: Historical and Anthropological Perspectives*, ed. Fiona Bowie, Deborah Kirkwood, Shirley Ardener, 6 (Providence: Berg, 1993).

2 Davidson diary typescript, Brethren in Christ Archives, Grantham, Pennsylvania, July 17, 1909, 169. Emphasis added.

3 Analysis of this dynamic in all its ambiguity is based on rejecting the dichotomized colonizer/colonized trope as a fruitful line of inquiry. Being concerned with the tensions of empire does not render one insensitive to the brutal nature of colonial rule. Rather, "it is . . . to broaden our analytic compass; to take in its moments of incoherence and inchoateness, its internal contortions and complexities." John Comaroff, "Images of Empire, Contests of Conscience: Models of Colonial Domination in South Africa," *Tensions of Empire: Colonial Cultures in a Bourgeois World*, ed. Fred Cooper and Ann Laura Stoler, 165 (Berkeley: University of California Press, 1997).

4 Margaret Strobel, "Gender, Sex, and Empire," *Essays on Global and Comparative History*, foreword by Michael Adas (Washington: American Historical Association, 1994), 4.

5 See, in particular, on American women missionaries, Patricia Hill, *The World Their Household: The American Woman's Foreign Mission Movement and Cultural Transformation* (Ann Arbor: University of Michigan Press, 1985); and Jane Hunter, *The Gospel of Gentility: American Women Missionaries in Turn-of-the-*

Century China (New Haven: Yale University Press, 1984). For a British-based study, see Bowie, Kirkwood, and Ardener, eds., *Women and Missions Past and Present.*

6 Jane Hunter observed that many female missionaries were "simultaneously both self-effacing and imperious," Hunter, *The Gospel of Gentility*, 29.

7 Davidson diary, June 17, 1909.

8 Wendy Urban-Mead, "Religion, Women, and Gender in the Brethren in Christ Church, Matabeleland, Zimbabwe, 1898–1978" (Ph.D. diss., Columbia University, 2004), chapt. 2, and Sider, *Nine Portraits.*

9 At the end of the nineteenth century, the BICC underwent a period of transformation, and Davidson's case can be seen as a lightning rod: in particular, for the BICC's divisions over the doctrine of sanctification and the controversial decision to sponsor foreign missions.

10 Carlton O. Wittlinger, *Quest for Piety and Obedience: The Story of the Brethren in Christ* (Nappanee, Ind.: Evangel Press, 1978), 214.

11 This religious body, also known as the River Brethren, is distinct from the better-known church, the Church of the Brethren.

12 Wittlinger, *Quest for Piety*, 60–68.

13 See Sider, *Nine Portraits*, and Urban-Mead, "Religion, Women, and Gender."

14 "Female preachers [at home] were dismissed as 'manly' women, but female missionaries were portrayed in glowing terms as models of heroism and piety." Catherine A. Brekus, *Strangers and Pilgrims: Female Preaching in America 1740–1845* (Chapel Hill: University of North Carolina Press, 1998), 301. Davidson's case shows that even women regarded as heroic missionaries could struggle with unwomanliness. Before they left for Africa, Davidson was frequently invited to speak. Anxious about church teachings on the silence of women, Davidson at first declined: "After coming home, I asked Bro. E. what he considered proper under the circumstances; and he seemed to think that it would be all right for any of us to do that kind of work." Diary, January 3, 1898, 41.

15 Sider, *Nine Portraits*, 166.

16 Matabele was the term used most commonly in the 1890s to refer to the people now known as the Ndebele. Matabeleland was the territory north of the Limpopo River where the Ndebele state was located, formerly ruled by Mzilikazi (1840–68) and his son, Lobhengula (1870–93.) The South African Republic, also known as the Transvaal, was an independent republic established by Dutch-descended settlers of the Cape region.

17 Sider, *Nine Portraits*, 167–68. Sider's source for this was Davidson's diary, December 11, 1897. See Ian Phimister, "Rhodes, Rhodesia and the Rand," *Journal of Southern African Studies* 1, no. 1 (October 1974), 87; Terence Ranger, *Revolt in Southern Rhodesia, 1896–97: A Study in African Resistance* (London: Heinemann, 1967), 90. National Archives of Zimbabwe, Harare, "Permit of Occupation," L2/1/24–61. Other mission societies such as the Seventh-day Adventists and

Roman Catholics also received land. C. J. M. Zvobgo, *A History of Christian Missions in Zimbabwe, 1890–1939* (Gweru: Mambo Press, 1996), 11, 66–67.

18 Frances Davidson, *South and South Central Africa: A Record of Fifteen Years' Missionary Labors among Primitive Peoples* (Elgin, Illinois: Brethren Publishing House, 1915.)

19 National Archives of Zimbabwe, Harare, letter from Jesse Engle to the Civil Commissioner, June 7, 1898, L2/1/24–215.

20 Government Inspector's Report, J. B. Brady, August 27, 1909. Cited in John Norman Hostetter, "Mission Education in a Changing Society: Brethren in Christ Mission Education in Southern Rhodesia, Africa. 1899–1959" (Ed.D. diss., SUNY Buffalo, 1967), 43. The nearby London Missionary Society missions used Ndebele-language materials, not Zulu. Personal communication, Marieke Clarke.

21 "Matoppa Mission" *Evangelical Visitor* (hereafter EV), July 25, 1903, 13. Compare this to writings about the Matopos by other white settlers in Terence Ranger, *Voices from the Rocks: Nature, Culture and History in the Matopos Hills of Zimbabwe* (Bloomington: Indiana University Press, 1999), 39–66.

22 Davidson, *South and South Central Africa*, 40.

23 Sara Cress, "Letter from Sister Cress," Bulawayo, S.A. August 22, 1899, EV, November 1, 1899, 419–20.

24 Amy Kaplan, *The Anarchy of Empire in the Making of U.S. Culture* (Cambridge, Mass.: Harvard University Press, 2002), 179.

25 Minutes from the General Conference of 1913. Flat File: Executive Board and Conference, 1907–1946, Brethren in Christ Church Archives, Bulawayo, Zimbabwe.

26 Nayan Shah, *Contagious Divides: Epidemics and Race in San Francisco's Chinatown* (Berkeley: University of California Press, 2001), 5.

27 See Heather Beal, " 'A Lighthouse for African Womanhood': Inanda Seminary, 1869–1945," *Women and Gender in Southern Africa to 1945*, ed. Cherryl Walker, 197–220 (Cape Town: David Philip, 1990). See also Deborah Gaitskell, "Race, Sex and Imperialism: A Century of Black Girls' Education in South Africa," *Benefits Bestowed? Education and British Imperialism*, ed. J. A. Mangan (Manchester, Eng.: Manchester University Press, 1988), 150–73.

28 Diary, March 11, 1902. Sider, *Nine Portraits*, 175.

29 Norman Etherington, "Gender Issues in South-East African Missions, 1835–85," *Missions and Christianity in South African History*, ed. Henry Bredekamp and Robert Ross, 135–52 (Johannesburg: University of Witwatersrand Press, 1995). See also Emily Rosenberg on Jane Hunter and Patricia Hill, in "Gender," *Journal of American History* 77, no. 1 (June 1990), 117. See also Jeff Guy, *The View Across the River: Hariette Colenso and the Zulu Struggle against Imperialism* (Charlottesville: University Press of Virginia, 2001), 34–42, for an account of Hariette Colenso, the influential daughter of the Anglican bishop John Colenso. Hariette became active in protecting the rights of the Hlubi people against the expansionist aims of Natal Colony.

30 From the beginning, Davidson sought intellectual companionship outside of her group of fellow missionaries (Diary, December 9, 14, 1897).

31 Diary, August 11, 1900.

32 Davidson, *South and South Central Africa*, 140.

33 Diary, May 17, 1902. This differs from Jane Hunter's observation that most single women missionaries in China clung to their relationships with fellow single women missionaries and their correspondence with home folks for their sense of well-being. Hunter, *The Gospel of Gentility*, 59.

34 Diary, March 10, 1898, 45.

35 Diary, passim.

36 *Isangoma* (pl *izangoma*) has been translated as "medicine man" (Ngwabi Bhebe), *Christianity and Traditional Religion in Western Zimbabwe, 1859–1923* (London: Longman, 1979, 6) or as "witchdoctor" (*A Practical Ndebele Dictionary*, 2d ed.; Harare: Longman Zimbabwe, 1996). For the senior Ndlovu's role as witchdoctor, see also Anna Engle, John Climenhaga, and Leoda A. Buckwalter, *There Is No Difference: God Works in Africa and India* (Nappanee, Ind.: Evangel Press, 1950), 194.

37 See also Davidson, *South and South Central Africa*, 66, 118, 139, and Diary, December 31, 1903, 110.

38 December 15, 1905, 15.

39 H. J. Frey, "Africa, chapter VII. Native Religions (Continued). Magic." *EV*, June 2, 1913, 7.

40 Robert A. Hess, "Brethren in Christ Schools and Acculturation in Matabeleland," *Brethren in Christ History and Life* (December 1979), 3–20.

41 Bhebe, *Christianity and Traditional Religion*, 165.

42 Davidson, "Dwellers in Darkness," *EV*, September 1, 1900, 339.

43 Davidson, *South and South Central Africa*, 109. Emma Long Doner wrote, "On Christmas eve several of our boys became burdened about their souls, likewise our girls. Going to Sister Davidson's hut they commenced to confess out their sins." "Sister Doner Tells of the African Children," *EV*, April 1, 1902, 133.

44 Davidson, *South and South Central Africa*, 109.

45 Ibid., 118.

46 Emma Long Doner, "Mapane Mission," *EV*, October 15, 1904, 6.

47 Davidson, *South and South Central Africa*, 168.

48 Ndhlalambi's *isibongo* (praise-name), or surname—Moyo—was the royal "heart" clan of the Mambo people.

49 Davidson, "One More Day's Work for Jesus," *EV*, November 15, 1905, 14. Meredith McKittrick emphasizes the importance of generations in understanding the impact of Christianity. *To Dwell Secure: Generation, Christianity and Colonialism in Ovamboland* (Portsmouth, N.H.: Heinemann, 2002).

50 Davidson, *South and South Central Africa*, 199.

51 Ibid., 179. See also Wendy Urban-Mead, "Sitshokupi Sibanda: 'Bible Woman' or evangelist? Ways of Naming and Remembering Female Leadership in a Mission

Church of Colonial Zimbabwe," special issue "Transnational Bible Women: Asian and African women in Christian mission" Guest editors: Deborah Gaitskell and Wendy Urban-Mead, *Women's History Review* vol. 17, no. 4, September 2008, 653–70.

52 Davidson, *South and South Central Africa*, 240, 273. Emphasis added.

53 Manhlenhle Khumalo, educated at Matopo Mission and later ordained minister, referred to Davidson as his "mother in Christ." Engle et al., *There Is No Difference*, 184.

54 Letter from Levi Doner to EV, May 15, 1904, 14.

55 EV, July 1, 1904, 2.

56 EV, April 15 1904,10.

57 EV, June 15, 1904, 3.

58 EV, June 15, 1905, 12.

59 Letter from Matshuba Ndlovu to Davidson, EV August 1, 1904, 13.

60 A letter by Ndhlalambi Moyo published in EV August 1, 1904, 13–14.

61 Mrs. Thomas Jenkins, a missionary in Natal, South Africa, expressed her relationship with Mpondo Chief Mgikela in maternal terms as well: Mgikela was "her child." "The Mpondo chiefs and people accorded her all the respect due to an aged mother." Etherington, "Gender Issues," 140.

62 See Martha M. Long, "Adda Taylor: Pioneer Missionary," in *Brethren in Christ History and Life*, vol. 7, 1 (June 1984), 66. Thanks to E. Morris Sider for this reference.

63 Diary, August 8, 1899, 65. Emphasis added.

64 Stephen Volz, "Written On Our Hearts: Tswana Christians and the 'Word of God' in the Mid-Nineteenth Century," *Journal of Religion in Africa* 38, no. 2 (2008), 112–40.

65 Diary, June 17, 1909, 168.

66 See Sider, *Nine Portraits*, 198–202.

67 Samuel Mlotshwa recalled how he was expected to remove his shoes when entering the office of the BIC white mission superintendent during the 1930s. Interview, Samuel Mlotshwa, May 22, 1999, Mayezane, Zimbabwe.

68 Sider, *Nine Portraits*, 204.

69 Sithembile Nkala (MaNsimango) interview, August 15, 2000, Bulawayo. Also Sadie Book, "What Hath God Wrought!" EV, November 8, 1926, 12. Nellie Mlotshwa interview, August 23, 1997, Wanezi Mission, Zimbabwe.

70 Sider notes that in spite of turmoil throughout her career, Davidson maintained firm loyalty to the church. Sider, *Nine Portraits*, 207.

71 Diary, September 17, 1893, 10.

72 Antoinette Burton, "The White Woman's Burden: British Feminists and 'The Indian Woman,' 1865–1915," in *Western Women and Imperialism*, ed. Napur Chaudhuri and Margaret Strobel (Bloomington: Indiana University Press, 1992), 137–57.

Gertrude Howe, Kang Cheng, and Cultural Imperialism in the Woman's Foreign Missionary Society, 1872–1931

Connie A. Shemo

In 1872, twenty-six-year-old Gertrude Howe arrived in the Chinese treaty port city of Jiujiang. She was one of the first missionaries of the newly created Woman's Foreign Mission Society (WFMS) of the Methodist Episcopal Church, and her initial task was to open a school for Chinese girls. She faced immediate hostility to this project from the local population. Few families were willing to entrust their daughters to her. Frustrated by her lack of access to the girls of Jiujiang and intensely lonely, Howe adopted a Chinese baby girl.[1] The relationship between Howe and her daughter, Kang Aide, who would achieve considerable prominence in the United States as Dr. Ida Kahn, would be repeatedly celebrated in later missionary periodicals. Howe gave Kang English lessons and provided her with intensive socialization in American missionary culture, ensuring that she would grow up bilingual and bicultural. Kang became one of very few Chinese Christians, male or female, to become a regularly appointed missionary (as opposed to an assistant to American missionaries). A missionary colleague wrote in an essay praising Kang that she "seemed to us all so thoroughly American that racial distinctions disappeared."[2]

Kang's colleague could hardly have been more obliging in presenting later scholars with evidence of American missionary "cultural imperialism."[3] Indeed, this comment supports interpretations of women missionaries as being particularly culturally aggressive.[4] Scholars in both the People's Republic of China (PRC) and the United States have used the

Gertrude Howe, undated photograph. By permission of the General Commission on Archives and History, The United Methodist Church.

Kang Aide / Kang Cheng / Dr. Ida Kahn, undated photograph. By permission of the General Commission on Archives and History, The United Methodist Church.

relationship between Howe and Kang as an example of how American women missionaries could use their close contact with their converts to culturally transform them, making them "almost American." One essay written in the PRC even extrapolates from Howe's relationship with Kang a broader policy of single women missionaries adopting Chinese children in order to practice "cultural aggression."[5]

In this essay I argue that the relationship between Howe and Kang shows instead the profound ambiguity American mission boards could have toward single American women missionaries as agents of cultural transformation. An understanding of this ambiguity is essential to answering the question of how American women missionaries contributed to the development of an American empire and indeed for grasping the inherent contradictions in the very concept of American empire. Turning out "thoroughly American" converts was not the goal of American mission boards, and Howe faced censure and rejection from the missionary community in Jiujiang both for her decision to adopt Kang and for the education she gave her adopted daughter.

Recent scholarship has suggested that ideologies of race, traditionally associated with American expansion, also served as an anti-imperialist force.[6] Similarly, racial segregation in missionary communities effectively put a brake on missionary goals of cultural transformation and inspired mission board policies and attitudes that counteracted the potential of single American women missionaries to become cultural imperialists. Howe's relationship with Kang demonstrates the potential loss of privileges associated with American citizenship that American women missionaries who violated these conventions could face.

The kind of adoption practiced by Howe not only threatened American missionary communities in China, but also had the potential to render the boundaries of the United States more permeable to Chinese immigration. In 1882, soon after Howe had adopted Kang, the first Chinese Exclusion Act passed in the United States. Even as Americans were traveling overseas in growing numbers and spreading American culture, this act and those that followed showed that U.S. officials who made foreign policy were determined not to let the United States become vulnerable to foreign influences. Had the growing number of single female missionaries begun to adopt Chinese children in droves, bringing them to the United States when they returned, the ability of the United States to exclude people of Chinese descent would have been compromised.

To be sure, most late nineteenth-century American Protestant missionaries deplored the anti-Chinese rhetoric that led to the Exclusion Acts and protested the acts themselves. From the mid-nineteenth century onward, many Protestant missionaries insisted vigorously on principles of racial equality.[7] The Methodist Episcopal Church stood out among mainline Protestant denominations involved in foreign missions for its commitment to equality among all baptized Christians and invested Chinese Methodist pastors and baptized church members with more authority than most other denominations.[8] A commitment to these principles of equality can be seen in the WFMS funding of medical education in the United States for four Chinese women, including Kang Aide, who returned to China to open dispensaries and, later, hospitals for women and children. These women, referred to collectively as "The Doctors" in one history of Chinese students in the United States, were the first Chinese women to come to the United States to study. They were vital in opening the medical profession to women in China.[9]

Yet the adherence of most missionaries to a Christian universalism did not preclude a belief that people of Anglo-Saxon descent were more fit than others to rule, both on a global scale and within mission institutions.[10] In Protestant mainline denominations, even in the Methodist Episcopal Church, the majority of Chinese Christians who worked with missionaries formed, to borrow a phrase from a British official in India discussing his hopes for English education in that country, a "class of interpreters" who enabled missionaries to function in Chinese society but who could not enter fully into missionary social life.[11] Especially in treaty port mission stations and urban centers, most missionaries, up until the late 1920s and in many cases beyond, lived in compounds segregated from the Chinese Christians with whom they worked, ate different foods, and controlled all the funds of the mission. Indeed, Kang's colleague's description of her as "so thoroughly American that racial distinctions disappeared" is notable as a rare admission among missionaries that racial distinctions structured most relationships between missionaries and Chinese Christians.

This essay traces how Howe and Kang fit into the broader American mission community from Howe's adoption of Kang as an infant to Howe's death in 1928. It explores the barriers of American missionary communities to inclusion of Chinese Christians. Howe actually adopted three Chinese girls after Kang.[12] These other girls did not become missionaries themselves and thus few records of their lives or relationship with Howe remain. Kang and Howe, however, lived together for almost all of Kang's life. As both were WFMS missionaries, their annual reports, WFMS minutes, and the letters of their missionary colleagues offer insight into their later relationship. Despite an official espousal of spiritual equality and despite the iconic status Kang and Howe achieved among missionaries in China and among Americans interested in foreign missions, the two women faced barriers in their inclusion in the mission community as well as difficulties with the travel to the United States essential to raising funds for mission work. Later, in 1927, during the crisis following the Nanjing Incident, the potentially life-threatening nature of this exclusion would become clear. This essay reveals the dominant attitudes and policies that ensured that Protestant American women missionaries would not, with all their potential as agents of cultural expansion, become conduits of contamination.

ADOPTION AND EARLY EDUCATION

In 1872, three years after the WFMS was established, Gertrude Howe arrived in Jiujiang with another American woman missionary, Lucy Hoag, as a companion. As some of the earliest WFMS missionaries, Howe and Hoag did not have access to the communities of single women missionaries that would form such a significant part of the experience of later women missionaries.[13] While their living arrangements are not recorded, in later discussions Howe recalled both intense loneliness and great frustration at the hostility expressed by the local population toward her school for girls. She had come to reach Chinese girls, and yet had no opportunity to do so. She found a solution when her Chinese language teacher arranged for her to adopt a Chinese baby girl. The girl kept her natal family's name of Kang, and Howe gave her the first name of Ida, after a beloved deceased sister. This translated well into the Chinese name Aide (Love Virtue). She would take the name Kang Cheng (To Become Healthy) in adulthood, as a literary name.[14]

The adoption caused great controversy among Howe's missionary colleagues, both in the WFMS and in the parent Methodist Board of Foreign

Missions. Scholars have discussed the destabilizing impact that relationships between male colonial officials and women in colonized countries could have on the boundaries between colonial society and the local population, suggesting that children from these unions "called into question the very criteria by which Europeanness could be identified, citizenship should be accorded, and nationality defined."[15] When American Protestant mission boards first sent single male missionaries into foreign fields in the 1810s, they also feared that a "powerful law of nature" ensured that men could not live without female sexual companionship and caretaking for long, and so as a rule insisted on male missionaries marrying before traveling overseas.[16]

Mission boards in the 1830s did express the fear that single women missionaries would seek foreign husbands.[17] However, when American mission boards began to set up women's boards in the 1860s and 1870s to oversee the sending of single women missionaries, mission boards viewed the lack of attachment of single American women in positive terms. Unlike the wives of male missionaries, they would not have to devote the majority of their time to household cares and child rearing.[18] Yet American women missionaries faced a different kind of temptation, potentially equally destabilizing to the boundaries of the missionary community. Viewing themselves as liberators of women oppressed by "heathenism," many were inclined to "rescue" Chinese girls from such oppression through adoption.

Almost all of these adoptions consisted of the missionary supporting the child in the home of a Chinese Christian family. Mission boards placed great importance on ensuring that Chinese converts would be able to remain part of their Chinese culture, especially Chinese Christian girls, who were expected to marry and raise the next generation of Chinese Christians.[19] The WFMS bylaws officially prohibited American women missionaries from adopting Chinese children beginning in 1900.[20] In her adoption of Kang, Howe was insisting on an intimacy that violated the unspoken but powerful traditions of segregation. With the adoption and with the education she provided Kang, Howe would force debates on how much transformation was appropriate for Chinese girls.

Howe not only lived with Kang, but also took her and another adopted daughter on furlough to the United States in 1879. This trip, during which Kang became fluent in English and learned a great deal about American culture, contributed in great measure to Kang's becoming "so thoroughly

American." By 1882, the Chinese Exclusion Act would have foreclosed the option of bringing Chinese adopted children to the United States, even if women missionaries were willing to brave the censure of their mission boards.

Why did Howe transgress the established boundaries of missionary communities? One account of Howe's mission work describes her belief that "to take little children, save them from heathenism . . . and let them grow up Christian was better and more lasting, than to work among people grown up, who were imbided with habits of superstition and ignorance."[21] The rhetoric of saving Chinese girls from heathenism and descriptions of the "superstition and ignorance" of Chinese customs commonly appeared in essays written by American women missionaries for American women supporters of foreign mission work in many Protestant denominations. However, by insisting on the importance of Chinese children being raised in Chinese Christian homes, the dominant mission practice emphasized how necessary it was for these children to learn to fit into their culture, a clear difference between introducing Christianity and Americanizing their converts.[22] By removing her adopted daughters from this kind of socialization and even bringing them to the United States, Howe was collapsing this distinction.

At the same time, Howe's very cultural aggressiveness led her to oppose the segregation inherent in the culture of the Methodist compound. When Kang wrote a Chinese language obituary for her adopted mother after her death in 1928, she emphasized that Howe had "no notions of racial hierarchy at all."[23] Implicitly suggesting that this attitude was not uniform among American missionaries, Kang was addressing the distance between the WFMS theories of spiritual equality, of a Christian fellowship in which the physical body was irrelevant, and missionary practices that for all practical purposes enforced racial segregation.

A more detailed description of Howe's divergence from other missionaries can be found in another obituary for Howe written by Shi Meiyu, Kang's "companion from babyhood."[24] The daughter of the first Chinese Methodist pastor in Jiujiang, Shi attended medical school with Kang, practiced medicine with her immediately after their return to China, and eventually established her own mission hospital for women and children. In this obituary, Shi focused on the amount of time she and Kang spent with Howe in "long talks" and walks. She specifically recalled that during the hot summers when "the other Missionaries fled for much-needed rest to beautiful Kuling [a mountain resort for missionaries] . . . where Chinese residents were not tolerated," Howe would stay with her children in a "little hut like home in the hot foothills."[25] Shi's description of Chinese as "not tolerated" is an indictment of missionary practices of exclusivity and fits in well with a more general protest of Chinese Christians in the late 1920s against what many Chinese had come to see as missionary racism.[26]

Howe's relationship with the Shi family, especially with Shi's father, persuaded her to teach classes that prepared the two girls for medical school. Howe had not originally intended to raise Kang to become a missionary herself. Howe adopted three other girls after Kang, and all became wives of prominent Chinese Christians, Howe's original goal for Kang.[27] The influence of Pastor Shi on Howe shows how prominent Chinese Christians could influence mission policy by forming close relationships with single women missionaries.

The Shi family had decided against binding Shi Meiyu's feet. Believing this would make it difficult for her to marry well, Shi Tseh-yu, inspired by an American woman missionary physician who had run a dispensary for women in Jiujiang from 1879 to 1882, decided that he wanted his daughter to receive training to become a missionary physician ministering to Chinese women. According to Shi Meiyu's obituary of Howe, her father asked Howe to provide her with training that would enable her to attend an American medical school and come back to practice medicine among Chinese women and children.[28] Howe agreed, setting up classes in English, sciences, and other subjects that would be helpful in getting accepted at an American medical school.

Numerous studies of missionary work in a variety of cultural contexts have commented on how converts "scrambled the message" of Western missionaries.[29] Yet Shi's father did not so much scramble the message of the Jiujiang missionaries as take it to its logical conclusion. Official WFMS ideology, like that of most mission boards for women, held that the source of the oppression of women was heathen religion and that therefore Chinese girls who converted to Christianity would be liberated and able to grow up to take positions of authority within the mission community, such as missionary physician.

However, when Howe agreed to Shi's request and began providing Meiyu, Aide, and three Chinese boys with special classes in English and some sciences, the other missionaries were horrified.[30] Shi remembers Howe facing "ostracism from close circles" both for her decision to adopt Chinese daughters and for offering these classes. Scholars have discussed the tendency of Protestant missionaries to view devolution—turning control of mission institutions over to Chinese Christians—as something that would happen far in the future, throughout the late nineteenth century and early twentieth, until Nationalist pressures after 1927 made it impossible to put off any longer.[31] In the early 1880s, concern about imposing Western cultural norms along with Christianity precluded offering the kind of education that would prepare converts to take over positions of authority in mission institutions. For Chinese Christian girls, whom missionaries expected to grow up to become Christian wives and mothers producing the Christian families that would be the bedrock of a Christian China, the arguments for avoiding alienation were especially compelling.

At the same time, Shi Tseh-yu was far from alone in desiring a more thorough mission education for his daughter. During the 1880s in Fuzhou, another treaty port city in central China, Chinese Christians were demanding that English be taught in schools for both boys and girls.[32] They argued against missionaries who promoted evangelism over education, who saw conversion in purely spiritual terms and did not pursue the broader cultural transformation of converts. One of those arguing was the father of Xu Jinhong (a.k.a. Hu King Eng), one of the other Chinese young women to study medicine in the United States under the auspices of the WFMS. Like the Shi family, the Xu family was close to a single woman missionary who pushed the WFMS to fund Xu Jinhong's overseas education.[33] Even before English was commonly taught in mission schools for girls, a few Chinese pastors were pushing individual women missionaries to provide such education for their daughters.

By 1883, the opposition to Howe's adoption and teaching in English had reached a point where she left with her daughters for the interior station of Chongqing. While treaty port cities such as Jiujiang had a substantial foreign population and large mission stations, more interior cities such as Chongqing usually had only one small mission station. In this case, Howe and one other single woman missionary appear to have been the only American Methodists in the city and therefore had much greater freedom in regard to their living arrangements. They also had less protection, as became clear when an antiforeign riot erupted after reports about the bad treatment of Chinese in the United States. According to a report from Howe's fellow missionary, during the riot "every missionary was compelled to fly for his life, every vestige of mission property was destroyed."[34]

When Howe returned to Jiujiang in 1885 after fleeing from this danger, the WFMS invited her to take over the girls' school again and publicly praised her in its annual report. Howe seems to have resumed her former special classes for Kang, Shi, and the three Chinese boys.[35] By the 1890s, among the larger Protestant mission boards, the offering of English and Western science in schools for girls and boys was becoming common, so Howe's early experience in teaching these subjects put her in the vanguard of mission education for girls in China.[36] The WFMS showed their support of Howe's goals by funding the medical education of Kang and Shi at the University of Michigan in 1892–96, where they graduated with honors.[37] Yet a widespread program of training Chinese to take over mission institutions never developed, despite the growing educational attainments of Chinese girls.

While Howe's early teaching of English and science to Chinese girls gave her the reputation in the mission press of possessing "all the vision of a prophet and a seer," her style of adoption never became an acceptable practice.[38] The memoirs of Ruth Hemmenway, a woman medical missionary who practiced in China between 1925 and 1941, report similar opposition in treaty port cities to her adoption of Chinese girls. In an interior, rural mission station, she was able to live with her adopted daughters. When she visited treaty port cities, other missionaries would not let her bring them to stay in their homes. Hemmenway does not report what justification the missionaries used but attributes their refusal to "feelings of racial discrimination."[39]

Far more than teaching English and Western science, the issue of adoption involved the transgressing of boundaries set up by American missionaries to segregate themselves from the Chinese among whom they worked. Howe was practicing the kind of expansive domesticity that Amy Kaplan notes in her essay "Manifest Domesticity." Kaplan notes that Catharine Beecher, writing with her sister Harriet Beecher Stowe in the *American Woman's Home*, advocated that unmarried women set up "Christian neighborhoods" in the southern and western United States. On the West Coast, these neighborhoods would work to introduce Christianity to the

Chinese "sojourners." This vision of Beecher and Stowe called for American single women to adopt "native children," as Howe did. Yet, as Kaplan observes, Beecher's writings and similar works "evoked anxiety about the opposing trajectory that brings foreignness into the home."[40] This anxiety explains why the kind of adoption proposed by Beecher and Stowe would prove so problematic when implemented by Howe.

The restrictions against what the WFMS would consider out-of-control maternal instincts were usually unofficial and seem to have been largely unspoken. The case of Gertrude Howe helps make visible the potential threat single women missionaries could pose to traditions of segregation and the possibility of expulsion that women who violated these traditions could face. However attractive the option of single American women engaging in Americanization through adoption might have seemed to writers such as Beecher and Stowe in the post–Civil War era, it was not a feasible option for most American women missionaries in China.

HOUSING AND TRAVEL

Yet in 1896, when Kang and Shi returned to China after graduating from the medical school of the University of Michigan, the vision of Shi Tseh-yu and Howe could seem to have been dramatically vindicated. Kang and Shi became regularly appointed missionaries. They received an annual salary of 450 gold (although less during the first two years in order to pay back the WFMS). This was less than the salary of American women missionaries (600 to 700 gold) but much higher than the salaries of most Chinese who worked for the missionary community.[41] They wrote their own reports of their medical work and had access to the American community of foreign mission supporters for raising funds for their work.

Despite these official signs of acceptance, Kang and Shi initially lived not with the other missionaries, but in a small house outside the mission compound. In her obituary for Howe, Shi pointedly reminisced that after she and Kang returned to China, Howe "left the beautiful home of the missionaries and came to live in a little Chinese home that she built for us out of her own money."[42] Upon their return to China, Kang and Shi were the focus of celebration in periodicals aimed at American supporters of foreign mission.[43] Yet not only were they not welcomed into the living space of the missionary community, but Howe had to again shed the privileges that came with the status of an American WFMS missionary in order to live with them.[44]

Kang left for Nanchang in 1903 at the invitation of gentry in that city, led by the husband of a woman whom she had successfully treated. She was soon joined by Howe. The WFMS agreed to her going but did not fund her medical work beyond paying her salary. Kang and the WFMS both seemed to have hoped that, because she was working in the wealthy capital supported by gentry, her work could become self-supporting, drawing on local sources of funding rather than on the mission society.[45] However, the gentry support for Kang's medical work was limited, especially initially, by her refusal to sever her ties with the Methodist Episcopal mission board.[46]

In reports from the time and even more in Kang's later reminiscences, the first years of her medical work in Nanchang emerge as a time of great financial stress. Howe and Kang lived on the second floor of Kang's dispensary and experienced problems with leaky roofs and difficulty paying rent. Howe donated her personal money to the medical work, and Kang sold her "small stock of jewelry" to raise money.[47] Kang and Howe seem to have been in a kind of liminal space, not adequately supported by either the WFMS or the gentry.

Their financial problems were exacerbated by the fact that neither Kang nor Howe had regularly scheduled furloughs. Usually scheduled every seven years, furloughs allowed missionaries to travel from church to church raising funds for such projects as building schools and hospitals. These tours gave American women missionaries access to American women willing to donate to foreign missions. Despite her status as a regularly appointed WFMS missionary, Kang could not cross national boundaries with the same ease as her American colleagues. After taking Kang to the United States in 1880, Howe had not returned there except to accompany Kang to medical school and live with her in 1892–94. While she never explained the reasons, it would seem that, just as Howe lived in a small Chinese house in order to remain with her adopted daughter, she also refused to leave Kang in order to travel.

By 1907, their situation had improved markedly. Kang's relationship with the Nanchang gentry had deepened: they donated a large piece of land within the city gates (and outside the mission compound) for Kang's home and hospital. At the same time, the upper echelons of the Methodist Episcopal Church seemed to grow increasingly embarrassed at Kang's and Howe's poor accommodations. Kang remembered that when the bishop in charge of Methodist Episcopal missionary work in central China visited Nanchang, he was "not so well pleased" at Kang's and Howe's living arrangement. When an American woman gave this bishop five thousand dollars to build a memorial to her sister, he chose to use the money to build Kang and Howe a home, which was completed in 1907. This house, described by one observer as a "splendid residence," reflected and enhanced the status Kang and Howe had achieved both among the elite of Nanchang and in the missionary community.[48] Yet as the house was outside the mission compound, the missionary policies of racial exclusion remained intact. No way was established for other women missionaries to emulate Howe and adopt Chinese girls themselves.

In 1907, the board approved a trip to the United States for Howe and Kang together, a tour during which they could rest and raise funds for Kang's medical work. Kang and Howe spoke to congregations to raise money, and Howe solicited two separate five-thousand-dollar donations for Kang's hospital in the year she spent with Kang in the United States.[49] When Kang returned in 1911 after two years of study in the United States, her hospital was almost built, having been carefully supervised by Howe, who had returned to China in 1909.

Despite the fruits of the trip, Howe's return to the United States underscored her feeling of alienation from many potential supporters. "Fifteen years absence on a stretch puts one out of touch with one's original kind," she mused in her annual report for 1909, noting an "assumption on my part that matters familiar to me need not take the form of an illustrated primer for presentation" that hindered her ability to raise funds: "What to me were illuminated peaks of interest in the mission horizon, could be seen only as banks of fog by many I would have inspired by them."[50] While Howe greatly understated her fundraising ability (perhaps with a view to soliciting more donations), her long absence from the United States undoubtedly did make it harder to relate to audiences of American churchgoers. Howe's experience in speaking to American audiences seems to have brought home the costs of her refusal to travel to the United States without Kang and thus remain out of the country for so many years at a time. While the WFMS minutes "heartily" welcomed Howe back to the

United States, no provision was made to offer Kang and Howe regular furloughs from that point on.[51] The two women returned to the United States only one more time, in 1919–20.

Moreover, the trip demonstrated the difficulties that any Chinese woman who became a WFMS missionary would face in crossing national boundaries. As the WFMS minutes reported, Kang was initially turned back when she attempted to leave China to go to the United States for "some trouble of the eyelids," a probable reference to the trachoma test, which, as one scholar suggests, had become "a byword among Chinese for arbitrariness and extortion."[52] In her annual report Howe wrote acidly that she and Kang had then decided to take the "long Siberian route by rail, lest haply another occasion for turning Dr. Kahn back should develop via the Pacific."[53] Kang's status as a missionary would probably have protected her from the charge of prostitution that many Chinese women coming to the United States had to face, whatever their class background.[54] Yet Kang and Howe clearly both feared that immigration officials would look for a way to exclude Kang.[55]

When Kang landed in the United States, WFMS officials had contacted President Theodore Roosevelt regarding their arrival, and he had given specific instructions to expedite their landings. Exercising power probably not available to smaller mission boards, the WFMS had spared Kang the "Kafkaesque drama" that awaited most Chinese, even officials and businessmen important to the China trade, entering the United States.[56] When Shi Meiyu had traveled to the United States two years earlier, in 1906, the WFMS had also contacted the president.[57] The American leaders of the WFMS took considerable trouble to avoid a clash between the missionary ideology of a Christian community that transcended national boundaries and the racialized conception of citizenship and belonging reflected in the typical encounter between American immigration officials and people of Asian descent attempting to enter the United States.

The work of the WFMS in protecting Kang and Shi from the harassment of immigration officials fit in well with the broader criticism by American Protestant missionaries of abuse by these officials. Officially, Protestant missionaries advocated as much contact between the United States and China as possible. Even Chinese laborers moving back and forth, the target of so much opprobrium from anti-immigration groups, could be seen by American missionaries as a force that would work toward transforming China into a Christian nation.[58]

However, as an action taken by the WFMS in 1917 indicates, the organization was unwilling to be a conduit of unfettered movement of Chinese Christians between China and the United States. The WFMS board voted that Chinese who became missionaries would not be granted travel to the United States.[59] WFMS officials may have perceived that they could make only so many phone calls to the White House. While they could ameliorate the process of entering the United States for a few missionary heroines such as Kang and Shi, no mission agency could change the fact that crossing into the United States would be a humiliating ordeal for the majority of Chinese who made the trip. WFMS missionaries could not Americanize their converts in the sense of extending an important privilege of citizenship in a powerful nation—free movement across the boundaries of other nations. And lacking this free movement, Chinese women who became WFMS missionaries would not have access to the same resources enjoyed by American women missionaries. The idea of Anglo-Saxon leadership that justified imperialism on the global stage would necessarily continue to be reproduced within the WFMS.

In 1919 the minutes of the WFMS board meetings noted with pride the fact that four of the eleven WFMS hospitals were run by Chinese women medical missionaries.[60] The minutes correctly mentioned as well that no other mission board had any hospitals controlled by Chinese. Appointing Chinese Christians to positions of power was an important goal of the WFMS. However, what the minutes do not make clear is that the last Chinese woman to assume control of a mission hospital was Li Bi Cu in 1905, after graduating from the Woman's Medical College of Pennsylvania.[61] There had been no subsequent progress in Chinese women taking over mission institutions. Even though the teaching of English and Western science in mission schools for Chinese girls in theory should have produced a greater pool of candidates for positions of authority in the WFMS, the WFMS had not funded the medical education of any other Chinese girls. While the WFMS leadership celebrated the fact that four Chinese women were running their mission hospitals, they did not institute any programs that would have helped continue and expand this trend.

In the celebration of Chinese women taking over its mission hospitals, the WFMS officials demonstrated their rejection of the idea that race could impact the leadership ability of Chinese women. However, fully integrating Chinese women into WFMS leadership would have required structural change within the WFMS and the broader Methodist Episcopal community. The importance of travel across national boundaries to the work of missionaries would have required the WFMS to challenge the exclusionary policies of U.S. immigration officials. WFMS officials were willing to intervene in special cases but not, as the 1917 decision to restrict the travel of Chinese women who worked for the WFMS shows, confront the policy on a wholesale basis. While the WFMS did not practice discrimination based on the physical body, the "nonvisual and more salient distinctions of exclusion on which racism rests" effectively prevented large-scale progress toward sharing leadership with Chinese women.[62]

MISSIONARIES' DEPARTURE FROM NANCHANG IN 1927

By the late 1920s, Howe, now in her eighties, appears to have been suffering from some form of dementia, or perhaps what today would be diagnosed as Alzheimer's disease. One missionary, in a private letter, referred to Howe as having "practically no mind at all."[63] Kang was completely responsible for her care, a fact celebrated in mission periodicals. As one obituary notice for Howe stated, "One of the most beautiful stories in our missionary annals is this, of the loving care bestowed by her Chinese 'daughter' on one who 'threw her life away on the Chinese.'"[64] Despite these kinds of moving tributes to Howe's and Kang's relationship, the events of 1927 demonstrated the potential dangers American women missionaries who chose to leave mission compounds to live with a "Chinese 'daughter'" could face.

In 1926 the Nationalist party had launched what is known as the Northern Expedition, an effort to unite China under one strong government that would be able to combat imperialism. The armies marching to unite China were ideologically quite diverse, containing both Communists and Communist sympathizers and more conservative nationalists, some of whom were sympathetic to missions. Initially in Nanchang, the more conservative wing was ascendant. Kang's hospital, protected both by its connection to a foreign missionary society and by Kang's connections with prominent Chinese military leaders, was one of the few major institutions the soldiers did not loot.[65] Kang was able to smooth relationships between the mission community and the incoming military by throwing banquets for the officers so that, in the words of a woman who had been a child of American missionaries in Nanchang during this period, the soldiers would "leave us alone."[66] The skills Kang had developed as a cultural broker served her well in this crisis.

In March 1927, Nationalist troops in Nanjing attacked the American, British, and Japanese embassies. A number of foreigners were killed, and American and British destroyers shelled the city in order to allow foreigners to escape unharmed, killing several Chinese in the process.[67] Fury erupted all over China, and the vast majority of foreign missionaries fled their stations for the safety of the foreign concessions of Shanghai, and then in many cases their home countries, fearful of a further attack in the cities in which they were stationed. Kang's patriotism, long the source of her good relations with her nationalist supporters, came under attack.[68] While Kang retained important support among Chinese officials and gentry in Nanchang throughout her life, by 1927 she was publicly branded a "running dog of imperialism."[69]

The night of the Nanjing Incident, all the foreign missionaries—except, significantly, Gertrude Howe—left Nanchang, accompanied by the American navy. They did not tell any Chinese but sent a note with a servant after they left, explaining that "the American representative gave positive instructions that this information be held strictly confidential among the foreigners," and that they were "therefore at the time unable to explain our sudden departure." The note assured the Chinese Christians that while the missionaries would "willingly give ourselves to whatever hardship might come to any of us personally," they had left to ensure the safety of the city as a whole.[70] Kang recorded her reaction to the missionaries' sudden departure in her annual report for 1927: "We woke up one morning to find that all our missionaries had left. . . . I can never describe the pain of that moment."[71]

This moment of crisis exposed the fault lines of the position Kang and Howe occupied in the Methodist mission community in Nanchang. In their fellowship with Kang, missionaries could point, as indeed the missionary quoted at the beginning of this chapter did, to an example of "racial distinctions" ceasing to matter, of the ideal of a community based on common spiritual aspirations coming to fruition. Yet as Kang discovered when she awoke to find that her colleagues had abandoned the mission station in the middle of the night, there were circumstances in which national identity would supersede this ideal. Despite the claim that she was "thoroughly American," Kang's missionary colleagues knew that when push came to shove she was not entitled to the privileges of American citizenship.

That Howe was left behind is more surprising. It would have been impossible to remove Howe without Kang's knowledge. The missionaries therefore faced a choice: tell Kang about their leaving and invite both Kang and Howe to come along, or leave Howe behind while saying nothing to Kang. The fact that the missionaries chose the second path suggests that in deciding, years back, to live with Kang rather than on the mission compound, Howe had lost some of the protection available to citizens of the United States. The physical segregation of the American missionary community was essential to the ability of the American navy to round them up and herd them away from danger.

The danger in which the missionaries' decision put Kang and Howe can be seen from a brief look at the situation of other prominent Chinese Christians in public positions during this time. Xu Jinhong, the woman medical missionary in Fuzhou mentioned above, was traumatized when soldiers burned her hospital and destroyed her home and possessions, an experience from which she never recovered.[72] In Nanchang, as reported by one foreign missionary, Chinese pastors suffered beatings and kidnappings.[73] Kang and Howe were not physically attacked, and while Nationalists did target her hospital in their anti-imperialist campaigns, Kang was able to use her contacts with important military leaders to secure some protection for her compound.[74] By early 1928, American missionaries began to return, reestablishing the Methodist mission community, and appear to have reestablished a warm relationship with Kang and Howe.[75] However, Kang's and Howe's safety was by no means assured when the American missionaries decided to leave them in Nanchang in March of 1927.

One of numerous obituaries in the mission press for Howe at her death at the end of 1929 (of natural causes) lionized her as "the only Protestant missionary to remain at her post inside the walled city of Nanchang" in 1927.[76] In fact, she was the only Protestant missionary to live inside the walled city in the first place. Traditions of segregation in the missionary community, at least in treaty port cities and urban areas, remained intact until the Sino-Japanese War in 1937 forced most American missionaries still in China to move to western China with the Nationalist government. Ironically, Ruth Hemmenway remembers that during 1936, when she worked with a Chinese woman doctor at the Nanchang hospital after Kang's death, an American woman missionary refused to let Hemmenway's Chinese adopted daughter take her meals with the foreigners.[77]

The idea of liberation and transformation, so prevalent in American thinking about women in China in the late nineteenth century and early twentieth, is integral to understanding American empire during this period. Yet American missionary ideas about transforming and liberating non-Christian women cannot be characterized as a simple and straightforward desire for their converts to become "American." Engaging in attempts at cultural transformation among Chinese women involved the WFMS in contradictions and controversies over what the liberation promised by Christian conversion would entail. In theory, in a community of converted individuals, the physical body would be irrelevant, and Chinese Christians would have as much chance for leadership positions as Americans. In practice, the status of a WFMS missionary, like that of most mainline Protestant denominations, was bound up with privileges that arose from their American citizenship, ranging from superior housing to free movement across national boundaries. The privileges of American citizenship in turn were tied to race. People of Chinese descent could not become American citizens after 1882, and similarly by the 1890s the rights of most African Americans were becoming increasingly circumscribed.

On a daily basis, the power and privileges of white American missionaries seemed natural enough that most missionaries did not have to face this contradiction. The story of Howe and Kang provides an example of contradiction rising to the surface. While Kang demonstrates the possibility of crossing the boundaries that kept Chinese women from running institutions, she also demonstrates the great difficulty in doing so. And while she achieved the status of heroine missionary, Gertrude Howe and her story illustrate the tenuousness of the privileges of American citizenship to those who violated conventions of segregation. For American women missionaries, crossing boundaries could result in becoming less "thoroughly American."

136 *Connie A. Shemo*

NOTES

1 This story is told in various articles appearing in both the "Gertrude Howe" and "Ida Kahn" files, Missionary Biographical Files, United Methodist Archives, Madison, N.J. (hereafter UMA). See also "Ida Kahn" chapter in Margaret Burton, *Notable Women of Modern China* (Chicago: Fleming H. Revell, 1912).

2 J. G. Vaughn, "Dr. Ida Kahn," Missionary Biographical Files, Ida Kahn file, UMA.

3 The classic essay linking missionary work to "cultural imperialism" is Arthur Schlesinger Jr., "The Missionary Enterprise and Theories of Imperialism," *The Missionary Enterprise in China and America*, ed. John Fairbank, 336–73, 365 (Cambridge, Mass.: Harvard University Press, 1974). See also Paul Harris, "Cultural Imperialism and American Protestant Missionaries: Collaboration and Dependency in Mid-Nineteenth-Century China," *Pacific Historical Review* 60 (1991), 309–38.

4 As scholarship on American women missionaries has pointed out, because American women missionaries could not preach, they were therefore involved in educational and medical ventures, the very kind of work most implicated in cultural imperialism. See Jane Hunter, *Gospel of Gentility: American Women Missionaries in Turn-of-the-Century China* (New Haven: Yale University Press, 1984); Patricia Hill, *The World Their Household: The American Woman's Foreign Mission Movement and Cultural Transformation, 1870–1920* (Ann Arbor: University of Michigan Press, 1985); Dana Robert, *American Women in Mission: A Social History of Their Thought and Practice* (Macon, Ga.: Mercer University Press, 1992). For a good biography of a woman missionary during this period, see Kathleen Lodwick, *Educating the Women of Hainan: The Career of Margaret Moninger in China, 1915–1942* (Lexington: University of Kentucky Press, 1995). For a work that focuses on Chinese Christian women and makes a similar point, see Kwok Pui-lan, *Chinese Women and Christianity, 1860–1927* (Atlanta: Scholars Press, 1992). For a recent reconsideration of the question of women missionaries and cultural imperialism, see Carol Chin, "Beneficent Imperialists: American Women Missionaries in China at the Turn of the Twentieth Century," *Diplomatic History* 27 (June 2003), 327–52.

5 Chin, "Beneficent Imperialists," 331, 342; Duan Qi, "Qingmo Minchu Meiguo nü Chuanjiaoshi zai Hua de Chuanjiao Huodong ji Yingxiang," *Jidujiao yanjiu*, no. 3 (1994), 32–40, 39. For similar perspectives, see Dong Xuhua, "Zhongguo Jindai Nüxue de Xingqi," *Funü xueyuan*, no. 3 (1995), 40–41; Guo Weidong, "Jiduxinjiao yu Zhongguo Jindai Nüzi Jiaoyu," *Lishi Dang'an*, no. 4 (2001), 98–104; Liu Huiying, "Ershi Shiji chu Zhongguo Nüquan Qimeng zhong de Jiuguo Nüzi Xingxiang," *Zhonguo Xiandai Wenxue Yanjiu Congkan*, no. 2 (2002), 156–79.

6 Eric Love, *Race Over Empire: Racism and U.S. Imperialism, 1865–1900* (Chapel Hill: University of North Carolina Press, 2004); Amy Kaplan, "Introduction," *The Anarchy of Empire in the Making of U.S. Culture* (Cambridge, Mass.: Harvard University Press, 2002), 16.

7 Jennifer Snow, *Protestant Missionaries, Asian Immigrants, and Ideologies of Race in America* (New York: Routledge, 2007).

8 Dana Robert, "The Methodist Struggle Over Higher Education in Fuzhou, China, 1877–1883," *Methodist History* 34, no. 3 (1996), 173–89, 178–79, 183. Robert points out that the Methodists in China set up a "conference structure" in which the votes of Chinese pastors were in theory equal to those of Western missionaries, although, as she points out, the missionaries' control of the "resources of the mission board" could give them more power. See also Ryan Dunch, *Fuzhou Protestants and the Making of a Modern China, 1857–1927* (New Haven: Yale University Press, 2001), 24.

9 Weili Ye, *Seeking Modernity in China's Name: Chinese Students in the United States, 1900–1927* (Stanford: Stanford University Press, 2001), chap. 4.

10 Catherine Hall makes this point about English missionaries in *Civilizing Subjects: Metropole and Colony in the English Imagination, 1830–1867* (Chicago: University of Chicago Press, 2002), 17.

11 Homi K. Bhabha, "Of Mimicry and Man: The Ambivalence of Colonial Discourse," *The Location of Culture* (London: Routledge, 2000), 87. For more on the importance of Chinese Christians in enabling missionaries to function in Chinese society, see Dunch, *Fuzhou Protestants*, 33.

12 Although most mission sources focus exclusively on Howe's and Kang's relationship, several references to these girls are made in articles in the Gertrude Howe file, UMA. See Mary Stone, "Miss Gertrude Howe," for the most detail about Howe's other daughters.

13 Hunter, *Gospel of Gentility*, chap. 3.

14 For another perspective on Kang's names, see Hu Ying, "Naming the First 'New Woman,'" *Rethinking the 1898 Reform Period: Political and Cultural Change in Late Qing China*, ed. Rebecca Karl and Pater Zarrow, 180–209 (Cambridge, Mass.: Harvard University Press, 2002).

15 Ann Laura Stoler, "Sexual Affronts and Racial Frontiers," in *Tensions of Empire: Colonial Cultures in a Bourgeois World*, ed. Frederick Cooper and Ann Laura Stoler, 198–237, 199 (Berkeley: University of California Press, 1997).

16 Patricia Grimshaw, *Paths of Duty: American Missionary Wives in Nineteenth-Century Hawaii* (Honolulu: University of Hawaii Press, 1989), 6–7; Grimshaw, "Faith, Missionary Life, and the Family," *Gender and Empire*, ed. Philippa Levine, 260–80, 265 (Oxford: Oxford University Press, 2004). The need for missionary men to be married was more pronounced in Hawaii, where local women were more sexually available, than in China, but the basic principle remained.

17 Grimshaw, *Paths of Duty*, 6–7. Later in the nineteenth century, in the British empire in India, relationships between Western women and Indian men continued to cause great consternation among colonial officials. See Kumari Jayawardena, *The White Woman's Other Burden: Western Women and South Asia During British Colonial Rule* (London: Routledge, 1995), 3–4.

18 Hunter, *Gospel of Gentility;* Hill, *The World Their Household.*

19 Hunter makes the point in *Gospel of Gentility,* 194–97.

20 WFMS Constitution and Bylaws, UMA. For a sample of the language, see page 256 of the bylaws of 1903. The bylaws of 1907 emphasize this point at greater length. My gratitude to Mark Shenise, UMA archivist, for this information.

21 "Miss Gertrude Howe and Dr. Ida Kahn," Missionary Biographical Files, Gertrude Howe file, UMA. The manuscript is not dated, but internal evidence would put it after the turmoil of 1927 and before Howe's death at the end of 1929.

22 William Hutchison refers to this as the " 'Christ and culture' dilemma" in *Errand to the World: American Protestant Thought and Foreign Missions* (Chicago: University of Chicago Press, 1989), 4.

23 *Hao Nuzi* (Miss Gertrude Howe), Missionary Biographical Files, Gertrude Howe file, UMA. Hu Ying, in making reference to this biography, has translated this passage as Howe having "no idea of race." I have chosen "racial hierarchy" because I think it more accurately reflects Kang's meaning. See Hu, "Naming the First 'New Woman,' " 208.

24 Burton, *Notable Women,* 119–20.

25 Mary Stone, "Miss Gertrude Howe," Missionary Biographical Files, Gertrude Howe file, UMA.

26 Daniel Bays, "Rise of an Indigenous Christianity," *Christianity in China: From the Eighteenth Century to the Present,* ed. Daniel Bays, 267–68 (Stanford: Stanford University press, 1996).

27 See articles in the Gertrude Howe file, UMA. Shi Meiyu provides the most extensive discussion of Kang's adopted sisters in her obituary for Howe.

28 Stone, "Gertrude Howe," 2–3.

29 For a survey of such works, see Ann Laura Stoler and Frederick Cooper, "Between Metropole and Colony: Rethinking a Research Agenda," in *Tensions of Empire,* 1–56, 7–8.

30 See numerous articles in Gertrude Howe file, UMA.

31 Jessie Lutz, *China and the Christian Colleges, 1850–1950* (Ithaca: Cornell University Press, 1971), 231; Jessie Lutz, *Chinese Politics and Christian Missions: The Anti-Christian Movements of 1920–1928* (Notre Dame: Cross Cultural Publications, 1988), 82–88; Bays, "Rise of an Indigenous Christianity"; Hutchison, *Errand to the World,* 95.

32 Robert, "The Methodist Struggle," 173–89, 178–79, 183.

33 For more on Xu, see Hu King-Eng file, Alumnae files, 1894, Special Collections and Archives on Women and Medicine, Medical College of Pennsylvania, Philadelphia (hereafter SCAWM); Burton, *Notable Women;* Dunch, *Fuzhou Protestants,* 44, 193–94.

34 WFMS Minutes, 1886, 36–37.

35 WFMS Minutes, 1886, 35.

36 Robert, *American Women in Mission;* Heidi Ross, " 'Cradle of Female Talent': The McTyeire Home and School for Girls, 1892–1937," *Christianity in China: From the*

Eighteenth Century to the Present, ed. Daniel Bays, 209–27 (Stanford: Stanford University Press, 1996); Judith Liu and Donald P. Kelly, " 'An Oasis in a Heathen Land': St. Hilda's School for Girls, Wuchang, 1928–1936," in Bays, *Christianity in China,* 228–42.

37 "Drs. Ida Kahn and Mary Stone," *China Medical Missionary Journal* (1896), 181–85.

38 Gertrude Howe file, Missionary Biographical Files, UMA.

39 Ruth Hemmenway, *A Memoir of Revolutionary China* (Amherst: University of Massachusetts Press, 1977), 129.

40 Amy Kaplan, "Manifest Domesticity," *American Literature* 70 (September 1998), 581–606, 589–90.

41 Reports of salary for WFMS missionaries can be found in the Methodist Episcopal Church Woman's Foreign Missionary Society, housed in the UMA. "Gold" refers to the Mexican gold standard in the form of the peso. The Methodist Episcopal mission board paid its missionaries in this currency because it was one of the more stable international currencies at this time. My gratitude to Mark Shenise of the United Methodist Archives for this information.

42 Stone, "Miss Gertrude Howe," 6.

43 See various articles in Missionary Biographical Files, Mary Stone and Ida Kahn folders, UMA; "Drs. Ida Kahn and Mary Stone."

44 For an example of the reluctance of a Presbyterian mission board to incorporate women of Chinese descent into missionary communities, see Judy Tzu-chun Wu's analysis of this mission board's rejection of the application of a Chinese American woman physician, Margaret Chung, in *Doctor Mom Chung of the Fair Haired Bastards: The Life of a Wartime Celebrity* (Berkeley: University of California Press, 2005), 49–50.

45 Ida Kahn, "Self-Supporting Medical Missionary Work," *China Medical Missionary Journal* (November 1905), 223–26.

46 Central Conference Minutes, 1903, 8–9. For more on the Nanchang gentry's opposition to Kang's Christianity, see Missionary Biographical Files, Ida Kahn file, UMA.

47 Ida Kahn, "A History of Nanchang Hospital," Central Conference Minutes, 1929.

48 See numerous articles in Ida Kahn file, UMA, especially Fletcher Brockman, "Daughter of Confucius," *Christian Advocate* (1914); J. G. Vaughn, "Dr. Ida Kahn." Kang's home was described as a "splendid residence" by Ruth Hemmenway, who lived in the home briefly in the 1930s. Hemmenway, *Memoir,* 153–54.

49 The donations are discussed in William Johnson to "My Dear Trindle," December 19, 1909, folder 184, box 11, William R. Johnson Papers, Yale Divinity School, Yale University, New Haven (hereafter WRJ).

50 Central Conference Minutes, 1909, 46–49.

51 WFMS Minutes, 1908, 145.

52 Michael Hunt, *The Making of a Special Relationship: The United States and China to 1914* (New York: Columbia University Press, 1983), 246.

53 WFMS Minutes, 1908, 144–45; Central Conference Minutes, 1909, 46–47.

54 For more on the specific problems that Chinese women entering the United States frequently encountered, see Sucheng Chan, "The Exclusion of Chinese Women, 1870–1943," *Entry Denied: Exclusion and the Chinese Community in America, 1882–1943*, ed. Sucheng Chen (Philadelphia: Temple University Press, 1991).

55 As Nayan Shah has argued, Chinese immigrants faced medical policing even after their arrival on American soil. See Nayan Shah, *Contagious Divides: Epidemics and Race in San Francisco's Chinatown* (Berkeley: University of California Press, 2001).

56 This term is used by Hunt in *Special Relationship*, 227–28.

57 Mary Wilton, "Mary Stone, M.D.," *Christian Advocate*, July 13, 1916, Mary Stone file, UMA.

58 See Derek Chang's essay in this book for more on this point.

59 Woman's Foreign Mission Society Annual Report, 1917, 278.

60 Ibid., 1919, 4.

61 For more on Li Bi Cu, see her alumna file, 1905, SCAWM.

62 The quotation is from Ann Laura Stoler, "Sexual Affronts and Racial Frontiers," in *Tensions of Empire*, 203.

63 Evaline Gaw to "Dear Furloughers," October 20, 1927, folder 229, box 13, WRJ.

64 "Coronation," *Friend*, April 1929, Gertrude Howe file, Missionary Biographical Series, UMA.

65 Ibid.

66 Interview with Hester Brown Hill, Ann Arbor, July 1998.

67 For more on the Nanjing Incident, see Lutz, *Chinese Politics and Christian Missions*, 232–38; James Sheridan, *China in Disintegration* (New York: Free Press, 1975), 180–81.

68 For more on this change, see Dunch, *Fuzhou Protestants*, 200.

69 Kiangsi Annual Report, 1927, 29.

70 "Letter from the Missionaries to the Chinese Christians," March 26, 1927, folder 3, box 2, series IV, Fred R. Brown Papers, M. E. Grenander Department of Special Collections and Archives, State University of New York at Albany, Albany, New York.

71 Kiangsi Conference Annual Report, 1927, 29.

72 Dr. Hu King Eng file, SCAWM; Dunch, *Fuzhou Protestants*, 193–94.

73 Fred Brown, in a letter of December 5, 1927, reported that some preachers had "suffered beating as well as reviling" and that "church members had been captured and held for ransom." Folder 3, box 2, series IV, FRB.

74 Kiangsi Conference Annual Report, 1927, 30–31.

75 American missionary colleagues of Kang frequently expressed concern for her in 1927. Strikingly, however, no correspondence I came across showed any sense of how their own actions may have put her in jeopardy. For more detail, see Connie Shemo, "An Army of Women: The Medical Ministries of Kang Cheng and Shi Meiyu, 1873–1937" (Ph.D. diss., Binghamton University, 2002), chap. 9.

76 "Gertrude Howe—Pioneer China Missionary," *Christian Advocate*, March 21, 1929, Gertrude Howe file, UMA.

77 Hemmenway, *Memoir*, 153.

American Women Missionaries
and the "Woman Question" in India,
1919–1939

Susan Haskell Khan

In "Sisters Under the Skin," an article published in an American women's mission magazine in 1922, Elizabeth G. Lewis told the story of an Indian woman who decided to become a nurse after many years of raising children. Lewis, an unmarried, professional medical missionary herself, interpreted the story as evidence that the desire to transcend familial responsibilities was universal. "From East to West," she exclaimed, "we hear the cry of overworked mothers!" Lewis's suggestion that the differences between women were only skin-deep resembled the facile universalist statements that often appeared in missionary writings, but she introduced a crucial difference: Lewis interpreted this "sisterhood" of Indian women and missionaries as an exchange, in which the missionary as well as her Indian sister had something to gain. Instead of approaching Indian women as "redeemer," the missionary should approach them as a friend or partner. The magazine editor, conscious of her American readers' expectations, recast the article in a more conventional missionary mold by praising Lewis in the preface for having "penetrated into the very hearts of India's suffering women." The point of Lewis's article, however, was to challenge the very assumption that India's women were suffering—or that the missionary, as a westerner, could really understand Indian women, let alone penetrate their hearts: "I sit and think of what their lives are—as I see them. That is the great point—as I see them. It is so possible, even more, probable, that I do not see them as they really are. But even as I see them may not some of my ideas be in need of changing as well as theirs?"[1]

The message of women missionaries in India to their supporters in the United States became increasingly complex after the First World War. Women missionaries had long justified their work in India by contrasting the supposedly liberated Christian woman of the West with her oppressed "heathen sisters" in the East.[2] Now they commonly praised the work being done by Indian women for themselves and even emphasized the sources within Hinduism of their strength. In response to objections from their readership that such statements undermined the very purpose of women's mission work overseas, women like Elizabeth Cole Fleming, a former missionary in India, insisted that Christianity's influence abroad depended on adaptation to shifting conditions in the mission field, particularly to the needs of India's educated and civic-minded New Woman.

The adoption of a language of friendship reflected changes at home: the influence of racial liberalism within certain facets of the Progressive movement as well as the expansion of women's professional opportunities. Just as important, however, were pressures in the mission field during the interwar period—pressures that have not received sufficient attention in the historiography of the women's mission movement.[3] In India, where American missionaries were eager to appeal to nationalizing elites, a nationwide discussion of women's status elevated the importance of missionaries' institutions of higher education for women, while simultaneously challenging their westernizing and evangelizing focus. In response, women missionaries found themselves in the ironic position of claiming rights for Indian women that they themselves did not possess in their churches back home and of criticizing stereotypes of Hinduism and Indian women on which missionaries had historically depended. (They also found themselves defending nationalist aspirations, despite the threat this posed to American missionaries' status as so-called guests of the British empire, a point that will have to be taken up elsewhere.) The irony of their position became acute in 1927, when the American journalist Katherine Mayo published *Mother India*, a British-funded diatribe against Indian nationalism that relied on the same depictions of Indian women that missionaries had employed for over a century. In the American press, missionaries condemned the book for the considerable embarrassment it caused their efforts to establish a relationship of friendship with India's women.

The politicization of women's issues in India after the First World War is essential to understanding two major, interconnected changes in the way American missionary women described their work in India. First, it allowed them to demonstrate the value of their work to the future nation and demand a larger role for women in missions—a move supported by a male missionary leadership eager to attract nationalizing, modernizing Hindu elites to Christianity. Second, presenting themselves as vital to the resolution of India's "woman question" required that missionary women reject the denunciations of Indian female agency and Hindu reform efforts that had often characterized their work. This effort was often fraught with contradictions, as missionary women claimed partnership with Indian women and male Hindu reformers, while at the same time insisting that their presence in India was indispensable to the progress of Indian women, an assertion that continued to rest on assumptions of cultural superiority often inflected with racial bias.[4] Nevertheless, their struggle helps explain how missionary women, by the Second World War, had come to play a prominent role in ecumenical Protestant efforts to promote international cooperation and challenge overt forms of racism in the United States.

THE CHALLENGE OF THE
WOMAN QUESTION

When Muthulakshmi Reddy, a prominent leader in the new national women's movement in India, gave her annual address to the All-India Women's Conference in 1931, she especially highlighted the contributions of Christian missionaries. Missionaries, Reddy suggested, had done more for women's education in India than the British government, providing models for indigenous efforts. Reddy demanded that national attention be given to the problem of women's education, lamenting that Christian missionaries still made up the majority of professional educators in India.[5] Missionaries received Reddy's words with pleasure and quoted her widely as evidence that the fruits of Christianity in India and of women's missionary work in particular were being realized.[6] At the same time, however, they gradually recognized that Christianity was not the only or even the most central force acting for women's interests in India. Indeed, they confronted the possibility that their schools would become obsolete in the context of invigorated indigenous efforts on behalf of women's education.

American missionary women had built some of the earliest and most critical educational institutions for women in India. Originating in the need to reach Indian women secluded by purdah and to train wives for native pastors, missions had raised funds in the United States for women's schools and attracted large numbers of young, mostly single women to serve as teachers. They built the second women's college in India, Isabella Thoburn College, and one of the first hospitals and medical training colleges for women, Vellore Medical College.[7] The women who built these institutions had defied accepted gender roles back home and within the missionary community and justified their work in part by emphasizing the liberties Christian women enjoyed in contrast to Hindu women's supposed subjugation. The salvation of India and the strength of the Indian Christian community would depend, they insisted, on the uplift of its women.

Because women could not be ordained and could not partake in the ecclesiastical, church-building activities considered central to the mission project in India, women missionaries tended to define their work in holistic terms that emphasized the social over the evangelical.[8] By the 1920s, missionary literature sought to recruit professionally oriented women in America by emphasizing the educational and medical opportunities available to them in mission work. In what was often a difficult balancing act, this literature celebrated female missionaries' autonomy while simultaneously denying feminist aspirations. An article in a women's mission magazine entitled "A Man's Work" honored the accomplishments of Adelaide Woodard, an unmarried woman who had left a successful medical practice in Seattle to come to India as a mission doctor, but whose work was described in the decidedly domestic terms of creating "better homes, better mothers, and better babies."[9]

Just as the feminist movement in the West often based its legitimacy on white women's burden on behalf of their suffering sisters in the East, missionary women justified their autonomy in missions by denigrating Hinduism and Indian female agency.[10] The article concluded by urging the college-educated, independent-minded woman of America to come to India, where the suffering of India's "womanhood" would allow her to achieve her potential: "This challenge comes to you, young woman of the clear eye and trained mind! It comes to you who have interested yourself in city problems, in settlement-house work. . . . You want to count for all that is in you. Then do not let the moan of India's womanhood, oppressed, sin-blighted, superstition-cursed—be drowned by the traffic noise of your own city streets."[11] The "moan of India's womanhood," the article suggested, allowed Western women the opportunity to pursue their ambitions in a self-sacrificing, Christian spirit.

The emergence during the First World War of a charged debate in the Indian press over women's education turned a national spotlight on American women's mission work in India. In 1916, the British government issued a report that highlighted the leading role of missionary schools for women and offered to fund future initiatives in women's education. A proposal by the Hindu social reformer Dhondo Keshav Karve that an indigenous all-India women's university be established raised the question of what women's education in India should accomplish. "Few things are more remarkable than the rapidity with which the education of Indian women has taken a foremost place among public questions," noted the editor of the *International Review of Missions* in 1917 with clear delight.[12] Missionary women interpreted this new focus on women's education as a measure of the success of their efforts on behalf of their sisters in India.[13]

Missionaries also recognized, however, the challenge implicit in national debates over women's education. Women's status had always been a highly politicized issue in India. Hindu reformers during the nineteenth century made women's status a central concern, countering efforts by both missionaries and the British Raj to justify imperial rule in India on the basis of such supposed Hindu practices as *sati* (the self-immolation of widows on their husbands' funeral pyres), child marriage, and female infanticide.[14] By the end of the nineteenth century, a Hindu reformist ideology was in place that claimed a golden age in India's past when women were educated, married at a later age, and participated in society and politics. The end of this era was blamed on the threat posed to Indian women by Muslim invaders. The Indian woman was valued for her role in maintaining India's spiritual superiority over the West, and limited reforms were introduced on her behalf.[15]

During the First World War, Hindu reformers and nationalist leaders remobilized the woman question against British claims of cultural and religious superiority and recruited Indian women into the nationalist movement.[16] The prominence of the woman question in this period also reflected the efforts of Indian women themselves to expand their rights in

Indian society, efforts assisted by women's rights leaders from the West. The 1890s had seen the emergence, in select castes and social classes, of a New Woman in India, highly educated, increasingly mobile, and active in the public sphere.[17] Women's organizations led by women appeared throughout India in the late nineteenth century and early twentieth. As in the West, the First World War afforded women opportunities for service outside the home and spurred demand for greater rights. A nationwide women's movement first appeared among middle-class, educated women after the war, directing nationalist energies to the cause of women's suffrage, education, and social reform. By the mid-1920s, these women's organizations increasingly cooperated with Mahatma Gandhi's nationalist movement, which made resolution of the woman question a major plank of its platform and shaped the form in which women's goals were articulated. Gandhi would stress the importance of Indian women to the movement and call for limited reforms in women's roles. Women would actively participate in Gandhi's civil disobedience movement, even holding prominent positions of leadership. In 1925, a woman, Sarojini Naidu, a prominent leader of the women's movement, was elected president of the Indian National Congress.[18]

In this context, missionaries' schools for women came under close scrutiny. Schools with an evangelizing agenda were already under attack in nationalist circles. During the First World War, Indian social reformers fought for a "conscience clause" in the Indian Education Codes that would allow parents to claim exemption of their children from religious instruction in schools that received government aid. V. S. Srinivasa, president of the Servants of India Society, defended a conscience clause as a matter of national self-respect in 1915, arguing that religious instruction in mission schools threatened Hindu traditions.[19] Other reformers opposed a conscience clause out of fear it would lead missionaries to abandon their crucial educational work in India, insisting that a Bible hour in mission-run schools could hardly make inroads into Hinduism.[20] Neither suggestion—that religious education challenged national self-respect or that it was completely ineffective—pleased the missionaries, who viewed their mission schools as important agencies for evangelization and hoped to attract the children of nationalizing elites in particular.

Both male and female social reformers criticized mission schools for imposing Western ideals of womanhood and thus "denationalizing" their students. Naidu argued that "education for Indian girls can only be given by Indian Women. . . . it must be built up on the traditions we inherit, and instruction by foreigners can, for that reason above, never be so fruitful as that given by our own women."[21] For some Indian women and reformers, the need to educate Indian women along national lines meant preparing them to be better wives and mothers. For others, it meant expanding opportunities for higher education and civic involvement.[22] All seemed to agree, however, that Western forms of education for Indian women were inadequate and that indigenous models of women's education along national lines were required.

The consequences of these debates for women missionaries' educational institutions in India were decidedly mixed. Missionary schools for women (both American and British) expanded in this period, admitting an ever-larger percentage of non-Christian women. By 1932, Christian missions in India ran twelve of the existing twenty liberal arts colleges for women, and five of seven of the existing teachers' training colleges. Of the non-Christian families who sent their girls to college, two-thirds, according to a historian of educational institutions in India, reported a preference to enroll them in Christian schools.[23] By the end of the 1930s, British and American mission hospitals also trained a large majority of female nurses in India.[24] Many of the women occupying posts in the Congress Party or the nascent women's movement had received their training in these mission institutions.[25] At the same time, however, it was becoming clear that the success of mission schools in the future hinged on their ability to make allies of the New Woman of India.

CHALLENGING SEPARATE SPHERES
IN THE MISSION FIELD

In this context, many missionaries came to believe that it was time to dispense with separate spheres for men and women in mission administration and church polity. Ironically, the need to keep up with India's New Woman sometimes put the missionaries at odds with the churches at home, where women continued to occupy a subservient role. In fact, the changing demands of the mission field became a compelling line of argument in favor of raising women's status in the churches back home, and women missionaries would go on to occupy leadership positions in the women's movement that emerged in the churches by the 1940s.[26]

A study published in 1927 entitled "The Place of Women in the Church on the Mission Field" made the case for expanding women's roles in the church in India and other major mission fields. Two women missionaries, one American and one British, wrote the study, which was instigated by "requests from missionary leaders in several countries," to "consider the problems created by the rapidly changing position of women in all parts of the world."[27] Through questionnaires, missionaries were asked how well they thought the churches were adapting to women's changing roles and how they could maintain their claim to leadership in the cause of women's rights and education. The report demonstrated women missionaries' efforts to take advantage of nationalist currents and growing attention to the woman question in India (and elsewhere) to promote the significance of their work, break down the barriers separating male and female mission work, and expand women's roles in the churches overseas and at home.

The study gave Christian missions primary credit for the Indian woman's progress, accusing the imperial government of actually widening the gulf between women and men. The study acknowledged, however, that there were now factors promoting women's issues in India that were "not in the control of the mission." Having played a leading role in women's emancipation in India, Christian missions could still perform an essential function: to help the New Woman of India navigate her new freedoms. Of the various religions in India, the authors of the study insisted that Christianity was the best suited to take up this task. Whereas most religions contained teachings about the sphere of women, only in Christianity was there "no suggestion that courage, independence, self-reliance, and wisdom are to be the special ideals of men, while obedience, submission, subordination, patience and the like are virtues to be required of women." Indian women would find in Christianity "a religion that compliments them by ignoring them as women."[28]

Despite the egalitarianism thus claimed to be innate to Christianity, the churches in India had failed to promote women to positions of responsibility. The study placed the blame only partially on the traditional attitudes of Indian Christian men: "Usually the churches abroad have been started as reproductions of our own Western churches and they have inherited our traditions. From the point of control, the church has been a man's church, and recognition that has come to women has generally been along the line of privileges that have been granted to them, rather than as responsibilities that naturally belonged to them." The native Christian leadership had, in fact, indicated a willingness to go further than the Western churches in extending equal rights to women. India was not the only major mission field where this was so. In China, the Chinese Christian leadership had actually "pressed for theological training for women" and appeared to regard it as "only natural that men and women should work in an equal partnership." Only thus could the church hope to appeal to China's and India's New Women, many of whom had been educated in mission schools but rejected Christianity: "One wonders why the Church, which stands for the freedom of women and was the first to open up to women avenues of service, should not keep the lead in meeting the new situation."[29] But the study did not restrict its recommendations to the church on the mission field. Reforming gender relations in the Indian church required first a transformation on the part of missionaries themselves, to incorporate "woman's work"—long considered separate and subordinate to the work of the men—into the work of missions as a whole. This would have to be accompanied by a significant change in "attitude of mind," in which women's work would no longer be viewed as "a department, separated from the rest of the work by a clearly defined line and to be developed or not as funds permit." The very success of Christian conversions in India depended on such a change in the relationships between male and female missionaries: "Attention is drawn to all that women owe to Christianity, and also to the urgency of winning the women of a country—the keepers of its traditions—if Christianity is not to remain a veneer."[30]

Male missionaries, too, were alert to the salience of the woman question in India after the First World War and to the need for Christian missions to compete with indigenous reform activities and women's organizations. Oscar MacMillan Buck, writing for an American missionary magazine in 1932, described the attention women's mission schools in India were receiving but regretted that their leadership was "largely gone from the women's movement in India." He blamed the fact that women's missionary work had been "too suspicious of the nationalist movement, too unwilling to trust that movement with its traditions and ideals out of the past of India." Nevertheless, he thought there was time to reverse this trend. "We still hold a very strategic place in the women's movement," he asserted.[31]

FROM REDEEMERS TO PARTNERS

Capitalizing on their strategic place at the vanguard of women's education in India required that women missionaries present themselves as allies, rather than saviors, of Hindu women, dispensing with the portrayals of Indian women on which missionary women had based their authority. Missionary women's gestures of friendship with the New Woman of India were equivocal and often contradictory. They did not necessarily translate into more egalitarian relationships on the mission field but did create tensions between missionary women and their female supporters in the West, who continued to heap scorn on indigenous women's reform movements. To defend their position, missionaries drew on social scientific criticisms of racism being articulated in the United States by such scholars as Franz Boas and Robert E. Park.[32] The impetus for their language of partnership, however, came principally from pressures encountered in the mission field.

The gradual, often begrudging transformation in women missionaries' characterization of their work during the 1920s and 1930s can be seen in the writings of Alice Van Doren, a single missionary, prominent educationist, and leader in the National Christian Council of India. In her first major work, *Lighted to Lighten the Hope of India: A Study of Conditions Among Women in India*, published in 1922, Van Doren emphasized the strength and heroism portrayed in the women of Indian folklore and drama—in the stories of Rama and Sita, Nala and Damayanti. Yet her praise was tempered by more conventional attitudes: the virtues of these heroes were, she interjected, limited: "Obedience, chastity, and an unlimited capacity for suffering largely sum them up." "They would scarcely satisfy," she continued, "the ambitions of the new woman today." Still, the Western woman, she suggested, might learn from the Indian woman's more modest virtues. Instead of blaming the condition of women in Indian society entirely on Hinduism, she accepted uncritically a Hindu polemic that it was not Hinduism but Muslim invaders who had brought purdah and turned Calcutta into a "city of men." Hindus, she claimed, were now changing, if largely in response to the Christian example. Hindu social reformers were criticizing child marriage and compulsory widowhood. Women like Sarojini Naidu were participating in the nationalist movement and setting shining examples for India's womanhood.[33]

Van Doren also took the unprecedented step of giving voice to Indian Christian women themselves, incorporating into her text pages of quotes from Indian Christian students, some criticizing the narrow-mindedness of traditional missionary tactics. Van Doren used these quotations to demonstrate the importance of allowing Indian Christian women to develop a nationalist consciousness alongside their identity as progressive women. These quotations emphasized the unique cultural genius that Indian women brought to their new freedoms—their gifts, which Western women were said to lack, of poise and modesty. "Freedom does not mean simply coming out of purdah and taking undue advantage and misuse of liberty," wrote one student. "We who have done away with our purdah should not be stumbling blocks to others. Freedom guided and governed by the Spirit of God is the only freedom and every true citizen ought to help to bring it about." Van Doren included biographical descriptions of leading Indian Christian women in the church and emphasized the importance of raising more such leaders who could gradually take over the missionaries' work.[34]

While downplaying the role of missionaries and highlighting Hindu accomplishments, Van Doren nevertheless insisted that Christianity remained vital to the real emancipation of India's women. The rate of literacy among Christian women remained far higher than that among Hindus and Muslims, and Christians were doing more, she argued, on behalf of women of lower castes. Despite her praise for indigenous reform efforts, she expressed deep suspicions of the motives of male Hindu reformers. Too often the Hindu reformer, "however well-meaning and sincere, talks out his reformation in words rather than deeds," Van Doren explained. The male Hindu reformer, she suggested, unlike the female Christian missionary, did not have "India's women's best interests at heart." In a metaphor that betrayed the racial tensions still underlying the conflict between white missionary woman and the male Indian reformer, Van Doren compared him to the "darky preacher who exhorted his audience 'Do as I say and not as I do.' "[35] In the title of her book, *Lighted to Lighten*, Van Doren appealed to a sense of racial and cultural superiority among her readers by drawing on a standard missionary metaphor that depicted Christian civilization as a lamp illuminating the darkness of heathenism.

Van Doren's skepticism about Hindu or indigenous-based reform did not go far enough, however, to satisfy her publishers in the United States. The foreword to her text was written by the publications committee in the United States, and the vitriol of its attack against Hinduism and Indian culture stands out from Van Doren's more conciliatory prose. "Miss Van Doren," the publishers advised, "has given emphasis in the book to the privileged young woman of India. [S]he shows the possibilities, and yet you will see in it something of the black shadow cast by that religion which holds no place for the redemption of woman." The reader was to understand that the culture Van Doren described was "revolting, sickening, shameful."[36] Van Doren's publishers in the United States recognized that a sympathetic treatment of Indian reform efforts threatened to undermine the very support on which women's missionary work in India depended.

By 1929, Van Doren characterized the female missionary task in India in terms of friendship, which meant playing a supporting role to indigenous women's activism. Indian women still needed the help of Western women missionaries, Van Doren suggested, but new missionaries would have to help them on their terms—on terms defined by Indian women. Missionary women should offer their guidance to organizations under the leadership of middle-class Indian women and engage in constructive social work: "In all these the Westerner is welcomed for her experience and organizing ability, provided only that she be free from the attitude of superiority and desire for domination." The new goal of mission work for women in India was "to strive for the give and take of Friendship." Missionaries were to focus on those problems affecting India's women which Indian nationalists such as Gandhi highlighted: literacy, poverty, "unhygienic living," and ecumenical religious teaching. In other writings, Van Doren criticized the tendency among American missionary women to create a "little America" in their homes; she urged them instead to adopt native furnishings and customs to make Indian women feel welcome.[37]

Van Doren was not the only female missionary revising her approach to Indian women in the 1920s and 1930s in ways that created tensions both with her fellow missionaries and with missionary supporters at home. Elizabeth Cole Fleming advised novice Presbyterian missionary young women to "seek the valuable companionship and advice of some older, intelligent, Christian Indian woman, respect her sympathy and affection, appreciate her spiritual stimulus." She also suggested that missionaries entertain their "native friends with other guests" and "not segregate them. You can get as close to them as you wish to, it all depends on how much you love them."[38] Welthy Honsinger Fisher, formerly a missionary in China, who had recently married a bishop of the Methodist Church in India, encountered both surprise and resistance from her fellow female missionary colleagues when she suggested that Indian Christian women should be encouraged to speak in meetings rather than allowing missionary women to speak for them.[39]

Disagreements over the missionaries' relationship with Indian women often reflected generational differences. Lucy Peabody, for example, a former Baptist missionary to India during the 1870s and 1880s, now turned a prominent figure in the home base of the women's foreign mission enterprise, was shocked by the view that any compromise with non-Christian cultures or faiths was possible when it came to women's uplift. Gandhi and other Hindu reformers, she insisted in 1933, had "done nothing to remedy the terrible physical, moral and mental conditions of women which are due directly to the religious life and beliefs of Hinduism."[40] Peabody's perspective, though still shared by a large segment of the mission community in India, harkened to an earlier era in missionary discourse. For the younger generation of missionary women in India, such statements threatened to alienate Hindu elites and render their institutions obsolete.

RESPONDING TO KATHERINE MAYO'S *MOTHER INDIA*

Missionary women's struggles to root racial and cultural stereotypes of Indian women from their texts are striking when held in contrast to prevailing attitudes toward India and Indian immigration in the United States during the same period. Jim Crow racism and xenophobic immigration laws were on the rise in the 1920s. In 1923, Bhagat Singh Thind, a Punjabi Sikh who had arrived in the United States in 1913 and fought with the American forces in the First World War, made the argument before the Supreme Court that Indians were in fact white and therefore immune to anti-Asian immigration laws. The Supreme Court, however, rejected his claim, a decision that resulted in efforts to remove property from Indians residing in the United States. When the Hindu poet and reformer Rabindranath Tagore visited the United States in 1929 for a lecture tour, he canceled his tour and returned home in response to rude treatment by American immigration officials.[41] Word of the treatment of Indians and other racial minorities in the United States spread quickly in the Indian press, and missionaries regularly spoke of the burden such perceptions placed on their efforts to demonstrate the superiority of Christian civilization in India. "The whole wide world has now become a whispering gallery," noted the popular American missionary E. Stanley Jones, "and India is listening in. . . . What we are doing in legislative halls and in the seemingly obscure incidents of racial attitudes is being broadcast to the rest of the world—and there is a loud speaker at the other end."[42]

The most influential attack on India and Indian culture in the United States—and therefore the most awkward for the missionary community—was *Mother India*, a book published in 1927 by Katherine Mayo. From the 1920s through the 1950s, Mayo's book went through twenty-seven editions in the United States and sold over a quarter of a million copies. According to a survey of 180 prominent Americans during the 1950s, Mayo's book was second only to Rudyard Kipling in shaping their early impressions of India.[43] In *Mother India*, Mayo depicted Indians as unfit for self-rule, principally because of relations between the sexes. Oversexed, tyrannical Hindu men, Mayo argued, left Hindu women so morally and physically degraded that they were incapable of raising strong, sturdy boys, resulting in a cycle of degeneracy.

The significance of Mayo's book extended beyond the United States. A storm of controversy in both India and the West followed its publication. Gandhi referred to it as a "Drain Inspector's Report"; Indian nationalists living in the United States published satirical responses under titles like "Uncle Sham"; and sympathetic liberals asked how Americans would like it if their divorce rates and crime statistics were paraded before the world.[44] Mrinalini Sinha has argued that the publication of Mayo's book marked a turning point in both the nationalist movement and the women's movement in India by remobilizing the woman question in India and encouraging a closer alliance between nationalists' and women's goals.

Reaction against *Mother India* "laid the foundations of an alliance that gave modern Indian nationalism its distinctive character, captured in the popular nationalist slogan: 'India cannot be free until its women are free and women cannot be free until India is free.' "[45]

Mother India also galvanized efforts within the American Protestant missionary community to adopt a more cooperative approach to women's issues in India and to distance themselves from the outspokenly racist and chauvinist views of their supporters in the United States. Historians writing about U.S.–India relations have often assumed that Mayo's perspective was typical of the missionary view of India, or at least have made no effort to distinguish Mayo's perspective from that being promoted by the most widely published mission leaders of the 1920s and 1930s.[46] Though it was not acknowledged at the time, Mayo's so-called investigation had been subsidized by the British government as propaganda to counteract suspected pronationalist activities in the United States.[47] Mayo's book was, in fact, a source of deep embarrassment to missionaries in India. The National Christian Council of India, the most important mission body in India, condemned Mayo's book as being untrue and unjust in a statement that was widely reprinted in the Indian press. Missionaries also wrote letters and articles for the Christian and secular press back home as well as letters to their friends and family explaining the differences between their perspective on India and that of Mayo. "Here and there," noted the editor of the *Christian Century*, "missionary supporters are somewhat gleefully saying that Mrs. Mayo's book makes the same charges that once constituted the backbone of missionary propaganda, but that are now seldom heard from the missionary."[48]

Missionaries provided their own evidence to demonstrate the strength of Indian women and the moral character of Indian men. An article in the *Atlantic Monthly* by Alden Clark, a Congregationalist missionary in India, offered extensive evidence compiled from women medical doctors in India to show that the average age of Indian brides was actually around eighteen, that marriage at age eight was almost unheard of, and that Indian women were predominantly sturdy and healthy. He described Mayo's claim that Indian men were physically weak and sexually degenerate as "grotesque" and countered with his own experience of playing tennis on Sundays with Indian men "who can beat any pair from among the British military officers and civilians of the town, young or old."[49] In correspondence with her home church, the American missionary Lillian Picken also took issue with Mayo's characterization of Indian men, describing examples of male Hindus she knew who were leaders in reform movements dedicated to women's causes.[50] The female missionary J. H. Orbison, writing in the pages of an American women's mission magazine, contrasted Mayo's stereotypes with the New Woman of India: "The educated women of India are more awake, alert and courageous than ever. . . . We wish that Miss Mayo in her book, Mother India, had given more prominence to these very significant reform movements."[51]

Missionaries accused Mayo of writing a biased account based on a superficial knowledge of the country. "Miss Mayo," declared a signed statement by India missionaries in the *Christian Century*, "saw only part of India and did not see that part in proper perspective. As Americans who have lived in India for a number of years and have moved with all classes of people, we have no hesitation in protesting vigorously against the unfairness of Miss Mayo's book."[52] Clark described Mayo's "whirl-wind tour" as "very American."[53] While acknowledging that Mayo's perspective was often out of date and overdrawn, India missionary Phila Linzell thought it a valuable corrective to recent efforts by some missionaries to depict India and Indian nationalism in an overly positive light. Still, Linzell objected strongly to Mayo's suggestion that India was beyond reform and criticized Mayo for the callousness of her account. Mayo, Linzell argued, "was not there long enough to acquire the love that springs from service. She only had time to probe and lacerate. She did not tarry to help in the healing."[54]

Even when they accepted aspects of Mayo's account, missionaries objected strongly to the ill will Mayo had brought to her subject matter, which missionaries feared had damaged their cause by interfering with their efforts to cultivate a relationship of friendship and cooperation. "If she had pictured the encouraging aspect of things with the same emotional effect which was given to the evils that still exist," wrote Clark, "we, who have been working for decades for India's physical and social progress, would have welcomed the book as an ally. As it is, Mother India has struck a blow both against truth and against interracial understanding and good will."[55] Missionaries widely agreed that the book had made their task in India far more difficult.

CONCLUSION: RESHAPING AMERICAN
WOMEN'S MISSION TO INDIA

Despite their efforts to present Indian womanhood and Hindu reform in a more sympathetic light, women missionaries probably did not succeed in overturning the degrading images of Indian womanhood that continued to circulate in American popular culture during the interwar period. After all, they themselves had depended for over a century on these images to raise money and support for their work in India. As they sought to challenge the very perceptions they once helped propagate, missionaries came into conflict with their publishers and other supporters in the United States. The widening rift between missionary women's agenda during the 1920s and 1930s and that of their supporters in the United States no doubt contributed to the decline of the women's foreign mission movement in this period—which in turn narrowed their audience among American Protestant women back home. Missionaries' campaign to denounce Mayo's portrayal of India as a land of child brides and Hindu tyrants, for example, did not prevent *Mother India* from selling hundreds of thousands of copies and creating a lasting impression on American minds.

Taking a longer view, however, women missionaries made a substantial impact on American culture and national identity through their participation in the emerging Protestant ecumenical movement in the United States. In the decades following the Second World War, ecumenical institutions such as the National Christian Council of Churches in America and the World Council of Churches played fundamental roles in shaping America's ideology of friendship to the "Third World" as well as the early civil and human rights movements. The large role of missionaries, above all, missionary women, in building these institutions and shaping their agendas has not received sufficient attention in the history of the women's foreign mission movement.

Also unrecognized is the prominent role missionary women came to play in nationalist India and in shaping U.S.–India relations in the postwar period. By this time, the educational and medical mission work long conducted by women missionaries had moved to the center of mainline American Protestant mission priorities in India. Women missionaries contributed to a broader shift in mainline Protestant missions from a focus on conversion to a focus on humanitarian service and cross-cultural exchange. This shift emerged in part as a response to mounting criticisms on the mission field from sympathizers with the nationalist movement and indigenous women's organizations, who welcomed missionaries' humanitarian activities while rejecting both their proselytizing activities and their expressions of hostility toward Hinduism and Indian culture. During the early Cold War, this new mission of partnership in India would gain the financial and moral support of American governmental and philanthropic agencies looking for ways to expand American influence in India.[57]

By the 1940s, women missionaries had become leading educational and medical experts, particularly on the subject of rural India. For this work they received recognition from Indian nationalists, and, after the Second World War, American governmental and nongovernmental organizations. Irene Mason Harper, for example, became a widely cited authority on progressive rural education.[58] Charlotte Wiser, with her husband, Arthur, published an anthropological study of village India that became a touchstone for community-oriented development programs in the 1960s and is still read by anthropologists today.[59] Alice Van Doren became a prominent authority on women's issues and rural high schools in India during the twenties and thirties and helped shape mission policy in ecumenical directions as secretary of the National Christian Council of India.[60] Welthy Honsinger Fisher became an active supporter of Gandhi's nationalist movement and published literacy materials for Indian youth and women geared toward building national citizenship.[61] Fisher would go on to found one of the most important village literacy programs in India after independence, prompting the Indian government to issue a postage stamp in her honor in the 1980s. The work of these women missionaries would pave the way, in direct and indirect ways, for postwar development and technical assistance programs, including governmental agencies like the Peace Corps and nongovernmental agencies like CARE and World Literacy, Inc.[62]

These women may have headed to India with visions of redeeming Indian women from the oppressions of Hinduism, but during the 1920s and 1930s, they came to define their roles in very different ways. The assumption that women missionaries contributed only to negative portrayals of non-Western cultures at home fails to capture the complexities of the missionary message after the First World War and the impact of changes in India on women missionaries' roles. American ecumenical

Protestants' new humanitarian mission overseas would reproduce many of the characteristics associated with the women's foreign mission movement but also diverge in key respects. Understanding these complexities requires taking seriously the impact of India on the missionaries themselves. With the politicization of women's issues in India after the First World War, Indian reformers succeeded in pressuring many missionaries to come to India's aid as partners rather than as redeemers. Pressures in India also had the unanticipated effect of expanding women missionaries' roles and encouraging them to advocate for equal rights with men in the churches and mission administration. The irony of American women finding their voice in India, so long depicted in missionary literature as a bastion of female oppression, is a reminder that although missionaries went abroad to effect change, they themselves were often transformed by their encounters.

NOTES

1 Elizabeth G. Lewis, M.D., "Sisters under the Skin," *Woman's Work*, October 1922.

2 Joan Jacobs Brumberg, "Zenanas and Girlless Villages: The Ethnology of American Evangelical Women, 1870–1910," *Journal of American History* 69, no. 2 (1982), 347–71.

3 Dana Robert describes this rhetoric of friendship among liberal Protestant missionaries after the First World War but does not emphasize the significance of the mission field context. Dana Lee Robert, *American Women in Mission: A Social History of Their Thought and Practice, The Modern Mission Era, 1792–1992* (Macon, Ga.: Mercer University Press, 1996). For studies that do stress the dialectical relationship between home and mission field (though not in regard to American women in India specifically), see Daniel H. Bays and Grant Wacker, *The Foreign Missionary Enterprise at Home: Explorations in North American Cultural History* (Tuscaloosa, Ala.: University of Alabama Press, 2003); Ruth Compton Brouwer, *Modern Women Modernizing Men: The Changing Missions of Three Professional Women in Asia and Africa, 1902–69* (Vancouver: University of British Columbia Press, 2002); Xi Lian, *The Conversion of Missionaries: Liberalism in American Protestant Missions in China, 1907–1932* (University Park: Pennsylvania State University Press, 1997).

4 For evidence that missionaries often defied their own universalist rhetoric in practice, discriminating against indigenous Christians in mission institutions and continuing to feed racist perceptions in the United States, see the essays by Connie Shemo and Derek Chang in this volume. Jeffrey Cox, too, in his study of the missionary encounter in the Punjab, suggests that "imperial fault lines"

continued to characterize missionary relationships with Indian Christians and non-Christians into the 1940s. Jeffrey Cox, *Imperial Fault Lines: Christianity and Colonial Power in India, 1818–1940* (Stanford: Stanford University Press, 2002).

5 Quoted in Aparna Basu and Bharati Ray, *Women's Struggle: A History of the All-India Women's Conference, 1927–2002*, 2d ed. (New Delhi: Manohar, 2003).

6 See, for example, Oscar MacMillan Buck, "Self-Criticism of Missions Today," *Missionary Review of the World* (April 1932), 209–12.

7 Maina Chawla Singh, *Gender, Religion, and "Heathen Lands": American Mission-ary Women in South Asia, 1860s–1940s* (New York: Garland Publishing, 2000), 245–60, 281–311. See also Geraldine Forbes, *Women in Modern India*, ed. Gordon Johnson et al., vol. 4, *New Cambridge History of India* (Cambridge: Cambridge University Press, 1996), 43.

8 Robert, *American Women in Mission*, 188.

9 Mildred B. Ogden, "A Man's Job," *Woman's Work*, April 1921, 83.

10 Antoinette Burton, *Burdens of History: British Feminists, Indian Women, and Imperial Culture, 1865–1915* (Chapel Hill: University of North Carolina Press, 1994).

11 Ogden, "A Man's Job."

12 Editor, "The Year 1916—British India," *International Review of Missions* 6 (1917), 26.

13 Missionaries probably had only an indirect influence on the emergence of femi-nism in India. Maina Chawla Singh has described the complexities of the rela-tionship between professional American missionary women and Indian female agency. Interviews with South Asian women educated in American mission schools indicate, on the one hand, a high degree of affection for their missionary teachers, and appreciation for their encouragement to pursue work outside the home. At the same time, however, Singh found that the missionaries' relation-ships with their female students tended to be matriarchal in character, with the students raised, usually in a boarding situation, under the missionary's protective wing and isolated from supposed harmful influences in their native culture. Singh, *Gender, Religion, and "Heathen Lands,"* 10, 205. See also Leslie A. Flem-ming, "New Models, New Roles: U.S. Presbyterian Women Missionaries and Social Change in North India, 1870–1910," *Woman's Work for Women: Mission-aries and Social Change in Asia*, ed. Leslie A. Flemming, 35–57 (Boulder: West-view Press, 1989).

14 Lata Mani has argued that the problem of *sati* in the early nineteenth century became an important focus for debates between Hindu reformers and British missionaries and officials over competing views of tradition and modernity—debates that largely excluded the needs and voices of women themselves. Lata Mani, *Contentious Traditions: The Debate on Sati in Colonial India* (Berkeley: University of California Press, 1998).

15 Forbes, *Women in Modern India*, 14–18.

16 Mrinalini Sinha, "Gender in the Critiques of Colonialism and Nationalism:

Locating the 'Indian Woman,'" *Feminism and History*, ed. Joan Wallach Scott, 477–503 (Oxford: Oxford University Press, 1996).

17 Forbes, *Women in Modern India*, 28–31, chap. 3.

18 Ibid., chap. 3. See also Basu and Ray, *Women's Struggle*; Madhu Kishwar, "Gandhi on Women," *Race and Class* 28, no. 1 (1986), 43–61; Gail Minault, ed., *The Extended Family: Women and Political Participation in India and Pakistan* (Delhi: Chankya Publications, 1981).

19 Editor, "A Conscience Clause in the Indian Education Codes," *Indian Social Reformer*, September 12, 1915. See also M. A. Master, "Letter to the Editor," *Indian Social Reformer*, October 10, 1915.

20 Editor, "Christian Missionary Education in India," *Indian Social Reformer*, September 19, 1915; Editor, "A Conscience Clause."

21 Sarojini Naidu cited in R. Gunniah Sastri, "Letter to the Editor," *Indian Social Reformer*, October 10, 1915.

22 See, for example, the issues for November 26, 1916, and December 16, 1917, of the *Indian Social Reformer*.

23 Aparna Basu, "Mary Ann Cooke to Mother Teresa: Christian Missionary Women and the Indian Response," *Women and Missions, Past and Present: Anthropological and Historical Perceptions*, ed. Fiona Bowie, Deborah Kirkwood, and Shirley Ardener (Providence, R.I.: Berg, 1993), 197. Basu also notes that because of mission schools, Indian Christian women were better educated, on the whole, than their Hindu and Muslim counterparts. Despite the fact that in 1932 Christians made up less than 2 percent of the population as a whole, 726 of the 2,966 women attending colleges were Christian, and 100 of the 157 students in teachers' training colleges were Christian.

24 Cox, *Imperial Fault Lines*, 185. See also Kenneth Scott Latourette, *Advance through Storm; A.D. 1914 and after, with Concluding Generalizations* (New York: Harper and Bros., 1945), 297. Latourette cites mission sources from the period suggesting that 150 out of 400 female physicians in India in 1930 were Protestant missionaries, that 43 percent of women medical students were in mission hospitals, and 85–90 percent of nurses in India were Indian Christians trained in mission institutions.

25 Basu, "Mary Ann Cooke to Mother Teresa."

26 On the history of the women's movement in the mainline Protestant churches, see Gladys Gilkey Calkins and the National Council of the Churches of Christ in the United States of America. Department of United Church Women., *Follow Those Women: Church Women in the Ecumenical Movement, a History of the Development among Women of the Protestant Churches in the United States* (New York: Office of Publication and Distribution, 1961); Margaret Shannon, *Just Because: The Story of the National Movement of Church Women United in the U.S.A., 1941 through 1975* (Corte Madera, Calif.: Omega Books, 1977).

27 International Missionary Council, *The Place of Women in the Church on the Mission Field* (International Missionary Council, 1927).

28 Ibid., 37.

29 Ibid., 56–57.

30 Ibid., 12–14.

31 Buck, "Self-Criticism of Missions Today."

32 See, for example, references to social scientific criticisms of racism in the writings of Daniel Johnson Fleming, a mission theorist and India missionary frequently cited by women missionary authors. Daniel Johnson Fleming, *Devolution in Mission Administration, as Exemplified by the Legislative History of Five American Missionary Societies in India* (New York: Fleming H. Revell, 1916).

33 Alice Boucher Van Doren, *Lighted to Lighten the Hope of India: A Study of Conditions among Women in India* (West Medford, Mass.: Central Committee on the United Study of Foreign Missions, 1922).

34 Ibid., 72.

35 Ibid., 28.

36 Ibid., 3.

37 Alice B. Van Doren, "The Women of India," in *The Christian Task in India*, ed. rev. John McKenzie (London: Macmillan, 1929), 43–65.

38 Elizabeth Cole Fleming, "School of the Presbyterian Prophets," *Woman's Work*, (August 1923), 172.

39 Welthy Honsinger Fisher, *To Light a Candle* (New York: McGraw-Hill, 1962).

40 Mrs. Henry W. Peabody, "A Woman's Criticism of the Laymen's Report," *Missionary Review of the World*, January 1933, 40.

41 Gary R. Hess, "The 'Hindu' in America: Immigration and Naturalization Policies and India, 1917–1946," *Pacific Historical Review* 38, no. 1 (1969), 59–79; Mrinalini Sinha, *Specters of Mother India: The Global Restructuring of an Empire* (Durham: Duke University Press, 2006), 100.

42 E. Stanley Jones, *The Christ of the Indian Road* (Cincinnati: Abingdon Press, 1925), 132.

43 Harold Robert Isaacs, *Scratches on Our Minds: American Images of China and India* (New York: J. Day, 1958); Manoranjan Jha, *Civil Disobedience and After: The American Reaction to Political Developments in India During 1930–1935* (Meerut: Meenakshi Prakashan, 1973).

44 On the controversy surrounding the publication of Mayo's book, see C. Seshachari, *Gandhi and the American Scene: An Intellectual History and Inquiry* (Bombay: Nachiketa Publications, 1969); Mrinalini Sinha, "Introduction," *Mother India*, ed. Mrinalini Sinha (Ann Arbor: University of Michigan Press, 2000); Sinha, *Specters of Mother India*.

45 Sinha, "Introduction," 2.

46 For example, Andrew Rotter, a historian of U.S.–India relations, while acknowledging that missionaries were the "eyes and ears [of the United States] in South Asia" and giving significant attention to the role of religion in shaping American attitudes toward India, does not actually examine any of the leading missionary texts from the period, taking the views of John Foster Dulles (descended from

missionaries, though not a missionary himself) as representative. Andrew Jon Rotter, *Comrades at Odds: The United States and India, 1947–1964* (Ithaca: Cornell University Press, 2000). See also Kenton J. Clymer, *Quest for Freedom: The United States and India's Independence* (New York: Columbia University Press, 1995). For an account of the Mayo controversy that does acknowledge missionaries' critical response to Mayo, see Sinha, *Specters of Mother India.*

47 Sinha, "Introduction," 24–25. See also Jha, *Civil Disobedience and After.*

48 Editor, "The Missionary's Changing World," *Christian Century,* November 17 1927, 1350.

49 Alden H. Clark, "Is India Dying? A Reply to 'Mother India,' " *Atlantic Monthly,* February 1928, 2H.

50 Letter Lillian Picken to "Friends." February 1928. Lillian Picken Papers, RG 159, 1:1. Yale Divinity School Archives.

51 Mrs. J. H. Orbison, "Straws Which Show the Wind," *Woman's Work* (October 1929), 270.

52 *Christian Century* statement quoted in J. T. Sunderland, "Miss Katherine Mayo's 'Mother India' Weighed in the Balance, What Is the Verdict?," *Modern Review* (January 1929), 1–6. See also Herbert L. Willett, "Review, Mother India," *Christian Century,* November 10, 1927, 1329–30.

53 Clark, "Is India Dying? A Reply to 'Mother India.' "

54 Phila Keen Linzell, "The Three Indias," *Christian Century,* December 29, 1927, 1548–49.

55 Clark, "Is India Dying? A Reply to 'Mother India.' "

56 Quoted in Editor, "The Missionary's Changing World." See also quotes in Sunderland, "Miss Katherine Mayo's 'Mother India,' " and Lillian Picken to "Friends." February 1928. Lillian Picken Papers, RG 159, 1:1. Yale Divinity School Archives.

57 Susan Haskell Khan, "The India Mission Field in American History, 1919–1947" (Ph.D. diss., University of California, Berkeley, 2006).

58 Irene Mason Harper, "Tendencies in the Religious Education of India," *International Review of Missions* 17 (1928), 515–27.

59 William Henricks Wiser, Charlotte Viall Wiser, and Susan S. Wadley, *Behind Mud Walls: Seventy-Five Years in a North Indian Village,* rev. ed. (Berkeley: University of California Press, 2000).

60 Alice Boucher Van Doren, *Projects in Indian Education: Experiments in the Project Method in Indian Schools* (Calcutta: Association Press, 1930).

61 Fisher, *To Light a Candle.*

62 See Khan, "The India Mission Field in American History," chap. 4.

III   MISSION

SETTLER COLONISTS, "CHRISTIAN CITIZENSHIP," AND THE WOMEN'S MISSIONARY FEDERATION AT THE BETHANY INDIAN MISSION IN WITTENBERG, WISCONSIN, 1884–1934

Betty Ann Bergland

Pearl Archiquette, a young Oneida woman writing in 1921 about her experiences at the Bethany Indian Mission in Wittenberg, Wisconsin, contrasted her life there with the renowned government school, Haskell Institute in Lawrence, Kansas. At Haskell, she wrote, they obeyed through coercion ("fear of punishment" in her words); at Bethany, they obeyed through persuasion ("God's desire that we should do that which is right," she wrote). Eight years earlier, at the age of eleven in 1913, Archiquette had entered the Bethany Indian Mission, received secular and religious instruction, was confirmed in the faith, and pursued her studies at Haskell. Feeling a sense of gratitude for the mission, she appealed to readers for help in the form of prayers and gifts to enhance its work among "my people." Aligning herself as Indian, she nevertheless embraced the work of the mission, claiming even elders now endorsed it and sent their children to be "cared for, fed, clothed and instructed in all things pertaining to good Christian citizenship."[1] Archiquette's short essay, dated November 25, 1921, was published and circulated by the Women's Missionary Federation (WMF) of the Norwegian Lutheran Church in America to provide information on the church's work with Indians to its immigrant church members, settler colonists in the Upper Midwest. Archiquette's affirmation of tribal identity as well as "Christian citizenship," through the mediation of the WMF, illuminates the complex relationships and ambiguities surrounding the Bethany Indian Mission.

The Bethany Indian Mission is distinguished in three important ways. First, the mission was established and staffed by first- and second-generation immigrants, themselves marginalized within the nation-state and part of a relatively small, immigrant church. They shaped neither Indian nor racial policy; however, because they were considered white and European, they benefited directly and indirectly from those policies.

Second, they were settlers and colonists occupying the land. Unlike the missionaries sent to China, Africa, and India, those at Bethany were not sojourners in a foreign land but settlers, displacing those whom they would convert and Americanize. Third, the Bethany Indian Mission was not a product of New England missionary societies or European efforts to Christianize Indians; rather, it emerged organically as a few immigrants saw vulnerable people in their midst. As a consequence of these distinctive features of the mission, its workers developed contradictory and ambiguous relationships with the Indians, with the nation, and with empire. As immigrants and settler colonists adopted the language and culture of the American nation and empire, they, the foreign, helped make Wisconsin Indians, the indigenous, aliens in their own land. As they Americanized Indians and helped facilitate federal policies, they made the occupied lands what they called their western home. Yet the missionaries also served as mediators between policies effected by governmental bodies and vulnerable Wisconsin tribes and families. These complex relationships make the Bethany Indian Mission a meaningful focus of study on the complexities of women, mission, nation, and empire.

The Bethany Indian Mission was neither merely an apparatus of state or imperial power nor simply a mitigating force for Wisconsin Indians. In this essay I argue that the Bethany Indian Mission and the WMF in particular not only served the interests of the nation and empire in its efforts to Americanize and Christianize Wisconsin Indians, but also mediated between the state and tribes, mitigating the harsher effects of Indian policy. It is this essentially ambiguous dimension of the mission that makes it so compelling as an object of inquiry to illuminate the complex processes of empire building in the context of diverse national communities. I explore ambiguities surrounding the Bethany Indian Mission through an examination of the discursive practices of pamphlets issued by the WMF of the Norwegian Lutheran Church in America from 1920 to 1934. To that end, I examine contested concepts, provide brief historical contexts of the mission, explore gendered dimensions of the church and state, analyze discursive practices to expose ambiguous identity formations, and examine negotiations of race, identity, and survival in Indian testimonials and biography.

CONTESTED CONCEPTS:
CHRISTIAN CITIZENSHIP, EMPIRE,
AND CULTURAL IMPERIALISM

Pearl Archiquette did not define what she meant by "Christian citizenship," but she did state that "all things pertaining to" it were taught at the mission. Whether she reproduced a concept heard at Haskell or elsewhere remains unclear. The expression does not appear elsewhere in WMF pamphlets, dispelling notions that Archiquette merely reproduced the words of mission workers. Conceivably, she captured a conceptual framework of survival for her people. Certainly, she heard discussions of citizenship within the Oneida community, for by the time she wrote, in 1921, citizenship rights for Indians were expanding and the idea of citizenship for Indians existed in the discourses of tribal life. Federal legislation enacted in 1924 (43. Stat. 253) declared all Indians born on U.S. territory to be citizens and contained language that permitted retention of tribal property rights and membership.[2] Thus citizenship and tribal alliance were not mutually exclusive but involved complex concepts of identity.

Archiquette's qualifier, "Christian," complicates the matter. What she meant by "Christian citizenship" is unknowable, but the term can be situated in the broader context of Christianity and empire. The scholar Vine Deloria Jr. has written extensively about the effects of Christianity on native peoples.[3] He views the missionary as central to his critique: "One of the major problems of the Indian people is the missionary. It has been said of missionaries that when they arrived they had only the Book and we had the land; now we have the Book and they have the land."[4] Deloria foregrounds the relationship between Christianity and empire in the American context, exposing the unequal exchange of "land for religion," an "exchange" that occurred in all European conquests.[5] In the settler colony of British North America, the policies of the British empire persisted after the American Revolution along with the goals, namely, the extinction of

Bethany Indian Mission students and staff, ca. 1895.
By permission of ELCA Region Three Archives, Luther Seminary, St. Paul, Minnesota.

native title to the land in favor of whites and transformation of Indian ways into white models. As Robert Berkhofer Jr. has argued, the only shift in postrevolutionary, U.S. Indian policy was the ideology of Americanism.[6]

The new national identity required an ideology distinguishing it, or its empire, from other sovereigns, in this case Indian nations and European empires. The concept of manifest destiny, a belief in America's providential claim to national expansion, served that purpose, and that framework remains, according to Thomas Hietala, America's "invaluable legitimizing myth."[7] In this mythology Indians were antithetical to Americans and required removal, isolation, or Americanization. Amy Kaplan's recent work on nation and empire, linking the domestic and the foreign, posits that Indians, like other peoples brought under U.S. authority in conquest, threatened the national spaces with their presumed foreignness. Indians posed distinctive problems as the foreign within the domestic or national territory.[8] This difficulty was exposed when the U.S. Supreme Court declared tribes to be "domestic dependent nations."[9] Missions, then, contributed to Americanizing the foreign within the domestic space of the nation. Bethany was no exception.

For many scholars of North American Indian history, Christianity and empire remain inseparable, as missions signify cultural imperialism.[10] Archiquette used the term "Christian citizenship" to frame an identity that evokes both the spread of Western religious culture and the nation-state, indicators for many of cultural imperialism. Other cultural critics and historians will argue that such concepts may be contested, that oppressed or dominated groups may appropriate concepts and use their own meanings.[11] Christian citizenship can be understood as a contested concept. Many Indians embraced citizenship while retaining tribal affiliation; others embraced Christianity and citizenship while claiming Indian identity. Archiquette's words, though contested, may have implied modernity, sovereignty, and survival.

HISTORICAL CONTEXTS OF THE MISSION: INDIAN POLICY, MIGRATION, AND SETTLER COLONISTS

Norwegian immigration history and Wisconsin Indian history converge in profound ways in the nineteenth century and offer the broadest contexts for understanding the Bethany Indian Mission. In 1837 a series of treaties signed by several tribes residing in what was then Wisconsin Territory ceded vast parcels of lands to the federal government.[12] This opened the floodgate of immigration. In 1838 the first Norwegian immigrants arrived in Wisconsin Territory; subsequently, the Pre-emption Act of 1841, which provided free land, further stimulated migration. By 1850, some eighty-six hundred Norwegians resided in Wisconsin, and by 1900 Norwegians constituted the second largest foreign-born population in the state.[13]

As immigrants flooded into Wisconsin, federal Indian policy shifted. The Indian Removal Act of 1830 sought to move tribes west of the Mississippi River; however, many tribes, especially the Ho-chunk (Winnebago), refused, and tribes already removed to the area refused to be uprooted again. Resistance took other forms: taking up arms in the Black Hawk War; selling a parcel at a time; returning to ancestral homelands after removal; and "by protracted bargaining and their ineffable talent for obfuscation and delay."[14] Also, policy-makers began to fear the consequences of removal: organized resistance in one great Indian Territory in the West could threaten white settlers. This shifting Indian policy meant Wisconsin tribes experienced diverse relations with the federal government.[15] Wisconsin became "a kind of natural laboratory for most of the government policies and programs."[16] The complexity was reflected also at the Bethany Indian Mission.

The national Indian policy of the General Allotment Act (1887–1934) aimed at assimilation of indigenous peoples. The logic was that by allotting individual parcels of existing reservation land to Indians, they would become farmers and citizens and assimilate, and the trust relationship with the federal government could end. The central effect was the dispossession of the land: nationally, about two-thirds of reservation land was lost from 1887 to 1934 (from 138 million to 52 million acres); in Wisconsin, approximately half of the land was lost.[17] This dispossession was achieved through white manipulation and unethical Indian agents, as well as legal land sales. This policy coincided with the years during which there was a boarding school at the mission (1884–1934). Not surprisingly, the policy assumptions, strategies, and goals of the U.S. government were to be found also at the mission, including farming as a way of life and assimilation as vital to survival. The settler-colonists who worked at the mission embraced this vision both for themselves and for the Indians—with obviously different consequences.

The Norwegian immigrants who settled Wisconsin in the nineteenth century had deep roots on the land: most had migrated from rural areas and sought land to preserve a way of life. Striving to reach that goal, they homesteaded on public lands and established permanent settlements. Among the immigrants was Even Johnson Homme, from the county of Telemark, Norway, who migrated as a child, attended public schools in Wisconsin, Luther College in Iowa, and the Lutheran Seminary in St. Louis, Missouri. Seeking to establish homes for orphans and the elderly, Homme explored Wisconsin for a site and discovered another vulnerable population, Indians. He determined to begin a mission.[18] The Norwegian Synod in America initially rejected his proposal, so Homme and his colleagues proceeded without the sanction of the synod: they purchased forty acres near Wittenberg, erected a modest building, and organized the Bethany Evangelical Lutheran Indian Mission in 1883. Later, acting on an appeal, the synod voted unanimously to support the mission. A call was issued to Erick Olson Morstad, a graduate of Luther College, and on August 30, 1884, he began mission work.[19]

Unlike the founding of most Protestant Indian missions in North America, that of the project started by Homme was more organic in that it was a response to immediate and real needs, a local initiative, rather than an abstract call to distant pagans. Homme's persistence in defiance of the synod accentuates the difference.[20] In addition, the arguments made by the church members as they moved to finally endorse the mission suggest, in the multiplicity of reasons they stated, a distinctive grassroots effort: (1) work "among the heathens has had a beneficial effect on the church"; (2) it "is right to begin a mission among the Indians since we occupy the land which was once their land, and we are obligated to them"; (3) it "would be well to forget some of our abominable church strife by serious participation in such a mission"; (4) it would be beneficial to indigenous children to be away from "pagan influence" and also to receive food, clothing, and schooling; and (5) the cynical commentary on federal policy —that it was now "cheaper to give them the gospel than to kill them"— reveals a consciousness of brutal conditions.[21] Thus, several reasons given for establishing the mission—the implied critique of federal policies, the immigrants' recognition that they occupied the Indians' land, and the stated benefits of a mission providing basic needs—convey humanitarian and practical motives. No monolithic view prevails. The diverse arguments suggest complex motivations for support of the mission and a grassroots origin.

In *Missionary Conquest*, George Tinker observes that most Lutherans did not establish Indian missions but rather took the best land.[22] By contrast, the Norwegian Lutherans did both: they established a mission and acquired the best land. The Bethany Indian Mission at Wittenberg, Wisconsin, became the only formal outreach to Indians sponsored by the Norwegian Synod, and from 1884 until 1955 the mission served the tribes of Wisconsin, mostly Oneida and Winnebago (Ho-chunk) but also Potawatomie, Ojibwe (or Chippewa), Menominee, and Stockbridge-Munsee.[23] Like most North American Protestant missions, the Bethany Indian Mission provided religious and secular instruction; in one respect, however, it differed from other North American missions: authority, responsibility, and structure remained among settler-colonists in the decentralized, immi-

Bethany Indian Mission, c. 1900.
By permission of ELCA Region Three Archives, Luther Seminary, St. Paul, Minnesota.

grant church. Its relationship to the state shifted over time. In the formative period, 1884–88, the mission was operated by the church with no state involvement; from 1888 until 1900, the synod contracted with the federal government on a per-pupil basis; from 1900 to 1917 the federal government owned the land and buildings and hired the settler-colonists to operate it; from 1918 to 1933, the synod owned and operated both the mission and the school; and from 1934 to 1955, the boarding school was closed, but the mission and synod offered religious instruction and assistance to the members of tribes in the area.[24] These shifting patterns reveal the continuity of the church and the immigrant staff—and the discontinuity of the state. The period when the school and mission flourished under ownership and operation of the church (1918–33) occurred when the WMF acquired responsibility for mission work—and the Bethany Indian Mission.

STATE, CHURCH, AND GENDERED
FRAMEWORKS OF MISSION WORK

To maintain social order, state and religious authorities both tend to preserve prevailing ideologies and their supporting structures, what Louis Althusser labeled Ideological State Apparatus (ISAs). In the late nineteenth-century United States that social order meant private land-

ownership; patriarchal domination of the administrative and juridical regimes; a racial hierarchy that privileged whiteness; and a cultural ideology
that promoted Anglo-Saxon, Western, and Christian identity formations.
Yet in the late nineteenth century, when the Bethany Indian Mission
emerged, authorities were also being challenged. Homme's defiance of
church authority became emblematic of a pattern: immigrants challenged
religious authority in Norway simply by emigrating, while others joined lay
movements. Even the immigrant church (neither old world state church
nor mainstream American) challenged tradition by training clergy in the
United States. One might view these challenges within a broader terrain of
contested authority on the Wisconsin frontier. In that larger context, and
on another level, Wisconsin tribes defied federal policies by refusing to be
removed or, once removed, returning to ancestral lands. Challenges to
patriarchal authority also become visible in the work of the women.

   In the nineteenth century many viewed mission work as essentially
feminine; others affirmed masculine models of mission work based on, as
Susan Thorne writes, "religious piety, moral seriousness and a civilizing
mission at home and abroad."[25] Mission work challenged prevailing gender roles. Amy Kaplan's work exposes the gendered contradictions and
ambiguities of missions.[26] Connecting the realms of the domestic and the
foreign (conceptually separated in historical and cultural studies of nation
building and empire), she challenges the gendered dichotomies surrounding these and would shift the "cognitive geography of the nineteenth
century."[27] The cultural work of domesticity, she argues, actually linked
men and women in an alliance against the perceived foreign (alien, wild,
savage), as domesticating the foreign within the national borders linked
the imperial project of civilizing the other outside the national borders.
Thus, domestic Indian missions and foreign global missions both engaged
in empire building; men and women both participated. The central dichotomy was not gendered but racial, determined by concepts of the
foreign and not-foreign. These national discourses of empire helped shape
ideas of missions and created the contexts of gendered work at the Bethany Indian Mission.

   Women generated neither the federal Indian policy nor the church
polity that shaped the mission. In the church after the Reformation, as the
historian L. DeAne Lagerquist notes, "women were left with no official
role in the Protestant church beyond that of worshiper."[28] At the Bethany

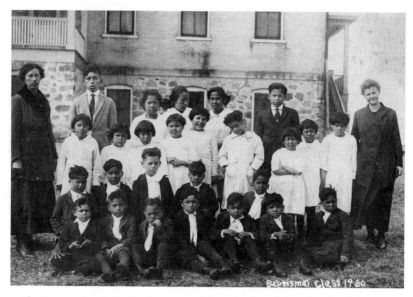

A baptism at Bethany Indian Mission, 1920, with Agnes Jacobson (*right*) and unidentified woman.
By permission of ELCA Region Three Archives, Luther Seminary, St. Paul, Minnesota.

Indian Mission, the pastors and school superintendents were men, but both men and women staffed the mission. Male and female Indian students were also employed. Yet with the merger in 1917 of Norwegian American church bodies, women assumed the responsibility for missions, represented by the WMF. The institutions of church and state in which the federation operated (the Norwegian Lutheran Church in America and the Bureau of Indian Affairs) provided structures in which women assumed both responsibility and empowerment. The gendered and racial ideologies of the time provided the conceptual and discursive arenas in which the women worked and thought—ideologies they both participated in and challenged. Thus they navigated contradictory positions: subordinate in patriarchal institutions of church and state; equal in relation to each other; and authoritative in relationship to the Indians. The WMF at the Bethany Indian Mission illuminates the ambiguous roles of women in the gendered systems of church and state and exposes the vexed relationships that both fostered and challenged prevailing racial and gendered ideologies.

The appropriate place of women in mission work and in the church is stated clearly in the Constitution of 1917 of the Women's Missionary

Confirmation class, Bethany Indian Mission, with Rev. T. M. Rykken, ca. 1925. By permission of ELCA
Region Three Archives, Luther Seminary, St. Paul, Minnesota.

Federation (WMF). Women were "to create interest in and stimulate love
for the great cause of missions; to unite . . . all women's societies . . . for
missions; to promote . . . separate mission societies and children's societies . . . to disseminate knowledge of missions."[29] The promotion of missions was central to the WMF, but this must be accomplished in the
context of the established order of the church, in which women and
the WMF functioned as an auxiliary.[30] While all women should be a part
"of the Big Sisterhood," they would also act as "the Lord's Handmaid."[31]
The gendered regimes of the church meant support, subordination, and
submission.[32]

While religious ideology decreed that women be "handmaids," the
church also fostered the solidarity of the "Big Sisterhood." That unity was
possible because the WMF was embedded in church structure. Formed in
1917, the WMF was organized into nine extant districts, a complex network
linking WMF to congregations across the country and facilitating communication. As membership expanded in the 1920s to over a thousand
affiliates, the WMF reached tens of thousands of individuals with its literature. In 1925, 1,232 societies representing a membership of 31,098 were

reported.[33] Church spaces, therefore, could be cultivated to enhance the Big Sisterhood, as the women met regularly, elected officers, kept records, planned meetings, organized fundraising, arranged and oversaw conventions, wrote reports and pamphlets, distributed literature, spoke at church gatherings, recruited new members, supported missionaries, maintained mission cottages, and informed church leaders of their work. In the process the federation fostered sisterhood: a public presence, growing confidence, and leadership skills among women.[34] Women's mission work done in a discursive context of subordination also empowered women.

In 1920 the Mission Board of the Norwegian Lutheran Church in America (NLCA) gave budgetary responsibility for the Bethany Indian Mission to the WMF. The new responsibility was not surprising. The Norwegian American churches began to send missionaries directly to foreign fields, mostly to China and Madagascar, in the 1890s. By 1900 there were more women than men in those fields.[35] Both single and married women went, and women were identified with missions. When the three Norwegian American Lutheran synods merged in 1917 their three mission societies became the WMF, aligned in foreign and home missions. At the general board meeting of the WMF held on June 9, 1920, the board approved a resolution that "the taking over of [the] budget for Indian Mission be approved."[36] The president's report explains, "This work [Bethany Indian Mission] naturally falls to the Federation for the same reason that it is to accept schools and hospitals for the Foreign Missions."[37] By 1920 women were seen to have a natural relationship to the mission.

The first WMF president, Lena Dahl (1848–1922), guided the federation in thinking about missions and Bethany.[38] Like many female leaders in the mission, Dahl was the daughter and wife of pastors and an immigrant from Norway. By the time Dahl became WMF's first president, she was deeply familiar with immigrant congregations, women's missionary work, and women's appropriate places in the religious and civic hierarchies. As she steered the work of the mission, she explained in an address in 1920 how women were expected to think about its Indian mission work: "Think of the little brown-skinned . . . children . . . with their bright eager faces full of questioning wonder—they too need us so they may learn what Christian motherhood means. Ah, they all need us, they look to us for many things that mean comfort and uplift, a help that gives them new and noble impulses, strength to walk in godly ways."[39] Though she could be describing foreign missions, she was speaking of a domestic one, Indians at Bethany. Ironically, in the racial and imperial hierarchy, the truly foreign Dahl instructed women to help the indigenous foreign.[40] Being the not-foreign-foreigner in this ideology, she was permitted not only to settle but domesticate the genuinely indigenous people. At the same time, her conception of "Christian motherhood" led her to offer the "comfort and uplift" that disastrous federal policy had not provided. Dahl filled the ambiguous role not only of addressing the genuine needs among the Wisconsin tribes, but also of supporting the work of empire by helping assimilate Indians. Ironically, while Dahl saw the work as "Christian motherhood" (a gendered concept), Archiquette learned "Christian citizenship" (a nongendered concept).

The ideology of manifest destiny and the federal policy of allotment and assimilation gave women the conceptual framework for Indian mission work. The government expansion of the school buildings from 1900 to 1917 provided an enlarged capacity for the mission work when the federation assumed its responsibility. Thus, both the church and the state, though constraining women, provided the institutional structures to achieve sisterly solidarity and cultural authority. In the world of the mission, the immigrant women gained stature and authority by virtue of their position in the racial and cultural hierarchy. In the competing narratives surrounding sovereignty, nation, and race, immigrant white women possessed an advantage: representing the English language, Western culture, and Christian religion, they occupied positions of authority. At the same time, immigrant women missionaries occupied subordinate positions in relation to the church and state and positions of equality in the Big Sisterhood. Less visible and obvious is the role of mediator between the Indian students and families and their difficult historical conditions. That role is partially evident in the constructed knowledge of the mission literature.

CONSTRUCTING SELF AND OTHER IN
DISCOURSES OF WMF PAMPHLETS

The WMF acknowledged from the start the importance of disseminating knowledge: "First in importance is the literature by which it is possible to reach every member—sometime," wrote President Dahl in 1919.[41] The literature program became the core of its work. Pamphlets, published in English and Norwegian, Dahl argued, "will give a correct presentation of our mission fields at home and abroad and impart a general knowledge of existing conditions both here and in heathen lands."[42] This meant writers would define the mission project and Indians. The unstated aim of the pamphlets was to stimulate empathy for Indians, affirm legitimacy of the work, and raise funds. To achieve these ends, the pamphlets gave evidence of success, especially conversion. By referring to the Bethany Indian Mission as "our mission fields at home," the pamphlets offered a discourse of legitimacy while stimulating awareness of Indians. In this way the WMF literature was essentially ambiguous. Primarily concerned with the propagation of the Gospel and the saving of souls, the writers also constructed images of the Indians, missions, and themselves, helping to define what it meant to be civilized, American, and legitimate. Thus, while propagating the Gospel, they also served the interests of Indian policy (extinguishing Indian claims and reshaping Indians as Americans) and legitimated land occupation; yet they also gave witness to the plight of the Indians.

The WMF published only ten pamphlets on the Bethany Indian Mission between 1921 and 1935, yet the literature committee circulated thousands of these, reaching tens of thousands of Norwegian Lutherans across the country.[43] Their construction of Indians and descriptions of mission work helped shape attitudes toward indigenous people. Written by WMF leaders and clergy, the pamphlets showed little variation in content between the men and women, although the clergy foregrounded religion and included more historical and statistical information, while the women emphasized secular education and the experiential. WMF leaders—generally wives of ministers or church leaders, first- or second-generation immigrants, urban, and middle class—possessed knowledge of church policies, practices, and hierarchies.[44] They would have been familiar with the tensions and goals surrounding the merger of the three major Norwegian Lutheran synods in 1917.[45] These women also were aware of the anti-foreign and anti-immigrant hysteria that was prevalent around the time of the First World War.[46] The 100 percent American movement of the prewar period and postwar xenophobia would have sensitized them both to the ambiguity of their positions and to the urgency of their work—Americanization and nation building. These larger contexts provide the framework in which the women conceptualized mission work. The pamphlets represented that conceptualization; the testimonials of Indian students would signify its achievement.[47] The WMF literature on the Bethany Indian Mission conceptualizes four arenas: women's self-construction as missions workers, constructions of the Indians, and conceptions of the mission and of the land.

The mission worker is most often described as a mother (the word is often capitalized). The image places Indians in an obvious dependent relationship as children. The mother gives gifts, bestows virtue, sets standards, dispenses clothing, gives food, provides education—and expects gratitude. The relationship to the readers, however, is sisterly, one of equality in the grand project of civilization and uplift of Indians.[48] By inviting their sisters (the readers) into this noble project, writers implied they were gift-givers, a kind of inversion of the real relations between immigrants (recipients of land) and Indians (dispossessed of land). Mothers to the Indians and sisters to each other, the women might create solidarity among themselves and authority over the children (the Indians). The male clergy do not allude to a sisterhood but rather create solidarity with the women by referring to "our work" and "our mission."[49]

The Indians invariably are described as children—as students, they literally are—but also figuratively as lost, dependent, in darkness, needy, helpless, and little children of the woods. One pamphlet describes Indians coming "in from the woods," which was literally true, yet metaphorically suggesting darkness and ignorance, masking their history and culture. Another pamphlet reads, "In the past the Indian was at the mercy of his own ignorance and the white man's evil example."[50] In yet another, students are portrayed as part of a heathen community when they leave the mission, "little messengers of the Gospel [who] teach the truths of salvation to their relatives."[51] Traditional religious beliefs are denied, as Indians are perceived as lost or saved in a Christian context.[52] Racial constructions strengthen this dichotomy. In one pamphlet, in an effort to counter charges that Indians are "lazy" and "shiftless," the writer evokes racial hierarchy: "It should be borne in mind that the Indian is not a white man with a red skin. He has racial inclinations and propensities . . . we can hardly expect them to measure up to our standards in every respect, yet many of them do."[53] In a similar vein, attempting to present a sympathetic portrait, Albert Holm, a graduate of Luther Theological Seminary and a clergyman, uses racial language and blames white men for their failure to

Indianer Missionen
Wittenberg, Wis.

Elizabeth Stacy and her Grandmother

W M F

Published by
LITERATURE COMMITTEE OF THE WOMEN'S MISSIONARY
FEDERATION, N. L. C. A.
425 FOURTH ST. SO., MINNEAPOLIS, MINN.

1931

Pamphlet of Women's Missionary Federation, Bethany Indian Mission, 1931.
By permission of ELCA Region Three Archives, Luther Seminary, St. Paul, Minnesota.

understand Indian culture and to keep promises, for their introduction of "firewater" and peyote, and for their tendency to continue in "primitive" ways; yet his refusal to give Indians agency and his use of the reductionist, masculine, and singular term "the Red Man" perpetuate racial views.[54] In these constructions, the Christian vision of equal soul brothers and sisters competes with a hierarchical and racial construction of nation and empire, while emphasis on Christian conversion tends to create the dichotomies of us and them, saved and lost.

Yet some pamphlets candidly address historical realities and the tragic consequences of white incursions. Thorvald Rykken, a clergyman at the mission, writes in one pamphlet, "Many of our Indians are very poor and their land is swampy, making it difficult if not impossible, for them to make a living." Discussing the limited sources of Indian income resulting mainly from labor that men secured in farming or seasonal work such as road construction and wood cutting, Rykken laments the effects when no employment is available: "We are compelled to buy baskets and beads from the women."[55] Another pamphlet points to the exploitation that produces poverty: "What a blot upon the pages of American history is not the story of our treatment of the American Indian! The Indians of Wisconsin were no exception. They too were the victims of avarice." The writer notes that the land was sold for ten cents an acre, and Indians received swampy land that whites rejected.[56] Compassion also emerges: "Their poverty is distressing, their material condition deplorable. And then as a last straw the court has decided that the land that some of them bought shall be taxed and even back taxes are to be collected . . . many are unable to pay . . . and worried lest they lose their land."[57] Often the empathy leads to assertions of common humanity. Rykken acknowledges that the Savior "died also for our Red brothers and sisters."[58] One writer affirms that Indians "also have an immortal soul and are bought with the same blood as you and I."[59] Another refers to the Indians as "our heathen neighbors."[60] These constructions mask the inequity and injustice of empire, while they affirm a shared geography and humanity.

The mission project is invariably described as one involving education: the Indian child "learns to work, is given an education and . . . is taught to love Jesus."[61] This education contains culturally specific meaning, however: labor means gender-specific, vocational skills; knowledge refers to Anglo-Saxon or Western epistemology; and religion signifies Christianity.

Though Western, the constructs are presented as universal. The clergy emphasized religion, as illustrated by Reverend Rykken: "Our chief purpose is to Christianize"[62] and, "If it were not for this side [the religious], we should certainly not carry on work among the Indians, for the Government is far better equipped to support schools than the church is."[63] Subsequently, Rykken proposes the inseparability of education and religion, conceding, "The school building is the important building at the mission."[64]

Conceiving the homeland of Indians and immigrants also raises problems for the clergy, as Rykken reveals: "We live on the land which they once possessed and in return we should show them our gratitude and our love, especially by bringing them the Gospel of Jesus Christ."[65] Holm writes, "The land on which we live once belonged to them. Let us show them our gratitude and love by bringing them the Gospel of Jesus Christ!"[66] Trained clergymen and second-generation immigrants, Rykken and Holm recognized the land as central to their communities' survival. Neither explains how the so-called land exchange occurred, but both imply a natural and inevitable process: the land as gift requiring reciprocity, that is, the book for the land. As the spiritual authorities of their communities and representatives of the mission, these writers offered their readers a moral equivalence of land for religion. In the process they offered readers legitimacy on the land and alliance with the nation and empire. At the same time they gave testimony to fellow settler-colonists that the land was not empty, not unpeopled. In short, the pamphlets that would convey "a correct presentation of our mission fields" also helped legitimize land possession and Americanize Indians (the imagined foreign), while giving witness to the difficult living conditions and the suffering of Indians.

NEGOTIATING SURVIVAL, IDENTITY, AND RACE: INDIAN TESTIMONIALS AND BIOGRAPHY

Historians report several responses of Indians to Christian missionaries, including rejection, accommodation, and a divided response. All appear at the Bethany Indian Mission.[67] While few records of Bethany students exist, extant documents favor accommodation. Interviews with Ho-chunk women and former Bethany students reveal the complexity of that accommodation. Adhering to traditional ways and harshly critical of federal policy and *maixeta* (the Ho-chunk term for whites, meaning "big knives"), these women, nevertheless, speak affectionately of workers at the mission and consider themselves both Christian and traditional, American and Ho-chunk.[68] Such a pattern of accommodation and complexity also emerges in the testimonials of Indian students. Three testimonials by Indians published by the WMF offer historical evidence of that pattern. All are by former students who were confirmed at the mission and were affiliated with Oneida. (Part of the Iroquois Confederacy located in the area of New York, one contingent of Oneida came west.)[69] Having had extended exposure to Christian missionaries and American culture, the Oneida would have been more receptive to accommodation than tribes indigenous to Wisconsin that first confronted settlers in the nineteenth century.

The testimonials were by Pearl Archiquette, Ellen Hill, and Ferdinand Palladeau. Ambiguous in their nature, these publications affirm Indian student voices and the value WMF placed on them, while also testifying to mission work and legitimacy, as the students express their gratitude, appeal for support, and convey their accommodation.

Archiquette, whose testimonial was published in 1921, described herself as entering the Bethany School in 1913 at the age of eleven, spending three years there, receiving secular and religious instruction, and claiming her confirmation day to be the "greatest day for me." At Haskell, by contrast, she learned many things, academic and industrial, but not "to love Jesus." She reported on changed attitudes among Indians, asserting, "Older Indians are [now] really very interested in the work." Her gratitude emphasized the instruction "in all things pertaining to good Christian citizenship."[70] Archiquette accommodated but also discriminated, explaining subtle differences: institutional ones, among Indian schools; temporal ones in the attitudes of elders; and cultural ones in her accommodations to Western culture. In the process she does not deny her Indian identity, aligning herself with "my people the Indian race."[71] Rather than seeing Archiquette as a victim of cultural imperialism who lacks agency, one might interpret her term "Christian citizenship" as her affirmation not only of agency but also of her people. Such an accommodation permits survival and affirms her construction of Indian identity.

Ellen Hill, writing while a student at the Normal School in Canton,

South Dakota, conveyed similar sentiments in her testimonial, published in 1922: she contrasted Bethany with the government school and expressed her gratitude. Like Archiquette's narrative, Hill's is one of progress, good works, and success. Her continuing education confirms accommodation. In her gratitude, she refers to Bethany workers as "God's own people of the Norwegian Lutheran people of America."[72] Naming the ethnic and religious formation, Hill suggests the possibility of a complex ethnic identity for Indians also. Ferdinand Palladeau's pamphlet, published in 1931, reflects similar patterns: experience, gratitude, appeal for support, and affirmation of Indian and Christian identity. Together, the three testimonials constitute evidence that Indians define themselves as Christians. They also reconstruct identities. While they may reproduce prevailing views, the students reconstruct themselves as Indians, as Christians, and as citizens—that is, as complex persons with multiple identities not perceived as contradictory. The testimonials also help construct complex subjectivities in the readers. Though the Indian students may be read as racial others, because they identify as Christians, readers must confront commonalities. Furthermore, specific histories and identities humanize the students and challenge prevailing stereotypes. Though racial constructions seem to legitimize the settler-colonists' occupation of the land, the testimonies give witness to the real history of the occupied land and challenge simple, dualistic interpretations.

The WMF published one biography of a Bethany student, entitled "The Model Christian Matron: Nancy Smith Palladeau." Part of the series begun in 1937 entitled "Little Library of Lutheran Biography," the Palladeau biography represented the fruit of Bethany and home missions.[73] The inclusion in the series of two indigenous women (domestic and foreign) with four mission workers posits an ideal of affinities that crossed national and racial boundaries—an ideal Christian community of women that challenged racist constructions. Certainly that image is not unproblematic, blurring Christian with Western and an idealized, middle-class American.[74] In many ways the tensions of the mission and the empire converge in the portrait of Palladeau, representing domestication of the foreign within, yet the portrait also posits a vision of "spiritual solidarity," or "Christian citizenship," that transcends racial and national categories.

The biography of Palladeau was written by Mrs. Ernest W. Sihler (nee Mabel Wold, born in China to Norwegian Haugean Synod parents called to mission work). Sihler served with her husband at Bethany from 1935 to 1955, living and working closely with Indian families, sharing their lives and worlds. Organizing Palladeau's life into four parts ("Early Life," "Marriage," "Matron at the Mission," and "Closing Years"), Sihler emphasizes the image of her subtitle: "Christian Indian woman . . . [and] much loved matron at the Bethany Indian Mission."[75] Nancy Smith Palledeau (1878–1932), one of the first children at the mission, came to represent it, and the construction of her life represented the mission work.

Sihler quickly establishes the confluence of Palladeau's life and the mission: one of the first pupils, arriving at the age of ten in 1888, Palladeau grew with the mission. Four years later, she was confirmed and continued school through eighth grade.[76] She excelled in music, sport, and sewing and became a seamstress and baker at the mission. Palladeau is described as she appears in a photograph taken when she was sixteen: "She is dressed in the fashion of '94 . . . [and] looks quite as stylish and pretty as the attractive Norwegian girl with whom she was photographed."[77] While whiteness seems the standard of beauty here, the comparison also aims to evoke "equality" between Indian and Norwegian. The ambiguous and contested image of Palladeau suggests both an awareness of otherness and an effort to posit sameness.[78] Part two addresses her marriage to another Bethany student, William Palladeau, and foregrounds domestic life.[79] As a wife, Palladeau is described as a devoted homemaker, a "splendid housekeeper," "expert canner" with "well-stocked shelves," but also "fastidious about her own appearance." While secular, middle-class American values prevail, Palladeau also joined the Ladies' Aid of the Lutheran Church and was a member of the Mission Circle.[80] The implication that middle-class American values coincide with Christian values further illuminates the tensions between empire and mission, while Sihler's observations reveal Palladeau's accommodation to her dual worlds. Sihler, raised in China by Norwegian Lutheran missionaries and forced to accommodate to multiple cultures, inevitably recognized and admired that capacity in Palladeau.

Part three of the biography addressed Palladeau, the "Matron at the Mission." If her marriage signified domesticity, this period signified service. In 1905 both Palladeaus began working at the Bethany School—he as an instructor of carpentry; she as a matron.[81] The matron assisted the young Bethany children, tending to their physical, emotional, and spiritual needs. Palladeau was good with them, Sihler asserts, especially sensitive to the homesick and often making special food. This closeness to the students led directly to the "closing years" and her tragic death. In the winter of 1932 a scarlet fever epidemic ravaged the mission, touching all sixty of the girls who were enrolled, but Palladeau nursed everyone back to health. Nonetheless, as a result of her exertion she contracted pneumonia and died on March 3, 1932. Buried at the Bethany Indian Mission cemetery in Wittenberg alongside immigrant workers, Palladeau becomes one with them. Sihler writes of her as loving, wise, and comforting, concluding, "Her valuable life had been sacrificed for the sick children to whom she had given of herself unsparingly."[82] Palladeau's life and sacrificial death represented the model Indian. Anne McClintock, writing on the British empire, explores the way women are "ambiguously placed on the imperial divide" (as nurses, nannies, servants) and thus "served as boundary markers and mediators," making them "dangerously ambiguous and contaminating."[83] Indeed, Palladeau's position was ambiguous, mediating between the Indian pupils and the mission; yet she seemed neither "contaminating" nor "dangerous." Palladeau lived and died within these ambiguous spaces of the Bethany Indian Mission in Wittenberg, Wisconsin—between an American empire and her own ancestral worlds—and embraced the contradictory identities on that divide as Oneida Indian, as Christian woman, as model citizen.

CONCLUSION

The literature of the WMF focused on the Bethany Indian Mission presented to its readers in communities of immigrants or settler-colonists what the federation believed to be "a correct presentation of the mission field." With the institutions of the church and state acting as facilitating structures and authoritative bodies sanctioning this presentation, the WMF generated a conceptual map of the new world in which the foreign Americanizes the indigenous in ironic reversals. The mission workers, like mothers, provided Indians, like children, gifts of uplift and instruction in godly ways, as they also occupied this new land and empire as naturally and inevitably (they thought) as their mission to civilize Indians. In this way the mission and the WMF served not only the propagation of the Gospel, but also the national goals of Americanizing Indians, dispossessing them of land, and securing the American empire. Yet in their positions as caretakers and imperial instruments, they also acted as mediators (observers and reporters) of the disastrous effects of federal policies and racial thinking. In that role they inevitably also advanced Western imperialism by persuading themselves of their benevolence and cultural superiority. This central ambiguity illuminates the complex relationships that existed between immigrant settler-colonists and indigenous peoples in sustaining the American empire.

NOTES

1 "The B.I.M.: An Indian's Appreciation, Pearl Archiquette (An Oneida Indian)" (Minneapolis: WMF Literature Committee, 1921), 2. For the term *settler colonist*, see Michael Adas, "From Settler Colony to Global Hegemon: Integrating the Exceptionalist Narrative of the American Experience into World History," *American Historical Review* 106, no. 5 (2001), 1692–1720, and Annie E. Coombes, ed. *Rethinking Settler Colonialism: History and Memory in Australia, Canada, Aotearoa New Zealand and South Africa* (Manchester: Manchester University Press, 2006).

2 Vine Deloria Jr. and Clifford M. Lytle, *American Indians, American Justice* (Austin: University of Texas Press, 1983), 220–21. Deloria and Lytle note that during the allotment period "citizenship became a ceremonial event, something akin to religious conversion," symbolizing the determination of individuals "to cast aside traditions and customs and assume the dress, values, and beliefs," of the larger society.

3 See, for example, Vine Deloria Jr., "Missionaries and the Religious Vacuum," *For This Land: Writings on Religion in America* (New York: Routledge, 1999), 22–30. Originally published in Vine Deloria Jr., *Custer Died for Your Sins: An Indian Manifesto* (New York: Simon and Schuster, 1969).

4 Deloria, "Missionaries and the Religious Vacuum," 22.

5 See Robert F. Berkhofer Jr., *The White Man's Indian: Images of the American Indian from Columbus to the Present* (New York: Vintage Books, 1979), especially, part 4. For a survey of U.S. Indian policy, see Deloria and Lytle, *American Indians, American Justice.*

6 Berkhofer, *The White Man's Indian,* 135.

7 Thomas R. Hietala, *Manifest Design: American Exceptionalism and Empire,* rev. ed. (Ithaca: Cornell University Press, 2003), 255.

8 Amy Kaplan, *The Anarchy of Empire in the Making of U.S. Culture* (Cambridge, Mass.: Harvard University Press, 2002).

9 The Supreme Court declared Indians "domestic dependent nations" in its deci-

sion in *Cherokee Nation v. the State of Georgia* in 1831. See *Major Problems in American Foreign Relations*, vol. 1, ed. Dennis Merrill and Thomas G. Paterson (New York: Houghton Mifflin, 2000), 201–3.

10 The term *cultural imperialism* is often defined as "the use of political and economic power to exalt and spread the values and habits of a foreign culture at the expense of a native culture"; cited in John Tomlinson, *Cultural Imperialism* (Baltimore: Johns Hopkins University Press, 1991), 3. Tomlinson's book explores the problems surrounding the term, identifying *cultural imperialism* as a "politically and intellectually problematic" expression (among the "essentially contested concepts," a description used by the British theorist W. B. Gallie). These contested concepts, as Tomlinson writes, cannot be isolated from their discursive contexts or the "real processes" to which the concepts relate (4).

11 See, for example, Rob Kroes, "American Empire and Cultural Imperialism: A View from the Receiving End," *Rethinking American History in a Global Age*, ed. Thomas Bender, 295–313 (Berkeley: University of California Press, 2002).

12 Earlier treaties with Sauk, Fox, Ottawa, Potawatomi, Menominee, and Winnebago had already ceded much of what became Wisconsin Territory.

13 Robert C. Nesbit, *Wisconsin: A History*, 2d ed. rev., ed. Wm. F. Thompson (Madison: University of Wisconsin Press, 1989 [1973]), 157–58. Germans were the largest.

14 Nancy Oestreich Lurie, *Wisconsin Indians* (Madison: State Historical Society of Wisconsin, 2002 [1965]), 15.

15 More specifically: (1) Oneida and Stockbridge were formally removed to Wisconsin from the East; (2) other eastern tribes (Stockbridge-Munsee, Brotherton, and Potawatomi) migrated from the East into Wisconsin; (3) indigenous tribes (Sauk, Fox, Kickapoo and Santee Sioux, some Winnebago) relocated west of the Mississippi; and (4) other indigenous tribes (Menominee, Ho-chunk, and Ojibwe) resisted removal and were permitted to remain. By the time of the Indian Homestead Act of 1875, Wisconsin Indians could claim land in ancestral regions. See Lurie, *Wisconsin Indians*.

16 Lurie, *Wisconsin Indians*, ix.

17 Lurie, *Wisconsin Indians*, 36–37, and Janet A. McDonnell, *The Dispossession of the American Indian, 1887–1934* (Bloomington: Indiana University Press, 1999), vii. Lurie refers to this as the "great Indian land grab," 36.

18 Bethany Indian Mission pamphlets and synod minutes convey similar histories. The Homme Homes still serve these populations in Shawno County.

19 "Bethany Indian Mission (Lutheran) at Wittenberg, WI 1884-date," typed manuscript. History and Publicity Notebook 1, ELCA Region Three Archives, Luther Seminary, St. Paul, Minnesota.

20 A. E. Morstad, "Erik Morstad's Missionary Work Among Wisconsin Indians," *Norwegian American Studies* 27 (1977), 114. Initial skepticism emphasized the difficulties of such a project: other Lutheran synods (Augustana and Missouri)

started Indian missions but gave up, providing evidence that it was difficult to minister to nomadic peoples and to find a minister for this work.

21 Committee Minutes, in *A Brief History of the Bethany Indian Mission at Wittenberg, Wisconsin*, 4, June 25, 1944. Published for the 60th Anniversary Program. Luther Seminary, St. Paul, Minnesota. Also cited in Morstad, "Missionary Work," 114.

22 George E. Tinker, *Missionary Conquest: The Gospel and Native American Cultural Genocide* (Minneapolis: Fortress Press, 1993), 125n7.

23 Other efforts by the Lutheran synod to develop missions to the Indians are discussed in E. Clifford Nelson, *The Lutherans in North America*, rev. ed. (Philadelphia: Fortress Press, 1980), 72–73, 88–89, 183, 199–200, 283–84.

24 The Indian Reorganization Act of 1934 attempted to restore autonomy to Indian tribes and represented a significant shift in federal Indian policy.

25 Susan Thorne, "Missionary-Imperial Feminism," *Gendered Missions: Women and Men in Missionary Discourse and Practice*, ed. Mary Taylor Huber and Nancy C. Lutkehaus, 40 (Ann Arbor: University of Michigan Press, 1999).

26 Amy Kaplan, "Manifest Domesticity," *American Literature* 70, no. 3 (1998), 581–606.

27 Kaplan, "Manifest Domesticity."

28 L. DeAne Lagerquist, *From Our Mother's Arms: A History of Women in the American Lutheran Church* (Minneapolis: Augsburg Publishing House, 1987), 67.

29 Mrs. T. H. Dahl, "The WMF Pamphlet, 1919," in Convention Program and Reports, vol. 1, 1917–31. Women's Missionary Federation Collection, ELCA Region Three Archives, Luther Seminary, St. Paul, Minnesota.

30 Ibid., 5, 6.

31 Ibid., 11.

32 See Martha Reishus, *Hearts and Hands Uplifted: A History of the Women's Missionary Federation of the Evangelical Lutheran Church* (Minneapolis: Augsburg Publishing House, 1958), 124–38.

33 Report of the Fifth General Convention of the WMF of the NLCA, 1925. Bound vol. 1, WMF, ELCA Region Three Archives, Luther Seminary, St. Paul, Minnesota.

34 The pattern of women's empowerment through organizing is reminiscent of the abolition and the suffrage movements.

35 L. DeAne Lagerquist, *In America the Men Milk the Cows: Factors of Gender, Ethnicity, and Religion in the Americanization of Norwegian American Women* (Brooklyn, N.Y.: Carlson Publishing Inc., 1991), 187. Lagerquist does not discuss the Bethany Indian Mission here, but for a discussion of missionaries, see 185–93.

36 "Minutes of General and Executive Boards," vol. 2, 1918–23, 83. Women's Missionary Federation, ELCA Region Three Archives, Luther Seminary, St. Paul, Minnesota.

37 Mrs. I. D. Ylvisaker, "The President's Reports," 1921, 10. Convention Programs and Reports, vol., 1, 1917–31. Women's Missionary Federation, ELCA Region Three Archives, Luther Seminary, St. Paul, Minnesota.

38 Dahl was active in the Kvindernes Missionsforbund, the missionary society of the United Norwegian Church, formed in 1911. Mrs. Th. Eggen, *Some Marthas and Marys of the NCLA: Life Sketches of Pioneer Lutheran Women First in their Field*, series 1 (Minneapolis: Literature Committee of the W.M.F., n.d.[1929?]), 20. See also Lagerquist, *From Our Mother's Arms*, 54.

39 Mrs. T. H. Dahl, Presidential Report, Women's Missionary Federation of the Norwegian Lutheran Church in America, June 14, 1920, 6; Conventions Programs and Reports, vol. 1, 1917–31. WMF Papers ELCA Region Three Archives, Luther Seminary, St. Paul, Minnesota.

40 A biographer in the 1920s describes her as "a loving and sympathetic mother, a dutiful daughter . . . a busy housewife . . . [and] her husband's loving companion and wonderful helpmeet," found in Eggen, *Some Marthas and Marys*, 23.

41 Mrs. T. H. Dahl, "The Women's Missionary Federation of the Norwegian Lutheran Church of American" (1919), 8. Small pamphlet affixed to Convention Programs and Reports, vol 1, 1917–31. WMF Papers, ELCA and Regions Three Archives. Luther Seminary, St. Paul, Minnesota.

42 Dahl, "The WMF of the NLCA," 1919, 8.

43 The literature committee reported that in 1921 fourteen articles were written in English and Norwegian on home and foreign missions, totaling thirty-four hundred copies of pamphlets; in 1922 there were forty-one thousand copies published. Convention Programs and Reports, vol. 1, 1917–31, bound volume, Women's Missionary Federation, ELCA Region Three Archives, Luther Seminary, St. Paul, Minnesota.

44 The WMF executive board in 1920 was constituted of the wives of the church hierarchy: President, Mrs. T. H. Dahl; Vice President, Mrs. H. G. Stub; Recording Secretary, Mrs. I. D. Ylvisaker; Corresponding Secretary, Mrs. Edward Johnson; and Treasurer, Mrs. M. O. Bockman. Conventions, Programs and Reports, vol. 1, 1917–31. Women's Missionary Federation, ELCA Region Three Archives, Luther Seminary, St. Paul, Minnesota.

45 Paul Daniels, archivist of Luther Seminary Archives and ELCA Region Three Archives, has noted that after the merger in 1917 and resulting tensions, missions became a kind of unifying force within the church.

46 Much has been written about the Americanization movement of the first decades of the twentieth century and the anti-immigrant discourses during the First World War. For effects on Norwegian immigrants, see Carl H. Chrislock, *The Upper Midwest Norwegian-American Experience in World War One* (Northfield, Minn.: Norwegian-American Historical Association, 1981).

47 The three WMF presidents writing pamphlets were Mrs. Ylvisaker (1921), Mrs. Lydia Sundby (1929), and Mrs. Lawrence (1932). The three clergy who wrote were Thorvald Rykken, who served at the mission (and wrote two pamphlets, 1920s and 1931); O. E. Stavland, writing in Norwegian (1931); and Albert Holm, a recent graduate of Luther Theological Seminary (1935). With one exception, these writers were all second-generation Norwegian immigrants.

48 Mrs. I. D. Ylvisaker, "The Bethany Indian Mission," WMF pamphlet, 1921.

49 T. M. Rykken, "Bethany Indian Mission," WMF, n.d. [1920s], 1.

50 Ylvisaker, "The Bethany Indian Mission," 1921, 5.

51 Rykken, "Bethany Indian Mission," 1920s, 7.

52 Much has been written about alienation between Indian children at boarding schools and their relationships with parents and elders upon their return. See, for example, Brenda J. Child, *Boarding School Seasons: American Indian Families, 1900–1940* (Lincoln: Nebraska University Press, 1998).

53 Lydia Bredesen Sundby, "Glimpses of the Bethany Indian Mission," WMF, 1929, 8.

54 Albert H. Holm, "The Red Man for Christ," WMF, 1935. Also see Nancy Shoemaker, "How Indians Got to Be Red," *American Historical Review* 102, no. 2 (June 1997), 625–44.

55 Rykken, "Bethany Indian Mission," 5. Rykken makes clear that the WMF helps to sell these baskets.

56 Sundby, "Glimpses," 2.

57 Ibid., 4. One might add—losing the land again. The policy of taxing Indians for their land was an outgrowth of the policy of assimilation, starting in 1887.

58 Rykken, "Bethany Indian Mission," 1920s, 10.

59 O. E. Stavland, "*Indianer Missionern*, Wittenberg, Wi," WMF, 1931, 7. Author's translation.

60 Mrs. J. Lawrence, "Bethany Indian Mission," 1932.

61 Ylvisaker, "The Bethany Indian Mission," 1921, 5.

62 Rykken, "Bethany Indian Mission," 1920s, 4–5.

63 Ibid.

64 Ibid. He evokes the debate among missionaries on what to teach first, the Gospel or English. C. L. Higham reports that thinking on this changed over time: of course, English was a means to an end for missionaries.

65 Rykken, "Bethany Indian Mission," 1920s, 10.

66 Holm, "The Red Man for Christ," 1935, 14.

67 Carol Devens, *Countering Colonization: Native American Women and Great Lakes Missions, 1630–1900* (Berkeley: University of California Press, 1992), 4, argues that the divided responses often occurred when missions or economics affected men and women differently.

68 Interviews with Eleanor Johnson, Lillian Longtail, and Correne Soldier, May 29, 1998, at Ho-chunk Senior Center and July 9, 2005, Wittenberg, Wisconsin.

69 The Oneidas who moved West were led by Eleazar Williams, part Indian and an Episcopal lay reader; the move was financed by a land company seeking their New York land. The Oneida negotiated for land with Menominees, Winnebagos, and Chippewas in 1823. The present-day Oneida reservation was established in 1838 on part of the tract negotiated in 1823. See Lurie, *Wisconsin Indians*, 11.

70 Pearl Archiquette, 1921, 2.

71 Ibid., 1922, 2.

72 Ellen Hill, "Fruits of the Indian Mission," 1922, 4.

73 WMF Scrapbook, Women's Missionary Federation of the NLCA/ELC, ELCA Region Three Archives, Luther Seminary, St. Paul, Minnesota.

74 See Barbara Welter, "The Cult of True Womanhood," *American Quarterly* 18, no. 1 (1966), 151–74, as well as the large body of literature that emerges from the "productive paradigm" that Kaplan describes in "Manifest Domesticity."

75 Mrs. E. G. W. Sihler, "Nancy Smith Palladeau," WMF, ca. 1938, in series Little Lutheran Biography (Minneapolis: WMF of the NCLA, 1938?).

76 Ibid., 5–8. Palladeau was Oneida, and her mother is described as "well grounded in the teachings of the Episcopal Church" (6); Nancy's husband was raised Catholic. Indigenous Wisconsin tribes (Ho-chunk, Dakota, and Menominee) with less exposure to missionaries were more resistant to Christianity, as is evident in the mission records.

77 Ibid., 11.

78 The paradigm of the nineteenth-century idealized woman includes submission as one of the cardinal virtues. This "virtue" is also present in non–Anglo American cultures, including indigenous ones. See Nancy Shoemaker, *A Strange Likeness: Becoming Red and White in Eighteenth Century North America* (London: Oxford University Press, 2004), esp. 105–24.

79 Sihler, "Palladeau," 12–14. Sihler describes the wedding couple as seen in a photograph: "Palladeaus made a fine looking couple and all the years have proved that they were as fine as they looked."

80 Ibid., 14–15.

81 In 1905 the Palladeaus were employed by the federal government, and in 1918, when the state sold the school, they were transferred to North Dakota. In 1921 they were asked to return to Bethany.

82 Sihler, "Palladeau," 26.

83 Anne McClintock, *Imperial Leather: Race, Gender and Sexuality in the Colonial Contest* (New York: Routledge, 1995), 48.

Competing Models at the Door of Hope Mission in Shanghai

Sue Gronewold

In 1929 there was an important change at the Door of Hope Mission, a nondenominational rescue mission established in 1900 by Anglo-American missionaries in the International Settlement of Shanghai to save Chinese prostitutes. The bride doll, the most popular doll in a series made and sold at the mission since 1902, was updated. The traditional bride, in her red embroidered dress with beaded headgear hiding her face, was replaced by a more modern bride with a stylish hat that allowed her face to show.[1] Representing a month's careful work by trained residents of the Door of Hope, these dolls constitute material metaphors for the mission's reconstruction of girls. However, they can also be seen as embodiments of the multiple messages about womanhood presented to young Chinese women at the mission. By the 1930s, the dolls were being altered to conform to new icons of a changing China.

The Door of Hope, a mission to marginals in the semicolonial treaty port of Shanghai, stood in an uneasy relationship to its many worlds: elite Chinese officials and reformers, foreign treaty port businessmen and administrators, Anglo-American missionaries, Japanese imperialists, Christians increasingly divided between modernists and fundamentalists, and lower- and working-class Chinese women and their families who used the mission to further their own agendas. Located among the competing empires and nations that these worlds represented, the mission struggled, negotiating its own way to "save and transform, not merely reform" young

Chinese women and girls. In this essay I explore the multiple paths that emerged at the mission to satisfy the many kinds of women within and the many competing kingdoms without.

Beginning in the 1890s and intensifying in the 1920s and 1930s, debates about a New Woman were part of the dominant discourse around the world. In the West, the New Woman came to be linked to modern times—featured in mass media as both subject and consumer; symbolizing increasing physical, sexual, and political freedom; demanding full citizenship and equality with men.[2] Not surprisingly, the New Woman precipitated political, social, cultural, economic, and religious anxiety.

In China, the New Woman (*Nu Hsing*) was also highly contested. Born of the late imperial reform movement of 1898 and incubated during the last decade of the Ch'ing dynasty, the New Woman reached full flower in the great cultural revolution that began in 1919. In this so-called May 4th Era, Chinese were called upon to reject the failed past represented by the Confucian tradition, with its emphasis on the patriarchal, hierarchical extended family. There was deep concern about the fate of Republican China, a new nation emerging out of an old empire in an era of foreign imperialism, and about women's proper place within it.[3]

Missions such as the Door of Hope presented ideals and images somewhat at variance with dominant national discourses. Unlike institutions for elite Chinese women, the Door of Hope was established expressly for poor and needy women mired in "a sea of suffering," women whose life chances and choices were fundamentally different from elites targeted by other institutions.[4] It differed from other institutions for women in that both its staffing and support at home and abroad were dominated by evangelical Christians who had their own vision of the New Woman (although they would never have used the term) in what they envisioned as a saved and transformed Christian China. Chinese communities both inside and outside the mission had their own views about new but appropriate roles for poor young women. At the Door of Hope, Western imperial views and religious beliefs were joined and mediated by Chinese traditions of desirable womanhood at a time when both city and nation were undergoing great changes.

In what had been the exclusive British Concession after the Anglo-Chinese Opium War, rising U.S. influence created a truly international settlement in semicolonial Shanghai run by a multinational Municipal

Council and Mixed Court. The Door of Hope's symbiotic relationship with these institutions—the court remanded "wayward girls" to its care and the council granted a thousand dollars a year plus use of the mission as the women's jail, reform school, and welfare home—prompted a guidebook in the 1930s to label the mission "an arm of the state" in "the most cosmopolitan city in the world."[5] Indeed, for the approximately thirty-five thousand foreign residents of more than seventeen nationalities to whom extraterritoriality had granted privileged access to the best homes, businesses, clubs, and playing fields in this enclave, life was very different from that of the nearly one million Chinese crowded into the concession who lived their lives as second-class citizens.[6]

Both national and competing imperial events intruded on this myopic vision. The forging of a new Chinese national identity in the fire of anger over unequal treaties of the mid-nineteenth century and the imperial "melon slicing" of the late nineteenth century fueled anti-imperialist reactions during the early twentieth century, from strikes and boycotts to antimissionary actions. A series of events, from the Kuomintang's (KMT) Northern Expedition of 1927 to the Japanese bombing of Shanghai in 1932 and renewed hostilities between China and Japan in 1937, caused tremendous turmoil in Shanghai, as did the Japanese occupation that was complete by 1942. During the Nanking Decade, from 1927 to 1937, in between periods of open military conflict, the relatively small area of China actually controlled by the KMT (Nationalists) experienced the full force of its experiments in new government and society.[7] Central China in general, and Shanghai in particular—with a Nationalist government in charge of the greater Shanghai Chinese city and an International Concession dominated by the KMT's foreign allies—was the best test case of the new regime, as it tried to remake China and in the process create new Chinese men and women. But what did these New Women look like? What new visions for women were projected at the Door of Hope in 1920s and 1930s Shanghai?

SAVING CHINA, SAVING OURSELVES:
GENDER RELATIONS IN REPUBLICAN CHINA

The dominant voices at the mission belonged to two overlapping groups: evangelical Christians, both Chinese and Western, and Nationalist Chinese in positions of social and political power. If the Christians represented Anglo-American empire, secular and sacred, the Nationalists spoke for the new Chinese nation. The beliefs of both groups about woman's role and work shaped their approaches to uplifting young Chinese women.

Suffer the Little Children: Evangelicalism and Gender Relations

The Door of Hope was established in 1900 by an ecumenical group of women missionaries in Shanghai united in their concern with social purity, the need for vigilance, and their desire to rescue women from the "sins of others." By the 1930s, however, the Door of Hope had virtually been taken over by the evangelical China Inland Mission (CIM), headquartered in Shanghai.[8] Firmly nondenominational and a true faith mission (no direct solicitation of funds, equal work for men and women, a focus on conversion rather than on social work)[9], the CIM by 1920 was the third largest mission organization in China, focusing on common people in China's interior. Many of its administrators, traveling evangelists, and missionaries worked, volunteered, and donated time and money to the Door of Hope.

The work of the CIM at the Door of Hope opens a window onto its beliefs about relations between men and women, their roles and restrictions, and, even more important, about the interrelationship between gender, race, and class in a Chinese context.[10] The founder of the CIM, Hudson Taylor, firmly believed in using men and women alike in mission work. The CIM was the first mission organization to send unmarried women missionaries to the interior and give them full responsibility to open and staff mission stations. The CIM was home to large numbers of strong women, including powerful evangelists like Margaret King. Yet women had no power within the exclusively male administration of CIM. Women had responsibility and autonomy in the field, but within an institutional framework of dependence and subordination. Throughout the 1920s repeated calls by women for representation on the major decision-making bodies were rejected.[11]

Male administrators justified a limited role for women in the CIM as a matter of economics. A bigger administrative role for women, they reasoned, would have required higher levels of support since women, having ostensibly greater susceptibility to illness and homesickness, tended to cost the mission more. The women's physical examination form, for example, was much longer than the men's and paid considerable attention to what was baldly called women's "uterine function."[12] Women had to be carefully watched and controlled in this profoundly patriarchal para-church organization.[13]

CIM views of Chinese women added racism and imperialism to the already complicated patriarchy. For evangelicals, the main attribute of Chinese women was their supposed heathenness and idolatrous ways. In their view, women were far more susceptible to and responsible for per-petuating popular religion, for prostrating themselves before the "gilded Goddess of Mercy." CIM literature, like much missionary writing, con-stantly portrayed Chinese women as downtrodden, dark, and limited in mobility, education, and esteem. The kingdom of Christ literally lightened and whitened them.[14] "Woman's work for woman" was necessary to reach the women and children of China and "bring them into the light." Vic-timized "girls" represented more than the CIM's best test case; they repre-sented China itself, a China that had been feminized and infantilized at the Door of Hope, born again, and transformed. The girls who produced new Chinese women and girl dolls in this period reinforced the image of remade and reborn China and Chinese womanhood.

Mary Ryan has argued that "woman's work" involved women oppress-ing other women of another class, and other scholars have argued that middle-class Victorian women were effectively trying to colonize working-class women at home.[15] But class relations at the Door of Hope were different from those of many other mission projects. This mission relied on religious women who themselves were often of the working class to work with poor and marginalized women of China. For evangelicals at the Door of Hope, racism and colonialism more than class defined Chinese women as the other. Still, for these women, working in such a mission in China was qualitatively different from proselytizing in the Lower East Side of New York or the East End of London. At the Door of Hope, by the 1920s and 1930s, racist, imperial beliefs about women and mission were set, and new Chinese Christian women were evangelicals' Chinese success story.

Feminine, Not Feminized: The New Woman in KMT China

The beliefs about Chinese womanhood held by evangelical foreign mis-sionaries were not the only ideas prevailing at the Door of Hope. A vigorous debate among Chinese women added diverse visions of womanhood.[16] An early image of the New Woman was the modern girl of the early May 4th movement who cast off family and Confucian restraints to work for marriage reform, the abolition of polygamy, concubinage, and prostitution, female employment in the public sector, and legal reforms that would guarantee women's suffrage and property rights.[17] Yet while images of the New Woman initially celebrated her new freedom and release from China's patriarchal past, they came to be linked to both frivolous new temptations and new urban risks. One of the most popular films of the 1930s, *New Woman* (*Hsin nu-hsing*), offered a cautionary tale of an independent young schoolteacher-writer who, abandoned by her lover, ends up with an illegitimate child and commits suicide, the only action which allowed women to "atone for transgressing the boundaries of their gender."[18]

A second image of the modern woman, one promoted in cities and colleges, was the international image of the New Woman connected in the West to schooling and suffrage, the modern girl in the public arena—in offices and professions, newspapers, New Women's journals, and radio. Introduced during the Reform Movement of 1898, it developed and thrived in urban areas of China in the twenties and thirties; however, the Chinese version of Ibsen's Nora was not completely divorced from her traditional role of self-sacrifice. In the view of a Chinese Christian writer, the New *Chinese* Woman combined "what is best in China and supplement[ed] it with the best from the West. . . . Then will she be able to . . . make the best use of those desirable old Chinese ideals such as maternal love and wifely devotion." To be modern and Chinese (and sometimes Christian) was not easy, but many Chinese women's writings were cautiously confident, asserting that "a new day has dawned for Chinese women."[19]

Yet the educated women who were writing these words did not touch on the experiences or the likely futures of the lower-class women who passed through the Door of Hope. Chinese Communists offered an alternate set of images which called upon these women to stand up, speak out, and "serve the nation." With their direction of nonelite, mostly rural women's energies into women's federations, cooperatives, and other mass organizations, the Communists experimented with new social models throughout the 1920s and 1930s. In both city and countryside, educated women were key actors in the Chinese Communist Party, devoted to changing China through political revolution. They recognized that poor urban women were different from the commercialized, urban New Woman, yet tended to conflate them with urban males in their exhortations to organize along class lines.[20] In all probability, some of the women who came to the Door of Hope had been exposed to Communist thought, with its rhetoric of equality and its images of new, heroic revolutionary women proudly serving the new nation.

The Nanking Decade, however, marked the ascendancy of Chiang Kai-shek and the KMT in east central China. Confronted by Communist and Japanese imperial rivals for power, Chiang fashioned a new-style campaign to unite and improve the country. Equal parts Confucianism, Christianity, and militarism, this campaign to socially and morally rejuvenate China was dubbed the New Life Movement (*Hsin sheng-huo yuntung*) and was promulgated in cities and villages throughout China beginning in 1934.[21] The New Life Movement resurrected ancient Confucian virtues of propriety, loyalty, integrity, and honor and gave them a modern twist.[22]

A central figure in this new campaign was Madame Chiang Kai-shek. Although she appeared to epitomize the New Woman of urban China—educated abroad, powerful, independent, and wealthy—Madame Chiang functioned as the major spokesperson for her husband's New Life Movement. Directly challenging radical reformist and revolutionary minded political activists, she urged women to eschew politics in favor of using their roles as helpmates to aid in the regeneration of China, to care for "warphans," and to behave in decorous and modest ways. Madame Chiang threw herself into the reform of domestic habits—encouraging orderliness, cleanliness, simplicity, and frugality—and traveled around China promoting training programs to teach women literacy, public health, and technical skills. While emphasizing the traditional virtues of wives, mothers, and the household arts in the countryside and among the urban poor, she encouraged middle-class women like herself to develop a sense of social responsibility and found local movements for New Life rather than waste their time as "social parasites and butterflies."[23] Yet the campaign had little focus and insufficient funds. It is usually presented as degenerating in rural areas into public lectures about the dangers of flies and dirt and in cities into condemnations of cabarets and cigarettes, hair curling, and short, tight dresses.[24] Looked at more seriously in terms of its inherent messages, the New Life Movement offered women a careful update of traditional roles which would enable them to negotiate these new times in the building of a new nation—and inoculate them from the powerful revolutionary appeals of Chinese Communists. To poor urban women (and missionaries who were intent on molding them), it seemed an appropriate, accessible message.

Many Chinese intellectuals and students greeted the New Life Movement with skepticism and scorn. Crucial to the campaign were the aid and support of Chinese and Western evangelicals.[25] CIM missionaries became vocal proponents of the New Life Movement in their publications, rural outstations, and urban institutions such as the Door of Hope. Madame Chiang openly appealed to evangelicals, and her husband chose them to head local projects.[26] Both Madame Chiang and her mother were mainline Methodists (as was General Chiang after he publicly converted in 1929) and donated funds to the Door of Hope. They visited it in Shanghai, modeling the new path of service urged on urban elite women. For the New Life Movement, the Door of Hope served multiple purposes: it offered proper charity work for urban elite and middle-class women and produced docile women workers for the nation while satisfying Western imperialists.

The New Life Movement demonstrates the congruence of the beliefs about womanhood preferred by evangelicals and conservative Nationalists. Both wanted newness, not modernity, and thought the future of China rested upon the capacity of its women to become frugal, responsible wives, mothers, and workers.[27] In this context, the girls transformed at the Door of Hope were not marginals. Instead, they fit into the new social order as a necessary component and were encouraged to be obedient yet disciplined, dependent yet productive, dedicated to serving the needs of the new modern nation. Women, nation, imperialism, mission— all were conjoined in making new lives at the Door of Hope, just as its girls made new Chinese women dolls.

NEW LIVES FOR REMADE WOMEN:
THREE PATHS FOR THE FAITHFUL

Three roles for Chinese women were promulgated at the Door of Hope and illustrated in the dolls they manufactured: first, the wife and helpmate constructing a wholesome Christian home; second, and most likely, the disciplined and obedient Christian worker given skills useful in domestic or factory work; third, available only to a few, the Chinese Christian missionary and evangelist. In the 1920s and 1930s these models took on a different cast, one at variance with both the urban New Woman and the Communist robust worker but congruent with Chiang's New Life models and the mission's—and nation's—newly evangelical lower- and working-class women.

A Doll's House: The Construction of Christian Brides

The model of marriage was presented at the Door of Hope in a number of ways, not all of them verbal. The Door of Hope's frontline institution was its Receiving Home in the heart of the brothel district.[28] It was decorated with eight scrolls painted by a Chinese artist and given to the home in its first decade by Shen Tun-ho, a prominent Chinese official and strong supporter of the mission. The scrolls, seen by all who entered, depicted a girl's life as she progressed from being sold to a brothel by her parents during a famine, to escaping and running away to the mission, receiving the Word and converting, living and learning at the mission, and finally, in the mission's very own fairy tale, marrying a Chinese Christian man and setting up a Christian home.[29]

Perhaps the loudest nonverbal messages about womanhood and marriage, however, came from the dolls sewn in the First Year Home, the required residence for older girls brought or remanded to the mission. A central and symbolic part of their training was the sewing of exquisite, realistic dolls that portrayed an array of Chinese social types.[30]

The first dolls made and sold included a traditional bride and groom, a nursemaid with two babies, a Manchu lady with her distinctive dress, a mourner in funeral garb, a boy with tunic and trousers, an elderly gentleman of high rank, and a policeman. By 1922, new models included a grandmother and grandfather in modest traditional dress, a widow in plain garb, a farmer complete with grass raincoat, a Buddhist priest with long gown, and an upper-class family consisting of a wife and husband with two children, a schoolgirl and a small boy. During the twenties and thirties, over forty different dolls were produced.[31] The dolls reflected the ways in which missionaries wanted to portray Chinese society. (Dolls were often sent to donors.)[32] They also suggested multiple meanings to girls who lived at the mission.

The dolls represented attainment of a certain level of skill, combining knitting, stitching, embroidering, and other fine needlework. Girls were not allowed to work on the dolls until they had graduated from basic sewing. The dolls were as true to life as possible, could be dressed and undressed, and were outfitted with realistically detailed undergarments. They represented fine skills useful in the wider world of work and home. The dolls also represented an income, albeit small, in that girls were paid a few cents an hour for their work. They took approximately one month to sew, each girl making no more than a dozen a year. This painstaking process explains why the dolls in the 1930s cost the then-large sum of ten dollars. Probably no more than fifty thousand were made in the fifty-year history of the mission.[33] The prestige of having graduated from basic skills and being able to earn even a small wage was used as an incentive to the girls in the pressured environment of the First Year Home, which, according to one Western observer, "seemed so hard with its early hours, food so regular, sensible clothes, housework, sewing, and industrial work."[34] Just as important as a measure of the girls' skill and as a source of profit (rarely bringing in more than five hundred dollars a year), however, is the dolls' representation of Chinese society.[35] Their didactic messages had to do with the proper course of one's life; the proper observations of rituals and rites; the proper ordering of society from farmer to official, servant to wealthy couple. In the dolls, the whole panoply of ranks and life stages was laid out before the girls. Important in this regard were the most popular dolls, the bride and groom, particularly the bride doll.[36]

One of the most powerful messages was that the proper course of life involved marriage. In this respect, missionary values reinforced rather than conflicted with Chinese gender roles.[37] But the expectations for the girls at the mission to marry "well" did conflict with the girls' realities. Whereas young women of the poorest classes in Chinese society would have been expected to marry, their husbands would most likely have been equally poor. Just as likely, their parents would not have been able to negotiate a regular marriage for them but would have accepted instead some variant, perhaps an adopted daughter-in-law or a concubine arrangement. For girls at the mission, marrying a respectful, Christian husband was nothing short of miraculous.[38] Missionaries exploited that desire to achieve compliant behavior.

The prospect of marriage was the students' motivation to concentrate and learn to read so as to be able to effectively proselytize with one's

Christian husband. Marriage was the reason to learn to wield a needle and produce dolls and doilies, lace, and knitted wear. Marriage was the incentive in the Industrial Home to bend over the embroidery frame eight hours a day for many years. The afternoon classes at the First Year Home, where girls were shown how to make Chinese garments and knitting, were considered "all important for Chinese women and mothers." Marriage was the future which made acceptable the constraints of the home. Girls who ran away, were deceitful, or stole were reprimanded by telling them that they might lose their chance to marry.[39]

The message about marriage had not altered in the 1920s and 1930s. What had changed was the image of women as seen in the revamped bride doll. Her dress was quite traditional and she was still paired with a man, yet there is a hint of the new in her rounder, more Western eyes and modern hair decoration that no longer covered her face. Significantly, she no longer had the bound feet of traditional elite women. Like the bride dolls, girls at the mission were being re-formed into new kinds of Chinese women.

Working for Christ: Constructing Christian Workers

Almost all the girls from the mission eventually married, but the number of young women who left as Christian brides was never as large as the mission hoped.[40] Other paths, therefore, had to be presented to the majority. Although most who returned to their families probably married non-Christians, Door of Hope sources and curricula did not address this possibility, nor did they address the certainty that, given their class, the majority who exited, married or not, also needed skills for work. So much time at the Door of Hope was spent on needlework because work outside the home—domestic positions or factory jobs—was the likely fate of most young women leaving the mission. According to a survey conducted in 1929 by the Bureau of Social Affairs in Shanghai, 61 percent of the industrial workforce in Shanghai was female and most were concentrated in textile work.[41] The mission sources are opaque on this point; they state only that "positions were found" for some. Interviews with former residents confirmed that some found childcare positions inside private homes, but the dozen elderly women I interviewed in 1998 wanted to make it clear that girls from the Door of Hope had promising futures. "*No one* from the Door of Hope became just a maid," they told me proudly.[42]

Given the structure of employment in Shanghai during this period, most young women who left the Door of Hope probably returned to their neighborhoods and worked in jobs that used their skills. These skills also made them more attractive wives to working-class men, both as home-makers and wage earners. The continual use of the mission by Chinese families seems to bear this out.[43]

Girls and young women at the Door of Hope were known to the world as skilled seamstresses. By 1910, their fine needlework at the mission was exhibited in an exposition in Shanghai and other large cities in China. The annual report of 1940 exulted that "it really is a wonderful thing that girls who cannot even hold a needle when they come to us can learn in a few months to do such fine work . . . that later they can do the finest embroi-dered tea cloths, ladies lingerie and dainty baby dresses that win the admiration of ladies." By 1913, the young women had become so proficient in sewing that a regular Chinese teacher was employed for the embroidery frames and another woman had four pupils in a lace-making class. The young Pearl Buck briefly worked at the mission as a lace teacher. Con-centration on fine needlework paid off, as the wider Shanghai community used the services of these seamstresses more and more. By 1914 it was claimed that the Industrial Home was generally self-supporting and by 1921 it was entirely so, making an annual profit that was at least double that earned from the dolls.[44]

The mission inculcated more than just skills, as is apparent from its photographs of docile, disciplined residents—qualities also prized by in-dustrial employers. By 1934, the Door of Hope claimed that the "lessons learned while embroidering are invaluable in molding the characters of these older girls as they prepare to leave us for homes of their own." At least half of their day was spent in needlework. Yet the lessons in what was called needle discipline were too valuable to leave only for the older residents. Visitors to the mission commented on the quiet concentration of even the littlest residents. The supervisor of the Children's Refuge remarked on her return from furlough in 1927 that what struck her most was the kindergarten with its "50 well-trained little ones," who began their mornings by marching to their appointed places and doing activities that tested their concentration, like paper folding, weaving, and sewing cards.[45]

What was unique about the Door of Hope among mission refuges, most of which had what they called an industrial component, was the relative success of its preindustrial craft workshop. The mission constantly emphasized the links between the kind of work that was done and the Christian message. The production of Christian workers was explicitly stated as a goal, and the desirable qualities of discipline and devotion were reinforced in the religious images presented. "Workers for Christ" was a slogan that applied to them all, and the goal was to promote workers full of "industry and good will."[46] The mission equally served nations and empires, including the kingdom of Christ, in its production of new Chinese women.

Just as I Am, Lord: The Construction of Chinese Christian Missionaries
There was yet a third path presented to the women and girls at the Door of Hope, one appropriate for only a few, although by the late 1920s the number taking that path had increased dramatically: Chinese Christian missionaries. More and more of the young women, the most capable and the most called, advanced to higher-level Bible schools and training institutions, either working elsewhere in the mission field or returning to the Door of Hope. This image of Christian womanhood was embodied by the resident missionaries and Chinese staff members. Projecting their own image as Christian "helpers," teachers, and servers, most of these women did not marry but instead dedicated their lives to living and working for what they saw as a higher purpose. By 1930, nearly all the helpers and "dear Chinese assistants" at the mission had once been young charges in its homes.

The women missionaries who, with their female Chinese helpers, lived in the mission and supervised and performed the day-to-day work there were always a small group; foreign missionaries never exceeded twenty. Perhaps an equal number of Chinese lived and worked in support jobs never accorded the status of the missionaries. By the twenties and thirties, the primarily British and American resident missionaries at the Door of Hope tended to have evangelical backgrounds, come explicitly for rescue work, and stay a long time.[47] Their lengthy tenure symbolized the strength of their faith and their commitment to their work, arduous though it was. As models for the young Chinese residents, these workers presented a high standard of piety, charity, and purity.[48] By and large, they were not young, in robust health, or well educated.[49] Their education beyond high school, if any, was acquired at short-course Bible seminaries and institutes, like Moody Bible Institute in Chicago and Nyack Seminary in New York. Unlike their Methodist, Presbyterian, Episcopal, or even YMCA counterparts, they had not gone to colleges and universities, had not been professionally trained as doctors, teachers, or even social workers. Some had received medical training, but it was as nurses or midwives or even as nurses' assistants; others had worked only in similar rescue or religious missions at home.[50] Many of them were rejected by other mission boards because of their age (over thirty!) or questionable health (Door of Hope waived some of the usual requirements because working in Shanghai was not as arduous as itinerating in the Chinese interior). Many of them represented what one writer called the superfluous and another the "imperial ragbag of unemployed poor," those women for whom work and missionizing abroad offered an opportunity not available at home.[51]

Exemplifying this life pattern was Hattie Bailey, supported by the "Go Ye Bible" class of Paul Rader's Chicago Gospel Tabernacle, who worked at the Door of Hope for nearly three decades. Born in England in 1882, Bailey attended her village school for seven years and then worked for twelve in a dry goods store. She left England for Canada, settling in Calgary, Alberta, where her religious faith led her to mission work. After completing the standard two-year missionary training course at the Moody Bible Institute in Chicago, where she was described as "plain, reliable, steady, sweet, and positive. Will make a good missionary," Bailey, (who was thirty-six years old by then), was discouraged to find that "the door was shut" because of her age. After some correspondence, the mission accepted her, provided she could make her way to China.[52]

Once in China, her way paid by her Young Business Women's Class at the Chicago Tabernacle, Bailey went through intensive language training. Chinese was the language of the mission, and a Chinese lifestyle, including food and clothing, was adhered to as much as possible, another example of the way national and imperial boundaries were constantly crossed at the mission.[53] Like so many others who dedicated their lives to the Door of Hope's brand of rescue work, Bailey had no life outside the mission. Even while on furlough she worked for the mission, doing "deputation" work to spread the message (and to make known the need for funds) in the United States, her adopted homeland. For Chinese girls at the Door of Hope, the model of Christian womanhood presented by a Hattie Bailey was an inspiration for their own lives.

By the 1920s, while much of the mission field reflected the liberal Social Gospel, which stressed education and modernization, the Door of Hope attracted faith and holiness missionaries, who were coming to China in large numbers. For these women, piety still held pride of place. One of the most reliable women to join the mission in the 1920s was Inez Green, thirty-four, an independent missionary who came to live and work at the Door of Hope on her own, supported by her local church in rural southwestern Illinois.[54] In 1925, Green wrote that the Love School "is located five miles from Shanghai just at the edge of a typical native village, and as we pass through its narrow, dirty streets, . . . the faces of men, women, and children alike show signs of the hopelessness of heathenism. . . . How fortunate are we to have been born in a Christian land."[55]

Green's description of rural China touched all the familiar Western evangelical tropes: China was dirty, dark, and dangerous. Only Western missionaries could bring cleansing, light, and the progress of civilization. To missionaries like Green, imperialism was the Lord's work. And yet she was much beloved by many young women at the mission, as they testified to me in the spring of 1998. In a world in which family and filial duty were paramount, the dominant and powerful message of Green's life for these Chinese girls was that she had left her family to be with them. For many, her piety and her life of sacrifice became a model and a keystone for the kind of new Chinese Christian women they hoped to become.

Much of the work at the Door of Hope was not done by the resident missionaries, however, but was delegated to the Chinese staff, from the matron in the receiving home who dealt with each incoming girl to the teachers in the older girls' two homes and the women who lived with the younger girls in the "love cottages" of the Children's Refuge.[56] The homes were successful because of this extensive network, which combined Western missionaries with competent, committed Chinese women. Both the aloof and alien resident missionaries, seen as sacrificing so much for their piety, and the matronly, more approachable Chinese caretakers served as fitting models of a new kind of Chinese Christian woman.

Chinese staff members and their special talents and individual histories can be identified from stories and reports pertaining to the Door of Hope.[57] By 1930, for example, a Mrs. Kung had been working at the Door of Hope for sixteen years. She was married to a man who taught at mission schools, and her life was secure until he suddenly left his job, took on more secular work for higher pay, and gradually changed. He began coming home less frequently, eventually took a "small wife," and set up another house. When Kung became despondent and began gambling, her sister-in-law, Mother Bau, who worked at the Door of Hope, offered her a job there. Kung continued her work at the mission even after her husband's concubine died and he returned home, frequently working at the mission himself.[58] She became a mainstay of the mission, living with her family and working at the Receiving Home, interviewing and caring for the incoming young women.

Many former residents came back to the Door of Hope to work, testifying to the success of the mission in training girls to replicate its work. Their return also indicates the lack of attractive employment options for women in Shanghai and the appeal of working at the mission, particularly for those with some Western education.[59] By the 1930s, most of the Chinese women working in the Door of Hope had been young residents there, many returning from higher-level schools and training programs.[60]

Several young women were inspired by their experience at the Door of Hope Mission to go even further and become missionaries themselves. They worked among the Chinese as "Bible women," traveling evangelists, or they established their own orphanages and philanthropic institutions. In 1936, a "former girl" opened an orphanage for eighty children; another, Peace Chu, became a hospital administrator; a third, Blossom, founded the Home for Destitute Children and Lonely Widows.[61] These girls had been reshaped in the image of the missionary women whose new models of Christian service and authority they followed beyond its portals.

Yet one could argue that by setting up institutions independent of the mission and the Western missionary establishment, these women were in effect serving multiple masters. No longer solely identified with Western empires, they instead put their energies into expanding the kingdom of Christ in the context of an emerging Chinese nation. As is true of so much of the mission's work, it is ultimately unclear whose agenda was most served at the Door of Hope: deracinated missionary women far from home with their vision fixed on a kingdom of God; Western imperialists with their goals of profiting economically, politically, and even spiritually; Chinese Nationalists with their goal of developing a strong, secure—and anti-Communist—China for and by the Chinese; Chinese families attempting to care for their own in hard times. All were served in some fashion by Blossom's orphanage and by Peace Chu's hospital work, and all would claim them as part of the project in fashioning new Chinese Christian women.

Door of Hope missionaries intended to be subversive of Chinese society by advancing "woman's work" for Christ, but they "did more than they intended."[62] Working in Shanghai was not the same as working in San Francisco; in China they had to continually adjust to Chinese realities, and the result was a syncretic mix that was as much Chinese as Western, national as imperial. The fruits of their labors benefited the Chinese nation as much as or more than they did either Western imperialists or the kingdom of God, as continued Nationalist support of the mission attests. From the vantage point of poor Chinese women in Shanghai who lived life on the edge and whose possibilities were limited to relatively unskilled factory work, abusive marriages, brothel work, begging, and hunger at home, the mission did indeed offer a "door of hope."[63] But its hope was neither exclusively Western nor solely Chinese. Like the new Chinese bride doll, the foreign missionaries and Chinese Christians, evangelicals, and Nationalists continually crossed boundaries between competing kingdoms, empires, and nations at the Door of Hope Mission in Shanghai.

NOTES

1 Door of Hope, *Annual Report*, 1929, 1; Door of Hope, *Annual Report*, 1940, 13.

2 There is voluminous literature on the New Woman. See Elaine Showalter, *Sexual Anarchy, Gender, and Culture at Fin de Siècle* (London: Viking, 1990); Sarah Deutsch, *Women and the City: Gender, Space, and Power in Boston* (New York: Oxford University Press, 2000); and Sheila Rowbotham, *A Century of Women: The History of Women in Britain and the United States* (New York: Penguin Books, 1999), chaps. 1–3. For recent work on the New Woman's role in the imperial project, see the articles by Rebecca Stott and Carolyn Burdett in *The New Woman in Fiction and Fact: Fin de Siècle Feminisms*, ed. Angelique Richardson and Chris Willis (New York: Palgrave, 2000).

3 For the New Woman question in China, see Wang Zheng, *Women in the Chinese Enlightenment: Oral and Textual Histories* (Berkeley: University of California Press, 1999), and Louise Edwards, "Policing the Modern Woman," *Modern China* 26, no. 2 (April 2000), 115–47.

4 See, for example, Heidi Ross, " 'Cradle of Female Talent': The McTyeire Home and School for Girls, 1892–1937," *Christianity in China: From the Eighteenth Century to the Present*, ed. Daniel Bays, 209–27 (Stanford: Stanford University

Press, 1996); Judith Liu and Donald P. Kelly, " 'An Oasis in a Heathen Land': St. Hilda's School for Girls, Wuchang, 1928–1936," in Bays, *Christianity*, 228–42; Mary Jo Waelchi, "Abundant Life: Matilda Thurston, Wu Yifang, and Ginling College" (Ph.D. diss., Ohio State University, 2002).

5 *All About Shanghai: A Standard Guidebook* (Shanghai: University Press, 1934–35), 10, 1.

6 Tsou Yijen, *Chiu Shanghai jen-kou pien-chien te yen chiu* (Shanghai, 1980), 133.

7 Lloyd Eastman, *The Abortive Revolution: China under Nationalist Rule, 1927–1937* (Cambridge, Mass.: Harvard University Press, 1974); Marie Claire Bergere, "The Other China: Shanghai from 1919–1949," *Shanghai: Revolution and Development in an Asian Metropolis*, ed. Christopher Howe, 1–34 (Cambridge: Cambridge University Press, 1981). For the range of reforms, see Christian Henriot, *Shanghai 1927–1937: Municipal Power and Modernization* (Berkeley: University of California Press, 1993).

8 Sue Gronewold, "Encountering Hope: The Door of Hope Mission in Shanghai and Taipei, 1900–1976." Unpub. Ph.D.diss., Columbia University, 1996, chap 4.

9 Paul Rader, "Landing in China," *World Wide Christian Courier* (October 29, 1929), 8; Alvyn Austin, "Blessed Adversity," *Earthen Vessels: American Evangelicals and Foreign Missions 1880–1980*, ed. Joel Carpenter, 52–71, 55 (Grand Rapids: Eerdmans, 1990).

10 Rev. G. F. Fitch, *China Mission Yearbook*. See also Rhonda Semple, *Missionary Women: Gender, Professionalism and the Victorian Idea of Christian Mission* (Woodbridge, Suffolk: Boydell Press, 2003), 154–55. For discussions of fundamentalism and gender, see Letha D. Scanzoni and Susan Setta, "Women in Evangelical, Holiness, and Pentecostal Traditions," *Women and Religion in America*, ed. Rosemary Ruether and Rosemary Keller, 223–34 (San Francisco: Harper and Row, 1986); John Hawley, ed., *Fundamentalism and Gender* (New York: Oxford University Press, 1994), particularly the introduction by John Hawley and Wayne Proudfoot, Randall Balmer, "American Fundamentalism," and Laren McCarthy Brown, "Fundamentalism and the Control of Women."

11 China Inland Mission, Toronto Council Minutes 6/23/26; China Council Minutes 3/8/29, CIM correspondence files, Billy Graham Archives, Wheaton, Illinois (hereafter BGCA); *East Asia Millions* (October 1929), 229.

12 CIM application in correspondence files, BGCA, Wheaton.

13 By the 1920s, Bolshevism was added to the "potential hazards of modernism." See Edgar Strother, *Bolshevized China: The World's Greatest Peril* (Shanghai, 1927), esp. "Semi-Nude Girls Are Following Communist Army" and "Naked Body Procession," 14–15. Strother was a CIM missionary.

14 See Miss M. E. Skelelton, "The New Opportunity for Women's Work in China," *Chinese Recorder* (November 1913); Mrs. W. J. Hanna, "Methods for Reaching the Heathen Women of China" in *China's Millions* (1911). For an example of new scholarship on the connection between gender, race, mission, and imperialism, particularly in the post–Civil War South, home to many Door of Hope mission-

aries and supporters, see Edward Blum, *Reforging the White Republic: Race, Religion, and American Nationalism, 1865–1898* (Baton Rouge: Louisiana University Press, 2005), esp. chap. 7, "Global Missions, Religious Belief, and the Making of the Imperial White Republic."

15 Mary Ryan, "The Power of Women's Networks," *Feminist Studies* 5 (Spring 1979), 67; Martha Vicinus, *Victorian Women: Work and Community for Single Women 1850–1920* (London: Virago Press, 1985).

16 See the analysis of the debate by a prominent activist of the 1930s, Lu Yunchang, in Edwards, "Policing," 131–32.

17 For women's roles, see Roxane Witke, "Transformation of Attitudes towards Women during the May Fourth Era" (Ph.D. diss., University of California–Berkeley, 1970), 77–330. Among the many literary representations of women in this era are Ding Ling's early writings. Wendy Larson, "End of 'Funu Wenxue,'" *Gender Politics in Modern China*, ed. Tani Barlow, 68 (Durham: Duke University Press, 1993).

18 See Edwards, "Policing," 128; Kristine Harris, "The New Woman: Image, Subject, and Dissent in 1930s Shanghai Film Culture," *Republican China* 20 (1995), 55–79; Sherman Cochran and Andrew Hsieh, eds., *One Day in China* (New Haven: Yale University Press, 1983), 64–66. For the theme of May 4 female suicide, see "The New Woman Martyrs," *Women in Republican China: A Source Book*, ed. Hua Lan and Vanessa Fong (Armonk, N.Y.: M. E. Sharpe, 1999); and Bryna Goodman, "The New Woman Commits Suicide," *Journal of Asian Studies* 24 (2005), 67–101.

19 Quoted in *Chinese Recorder*, 1926. Also see Wang, *Women and the Chinese Enlightenment*; Pickowicz, "Theme of Spiritual Pollution"; P. S. Tseng, "The Chinese Woman, Past and Present," *Symposium on Chinese Culture*, ed. Sophie Chen, 281–92 (Shanghai: Chinese Institute of Pacific Relations, 1969); Ting Shu-ching, "What Chinese Women Are Doing," *Chinese Christian Yearbook* (1929), 107–11.

20 For women and the Chinese Communist Party, see Christina Gilmartin, *Engendering the Chinese Revolution* (Berkeley: University of California Press, 1995); Elizabeth Croll, *Changing Identities for Chinese Women: Rhetoric, Experience and Self Perception* (New York: Zed Press, 1995); Patricia Stranahan, *Yan'an Women and the Communist Party* (Berkeley: University of California Press, 1983). For a discussion of the conflation of gender and class analysis, see Meng Yue, "Female Images and National Myths," *Gender Politics*, ed. Barlow, 118–36.

21 Chiang, *Hsin sheng huo-yun tung tsu chih* (Nanking, 1935), 216–20. See also Arlif Dirlik, "The Ideological Foundations of the New Life Movement," *Journal of Asian Studies* (August 1975), 945–80; and Pichon Loh, "The Ideological Persuasion of Chiang Kai-shek," *Modern Asian Studies* 4, no. 3 (1970), 211–39.

22 Its impact on women has been little studied. See Elizabeth Croll, *Feminism and Socialism in China* (New York: Schocken, 1980); Norma Diamond, "Women Under KMT Rule: Variations on the Feminine Mystique," *Modern China* 1 (January 1975), 3–45.

23 Mme Chiang Kai-shek, *Messages in Peace and War* (Hankow, 1938).

24 See esp. Croll, *Feminism and Socialism*, 158–77.

25 James Thomson, *While China Faced West: American Reformers in Nationalist China, 1928–37* (Cambridge, Mass.: Harvard University Press, 1969), 171, 189, 195, 227; Charles Hayford, *To the People: James Yen and Village China* (New York: Columbia University Press, 1990); Chang Fuliang, *When East Met West: A Personal Story of Rural Reconstruction in China* (New Haven: Yale University Press, 1972), 42, 53–60.

26 See the speeches of both General and Mme Chiang in her *Messages in Peace and War* (Hankow, 1938) and his "The New Life Movement," in T'ang Leang-li, *Reconstruction in China* (Shanghai, 1935); see also descriptions of the New Life Movement in the *Chinese Recorder*, esp. the issue of May 1937, and George Shepherd Papers, Burke Library, Union Theological Seminary, New York, passim.

27 Other reform institutions also gave conflicting messages about the ideal of marriage and the reality of work. See Kathleen Aiken, "The National Florence Crittendon Mission, 1883–1925 (Ph.D. diss., Washington State University, 1980), chap. 2; Carol Devens, "If We Get the Girls, We Get the Race," *Journal of World History* 3, no. 2 (fall 1992), 219–37.

28 By the 1930s, the mission included a network of affiliated institutions: its Receiving Home, the children's Love School in a nearby suburb, the First Year Home for older residents, an Industrial Home for those who stayed, a hospital, day schools for local children, and preaching halls for sermons and revivals. Because of the growth of the mission and the turmoil in Shanghai, the locations changed over the years.

29 *Women's Work in the Far East* 38 (1917), 213–14.

30 Serious doll collectors know of these dolls. They are also held by museums, from the Field Museum in Chicago and the Newark Museum to the American Museum of Natural History in New York. Also see Web sites like www.lotzdollpages .com/ldoorh.html.

31 Door of Hope, *Annual Report*, 1916, 1922, 1940.

32 One doll sold in 2001 by Skinner auctioneers of Bolton, Massachusetts, retained "the provenance of its original child owner who received the doll through her Sunday School class [which] . . . had sent donations to the Mission which then responded by sending each child in the class a doll" (www.skinnerinc.com/ press, accessed January 10, 2006). Today these dolls sell for six hundred to fifteen hundred dollars.

33 Violet Mathews, *Escaped as a Bird* (Melbourne, Australia: Southland Press, n.d.), 36; Ann Coleman, *Collector's Encyclopedia of Dolls* (New York: Crown Books, 1980), 356–59; Patricia Planton, "The Door of Hope Reopened" in *The Doll Reader* (February/March 1980), 12–13; Patricia Smith, *Doll Values* (Lexington, Ky.: Collectors' Books, 1988), 68; Ashley Wright, "Door of Hope Dolls: A History of Their Origins" (paper); author's interview with Wright, Princeton, N.J., May 1990.

34 C. E. Darwent, *Shanghai: A Handbook for Travellers and Residents* (Shanghai: Kelly and Walsh, 1920), 154.

35 Door of Hope, *Annual Report*, 1926–30, 1938.

36 As I discovered while teaching at the American Museum of Natural History, children and adults alike find these dolls fascinating. Young women at the mission would have learned a great deal from these dolls, their bodies, their costumes, and their roles.

37 For a discussion of what Amy Kaplan calls "manifest domesticity," see her *Anarchy of Empire in the Making of U.S. Culture* (Cambridge, Mass.: Harvard University Press, 2005), 23–50; Patricia Hill, *The World Their Household: The American Women's Foreign Mission Movement and Cultural Transformation 1870–1920* (Ann Arbor: University of Michigan Press, 1984).

38 Maria Jaschok, "Chinese Slave Girls in Yunnan-fu," *Women and Chinese Patriarchy* (London: Zed Books, 1994), 183, argues that for many "the missionaries offered a rare escape route from lives of suffering and neglect."

39 Door of Hope, *Annual Report*, 1933, 9.

40 Estimates varied widely; in 1917 *Women's Work* stated that of a total of fifteen hundred girls only one hundred had married; Paul Rader in "Landing" reported in 1929 that one thousand of four thousand had married; the Door of Hope *Annual Report*, 1936, stated that over two thousand of five thousand had. I suspect that nearly all eventually married, just not at the mission or to Christian men.

41 Emily Honig, *Sisters and Strangers: Women in Shanghai Cotton Mills, 1919–1949* (Stanford: Stanford University Press, 1986), 23–24. See also Eleanor Hinder, *Life and Labor in Shanghai* (New York: YWCA, 1943).

42 My interviews in Shanghai, April 19 and 25, 1998; Mary Chang interview by TEAM's Door of Hope Center missionary Kathryn Merrill, Taipei, 1994. My alumnae informants were proud of their sewing skills; a woman who said she had learned how to knit there wore a sweater she had knitted while at the mission. These women, however, had all been in the Children's Refuge and were not part of the doll-making project. "A Memory of Hope: How Chinese Mission Alumnae Remember/Reinterpret Relations of Rescue," Berkshire Conference on Women's History, 2005.

43 For the uses of such institutions by residents, their families, and local communities, see Michael Katz, *In the Shadow of the Poorhouse: A Social History of Welfare in America* (N.Y.: Basic Books, 1986); Peter Mandlin, ed., *The Uses of Charity: The Poor on Relief in the Nineteenth Century Metropolis* (Philadelphia: University of Pennsylvania Press, 1990).

44 Door of Hope, *Annual Report*, 1910, 1913, 1914, 1921. For examples of Industrial Home proceeds, see ibid., 1929, 1931, 1934.

45 Ibid., 1927. They went on to make shoes and clothes, eventually working for the knitting department on orders from the community. Ibid., 1934, 1940.

46 The link between purity, work, and the needs of the market has been noted by

many critics of early capitalist industry and education, for example, Samuel Bowles and Herb Gintis, *Schooling in Capitalist America* (New York: Pantheon, 1977); Ed Bristow, *Vice and Vigilance* (Dublin: Gill and MacMillan, 1977), 71, who offers his notion of the "sanctimonious sweatshop"; Linda Mahood, *The Magdelenes: Prostitution in the Nineteenth Century* (London: Routledge, 1990), chap. 5.

47 For example, Beth Peck and Lois Sells worked from 1928 to 1938. Door of Hope Annual Report, 1928. Beth Peck (Rademacher), interview with author, Los Angeles, 1992; Peggy Dobson (Lois Sells's daughter), letters to author, 1991–92; Sells, "Footsteps," unpublished diary. Ethel Abercrombie, head of the Receiving Home, worked from 1908 to 1940; Gladys Dieterle, director of the Children's Refuge, worked from 1908 to 1952 in Shanghai and then in Taipei into the 1960s. For Abercrombie, see *Annual Reports*, 1908–40; *North China Herald*, February 7, 1940. For Dieterle, see Annual *Reports*, 1908–40; Mathews, "Escaped as a Bird"; Dieterle's "Christ in Our Midst" and "Elijah"; correspondence files, The Evangelical Alliance Mission (TEAM), Wheaton, Illinois.

48 Peggy Pascoe, *Relations of Rescue: The Search for Female Moral Authority in the American West, 1874–1939* (New York: Oxford University Press, 1990).

49 See Helen Barrett Montgomery, *Western Women in Eastern Lands* (New York: Macmillan, 1911); Jane Hunter, *Gospel of Gentility* (New Haven: Yale University Press, 1984), 29–51; Paul Varg, *The Home Base of American Missions* (Cambridge, Mass.: Harvard University Press, 1978), 80–81, 97; Martha Vicinus, *Independent Women: Work and Community for Single Women 1850–1920* (Chicago: University of Chicago Press, 1985), 21–30; Sonya Rose, *Limited Livelihoods: Gender and Class in Nineteenth Century England* (New York: Routledge, 1992).

50 Many had worked with the Salvation Army. See Pamela Walker, *Pulling the Devil's Kingdom Down: The Salvation Army in Victorian Britain* (Berkeley: University of California Press, 2001); Diane Winston, *Red Hot and Righteous: The Urban Religion of the Salvation Army* (Cambridge, Mass.: Harvard University Press, 2000).

51 Henry Haggard, quoted in Annie McClintock, *Imperial Leather: Race, Gender and Sexuality in the Colonial Contest* (New York: Routledge, 1995), 261.

52 Hattie Bailey, "Farewell Address," *Good News* (March 16, 1918), 3–4.

53 Hattie Bailey, Student files, Alumnae Office, Moody Bible Institute, Chicago.

54 See Green correspondence with Mr. and Mrs. Meaers, December 1967, in Door of Hope correspondence files, TEAM, Wheaton, Illinois; Mathews, "Escaped as a Bird" (1950), 62; Door of Hope *Annual Report*, 1925, 7.

55 Door of Hope, *Annual Report*, 1925, 26–27.

56 Western missionaries lived separately; Chinese workers lived with them. Interview with Elizabeth Peck Rademacher.

57 Called helpers, mothers, or matrons, Chinese workers were never regarded as equals, just as all residents were called girls. See Devens, "If We Get the Girls," 233; Nicole Rafter, "Chastising the Unchaste: The Social Control Functions of a

Woman's Reformatory," *Social Control and the State*, ed. S. Cohen and A. Skull, 299 (Oxford: Martin Robertson, 1983).

58 Door of Hope, *Annual Report*, 1930, 2; 1932, 2.

59 For limited options, see my *Beautiful Merchandise: Prostitution in China, 1860–1936* (New York: Haworth Press, 1982); Li Yu-ning, *Chinese Women Through Chinese Eyes* (Armonk, N.Y.: M. E. Sharpe, 1992), esp. 167–74, 175–81.

60 Tuition payments for them were always included in yearly budgets. For example, Door of Hope *Annual Report*, 1929, 1931, 1932, 1934, 1935.

61 Ibid., 1936, 29–30; for Peace Chu, my interviews in 1998 in Shanghai.

62 Adrian Bennett, "Doing More than They Intended," *Women in New Worlds*, ed. Rosemary Keller and Hilah Thomas, 249–67 (Nashville: Wesley Press, 1985).

63 How young women at the mission understood these ideas is a different matter. My interviews with alumnae suggest complex interactions between residents at the mission and those in charge, but it was clear that the missionaries were firmly fixed as models in their memories.

The Women's Ecumenical Missionary Movement and Tokyo Woman's Christian College

Rui Kohiyama

When North American evangelical women commemorated the jubilee of their foreign missionary enterprise in 1911, they celebrated the strength of their movement: thirty-six women's organizations with over eight hundred thousand contributing members had collected over three million dollars, supported more than two thousand missionaries, and operated some three thousand schools of various grades overseas.[1] Energized by their success, evangelical women launched their most ambitious project, the campaign for "seven women's colleges in the Orient" to support higher education for women in India, China, and Japan. By the end of the campaign in 1923, the women had raised another three million dollars. Most of the money was used to construct buildings, some of which still stand today. In this essay, I explore the ideals that inspired the campaign and show how the initiative was received and transformed in Japan by examining the founding of Tokyo Woman's Christian College (TWCC). TWCC became a site of contention where Japanese desires prevailed. Although American leaders of the campaign planned for a Christian leadership and curriculum, they were obliged to make compromises in the context of rising Japanese nationalism.

WOMEN'S ECUMENISM AND THE CAMPAIGN FOR
SEVEN WOMEN'S COLLEGES IN THE ORIENT

The jubilee in 1911 was led by Lucy M. W. Peabody, chairwoman of the Central Committee for the United Study of Missions, as a celebration of "woman's work for woman."[2] Its memorial book, *Western Women in Eastern Lands* by Helen Montgomery, had landmark sales of 132,603 copies by 1914.[3] Peabody and Montgomery, both Baptists, were close friends. In 1913–14 they made a world tour representing the newly organized Federation of Women's Boards of Foreign Missions (FWBFM) to promote the idea of sustaining ecumenical women's colleges overseas, in accordance with a resolution passed at the International Missionary Conference in Edinburgh in 1910.[4] During that tour, they visited Japan and met with a committee of North American women missionaries and several prominent Japanese Christians that had been established to advocate for a women's college in Tokyo.[5] Back in the United States, Peabody and Montgomery joined the cooperating committee for the Tokyo college.[6]

After a hiatus caused by global warfare, Peabody launched a campaign in 1919 to raise three million dollars to provide permanent buildings for the colleges, namely, in India, Isabella Thoburn College in Lucknow, Woman's Christian College in Madras, and Union Missionary Medical School for Women in Vellore; in China, Woman's Union Medical College in Peking, Yenching College in Peking, and Ginling College in Nanking; and, in Japan, Woman's Christian College in Tokyo (Tokyo Woman's Christian College).[7] "If there is anything larger on the face of the earth than this,—the question of Christian leadership for women in three great countries like Japan, China and India, I do not know what it can be," wrote Peabody, expressing the intensity of her feeling in leading the movement.[8] With a promise from the Laura Spelman Rockefeller Memorial Foundation to provide one million dollars if she raised the other two, Peabody took up this challenge and brought it to a triumphant success.[9]

Support from the Laura Spelman Rockefeller Foundation was of vital importance to the campaign. The Rockefellers were Baptists, and Laura Spelman Rockefeller supported Baptist women's interests overseas for some time before her death in 1915. Peabody, who had worked for the WBFMS after the death of her first husband (a missionary to India) in 1886, was acquainted with the Rockefellers.[10] Her rise in the ecumenical movement in foreign missions seems to have been due, at least partially, to this connection. Her second marriage to Henry Peabody, a wealthy Christian merchant, also enhanced her ability to raise funds.[11]

The importance of women's higher education was widely recognized among the first generation of college-educated women who emerged as examples of the New Woman and engaged in Progressive-era reforms. Montgomery, a graduate of Wellesley College, was a New Woman and a "college girl" in foreign mission circles.[12] Combining deep religiosity with higher education, she was an icon of pious womanhood and Progressivism. Elected in 1896 as president of the New York State Federation of Women's Clubs and in 1899 as the first woman member of the board of education in Rochester, New York, Montgomery's ability for conscientious leadership was widely recognized. She was elected president of the Northern Baptist Convention in 1921, the first woman to obtain such a position.[13] Although Peabody was not a college graduate, she joined the vanguard of well-educated womanhood by supporting Montgomery and working together with her.

"No nation can rise higher than its women" was the phrase Peabody emphasized in her campaign for the seven women's colleges in the Orient. It was her favorite phrase, reminiscent of Alexis de Tocqueville's observation about American women in the 1830s. The idea that national progress was associated with the status of women in society was still popular in the United States in the early twentieth century.[14] White, middle-class women like Peabody were proud of their role representing the supremacy of American civilization. Peabody enjoyed this sense of superiority and believed she had a responsibility to improve the status of women outside the United States. She also believed in the potential of women everywhere, regardless of nationality, to uplift the level of civilization.[15] As the title of one of her books indicates, she wanted to open up a "wider world for women," both in the United States and overseas.[16] Peabody and her supporters in North America expected the women's colleges in the Orient to contribute to the spread of higher education, Christianity, women's networks, and civilization. They planned to reshape societies in Asia. Their project was made possible by the combination of Rockefeller money (the fruit of the growth of U.S. capitalism) and evangelical enthusiasm.

Lucy Peabody and Helen Montgomery were home-based promoters.

After their initial visit, their connections to the seven colleges were indirect but nevertheless important. The women attended the regular meetings of the cooperating committee for TWCC in New York to resolve a number of important matters, particularly questions of finance. In 1917 Peabody chaired the candidates committee for TWCC and offered to staff the college with North American Christian women.[17] In Tokyo, the college began in 1918 in rented quarters and, thanks to the success of Peabody's building fund campaign, moved to a permanent site in 1923. The money Peabody raised provided the college with most of the initial buildings on the new campus.

WEAKENING MISSIONARY LEADERSHIP IN JAPAN AND THE ESTABLISHMENT OF TWCC

Seen from the Japanese side, the establishment of TWCC was not the expression of a high tide of missionary influence but the desperate attempt of missionaries to rally the leadership in the field of women's education in Japan. Since the first single woman missionary began a school for women in 1870, North American women missionaries had led "modern education" for women in Japan until the end of the 1880s. They were especially strong in secondary education for women because the Meiji government left the field largely to the private sector, in which Protestant missions figured prominently.[18]

Then in the latter half of the 1880s, Japanese nationalism surged, accompanied by a clear understanding of the Western idea of the order of civilization: "No nation can rise higher than its women." In 1899 when unequal treaties were rectified, the Ministry of Education issued Ordinance No. 12, which prohibited religious education in schools that sought recognition from the government. In 1899 the Ministry of Education also issued an ordinance to formally request each prefectural government to establish at least one public girls' higher school (Koto Jogakko) in its jurisdiction. The former ordinance mainly affected mission schools for boys; the latter affected girls' schools.[19]

The equal treaties not only ranked Japan among Western powers but also abolished foreign concessions, allowing foreigners to acquire land, live, and travel anywhere in Japan. This arrangement was called domestic cohabitation (Naichi Zakkyo) and stimulated Japanese sensitivities: while the popular imagination often expected a cheerful exchange among different peoples, the government was apprehensive about a full disclosure of Japanese lives.[20] The condition of ordinary women was one such inner reality. Now fully engaged in a politics of respectability, the government was determined to make efforts to produce a corps of educated middle-class women who could express the civility of the nation. Public girls' higher schools were to serve this end.[21]

At the same time, Japanese private initiatives emerged to pursue women's higher education. At the end of the nineteenth century, the government maintained only one such institution in Tokyo, the Higher Normal School for Women (Joshi Koto Shihan). In 1900, Tsuda Umeko, who had studied in the United States on a government appointment, began a private school to train women teachers of the English language. In the same year, Yoshioka Yayoi, who received a license to practice medicine in 1892, opened a medical school for women. In 1901, Japan Women's College was established by Naruse Jinzo, a male Japanese Christian educator.[22] These schools eventually achieved the status of a higher special school (Senmon Gakko), the highest kind of school for women according to Japanese government regulations before the Second World War. Although Naruse and Tsuda were Christians, they were not graduates of mission schools and sought no missionary connection.[23] Mission schools in Japan began to lag behind Japanese schools. By 1912, nineteen girls' mission schools had higher departments, two of which had the status of Senmon Gakko. However, the total enrollment in these higher departments was only 336, whereas the Government Higher Normal Schools in Tokyo and Nara had 450 students, Japan Women's College 450, and Miss Tsuda's school 140.[24]

By 1910, as Japanese national pride swelled following Japan's defeat of Russia in the Russo-Japanese War (1905), the government ordinance of 1899 on Koto Jogakko was in full swing. The number of Koto Jogakko tripled to 194, with an enrollment of 56,282 pupils, a nearly fivefold increase; by contrast, 38 mission secondary schools for girls in Japan enrolled 3,622 pupils.[25] In order to retain a curriculum that included religious education, several of the mission girls' schools did not apply for formal Koto Jogakko status, thereby obliging their graduates to take additional examinations if they wished to apply for Senmon Gakko.[26] Thus, the girls' higher school funded by the local government became the norm for respectable secondary education for women in each locality. The overall leadership in women's education that American women missionaries had once thought theirs was now lost to the Japanese.

The need to build a Christian system of education up to the highest level had thus increased by 1910, when the proposal to establish a union Christian women's college in Tokyo was made at the Edinburgh Conference. The opening of TWCC in 1918 was the result more of a sense of crisis on the part of the American missions in Japan than of a cry for help from the Japanese. In fact, in answering a questionnaire distributed in the 1920s on Christian education in Japan, Japanese Christian educators agreed that Christian schools for both men and women were inferior to national and public schools. They attracted inferior students; they were superior only in character building.[27] Japan was the antithesis of the assumption that women leaders of the ecumenical movement made, that civilization was a result of Christianity. Missionaries believed that Japan was "strong and virile but pagan" and thus a "menace to world peace."[28] The missions in Japan had to maintain a hold on education in Japan because "the only hope of a really democratic and liberal spirit coming to the front in Japan lies in the Christian education of the coming generation."[29] Yet the campaign for the women's colleges in the Orient could never discard the classic missionary rhetoric of helping backward peoples.[30]

Under these circumstances, the Woman's College Promoting Committee of Japan, in its statement of principles and methods of procedure, declared, "It shall be the aim of the movement to establish a College whose standard is not lower than the highest the govt or other non-christian [sic] schools are offering. As the higher Normal School for Women is the norm for the highest education at present being given in Japan it should be at least equal in grade to the type of work done there."[31] The basic plan of the college had not only to meet Japanese regulations to obtain at least the Senmon Gakko recognition but also to satisfy Japanese expectations. The situation was different from that in India, where the proposed women's colleges were incorporated under British–Indian law, and that in China, where the colleges were simply registered to the New York state regency.[32]

Campus of Tokyo Woman's Christian College, 1925. By permission of Tokyo Woman's Christian University.

NO AMERICAN WOMEN'S LEADERSHIP:
REISCHAUER, NITOBE, AND YASUI

Seen from the U.S. side, one of the most serious problems for the college in Japan was its leadership. In colleges in India and China, American missionary women became presidents and set the initial directions for the colleges. Their leadership was the most important symbol of American churchwomen's influence on the colleges, ensuring that sisterhood extended across national borders.[33] U.S. supporters expected the TWCC to have an American woman as president and a Japanese woman as dean.[34] Missionaries in Japan tried unsuccessfully to find a suitable woman missionary for the position.[35] As nationalistic antagonism against mission schools surged around the end of the 1880s, the number of missionaries sent to Japan was curtailed. As a result, by 1910 few experienced women missionaries with college degrees and fluency in Japanese resided in Japan. Although Lucy Peabody was willing to find well-educated American women to work at TWCC, none were qualified to assume leadership at the college, where subjects were taught in Japanese. When TWCC finally opened, a few women missionaries were on the board of trustees, but they were inconspicuous in terms of leadership. Contrary to the wishes of

A. K. Reischauer, ca. 1915.
By permission of Tokyo Woman's
Christian University.

Americans, Japanese educators expected women missionaries to teach English.[36] This posed a problem: in the absence of an American woman leader who could inspire the bonds of sisterhood, it was not easy to persuade North American women to give money.[37]

Inevitably, A. K. Reischauer, a male missionary of the Presbyterian mission in Tokyo, broke into the network of sisterhood and occupied a conspicuous position as general secretary for the college. Reischauer was sent to Japan in 1905 by the Board of Foreign Missions of the Presbyterian Church and was one of the most prominent of the third generation of missionaries in Japan. Reischauer's missionary approach was different from that of missionaries before him. First, he observed the world from the Japanese perspective. In a series of lectures Reischauer delivered in 1925 at Princeton Theological Seminary, he criticized Western imperialism, saying "From the standpoint of an awakened Orient the world situation looks very different. . . . there is a growing dissatisfaction with the fact that the 'Christian' White race has too large a share of the world's land and wealth, and there is even a more bitter resentment against the White Man for his 'superior' attitude in his dealings with the coloured races."[38]

To rectify the situation, Reischauer argued that missionaries should aim to do things with Japan rather than in Japan or for Japan, which invited patronizing attitudes.[39] In his opinion, "no missionary has any place in Japan today who cannot work on a plane of equality and as a 'fraternal helper' with his Japanese colleagues."[40] He put his opinion into practice. To place Christianity in the religious order in Japan, he studied religions in Japan, especially the Shin sect of Buddhism. Later, he was known as a Christian scholar of Japanese Buddhism, which he taught at Union Theological Seminary in New York.

The position that Reischauer took at TWCC was the epitome of his efforts to be a fraternal helper. As general secretary of the college, he took care of finances and the physical plant building by representing the Japanese needs to the North American supporters. He left educational matters, including the selection of staff members, entirely to the Japanese. He called himself "the janitor of TWCC."[41] He brought money to the college but abjured the power that accompanied the money. In terms of theology, he was the foremost liberal, being conciliatory to various religions and cultures. He was one of the rare missionaries who could maintain the most cordial relationship with the proud, highly educated ex-samurai Japanese Christians who often distanced themselves from missionaries.[42]

With Reischauer as intermediary, the leadership of the college was firmly assumed by the Japanese. Nitobe Inazo, the president, and Yasui Tetsu, the dean, were prominent educators of the day. The two leaders shared experiences that are important to the arguments I pursue here.[43]

First, both Nitobe and Yasui were products of the government education system. Nitobe attended the Sapporo Institute of Agriculture and the Imperial University of Tokyo; Yasui attended the Higher Normal School for Women in Tokyo. They were Christians but belonged to denominations that did not cooperate with TWCC: Nitobe was a Quaker and Yasui a Congregationalist. They were recruited outside of the missionary network, which was exceptional in mission fields and was possible, in my opinion, only because of Reischauer's liberal attitudes. Further, both Nitobe and Yasui were generally critical of missionaries.[44] The two had to be persuaded to take the initial leadership. Nitobe's reputation allowed TWCC to acquire instant recognition in Japanese society. His connection with the Ministry of Education was also necessary for negotiating governmental recognition and support. Yasui was also a member of the Japanese elite.

The second feature Nitobe and Yasui had in common was that they

Nitobe Inazo, ca. 1920s. By permission
of Tokyo Woman's Christian University.

Yasui Tetsu, ca. 1930. By permission of Tokyo
Woman's Christian University.

were nationalists from samurai families but had rich experience in the West. Nitobe enrolled at Johns Hopkins University in 1885, initially on his own and later on a government appointment. He took his doctorate from the University of Halle in Germany. In the United States, he met Mary Elkinton of a wealthy Quaker family in Philadelphia and married her in 1891. His international career culminated in his appointment as undersecretary for the League of Nations in 1920. Yasui's Western experience was also extraordinary, especially for a woman: she was sent to England by the government to study for three years. In 1907, she spent another year in England on her own.

Yet they were not merely admirers of the West. Nitobe was widely known as the author of *Bushido* (The warriors' manner, 1899), the result of his search for the source of the high standard of morality maintained by the Japanese that had developed outside of the Christian tradition. He insisted that *bushido* was the backbone of Japanese morality. The book was first published in English in the United States and was more a proclamation of Japanese authenticity vis-à-vis the West than an accurate report of Japanese tradition. It was an expression of the spirit of independence the Japanese began to put forward in the 1890s.

Yasui's occasional writings also revealed her patriotism. For example, remembering Nogi Maresuke, the general and hero of the Russo-Japanese War who immolated himself at the funeral of Emperor Meiji, Yasui wrote, "I always had a confidence in myself having sincere passion for the nation although I was such a small being. I believed that the spirit to love the nation and to be faithful to the monarch in its widest and deepest sense must be expressed in the ordinary and everyday life. In order to put my belief into practice, I examined the matter silently and carefully. I finally came to a conclusion that I should have a [Christian] faith. In the same spirit, I always admired General Nogi's supreme sincerity and simple and sober life. Unfortunately, the General did not understand my truthful devotion to the nation as a Christian."[45] In Yasui's mind, her Christianity coexisted with her patriotism. She distinguished between Christianity and Western culture and civilization.

Nitobe's and Yasui's third commonality was their involvement in Asia. Nitobe worked in Formosa as a top-ranking colonial government official between 1901 and 1903. He was recruited by the governor of the colony to develop a policy for agricultural engineering. He traveled widely during this period and thereafter in Asia, becoming a lecturer in colonization policy at the Imperial University of Tokyo in 1913. Also he served as dean of the Oriental Association Special School for Colonization (later, Takushoku [colonization and development] College) between 1917 and 1922.[46] Yasui worked in Siam from 1904 to 1907 on government appointment to help the Siamese Imperial Household found the Empress School for Girls. British women had been active in educating the imperial family as well as women in Siam. The school project was an intervention by the rising Japanese nation in Asia into the British sphere of influence, for "Oriental women were more suited for educating Oriental women."[47] Yasui thus worked as the vanguard of Japanese expansionism in Asia. Both Nitobe and Yasui, though to different degrees, were part and parcel of imperialist Japan. "No nation can rise higher than its women" was likely the idea that inspired Nitobe and Yasui to cooperate with TWCC, the missionary project they were not enthusiastic about at the beginning.[48]

CURRICULUM AND LIBERAL ARTS
EDUCATION AT TWCC

Reflecting the new trend of women's higher education in the United States at the beginning of the twentieth century, the Americans seem to have envisioned a gender-specific and practical education at TWCC; for example, they wanted to introduce domestic science and social work.[49] These subjects emerged out of American women's traditional roles as housewives and volunteer workers for benevolent associations. During the first half of the twentieth century, much of this work had been professionalized and established on scientific principles. The subjects were at the forefront of women's higher education and contributed to expanding women's sphere of professional work in the United States. At TWCC, they were put on the table for discussion several times, but, although partially pursued in the beginning, were never established in the formal curriculum on a long-term basis.[50]

The college was not prepared to offer these gender-specific subjects. The dominant language at TWCC was Japanese. New missionaries did not know Japanese, and the old missionaries, who did to some extent, were unfamiliar with the new subjects.[51] Key teaching staff at the college came from the Imperial University of Tokyo on a part-time basis in part to impress the public with the high quality of academic life at the college. They were all men, many of them educated in Europe, and they were indifferent to or ignorant of gender-specific subjects, showing no little disrespect for American scholarship.[52] This tendency was reinforced by Yasui's inclination toward highbrow academicism.[53]

When Nitobe left to go to Geneva in 1920, Yasui Tetsu became the second president of the college in 1923. The curriculum that was finally established at the college reflected her vision, which emphasized a liberal arts education modeled after the First High School (Daiichi Koto Gakko), a notable government school for boys where Nitobe was once principal. The First High School provided an elitist education, preparing future male national leaders to pursue more professional or specialized training at the Imperial University of Tokyo. Women were excluded from this educational system. Yasui was rejected by the Imperial University of Kyoto only because she was a woman. TWCC was thus to compensate women for lost educational opportunities. Educated in Japanese government schools and also in England, Yasui knew little about the women's culture in the United States that had fostered gender-specific and practical subjects and had no interest in replanting such a culture at TWCC. Reischauer's efforts to create a sisterly bond between Yasui and American women supporters were in vain.[54]

What was the use of such a liberal arts education for women at the time? Women had few opportunities for either vocation or leadership in those days in Japan. Many TWCC students aimed to teach English, Japanese, or mathematics at secondary schools and actually became teachers, and some were active in such professions as social work and writing.[55] But the majority married, and not a few married elite men. As highly educated women, they knew the value of knowledge and a liberal arts education as they aspired to obtain them. They might have admired men with such knowledge and education more enthusiastically than ordinary women. They might have helped such men realize what women themselves could not achieve in spite of having attained education and knowledge almost equal to those of the men. In short, their education might have prepared women to be ideal helpmeets to highly educated men, although at TWCC Nitobe and Yasui prepared women to live beyond the narrowness of the good-wife and good-mother principle widely inculcated at government girls' higher schools. In fact, creating "high-grade wives" was one of the aims of TWCC, according to Nitobe.[56] They helped create the culture of the new middle class in cities, a group made up of salaried white-collar workers who began to have nuclear-family households.[57]

High-grade wives were necessary in Japan not only to achieve social adjustment in accordance with the growth of capitalism but also to satisfy the country's imperialist ambitions: Nitobe understood the importance of such wives from the perspective of his colonial experience. Nitobe's thinking on colonial policy was complex, but he certainly believed that civilized races of excellence were justified in their colonial rule over lesser races, although such rule must be exercised in the spirit of benevolence and "public conscience." He was a paternalistic imperialist, and for him to justify Japan's rule in Formosa and Korea, it had to be proved that the Japanese belonged to the civilized races.[58]

Repeating the idea in the phrase "No nation can rise higher than its women," Nitobe in one of his writings encouraged educated women to join the Japanese expansion to the south and "show the model of Japanese womanhood to the world."[59] Yasui agreed with Nitobe, as she insisted in response to the celebration of the imperial year of 2600 that "in order to cooperate with the building of the new order in East Asia, we have to further raise the dignity of the nation. . . . I sincerely hope that highly educated women like the graduates of our college will be aware of their relationship with the nation on such an occasion . . . and make efforts to upgrade the dignity of the Japanese women."[60]

The practical and gender-specific subjects such as social work and kindergarten teaching that the U.S. supporters planned to introduce to TWCC were eventually incorporated into extracurricular activities like the college chapter of the YWCA. Moreover, the college took steps to be recognized by the government to automatically give licenses to its graduates of "specialty courses" to teach at secondary schools in several fields. The college incorporated the vocational aspect of education in the four-year specialty courses, which were in fact popular, attracting more students than the full collegiate course of six years.[61]

Nevertheless, TWCC's distinctive characteristic was its extension to women of a liberal arts education that heretofore was imparted to men only. The high-grade wives thus produced were most meaningful in the context of Japanese imperialism and colonialism. Japanese leaders grasped the theme "No nation can rise higher than its women" on their own and pursued it even more aggressively, together with intense nationalism, to place Japan in the upper echelons of the international order and to facilitate Japanese rule in Asia. American attempts to provide a practical, gender-specific education so as to produce in Japan what women's culture had produced in the United States, as well as strengthen connections with American women, were deemed unimportant by the Japanese. A practical education was given only token attention and located on the periphery of life at TWCC.

CHRISTIANITY

Christianity at TWCC was definitely liberal and modernist. Although the college maintained the demeanor of a Christian institution—it had chapel service, compulsory courses on Christianity, and a college chapter of the YWCA—not only students but also faculty members were left free to decide how to relate to religion. Exhortations were never made. Although she was known for her "sterling Christian quality," Yasui hated exhortations.[62] She was a city-bred intellectual from an ex-samurai family who found emotional evangelicalism distasteful.[63]

Many teachers at TWCC were Japanese non-Christians, and not all students were Christians. Most students came from government girls' higher schools, not from mission schools, in spite of the fact that the cooperating mission schools had abolished their higher departments so that they could send their students to TWCC. Because the government secondary schools produced many women who wanted higher education, the college had to screen applicants through an examination, one in which graduates of Protestant mission schools did not fare well. The Japanese side claimed that giving special favor to mission school graduates would damage the prestige of the college and its future growth.[64] This was a problem: TWCC was supposed to be the capstone institution for girls' mission schools to educate Christians. In comparison, at Ginling College in China, almost all the teachers and most of the students were Christian.[65]

Symbolically important in this vein, the word *Christian* was omitted from the Japanese name of the college. The name Tokyo Joshi Daigaku literally meant Tokyo Women's College, which sounded, as Reischauer happily reported, somehow related to the Imperial University of Tokyo (like Radcliffe to Harvard). But the word *Christian* was retained in the English name, Tokyo Woman's Christian College, so as to make the omission invisible to people in North America. In explaining the dropping of the single most important word, *Christian*, from the Japanese name, Reischauer wrote, "It might give the public the impression that the College is simply a school for teaching Christianity, a sort of Bible School. And if we had used a transliteration of the word 'Christian' we would have had a word that is hardly good Japanese."[66]

Further, liberal Christianity at the college provoked keen interest in social activism. The enthusiasm and atmosphere of the Social Gospel type at the college, together with rising interest in communism among university and college students in general, led some TWCC students to join the Communist Party, which was unlawful at the time. Some of them were arrested by police in 1929, and the incident was widely publicized, giving the college a "red" label.[67]

At the other extreme, the college had to face another difficult problem: how to deal with the emperor worship and Shintoism that the government forcefully tried to incorporate in the educational system of the empire. There had been numerous discussions and disputes since the 1890s over the relationship between Christianity and emperor worship combined with Shintoism. Christians and missionaries in the Japanese empire were divided in opinion, but the liberalist camp generally accepted, albeit reluctantly, the official government explanation that emperor worship and national Shinto were not religions but national rituals.[68] TWCC received from the government in 1938 a set of photos of the emperor and the empress to which everyone on campus had to pay respect in ceremonies. The photos were carefully kept in a specially built storage area on the roof of the main building and were hung on the front wall of the auditorium when ceremonies were held. Christianity coexisted with emperor worship on campus.[69]

The cooperating committee for TWCC in the United States began to receive complaints in 1922 that the college did not demonstrate enough Christian character; that it was by no means acting like a mission school. People who had given donations to the college occasionally visited Tokyo and the college and sent their comments to promoters in the United States. Some conservative Christians found liberalism at TWCC annoying.[70]

But then the fact that such conservatism was no longer the norm in the United States was also disclosed on the TWCC campus. The supporting committee for TWCC in the United States arranged a sister relationship between TWCC and Vassar College. In the 1920s Vassar regularly sent a representative to teach at TWCC for a year or two. One of these teachers, Mary Butcher, who taught English and hockey between 1929 and 1930, did not comply with the missionary standard of morality. According to a letter from Tokyo to Vassar College, she was "a real social climber. . . . Tokyo with its Legation and Embassy circles and a rather fast business crowd offers ample opportunities for such ambitions. She has spent three, four and five nights away from the campus at dances, card parties etc. and often the next day was too tired to do her work effectively. . . . She told a girl who is visiting us that she is not a Christian at all and that one religion is just as good as another etc."[71] The new generation of American college women was no longer comfortable with moral rigidity, an important visible marker that had long distinguished Christians from non-Christians. These young women, when placed at the mission women's colleges overseas, highlighted the contradiction and fueled disputes rather than reinforcing the Christian unity and sisterhood that the colleges were supposed to symbolize.

CONCLUSION

Despite the huge financial contribution they drew from the United States, missionaries and their American supporters had little presence at TWCC. As some missionaries and U.S. supporters feared from the outset, "the foreign element" was not "sufficiently large to develop the work along the lines of an American institution to the degree" they "felt desirable."[72] A. K. Reischauer was the only influential missionary on campus, but he worked more as an agent of the Japanese than of the committee for TWCC in the United States. At the beginning of the twentieth century, when Japan had strengthened its grasp on the people in terms not only of law and regulations but also of national spirit, missionaries had to listen to the Japanese and leave most of the actual decisions and implementations to them. Yasui Tetsu was well aware that the major financial support came from the United States. In her speech to commemorate the fifteenth anniversary of the college, she said that the college was built upon offerings from unnamed women in Canada and the United States and that these anonymous women contributed the money for young women in Japan willingly in the spirit of service and sacrifice.[73] She took the old principle of foreign missions, "disinterested benevolence," at face value. Consciously or not, by placing the financial matter in the higher domain of Christian love, Yasui seems to have contained the American power that should have naturally accompanied American money.

NOTES

Japanese names are given with the family name first.

1 Helen Barrett Montgomery, *Western Women in Eastern Lands* (New York: Macmillan, 1910): Appendix. The data are for 1909.

2 *The Story of the Jubilee* (West Medford, Mass.: Central Committee on the United Study of Missions, 1911).

3 *The First Bulletin of the Federation of the Woman's Boards of Foreign Missions of the United States* 1, no. 1 (March 1914), 32.

4 "Lucy Whitehead McGill Waterbury Peabody," *Notable American Women*, ed. Edward T. James, Janet Wilson James, and Paul S. Boyer, 37 (Cambridge: Belknap

Press, 1971); Louise Armstrong Cattan, *Lamps Are for Lighting* (Grand Rapids: Eerdmans, 1972), 66.

5 A. K. Reischauer, *Tokyo Woman's Christian College* (Tokyo: TWCC Academic Society, n.d.), 15–16; Hideko Omori, "Kirisutokyo Joshi Kyouikukai to Kirisu- tokyo Rengo Joshi Daigaku Undo," *Hyakunenshi Kiyo* 1 (June 2003), 19.

6 "Committee on the Tokyo Woman's Christian College," in the Woman's Chris- tian Union College (Tokyo) file, Missionary Research Library Collection (here- after MRLC), Burke Theological Library, Union Theological Seminary (hereafter BTLUTS).

7 Gordon Florence, *Building Women Leaders* (New York: Foreign Missions Con- ference of North America, 1942), MRLC, BTLUTS. The Women's Union Medical College in Peking was excluded from the subjects of assistance from the Laura Spelman Rockefeller Memorial Foundation (hereafter LSRM Fund) because the Rockefeller Foundation had already assisted Peking Union Medical College (a letter from Lucy Peabody to Richardson [March 18, 1921] in folder 86, box 7, series 3–2, Laura Spelman Rockefeller Memorial Archives (hereafter LSRM), the Rockefeller Archive Center (hereafter RAC).

8 Letter, Mrs. Henry W. Peabody to W. S. Richardson (December 7, 1920) in folder 85, box 7, series 3–2, LSRM, RAC.

9 Rui Kohiyama, "From Ecumenism to Internationalism: American Women's Cross-Pacific Endeavor to Promote Women's Colleges in the Orient," *Rediscover- ing America*, ed. Kousar J. Azam, 265–77 (New Delhi: South Asian Publishers, 2001); Rui Kohiyama, "Yujo no Teikoku," *Gurobarizeishon to Teikoku* (Tokyo: Minerva, 2006).

10 Letters, Lucy Peabody to W. S. Richardson (September 27, 1920, and October 18, 1920) in folder 85, box 7, series 3–2, LSRM, RAC; "Statement of the Laura Spelman Rockefeller Legacy from September 1915 to September 1920," ibid.

11 *Report of the Laura Spelman Rockefeller Memorial* (New York, 1923) in box 2, series 2, LSRM, RAC. The foundation began to concentrate on scientific social research for the betterment of society after 1922. See Olivier Zunz, *Why the American Century?* (Chicago: University of Chicago Press, 1998), 36–39.

12 Helen Barrett Montgomery, *From Campus to World Citizenship* (New York: Fleming H. Revell, n.d.), 114.

13 "Helen Barrett Montgomery," *Notable American Women*, ed. James et al.

14 Letter, Lucy Peabody, Margaret Hodge, and Elizabeth Bender to John D. Rocke- feller, Jr. (October 18, 1920) in folder 85, box 7, series 3–2, LSRM, RAC. In the 1920s, even the Ku Klux Klan used the expression. See Kathleen M. Blee, *Women of the Klan* (Berkeley: University of California Press, 1991), 46; Alexis de Tocque- ville, *Democracy in America*, trans. Arthur Goldhammer (New York: Library of America, 2004), 708.

15 Letter, George E. Vincent to John D. Rockefeller, Jr. (October 21, 1921) in folder 87, box 7, series 3–2, LSRM, RAC.

16 Lucy W. Peabody, *A Wider World for Women* (New York: Fleming H. Revell, ca. 1934).

17 Letter, Lucy Peabody to A. K. Reischauer (October 1, 1917) in Board of Trustees–Cooperating Committee Correspondence (hereafter BTCCC), stored at Tokyo Woman's Christian University (TWCU hereafter).

18 Rui Kohiyama, *Amerika Fujin Senkyoshi* (Tokyo: University of Tokyo Press, 1992), chap. 4.

19 A school that lacked government recognition could not get an exemption from conscription for its students. Also, graduates from such schools would not be automatically qualified to take examinations to enter high schools (Koto Gakko), a kind of preparatory school for Imperial Universities. These handicaps did not affect women's choices because conscription did not apply to women and because they rarely went to school above the secondary level. See Kirisutokyo Gakko Kyoiku Domei, *Nihon ni okeru Kirisutokyo Gakko Kyouiku no Genjo* (Tokyo: Kirisutokyo Gakko Kyoiku Domei, 1961), 77–82. For the ordinance for girls' higher schools, see Sakurai Tasuku, *Joshi Kyoiku Shi* (1943; rpt., Tokyo: Nihon Tosho Center, 1981), 122–30.

20 Inou Noritaro, *Naichi Zakkyo Ron Shiryo Shusei*, vol. 1 (Tokyo: Hara Shobo, 1992), 3–22. I have several copies of Naichi Zakkyo Sugoroku, a board game published in those days, which described cheerful exchanges between Japanese and non-Japanese living in Japan.

21 See Koyama Shizuko, *Ryosai Kenbo toiu Kihan* (Tokyo: Keiso Shobo, 1991).

22 Sakurai, *Joshi Kyoiku Shi*, 157–60.

23 It is well known that Tsuda Umeko did not like missionaries. See Barbara Rose, *Tsuda Umeko and Women's Education in Japan* (New Haven: Yale University Press, 1992), 43–44.

24 *The Need of a Christian College for Women in Japan*, ([1913]), 9–10, in Woman's Christian Union College of Japan (Tokyo) file, MRLC, BTLUTS.

25 Ibid.

26 The government regulation of Senmon Gakko issued in 1903 denied such privilege to graduates of girls' secondary schools that had no formal government recognition (Sakurai, *Joshi Kyoiku Shi*, 158). The process by which a Presbyterian girls' mission school in Tokyo made a difficult choice to get Koto Jogakko status finally in 1915 is described in Ohama Tetsuya *Joshi Gakuin no Rekishi* (Tokyo: Joshigakuin, 1985), 354–56.

27 "English Translations of Individual Replies from Japanese Educators to the First Educational Questionnaire," in the "Ed. Miss.—Japan College" file, MRLC, BTLUTS.

28 "Kobe College–Kobe, Japan," in folder 84, box 7, series 3–2, LSRM, RAC.

29 The Joint Committee on Women's Christian Colleges in the Orient, *Report of the Building Fund Committee of the Women's Union Christian Colleges in the Orient* (New York: Joint Committee, 1923), 24.

30 Peabody's campaign utilized such rhetoric. Some Japanese in the United States

took notice of it and sent complaints to TWCC. The Japanese did not want to see themselves grouped with India and China. See a letter from A. K. Reischauer to Charlotte H. Conant (December 29, 1922) in BTCCC, TWCC.

31 "The Promoting Committee of the Christian College for Women" (May 17, n.d.), in the Woman's Christian Union College of Japan (Tokyo) file, MRLC, BTLUTS.

32 Letter, Lucy Peabody to W. S. Richardson (October 25, 1920) in folder 85, box 7, series 3–2, LSRM, RAC.

33 Ida Scudder of Vellore Medical School represented the ideal type of such leadership.

34 "Report of the Promoting Committee of the Woman's Christian Union College of Japan" (July 1915), in the Woman's Christian Union College of Japan (Tokyo) file, MRLC, BTLUTS.

35 In 1916, Charlotte De Forest of Kobe College, a Congregationalist institution in Kobe, became the candidate for president. But this plan did not materialize because De Forest had a prior denominational commitment. See a letter of Isabelle Blackmore (February 10, 1916) in the TWCC file, Presbyterian Historical Society (hereafter PHS). For the response of Congregationalist women missionaries in Japan, see Noriko K. Ishii, *American Women Missionaries at Kobe College, 1873–1909* (New York: Routledge, 2004), 62.

36 In the questionnaire issued in the 1920s to Japanese Christian educators (mentioned in note 27), most of the responders favored Japanese leadership in teaching. Missionaries were expected to teach only the English language.

37 A letter to Reischauer (April 18, 1918) in the TWCC file, PHS.

38 August Karl Reischauer, *The Task in Japan* (New York: Fleming H. Revell, n.d.), 29–30.

39 Ibid., 47.

40 Ibid., 212.

41 Teiji Takagi, "A. K. Raishawa hakase to Tokyo Joshi Daigaku," in *Hakarinawa wa Tanoshiki Chini Ochitari* (Tokyo: Kyobunkan, 1961), 104–5.

42 Most recruits to Christianity during the Meiji period came from the former samurai class. Japanese Christian leaders were critical of missionaries in terms of character, education, morality, and even faith. They were sensitive to the arrogance of missionaries who were backed by financial ability. Uemura Masahisa, by far the most famous pastor and leader, was typical of such Japanese Christians. See Uemura Masahisa, "Gaikoku Senkyoshi," *Uemura Masahisa to Sono Jidai*, vol. 4 (1938; rpt., Tokyo: Kyobunkan, 1976), 534–38.

43 Brief biographies of the two leaders can be found in *Nihon Kirisutokyo Rekishi Daijiten* (Tokyo: Kyobunkan, 1988).

44 Aoyama Nao, *Yasui Tetsu Den* (Tokyo: Tokyo Joshi Daigaku Dosoukai, 1949), 42; Nitobe Inazo, *Bushido*, trans. Naramoto Tatsuya (1899; Tokyo: Mikasa Shobo, 1997), 160–61.

45 Aoyama, *Yasui Tetsu Den*, 164.

46 Kusahara Katsuhide, "Nitobe Inazo to Takushoku Daigaku," *Kokusai Bunka Kai-kan Kaiho* 13, no. 1 (spring 2002), 15–25.

47 Aoyoma, *Yasui Tetsu Den*, 104.

48 Nagao Hanpei, ed., *Souritsu 15-nen Kaisou-roku* (Tokyo: Tokyo Joshi Daigaku, 1933): 6–8; see also note 63 below.

49 Helen Lefkowitz Horowitz, *Alma Mater* (New York: Knopf, 1985), part 4; T. H. P. Sailer, "Some Suggestions for the Curriculum of a Woman's College in the Orient," in the TWCC file, PHS.

50 Details of early curricula can be found in *Tokyo Joshi Daigaku 50-nen Shi* (Tokyo: Kenbun-sha, 1968), 42–43, 49–53, 75–90.

51 Letter, A. K. Reischauer to Florence L. Nichols (April 22, 1918) in the Correspondence between the Board of Trustees and the Cooperating Committee, TWCU.

52 For the faculty, see Nagao, *Souritsu 15-nen Kaisou-roku*, appendix.

53 Yasui did not support the introduction of gender-specific, practical, American subjects like nutrition into the formal curriculum. See Amadatsu Fumiko, "Eiyo-ka Shunin Jiken," Aoyama, *Yasui Tetsu Den*, 73–79.

54 "Not [being] familiar with the American character," Yasui hesitated in accepting the position at TWCC (see Aoyama, *Yasui Tetsu Den*, 215). Reischauer negotiated an honorary doctor of philosophy degree from Mt. Holyoke College, and Yasui traveled to the United States to receive it in 1923. (Letter, Charlotte H. Conant to A. K Reischauer [May 17, 1923] in BTCCC, TWCU.) Very reserved and quiet, Yasui hardly evoked enthusiastic support among American women like Ida Scudder, president of Vellore Medical College in India (for Scudder's contribution to Peabody's building fund campaign, see a record of a meeting of Cooperating Committee, Woman's Christian College of Japan [October 16, 1922] in the TWCC file, PHS).

55 Approximately 223 of the 1,043 graduates had paid jobs around that time. See Hobo Fusa, "The Life Report," *Dousoukai Geppo* 2, no. 10 (December 1936), 20–22.

56 Nitobe Inazo, "Kirisutokyoushugi no Joshi Daigaku," *Shi Jokai* 1, no. 1 (1918), 21. Also see Yasui Tetsu, "Shisetsu Serarentosuru Tokyo Joshi Daigaku," ibid., 41.

57 For the new middle class, see Koyama Shizuko, *Katei no Seisei to Josei no Kokumin-ka* (Tokyo: Keiso Shobo, 1999). For the involvement of TWCC graduates in the creation of the culture of the new middle class, see Rui Kohiyama, "Fujin no Tomo ni okeru Yousou-ka Undo," *Higashi Ajia no Modern Girl to Shokuminchi-teki Kindai*, ed. Ito Ruri, Tani Barrow, et al. (Tokyo: Iwanami Shoten, forthcoming).

58 Kohiyama Rui, "Teikoku no Riberarizumu," *Teikoku to Gakko*, ed. Komagome Takeshi and Hashimoto Nobuya (Kyoto: Showa-do, 2007).

59 Nitobe Inazo, "Fujin to Nanpo Hatten," *Fujin ni Susumete* (Tokyo-sha, 1922), 387–95.

60 Yasui Tetsu, "In the Beginning of the Imperial Year of 2600," in *Dosoukai Geppo* 6, no. 1 (February 1935), 112.

61 For YWCA, see *Tokyo Joshi Daigaku Gakusei YWCA no Rekishi* (Tokyo: Institute

for Women's Studies at TWCU, 1992), 17. For "specialty courses," see *Tokyo Joshi Daigaku 50 nen Shi*, 75–79.

62 As Reischauer described her in *Tokyo Woman's Christian College*, 24.

63 As for Yasui's dislike of missionary exhortation and policy on Christianity at the college, see Aoyama, *Yasui Tetsu Den*, 42–43, 349–72.

64 Letters, T. H. P. Sailer to Robert Speer (August 14, 1922), A. K. Reischauer to Robert Speer (May 23, 1921), and E. W. Ross to Robert Speer (May 4, 1920) in the TWCC file, PHS.

65 Letter, T. H. P. Sailer to Robert Speer (August 14, 1922) in the TWCC file, PHS. Also see "Statistics for September 1922" in box 129–2649, RG11, Archives of the United Board for Christian Higher Education in Asia (hereafter UBCHEA) Collection, Yale University Divinity School Library. For the Ginling faculty, see "Denominational Affliation of Ginling Faculty," in box 134–2705, RG11, ibid.

66 Letter, A. K. Reischauer to Robert E. Speer (November 30, 1917), in the TWCC file, PHS. The English name, Tokyo Woman's Christian College, was changed to Tokyo Woman's Christian University in 1977.

67 The incident is analyzed in detail in *Sousetsuki ni okeru Tokyo Joshi Daigaku Gakusei no Shisouteki Keiko* (Tokyo: Institute for Women's Studies at TWCC, 1990).

68 There are numerous works on this topic. See, for example, Doi Akio, *Nihon Purotesutanto Kirisutokyo-Shi*, 5th ed. (Tokyo: Shinkyo Shuppan, 2004).

69 *Dousoukai Geppo* 4, special no. (November 1938), 117; *Tokyo Joshi Daigaku 50 Nen Shi*, 114–18.

70 Letters, Robert Speer to A. K. Reischauer (September 13, 1922) and Florence Hooper to Robert Speer (January 17, 1923), TWCC file, PHS.

71 A letter to Mrs. Bancroft Hill (June 13, 1930), in BTCCC, TWCU.

72 Letter, William Bancroft Hill to Robert Speer (July 14, 1922), TWCC file, PHS.

73 Quoted in Aoyama, *Yasui Tetsu Den*, 221.

Lillian Trasher and the Orphans of Egypt

Beth Baron

Lillian Hunt Trasher (1887–1961) felt called in her early twenties to serve as a missionary in Africa and accepted the invitation of a Pentecostal couple to join them in Egypt. Having solicited funds, she went out in 1910, accompanied by her sister Jennie but without the backing of a church board, to Asyut, a city located on the Nile in southern Egypt. Within months of her arrival, she went to pray for a dying young mother. Trasher returned to the Pentecostal mission home with the dead woman's baby, but her hosts soon lost patience with the infant's crying. Rather than give the baby back to its family, which did not have the means to feed it, she kept the child. Unfettered by the bureaucracy that would have come from being associated with a board, Trasher rented a home and started an orphanage. She believed that God would provide. The Assiout Orphanage, which later became affiliated with the Assemblies of God Division of Foreign Missions, grew into a village that at its peak was home to fourteen hundred children and widows and contained its own schools, church, clinic, bakery, dairy, dormitories, and swimming pool. During its first fifty years, roughly eight thousand orphans passed through its doors.[1]

Trasher's orphanage became the centerpiece of the Pentecostal mission in Egypt, producing many of its converts, preachers, and leaders. It surpassed in size and longevity most other foreign missionary projects, and whereas other missionaries were expelled or prevented from returning at critical moments Trasher enjoyed special privileges. She became one of the most recognized Pentecostal missionaries of the twentieth century. Her supporters followed her story through her letters to evangelical periodicals, features in magazines, biographies, and a movie (*The Nile Mother*).[2] These works frame her life and the success of her mission as an affirmation of evangelical Christian faith.

The story of Lillian Trasher's mission in Egypt embodies multiple marginalities. The Assemblies of God mission in Egypt has been overshadowed by the United Presbyterian Church of North America (UPCNA) mission. Standard accounts have marginalized women in both missions. American missionaries evangelized heavily in the region around Asyut, a city in southern Egypt two hundred and fifty miles up the Nile from Cairo that has received only a fraction of the attention of the capital. Pentecostals and Presbyterians targeted Orthodox Copts, a Christian minority of roughly 10 percent whose story has been muted in the nationalist narrative of Egypt. And Trasher chose the most marginal of people for her ministry: orphaned and abandoned infants and children with disabilities who lacked family in a society that considered the family its basis and saw family lineage as critical to creating and sustaining social and political bonds. Her marginality as well as that of her wards helped ensure her success even when Presbyterians and other missionaries in Egypt began to withdraw.

Trasher's orphanage sat at the intersection of colonial and national projects and of the colonial and postcolonial state. It was a busy and sometimes dangerous intersection. British colonial officials protected American missionaries, lending them security, material aid, and assistance. Yet the colonial presence engendered resentment on the part of nationalists, who saw missionary and colonial projects as being intimately linked. Given the shortage of social welfare services, locals often supported and patronized missionary institutions, in the process reshaping them. They created schools, hospitals, clinics, and orphanages in the image of the missionary institutions but also in reaction to their presence and agendas. The postcolonial state reversed the protectionism of the colonial state and nationalized missionary institutions that had not been handed over to local churches. Trasher carefully navigated the crosscurrents of anticolonialism, nationalism, and Islamism and the transition from colonial to postcolonial state, keeping her orphanage intact.

This essay focuses on Trasher's orphanage as a lens through which to chart how colonial projects protected and local environments reshaped American missionary projects. While this encounter was reciprocal, transforming American missionaries and Egyptians alike, it was not symmetrical, and the overwhelming evidence comes from the American side. The sources have been examined with an eye to unsettling the story of American missionaries in the Middle East by focusing on the foot soldiers—the women workers—and the view of missionaries from the ground.

PRESBYTERIANS PREPARE THE FIELD

Pentecostal evangelists in Egypt followed in the footsteps of Presbyterians, who had arrived in Egypt in 1854 and established a base in Asyut early on.[3] The fourth largest city in Egypt, Asyut was the capital of Upper Egypt and a stronghold of Eastern Orthodox Christians, who were considered by Presbyterians to be in need of reform and receptive to Protestant conversion. Indeed, a number of prominent Coptic families in Asyut, most notably the Wissas and Khayatts, became Protestants.

Hanna Wissa relates in his family memoir that his grandfather, Hanna Boktor Wissa, left the Coptic Orthodox Church in 1865 after a confrontation with the bishop of Asyut. His maternal grandfather converted to Protestantism while attending the Syrian Protestant College (later renamed the American University in Beirut). The conversions of the newly emerging landed elite stemmed from a desire to reform religious experience, gain access to education, identify with Western culture, and challenge the authority of the Coptic Orthodox hierarchy. A small circle of wealthy Copts found their interests served by Presbyterian missionaries and helped to finance their institutions. The Khayatts funded a girls' school and the Wissas a boys' school, each affixing their name to the school. The Wissas also contributed generously to the building of the Presbyterians' first church in Asyut, completed in 1870; a larger main church was built on a Wissa property thirty years later.

The Presbyterians enjoyed the support of the board and established self-sustaining, money-making operations such as schools and hospitals. The Pentecostals, by contrast, came out on faith, hoping to raise money from local supporters and those back home; they focused on preaching, prayer, and proselytizing through the distribution of Bibles, Arabic periodicals, and gospel literature. American Protestant missionaries tended to have different class backgrounds and geographic origins: the Presbyterians hailed from Pennsylvania, Ohio, and the northern heartlands; the Pentecostals generally came from the American South or West and states like Missouri and California. (Trasher was born in Florida and raised in Georgia.) The Presbyterians, better educated than the Pentecostals, were elitist and sought out converts from the wealthier classes; the Pentecostals were populists who spent more time with the poor. The groups had very different notions of conversion: Presbyterians focused on learning and indoctrination, Pentecostals on a religious experience that included "baptism by the Holy Spirit" and speaking in tongues. The two Christian sects also had differing notions of gender roles in church and society: the Presbyterians came out mainly as couples in the early days: wives often taught or directed Bible women (locals who read the Bible to illiterate girls and women), while single women mainly taught. The Pentecostals came out as couples or as singles, but missionary wives and single women could preach should they feel divinely chosen for this task. The early Pentecostals were faith healers and left medical evangelizing to the Presbyterians, who started hospitals in Asyut and Tanta and numerous clinics.

Egyptian Copts, whose own church unity was cracking along Orthodox, Catholic, and Protestant fissures, saw family resemblances, not stark sectarian differences, in the competing Presbyterians and Pentecostals in Asyut. "One of the weaknesses of the Protestant movement in Egypt," noted Hanna Wissa, writing toward the end of the twentieth century, "was that there were many different Protestant missions trying to do the same thing. They stepped on each other's toes and there were sometimes petty misunderstandings among themselves." This exacerbated tensions among the reformed Copts, "who were supposed to carry the torch" but who had their own squabbles.[4] American missionaries dominated a field crowded by Protestants and Catholics of various nationalities but were beholden to the British for imperial protection.

COLONIAL POLICY ENCOURAGES PRIVATE SOCIAL WELFARE

Providing benevolence was a religious obligation that individuals in the Ottoman empire fulfilled through acts of charity and the establishment of trusts. Rulers and the elite had a special social obligation to care for those in need and demonstrated largesse and power through the funding of soup kitchens, hostels, and hospitals. During the nineteenth century, the Ottoman–Egyptian state increasingly appropriated religious functions and funds, taking over trusts and the care of the poor. Social service was increasingly divorced from indigenous religious institutions. The British occupation of 1882 reversed the trend toward a welfare state, encouraging private social welfare and permitting foreign providers to compete in delivering health, education, and welfare.

Before the advent of orphanages in the nineteenth century, an orphan would most likely have been fostered by a male guardian, presumably a relative, who gave the "gift of care." Abandoned infants and orphans might have been informally or secretly adopted or could have been placed in a hospital–mosque complex such as Maristan Qalawun in Cairo, which contained a religiously endowed orphanage and foundling home for infants.[5] In Islamic family law, which Copts followed on inheritance, an orphan (*yatim* or *yatima*; plural, *aytam* or *yatama*) was defined as a child whose father had died. A foundling (*laqit* or *laqita*; plural *luqata'*) was not legally an orphan, since the infant's unknown father was probably alive but not married to the infant's birth mother. A foundling was often the product of an illicit sexual encounter or rape but could also have been abandoned when a mother died in childbirth. In the 1830s, the new state-sponsored School for Midwives (Madrasat al-Wilada) contained the first state-run home for foundlings and a rudimentary orphanage; the home hired wet nurses for the infants, and orphans were enrolled along with slaves as the first students in the school.[6] In the second half of the nineteenth century, abandoned children and orphans found refuge in Catholic and Protestant missionary homes in Alexandria, Cairo, and Port Said.[7]

Under the British occupation of Egypt, state management of the poor continued; but British imperial policy limited funds allotted to health, education, and other social services to less than 1 percent of the budget.[8] Eager to have private individuals and groups bear the burden of providing social welfare, the British encouraged private initiatives. Public health and social welfare became a patchwork of state, private, and foreign initiatives. The haphazard approach of the colonial authorities was reflected in the distribution of services among various ministries and reliance on efforts from local elites, missionaries, and colonial wives. For example, the British friends of Evelyn Baring, Earl of Cromer, vice consul from 1883 until 1907 and Lord Cromer from 1892, started the Lady Cromer Home, or Found-ling Hospital, in a wing of Qasr al-Ayni Hospital in 1898.[9] The British, like their Ottoman–Egyptian predecessors, often seemed more concerned with keeping the poor out of view and off the streets than with providing meaningful services and training. In Cairo and Alexandria, eighty-one children in "undesirable surroundings" were taken off the streets in 1908 and sent to a reformatory in Giza after British colonial officials passed a law dealing with vagrant children whom they suspected of criminality.[10]

British imperialists had an unspoken pact with Christian missionaries. This came in the form of assistance in the colonial setting, removal of obstacles to institutional growth, and protection for missionaries (but not converts). British officials interceded at critical moments to save the lives of those preoccupied with saving souls. Missionaries in turn supported British rule, lending it a veneer of respectability and moral purpose.[11] American missionaries saw their role as spreading the kingdom of God through American forms of Christianity and could not have built their extensive network of hospitals, schools, and orphanages without British imperial support for their projects.

WINNING LOCAL SUPPORT AND
AVERTING ATTACKS

When Trasher arrived in Upper Egypt, preachers were plentiful, but there were no orphanages in Asyut or its environs. She resolved to start one. Children initially did not come flocking to the Malja' al-Aytam al-Khayri bi-Asyut (shortened in English to the Assiout Orphanage). As Trasher wrote, "Then we took in a few children, but at first it was very hard to get them."[12] Egyptians suspected that Trasher planned to take the orphans to America as slaves. Given Asyut's historical role as a major depot in the slave trade, which ended only in 1877, and the destination for slave cara-vans on the "forty days road" (*darb al-arba'in*) from Darfur and Kordofan in the Sudan, as well as the American history of slavery, the thought was not that strange.[13]

The first year of the orphanage's existence was rocky. After a child with bubonic plague entered the home, the authorities closed it down tempo-rarily, and Trasher returned to the United States to convalesce. In North Carolina, where she had once worked in a faith-based orphanage, she became ordained as an evangelist.[14] Upon her return to Egypt, the Assiout Orphanage began to grow. "Every week I have to turn away four or five little ignorant children from lack of space who might be taught and led to Christ," Trasher wrote in 1913.[15] By the next year she had fifty children under her care. An unnamed Turkish woman taught rug making, and Sarah Smith, a missionary from Indianapolis, gave Trasher a hand.

With space tight, Trasher decided to move the home out of the city in 1915. She built across the river in Abnub on a half acre that Balsam Wissa sold her for $250.[16] Balsam, the eldest daughter of Wissa Boktor Wissa, had been one of the first students in the Presbyterian Khayatt Girls' School. Being based on the east side of the river, the orphanage had room to grow. At the same time, the orphans, whose status was often ambiguous, were removed from the center of town and physically marginalized.

Trasher received support from local elites as well as from foreign backers, raising funds through Pentecostal periodicals, but the Pentecostals had not picked the most propitious moment to launch their missionary effort in Egypt. They arrived after the founding of the first nationalist parties in 1907 and were oblivious to the growing nationalist and Islamic opposition to British occupation. When the Ottoman empire entered the war as an ally of Germany in August 1914, Britain severed Egypt's formal ties to Istanbul and declared it a protectorate. The British kept a tight hold on the country, hoping to avert an uprising in support of Ottoman troops, who twice attempted to cross the Suez Canal during the war. Egyptian notables active in the nationalist movement were silenced under martial law and sent into internal exile on their country estates.

During the war foreign missionaries became targets of anti-imperial dissent. All the Pentecostals, with the exception of Trasher, evacuated Egypt, leaving the nine or ten stations they had built in the hands of "native workers."[17] Trasher stayed on with her staff, which included Shakir Gadallah and two other Egyptian women. Feeding the children in the midst of a spike in prices that multiplied costs challenged their resourcefulness. After the May wheat harvest, when peasants had money, Trasher rode out to villages on a donkey, soliciting funds and food and staying in police stations along the way.[18] She gained the peasants' trust along with donations of food and cash. As Trasher roamed the countryside during the war asking for food for the orphans, the British pressed peasants into the military labor corps and requisitioned their farm animals and hay for transport and feed. Peasant women took to the fields in record numbers to keep crops coming in and families fed.[19] That people had something left over to give to the orphans reflects their willingness to share with the poorest of the poor. Trasher's meanderings in the Egyptian countryside made her a familiar figure to village mayors, who later wrote to ask her to take in their widows and orphans.

The orphanage doubled its numbers during the war from roughly fifty to one hundred children. To accommodate the new residents, rooms were added in a process that became a pattern at the home. Once the children got older, they participated in the brick making and laying process. At the end of the war an influenza epidemic that left many children orphaned increased the numbers even more. "We are glad to accept the most needy cases, and have had to enlarge our house, adding four new rooms which are about filled," Trasher wrote in early 1919.[20] The boys learned trades like carpentry and shoemaking, and the girls were taught sewing, child care, and housework.

As the war wound down and international peace talks were organized, Egyptian nationalists sought a place at the table. They had remained quiet during the hostilities in spite of the resentment they felt at being forced to contribute to the war effort. The British preferred to handle negotiations over Egypt's fate bilaterally with a handpicked government and turned down the request of a delegation of nationalist leaders (a *Wafd*) to attend peace talks in Paris. The delegation mobilized support with petitions and speeches, becoming the seeds of a new nationalist party. When Wafd leaders refused to go quietly to their estates, colonial officials arrested them. Massive protests erupted throughout Egypt, the protestors calling for the release of their leaders. The British acted quickly to restore order in the capital, where among those protesting were some of Trasher's staunchest supporters, notably Esther Wissa (the daughter of Balsam Wissa and Akhtukh Fanus and the wife of Fahmi Wissa).[21] In Asyut, events started peacefully but took a violent turn.[22]

Before the violence erupted an American Presbyterian minister had tried to persuade Trasher to take refuge with his group in one of the schools in Asyut, but she refused to leave the orphanage in Abnub. After communication with Cairo was severed and the banks limited access to funds, Trasher and Auntie Zakiya, the head matron, decided to send all of those children with family in Asyut and nearby villages to their relatives.

Fahmi and Esther Wissa and their first three children, (*from left*) Doussa, Gamil, and Adli (d. 1921), ca. 1918. By permission of Book Guild Publishing, Brighton, England.

The orphanage subsequently became cut off from town and came under attack by looters. A neighbor intervened. "Men, be ashamed!" he apparently said. "These are our own orphans, our own Egyptian children for whom the lady has given her life . . . and she has never done you any harm. Be ashamed and go somewhere else but to the home of our orphan babies."[23] While many other foreign institutions and businesses were attacked and burned in the revolt, the orphanage was spared.

When British reinforcements arrived in the region, they forced Trasher and the children to evacuate the orphanage. The boys were moved into one of the American Presbyterian schools in town; the girls and babies were sent to the American Presbyterian Hospital. Auntie Zakiya took charge of the children, awaiting permission to return with them to Abnub.

British officials forced Trasher to join other foreigners being evacuated to Cairo. Having been away from her family for seven years, Trasher decided to use the time of her enforced separation from the children to visit the United States. There she raised funds for the orphanage and registered as an evangelist of the Assemblies of God Church, beginning her official affiliation with a church that did not exist when she left for Asyut in 1910.[24]

ROYALS, NOTABLES, AND LOCAL EGYPTIANS HELP FUND THE HOME

In the wake of the Revolution of 1919, Egyptians started new orphanages, sensing that they needed to care for their own orphans and abandoned children rather than leave it to foreigners. 'Abd al-'Aziz Nazmi spear-headed the effort to open the Malja' al-Hurriyya (Shelter of Freedom) for boys, and Labiba Ahmad launched an orphanage through her Jam'iyyat Nahdat al-Sayyidat al-Misriyyat (Society of the Egyptian Ladies' Awakening).[25] Both efforts were based in Cairo and were modeled after missionary institutions; both sought to create good citizens and loyal nationalists.

Trasher's refuge had little competition in Asyut, to which she had returned in February 1920. She had more requests for entry than she could accommodate. "You cannot imagine how I feel when I have to refuse some [children entry]," she lamented. "There are no other orphanages within hundreds of miles from here and the other orphanages in Cairo and Alexandria will not take in new ones until some of the older ones leave."[26] Rather than continue to turn down children, Trasher decided to expand the home again. A gift in 1921 of fifteen hundred dollars from Sultan (later King) Fu'ad (r. 1917–36) helped make this enlargement possible.[27] His visit to the orphanage was one in a line of visits by Egyptian rulers and foreign royals and nobles, including a queen of Belgium and a lord from Scotland, who sought to demonstrate their benevolence and enhance their prestige through charitable giving.

Asyut's Coptic elite continued to support the refuge. In 1922, Balsam Wissa's brothers, Zaki and George, teamed up with Amin Khayatt and Bushra Hanna to buy two plus acres at $2,625 for the orphanage and equipped the land with water and electricity at the added cost of $1,000. In 1928, Amin's older sister, Amina Khayatt, the wife of Nassif Wissa, donated $3,100 to cover the purchase of two and a half plus additional acres for the orphanage.[28] This last gift came after Trasher had gone to the shariʿa court in Asyut in 1926 to establish a trust (*waqf*) for the lands and buildings of the Assiout Orphanage. Her strategy deviated from the standard practice of American missionaries, who accumulated property in the name of a board, which then controlled the property. According to the terms of the trust, Trasher could never sell the land but would remain head of the trust as long as she lived. She appointed a committee of interrelated Wissas, Khayatts, and Alexans along with her sister Jennie Benton to administer the trust after her death.[29] Trasher explained, "All those who have helped buy the land are absolutely satisfied, now that the land is made over 'Wafk' [*sic*], as I myself can never sell it."[30] Elite Copts now felt assured that they were giving to an institution that would serve Upper Egypt for the long term.

It was no accident that the refuge was located next to the Nile Sporting Club, for the same families who sold or donated land to Trasher for her orphanage provided land for the club. The playground of the Asyut elite, the club contained tennis courts, a nine-hole golf course, and a box for charitable donations that Trasher periodically emptied.[31] Women like Lily (Alexan) Khayyat and Esther (Fanus) Wissa, longtime supporters of the orphanage, took out subscriptions, started sewing circles, and sent gifts of wheat, beef, cooked meals, cotton, and cloth. They celebrated births, weddings, and major life events with donations, and adopted Trasher as one of their own. They invited her to meals, took her on outings, and sent her new dresses. "They realize that I have given my life for their children and show their appreciation in many ways," Trasher wrote in 1924, no longer having to ride out to villages on a donkey.[32] Esther's son Hanna Wissa remembered this "remarkable lady" from summer visits to his grandparents in Asyut.[33]

Middle-strata merchants and poor workers and peasants also gave gifts in kind or sums of money to the orphanage, ranging from free taxi rides for the children to stocks of soap and other items to wrinkled money. Trasher's letters are full of stories of local generosity, often from people of humble means. The community valued her commitment to caring for the orphans.

The support of royalty, notable families, and the general public was needed to fund expansions of space and the quotidian feeding of a constantly growing group of children. The orphanage charged no fees for the orphans it took in and accepted boys under ten and girls under twelve. Lillian wanted the children for the long term in order to be able to work the transformation to body and soul she envisioned. The orphanage set basic rules for admission that required relatives "to sign a paper that they give the children to us until they are eighteen years old," thereby granting the orphanage legal custody and preventing families from retrieving their children before the work of socialization and conversion was completed.[34] The orphanage also accepted children with disabilities, the offspring of lepers, and blind girls (but not blind boys, for whom there was already a home in Egypt).[35]

Egyptians increasingly turned to the orphanage for help. Fathers often brought in babies after their wives had died from complications of childbirth. Many infants left at the orphanage were thus not technically orphans but offspring of single fathers who had insufficient knowledge, will, or means to raise motherless children. In the days before there was an orphanage, such babies might have been given to a wet nurse, informally adopted by others, or abandoned. The orphanage also accepted foundlings: "About two weeks ago I had some one knock at my door about midnight and hand me a wee tiny baby, just a few hours old which they had found in the street," wrote Trasher in 1921. "We had one like this one a little while ago, but its head had been injured when it had been thrown away and it went quite blind and then it died."[36]

Another set of children arrived with widowed mothers who had no financial resources or willing relatives to help raise their fatherless offspring. The older children were separated from their mothers and placed in dormitories. "It quite often happens," Trasher explained, "that a child is received with its widowed mother, who earns her support by working in the orphanage, whilst the children receive full training along with the others."[37] Roughly 10 percent of the population of the orphanage at any given moment consisted of widows, who were indispensable to the orphanage, becoming its main labor force and replacing the servants hired earlier. They performed menial tasks such as doing laundry, cooking, baking, and cleaning (and later, when the orphanage began raising Jersey cattle donated by the American Presbyterian Mission, they milked the cows). Although they were the backbone of the institution, the widows were seen as *fellahat* (peasant women) and were not permitted to care for their own or other children once weaned "because they were still too

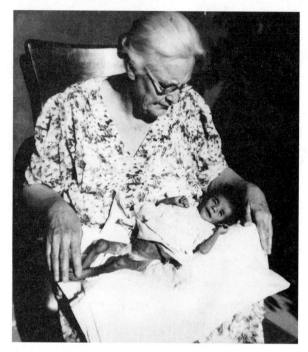

Lillian Trasher with infant, ca. 1950.
By permission of Flower Pentecostal Heritage Center P0264.

much like the village they had left," the American missionary Florence Christie noted. The older girls, who were taught to be "clean and cultured" and had been remade into Americanized Pentecostal Christians, cared for the younger ones.[38] For the widows, the orphanage provided an alternative to poverty and hunger, yet it came at a price: they had little say over the upbringing of their children and often experienced enforced separations.

A few "fallen" girls who did not or could not abandon their newborn infants also found refuge in the orphanage with their children. British officials in Cairo asked Trasher to give safe haven to one such unmarried mother: her boyfriend had been killed by her father and brother, both of whom had then been tried and executed, but the girl's mother and a younger brother still presented a threat to her safety. "We would be very grateful if you could see your way to admitting this girl to your home," the authorities requested, wanting "to give her a chance to lead a decent life and avoid the risk of assassination by her family." Trasher accepted the mother and child as well as girls in similar situations: "Others have come like this and have been wonderfully saved."[39] In such situations, while the British provided the mission with security, the missionaries helped the colonial authorities to care for individuals whose social networks had collapsed or did not exist.

Egyptians supported the orphanage in spite of its religious agenda, and in some cases because of it, for it provided a service others were unwilling to provide. The shame of illegitimacy hung over those children whose mothers were not married or whose fathers were unknown, making it hard for them to be accepted into the larger society and for society to care for them. Another set of stigmatized children who ended up at the home were those with physical disabilities, including children with birth defects and those injured in accidents. For the children, the orphanage became a large family.

THE ANTIMISSIONARY MOVEMENT
AND ITS AFTERMATH

Trasher opened the doors of the orphanage wide, not denying entrance based on religion. "I take into my orphanage Mohammedans, Syrians, Catholics—anyone. My work is not denominational, although I myself am Pentecostal," she explained.[40] Under the terms of the charitable trust written in 1926, the orphanage was established "as a home for the training and education of poor orphans, of any religion and of any denomination." The trust stipulated that Muslim children were to be trained in Islam, and Christian children "instructed in the teachings of the Assemblies of God."[41] Although it was difficult to ascertain the exact number of Muslims in the orphanage, Muslim children were a minority of roughly 10 percent. There is no indication that Trasher provided an Islamic education for her Muslim wards and no mention of going to mosques or bringing imams to instruct them. This may well have been a fictive strategy enacted in court to get the land placed in a trust and avoid state interference. Unlike Egyptians, who saw infants as born with a religious identity inherited from a father (or mother in the case of Jews), Pentecostal missionaries saw religious faith as something to be instilled, taught, and experienced.

Serving as matriarch and patriarch of the orphanage family, Trasher sought to save souls. In winter 1926, she claimed to see results. "After crying and praying like the sound of many waters, they began to testify," Trasher wrote. "One little Mohammedan boy got up on top of the bench and testified saying, 'In my village I was a sinner but now God has saved me and if I was cut in little pieces I would not serve idols.' . . . Souls are being saved and others baptized in the Holy Spirit."[42] The intensification of Protestant evangelizing in Egypt in the late 1920s and early 1930s led to a record number of revivals, conversions, and baptisms. But the open attempts to proselytize among Muslims as well as Christians led to a backlash that peaked in the summer of 1933.

An episode that began as a confrontation between a fifteen-year-old orphan girl named Turkiyya Hasan and a matron in the Swedish Salaam Orphanage in Port Said galvanized the country and led to investigations of missionary institutions. "I am very much in need of the prayers of all the Lord's children as there is a great stir among all of the Muslims against the missionaries here," Trasher wrote in a letter home on June 23, 1933.[43] A correspondent in Asyut for the daily Arabic newspaper *al-Jihad*, which prided itself on being in the vanguard of the antimissionary movement, called upon the authorities to investigate the orphanage.[44] Trasher admitted to the inspection officials sent by the governor that the Muslim children went to Christian services along with the other children. She explained that hers was a faith-based enterprise—"the Lord supplies our needs"—and she told them about her own "call to the work." She gave them copies of financial reports, pamphlets, and, upon request, a Bible. The governor subsequently called Trasher in for a meeting; while thanking her for what she had done for the poor children of Egypt, he informed her that they were going to take the Muslim children out of the orphanage and build new refuges for them.[45]

In a move celebrated by *al-Jihad*, government officials returned to remove the Muslim children. The newspaper reported, "July 8th, 1933, was a day of great joy at Asyut when about 64 Moslem boys and girls were taken away from Miss Lillian's Orphanage."[46] Although Trasher was relieved that she had not been forced out of Egypt like the matron of the Port Said orphanage, she lamented the loss of the children: "Words cannot describe the sad sight as they took them away! . . . Pray that the teaching of years will go with them and not die."[47]

The antimissionary movement transformed missionary orphanages in Egypt into institutions theoretically open only to Christians and Jews. The state protected Muslims from evangelizing but felt little compulsion to do the same for Orthodox Copts, many of whom were also troubled by Protestants' proselytizing. Although one could never know the identity of a foundling, the myth that the Christian orphanages served only Christians became convenient.

From the 1930s on, the large American Presbyterian mission began retrenching in reaction to the antimissionary movement in Egypt and decreasing support for foreign missions at home. But Pentecostals were not on the retreat. The orphanage that stood at the center of the mission in Egypt settled back into its routine. When the writer Jerome Beatty visited in 1939, there were 647 orphans and 74 widows, and the orphanage had grown into a virtual village.[48] Christie, who taught, delivered babies, and supervised the girls in this period, described working for Trasher: "She possessed a loving, but strong personality, which people sometimes found hard to follow. . . . She was known to be difficult to work for also because of her high expectations and demands." There was only one Mama. The other women, as Christie quickly learned, were Aunties.[49]

The orphanage instilled American Pentecostal culture and values. The children learned English in addition to Arabic and dressed in American-style clothes that were either sent from the United States or made at the orphanage. While cutting patterns and sewing clothes, they listened to hymns on the gramophone, including "Onward, Christian Soldiers!" "We Are Going Down the Valley," and "Joy to the World."[50] They did not play recordings of Umm Kulthum, the most famous Egyptian singer of the century, whose records were available from the 1920s.[51]

Along lines that were typical of industrial schools boys were taught artisan skills like carpentry and chair making, and girls were trained in such domestic tasks as infant care and sewing. Both had farming tasks, the girls feeding chickens and collecting eggs, and the boys working with barn animals. The boys attended primary and secondary schools at the orphanage and could continue on to college if they had the aptitude. They took up the trades into which they had been apprenticed or took up careers as teachers, clerks, and pastors. Some of the boys became active in the Assemblies of God Church in Egypt, forming its core. They evangelized in villages, started schools and churches, and staffed the missions scattered about Egypt.[52]

Girls attended a general school in preparation for marriage. Trasher made it clear that the girls were not to be hired out as domestic servants, the once-expected fate of female orphans; working in a home around unrelated men would compromise their reputations and hurt their chances for marriage. Even if they excelled in their studies, they were not offered the option of continuing their educations. In this, Trasher's goal differed from that of the American Presbyterians, who championed girls' education and started secondary schools and colleges for girls in Asyut and Cairo. And it contrasted with the agenda of Egyptian feminists, who endorsed girls' secondary and higher education as the main path to women's progress and pushed open the doors of Cairo University in the late 1920s. Most of the orphan girls married; some did not and stayed in the home as helpers. A few felt called to join American female missionaries in their work outside the orphanage. This was the only career path available to them.

Trasher maintained a strict gender segregation that was more Egyptian than American. Boys and girls had separate dormitories and schools and separate seating in church and the dining hall. With the exceptions of siblings, boys and girls were not allowed to talk to one another. When boys were ready to leave the orphanage, they approached Trasher to ask permission to marry one of the girls. She decided if they were suitable, allowing them to meet in her presence but not to date or court. She did this at a time when Egyptian elites were challenging such conventions, calling for meeting before marriage and endorsing the ideal of companionate marriage. Trasher also did not allow blind girls to marry, a policy Christie characterized as a practical approach to "an already severe problem."[53]

During the Second World War, American missionaries were evacuated from Egypt. Those in Asyut headed south to the Sudan. Trasher stayed on but sent Christie to America to raise funds, which were in short supply during the war. When cities such as Alexandria were bombed by the Germans, the orphanage opened its doors to those of its grown children who had become refugees. The orphanage survived the war intact but faced challenges in its wake, when cholera and malarial epidemics devastated the countryside. After the war, as Presbyterians were reducing their presence, Pentecostals sent reinforcements to help Trasher.

WEATHERING THE REVOLUTION OF 1952

"It is whispered around the city of Assiut that it is always good to give an offering to the orphanage when God has been good to you!" wrote Lester Sumrall in 1951.[54] With the donations it received from Egyptians and Americans, the Assiout Orphanage continued to expand. Trasher decided to transform the orphanage hospital into a nursery for babies over seven months of age and to build a new hospital for sick children. Ground was broken for the new building in late 1951, and it opened the following year.[55] That year marked a sea change in Egyptian politics.

Revolutionary winds transformed Egypt in 1952 when a group of officers led by Gamal Abdel Nasser (1918–70) toppled King Farouk (r. 1936–52) and inaugurated military rule by a Revolutionary Command Council (RCC). This effectively put an end to the British presence in Egypt as well as to the presence of most of the foreign missionaries they had assisted and protected. Nasser, who was born in Alexandria, had spent many summers and some school years in his father's natal village, Bani Murr, which was adjacent to Abnub and within walking distance of the orphanage. His sympathy toward the refuge and its founder helped to save it from the fate of other missionary institutions and its founder-director from expulsion.[56]

When the RCC toured Upper Egypt in March 1953 as part of an attempt to consolidate power by rallying popular support, they stopped at the orphanage. Prime Minister Muhammad Naguib led the entourage of government officials, local leaders, reporters, and photographers that visited Trasher and the children on the afternoon of March 24. Naguib's sister had stopped by the orphanage earlier that month to lay the groundwork for the visit. Its purpose was to soften the image of the colonels and generals who had come to power through a coup in July 1952, abrogated the Constitution in December, and banned political parties in January 1953, allowing only the Muslim Brothers, who remained a potent political force, to operate. The RCC also hoped to demonstrate through the visit to the orphanage their concern for the poor and their genuine interest in social welfare.[57]

Before departing, Naguib inscribed a message in the guest book, part of which read, "I call upon all those who are engaged in social reform and activities to visit this institution and learn from it what they should do if they really wish to achieve." The leading Arabic and English dailies—*al-Akhbar*, *al-Ahram*, and the *Egyptian Mail*—covered the visit, giving the regime a human face and the orphanage widespread publicity. The pieces transformed Lillian Trasher from a missionary into a social worker to fit revolutionary times and new social agendas.[58] Trasher noted that the nice things Naguib said "helped to give the people of Egypt a more friendly feeling toward us."[59] Trasher needed this political capital if she and her institution were to survive revolutionary transformations. Naguib himself did not survive the struggle for power among the revolutionary officers and was placed under house arrest.

In September 1952, the revolutionaries limited agricultural landhold-ings to two hundred *feddans* (a feddan is slightly larger than an acre) and later lowered the limit to one hundred feddans. They undercut the main sources of wealth of the elite landowning families such as the Wissas, Khayyats, and Alexans who were Trasher's original patrons. The authori-ties then began to appropriate and nationalize businesses, properties, hos-pitals, and schools (including, in the 1960s, the Khayatt Girls' School and the Wissa Boys' School, razing the latter). The Nile Sports Club, a favorite retreat of wealthy Upper Egyptians, became the Asyut Sports Club for police.[60] The new name and beneficiaries showed the clear shift of power from the landed elite to the military and security forces. The orphanage could no longer look to notable families as major benefactors. In any case, in the 1940s Trasher had already reconstituted the board of the orphanage, replacing deceased Coptic friends with orphans and representatives of the Assemblies of God.

The days of the American Presbyterians, whose infrastructure and friendship had aided Trasher, were numbered after the Revolution. In retreat from the 1930s, the Presbyterians gradually transferred most of their schools, hospitals, and other properties (including the Fowler Or-phanage) to the Egyptian Evangelical Church. This process of indigeniza-tion was meant to avoid confiscations. The Presbyterians phased out their mission in the 1960s.[61] In contrast, the Assemblies of God were on the upsurge in America, and their missionary zeal was strong.

When the United States decided not to fund Nasser's Aswan dam project, which was designed to power industrial development, strains in American–Egyptian relations grew. To raise funds for development,

Lillian Trasher with children of the Assiout Orphanage, ca. 1950.
By permission of Flower Pentecostal Heritage Center P1990.

Nasser nationalized the Suez Canal in 1956. The British, French, and Israelis quickly launched a tripartite attack to topple the regime. Americans were evacuated along with other foreigners from Egypt, but once again Trasher stayed put. "Thank God, everything with us is just the same as it has always been," she wrote to reassure her supporters in America. The ladies of the Women's Missionary Committee and other supporters continued to send supplies of clothing, linen, toys, and equipment.[62]

Trasher did not cut back her activities or plan to leave. At the start of 1957, the number of residents at the orphanage stood at 1,035, not including refugees from the Suez War.[63] The next year Trasher built a new school to accommodate the growing numbers, and supporters sent supplies. When a new car got held up in customs, she appealed directly to Nasser to waive the duties. His response—"I would like to tell you that your work for the orphans is very much appreciated by everyone in this country"—reassured Trasher. "I feel it will give me by far the greatest pristage [sic] I have ever had," she wrote, anticipating that Nasser's blessing would help her in dealing with the Egyptian authorities.[64] The Egyptian press recognized her as "Mother of a Thousand."[65]

No longer young, Trasher turned to carefully updating her affairs. She intended to run the orphanage as long as she could and then turn it over to a team of handpicked successors—a protégé from the orphanage and Assemblies of God missionaries from America. She subverted designs on the property by Habib Yunis, the Egyptian treasurer of the Assemblies of God in Egypt, whose motives she suspected.[66] "Everything has been settled as *we* wanted it in the [Ministry of] Social Affair[s]," she wrote to the head of the Foreign Board.[67] If earlier in her career she had recognized the power of Asyut elites, she now realized that power lay in the hands of the new military elite, which had its own social agenda. She made arrangements with the Asyut office of the Ministry of Social Affairs, the office responsible for inspecting and certifying the orphanage. Trasher's hope was that the orphanage, which numbered 1,340 in 1960, would survive under a system of checks and balances—officials of the local Ministry of Social Affairs, orphan successors, and advisors from the Assemblies of God Foreign Board—after her death.

Trasher cut short a trip to the United States in 1960 when she grew ill, not wanting to die and be buried away from Egypt and her orphans. She returned to Asyut, where she celebrated the fiftieth anniversary of the orphanage in February 1961. She died later that year on December 17, 1961. The Egyptian and Pentecostal press mourned the passing of a woman called alternatively a "saint," "virgin mother of thousands of Egyptians," "Nile Mother," and "Mama" Lillian. Many of the former residents of the orphanage returned for her funeral, the largest in Asyut's history: a six-horse carriage pulled the body through the streets of the city to a plot in the orphanage cemetery, where she was buried alongside helpers and many of her children. She had sought to instill American Christian culture and values in the orphans and abandoned children under her care; by the end of her life, after fifty years in Egypt, she considered Egypt her home, the orphanage her family.

CONCLUSION

Lillian Trasher's orphanage survived real and potential nationalist assaults at pivotal moments—the Revolution of 1919, the antimissionary movement of 1933, and the Free Officers Revolution in 1952—because it targeted an underserved community that sat at the margins of society. While Presbyterians were in retreat from the 1930s, Pentecostal enthusiasm for foreign missions grew, and the Assiout Orphanage continued to flourish, surpassing in size and longevity other, better-endowed foreign missionary projects. The orphanage proved to be the most enduring part of the Pentecostal mission in Egypt. It also became an important symbol of the power of faith for the Assemblies of God Church, one of the fastest growing churches in the world. In recent decades, the orphanage, which was sometimes known as Miss Lillian's Orphanage during her lifetime and became known as the Lillian Trasher Memorial Orphanage after her death, has become a destination for young North American volunteers, who give service to affirm their faith.

Lillian Trasher had an uncanny ability to navigate the crosscurrents of political change, thus ensuring the longevity and success of the mission. At critical moments British colonial officials and, later, American officials interceded with help, and a broad base of Americans and other Westerners supported the project with donations. Trasher found a niche in Asyut precisely because Egyptians of all classes supported the venture, though some felt strongly that the orphanage should not raise Muslims, who were removed from the home in the 1930s. While the colonial state relied on a patchwork of social welfare providers, the postcolonial state moved to take over many of these projects, ousting missionaries and foreigners. Trasher was permitted to stay on in Egypt when others were expelled or asked to leave because she had earned the trust and admiration of Egyptians at the highest levels.

The marginality of women and Pentecostals in the missionary field, Asyut and Copts in Egypt, and orphans in Muslim society all served to shelter Trasher's undertaking. While most of the children in the orphanage came after the death of one or both parents, the social shame associated with illegitimacy and birth defects surrounded them all and protected the mission of the orphanage. Trasher cultivated local support from Egyptians who preferred to subcontract the raising of such children to foreigners and foreign support from those who saw her mission as worthwhile. Her initial independence from a board or bureaucracy gave her broad scope for working with local inhabitants and foreign donors in launching and ex-panding the home. Ultimately the orphanage worked because the locals shaped it. The marginality of the missionary, the location, and the children allowed the orphanage to grow and flourish in unimagined ways. The children raised one another, the first generation of grown girls and boys in turn caring for the next, creating a sense of family for those without the bonds of kinship. This was crucial for their life within the orphanage and later in the larger society outside of it. The labor of widows was also critical to sustaining the home, but shelter came at a price: many of the widows were physically separated and socially distanced from their children. The widows, though, at least maintained ties with their transformed children. Those single mothers who felt forced by social circumstances to abandon their children at birth could not maintain ties: Trasher became the Nile Mother of their children.

Lillian Trasher's mission challenges the narrative of missionaries in Egypt and the broader Middle East. Historical accounts, based mostly on the memoirs, writings, and records of the male leaders of the Presbyterian and Congregationalist movements, show a distinction between evangelizing and modernizing and a shift from proselytizing to providing social services. While this shift may hold for male missionaries, it does not easily apply to the women, who composed the majority of the rank and file of the missionary movement from the late nineteenth century. They were engaged from the outset in social welfare projects, starting or working in schools, hospitals, clinics, and orphanages that consistently fused social work with proselytizing. The social welfare work cannot uncritically be characterized as modernizing. Trasher's mission endorsed certain medical treatments, gender roles, and religious rituals that were at odds with prevailing expectations of modernity. The trajectory of Trasher's work also challenges the periodization of mission history. While missionaries from liberalizing Protestant churches were in retreat from the 1930s, Pentecostals enjoyed an upsurge in the United States and abroad. Trasher's institution weathered the storms that came with decolonization and thrived.

NOTES

1 While Asyut is the preferred transliteration for the town, I will use the spelling for the orphanage (Assiout) that Lillian Trasher used for it. For background, see Beth Baron, "Orphans and Abandoned Children in Modern Egypt," *Between Missionaries and Dervishes: Interpreting Welfare in the Middle East,* ed. Nefissa Neguib and Inger Marie Okkenhaug, 12–34 (Leiden: Brill, 2008).

2 Jerome Beatty, "Nile Mother," *American Magazine* (July 1939), 55; Lester Sumrall,

Lillian Trasher: The Nile Mother (Springfield, Mo.: Gospel Publishing House, 1951); Beth Prim Howell, *Lady on a Donkey* (New York: E. P. Dutton, 1960); *Letters from Lillian* (Springfield, Mo.: Assemblies of God Division of Foreign Missions, 1983); Janet and Geoff Benge, *Lillian Trasher: The Greatest Wonder in Egypt* (Seattle: YWAM Publishing, 2004).

3 Heather J. Sharkey, *American Evangelicals in Egypt: Missionary Encounters in an Age of Empire* (Princeton: Princeton University Press, 2008).

4 Hanna F. Wissa, *Assiout—The Saga of an Egyptian Family* (Sussex, England: Book Guild, 1994), 122.

5 Mine Ener, *Managing Egypt's Poor and the Politics of Benevolence, 1800–1952* (Princeton: Princeton University Press, 2004), xi, 26.

6 Ibid., 42–45, 155 note 81.

7 Ibid., 103.

8 Beth Baron, "Women's Voluntary Social Welfare Organizations in Egypt," *Gender, Religion and Change in the Middle East: Two Hundred Years of History*, ed. Inger Marie Okkenhaug and Ingvild Flaskerud, 85–102 (New York: Berg, 2005).

9 British National Archives, Foreign Office (FO) 371/1362/15421, Kitchener to Grey, "Annual Report for 1911," Cairo, April 6, 1912, 37.

10 FO 371/661/12738, Gorst to Grey, "Annual Report of 1908," Cairo, March 27, 1909, 86; Ener, *Managing Egypt's Poor*, 114–15.

11 Sharkey, *American Evangelicals in Egypt*.

12 Trasher, *Word and Witness*, October 20, 1913, 2.

13 Muhafazat Asyut, *Asyut fi 10 Sanawat* (Cairo: Matbaʿat Nahdat Misr, 1962), 9.

14 Flower Pentecostal Heritage Center (FPHC), Lillian Trasher Personal Papers, File cards, 0504 074.

15 Trasher, *Word and Witness* (October 20, 1913), 2

16 Veronica Seton-Williams and Peter Stocks, *Blue Guide: Egypt* (New York: W. W. Norton, 1984), 475; Wissa, *Assiout*, 175–76.

17 Ghali Hanni, *Latter Rain Evangel* (October 1916), 4; Habib Yousef, *Weekly Evangel* (March 3, 1917), 13; idem, *Weekly Evangel* (May 19, 1917), 13.

18 Trasher, "The Miracle of the Assiout Orphanage," *Latter Rain Evangel* (August 1924), 22.

19 Beth Baron, "The Politics of Female Notables in Postwar Egypt," *Borderlines: Genders and Identities in War and Peace, 1870–1930*, ed. Billie Melman, 332–33 (New York: Routledge, 1998).

20 Trasher, *Latter Rain Evangel* (March 1919), 15.

21 Beth Baron, *Egypt as a Woman: Nationalism, Gender, and Politics* (Berkeley: University of California Press, 2005), chaps. 5–7.

22 *Muhafazat Asyut: al-ʿId al-Qawmi, 18 April 1982* (Cairo: Jumhuriyyat Misr al-ʿArabiyya, al-Hayʾa al-ʿAmma lil-Istiʿmalat, 1982), 7–8.

23 Trasher, "God's Protection through a Reign of Terror," *Latter Rain Evangel* (September 1919), 16.

24 Trasher, "God's Protection in Great Peril," *Latter Rain Evangel* (June 1919), 11; idem, "God's Protection through a Reign of Terror," *Latter Rain Evangel* (September 1919), 16; A. H. Post, "Alexandria, Egypt," *Christian Evangel* (June 28, 1919), 10.

25 Ener, *Managing Egypt's Poor*, 102, 117–19; Beth Baron, "Islam, Philanthropy, and Political Culture in Interwar Egypt: The Activism of Labiba Ahmad," *Poverty and Charity in Middle Eastern Contexts*, ed. Michael Bonner et al., 239–54 (Albany: SUNY Press, 2003).

26 Trasher, *Pentecostal Evangel* (July 18, 1925), 10.

27 Trasher, *Pentecostal Evangel* (April 2, 1921), 12.

28 FPHC, Lillian Trasher Personal Papers, Deeds, 0795 043.

29 FPHC, Lillian Trasher Personal Papers, Waqf Document in Arabic and English translation, 0795 043.

30 FPHC, Lillian Trasher Personal Papers, Explanation of Deeds, 0795 043.

31 Wissa, *Assiout*, 176; *Muhafazat Asyut*, map on page 38.

32 Trasher, *Latter Rain Evangel* (August 1924), 21.

33 Wissa, *Assiout*, 176–79.

34 Sumrall, *Lillian Trasher*, 22–23.

35 Trasher, *Pentecostal Evangel* (August 25, 1923), 12.

36 Trasher, *Pentecostal Evangel* (June 25, 1921), 13.

37 Trasher, *Pentecostal Evangel* (August 25, 1923), 12.

38 Christie, *Called to Egypt*, 45–46.

39 Trasher, "Thou God Seest Me," *Pentecostal Evangel* (December 13, 1930), 11.

40 Trasher, *Latter Rain Evangel* (October 1919), 7.

41 FPHC, Lillian Trasher Personal Papers, Waqf, 0795 043.

42 "A Big Revival in Egypt," *Pentecostal Evangel* (March 27, 1926), 11.

43 Trasher, *Letters from Lillian*, letter dated June 23, 1933, 20.

44 *Al-Jihad* (July 3, 1933) in Presbyterian Historical Society (PHS), RG 209, box 26, folder 38.

45 Lillian Trasher, *A Work of Faith and Labor of Love: The Assiout Orphanage, Assiout, Egypt* (Springfield, Mo.: Foreign Missions Department, General Council of the Assemblies of God, 1937), letter dated June 23, 1933, 19; idem, *Letters from Lillian*, letter dated July 20, 1933, 22; "Officials Commend Assiout Orphanage," *Pentecostal Evangel* (August 26, 1933), 9.

46 *Al-Jihad* (July 10, 1933) in PHS, RG 209, box 26, folder 38.

47 Trasher, *Work of Faith*, 20; *Letters from Lillian*, 22–23.

48 Beatty, "Nile Mother," 55; Noel Perkin, "Down in Egypt," *Pentecostal Evangel* (May 1, 1937), 9–11.

49 Florence Christie, *Called to Egypt* (Wichita Falls, Texas: Western Christian Foundation, 1997), 54.

50 Trasher, *Work of Faith*, letter dated March 8, 1935, 29.

51 Virginia Danielson, "Artists and Entrepreneurs: Female Singers in Cairo during the 1920s," *Women in Middle Eastern History: Shifting Boundaries in Sex and*

Gender, ed. Nikki R. Keddie and Beth Baron, 297–301 (New Haven: Yale University Press, 1991).

52 Samu'il Mishriqi, *Tarikh al-Madhhab al-Khamsini fi Misr* (Cairo: al-Majma' al-'Amm li-Kana'is Allah al-Khamsiniyya, 1985).

53 Christie, *Called to Egypt,* 53.

54 Sumrall, *Lillian Trasher,* 38.

55 Trasher, " 'Growing Pains' at Assiut," *Pentecostal Evangel* (December 2, 1951), 7.

56 Seton-Williams and Stocks, *Blue Guide: Egypt,* 476.

57 *Al-Ahram* (March 25, 1953); *al-Akhbar* (March 25, 1953); FPHC, Lillian Trasher Personal Papers, Scrapbook; Christie, *Called to Egypt,* 142–43; "General Naguib's Visit to Assiut," *Pentecostal Evangel* (February 13, 1955), 2.

58 *Al-Ahram* (March 25, 1953); *al-Akhbar* (March 25, 1953); FPHC, Lillian Trasher Personal Papers, Scrapbook; Christie, *Called to Egypt,* 142–43; "General Naguib's Visit to Assiut," *Pentecostal Evangel* (February 13, 1955), 2.

59 Trasher, *Letters from Lillian,* letter dated January 16, 1954, 92.

60 *Muhafazat Asyut: al-'Id al-Qawmi, 18 April 1982,* 37.

61 Heather J. Sharkey, "Missionary Legacies: Muslim–Christian Encounters in Egypt and Sudan during the Colonial and Postcolonial Periods," *Muslim–Christian Encounters in Africa,* ed. Benjamin F. Soares, 57–88 (Leiden: Brill, 2006).

62 Trasher, "A Letter from Lillian Trasher," letter dated August 20, 1956, *Pentecostal Evangel* (November 25, 1956), 25.

63 Trasher, "News from Lillian Trasher," *Pentecostal Evangel* (March 10, 1957), 23.

64 FPHC, Lillian Trasher Personal Papers, 1094 247, Gamal Abdel Nasser to Lillian Trasher, Cairo, October 13, 1959; Lill to Jen, Assiout, October 20, 1959.

65 Raymond T. Brock, "Mother of a Thousand," *Pentecostal Evangel* (June 26, 1960), 11.

66 Christie, *Called to Egypt,* 176.

67 FPHC, Lillian Trasher Personal Papers, 0795 043, Lillian to Brother and Sister Carmichail, March 25, 1960.

IV   NATION

Women, Mission, and Nation Building
in Ottoman Europe, 1832–1872

Barbara Reeves-Ellington

In March 1872, Evgeniya Kissimova resigned from the presidency of the women's association she had founded almost three years earlier. Her resignation was not voluntary. Announcements in the Bulgarian-language press suggest that unnamed members of the association in Turnovo, a town in the northern sector of the Ottoman province of Rumelia (present-day Bulgaria), had forced her departure. They reproached her for using "all the mannerisms of Protestant missionaries from beginning to end, but without their accuracy, intelligence, and dignity."[1] Kissimova's detractors accused her of ineffective emulation of Protestant missionaries, but their determination to remove her from the presidency of the association hints at deeper concerns about her activities.

In the three years from 1869 to 1872, Evgeniya Kissimova strode boldly into the public sphere, using Protestant strategies to organize Bulgarian Orthodox Christian women. In her speeches at the Turnovo women's meetings, she introduced new ideas she encountered in Protestant publications about women's education and the contributions that educated Christian women could make to Ottoman Bulgarian society. Rearticulating an American discourse of domesticity promoted by American missionaries, Kissimova began to advance a new Bulgarian understanding of female moral authority grounded in maternal influence. She urged the Turnovo townswomen to work for female education and organize schools for their daughters. Her activities publicly challenged the power of the

Bulgarian town council responsible for the provision of education in Turnovo. Ultimately, Kissimova was forced to yield to that power, but not before she and other literate urban women had crafted a Bulgarian discourse of domesticity that borrowed from the American version but was grounded in their own experiences.

The American discourse of domesticity emerged from an early nineteenth-century view that progress in any given society was associated with the status and education of women. Evangelical Christian Americans believed that the United States was at the pinnacle of progress as a Protestant Republic where Christian women were educated and charged with the responsibility of shaping the character of the home and the nation by raising future generations. Domestic discourse established the moral authority of white, middle-class Protestant women within the home as the household became the "empire of the mother."[2] Prominent antebellum female writers equated Christianity with Protestantism and helped shape an Anglo-American mission to domesticate and Christianize non-Protestant, non-European communities across the United States and around the globe.[3] Their discourse of difference became a colonizing tool. The question is: What happened to that discourse when American women missionaries took it abroad?

An analysis of Kissimova's published speeches and private correspondence helps answer that question as it relates to a part of the world that hosted the largest antebellum American mission.[4] In the Ottoman Empire, one can trace the connections between an imported American discourse of domesticity and a new Bulgarian discourse of women's rights, as some Bulgarian women worked to direct a developing awareness of women's changing social and political status. A discourse of difference was useful to them as they sought to differentiate themselves as ethnic Bulgarian Christians within the Ottoman Empire and looked outside the empire to Europe for comparisons of progress in their society. In this essay I illuminate the ways in which literate urban Bulgarian women rearticulated domestic discourse and used it to exercise their moral authority as women to fight for female education and include women in the process of nation building during a period of increasing Bulgarian nationalism (*Vuzrazhdane*) within Ottoman domains.

Historically, the Ottoman government did not recognize ethnic or national groups; instead, it organized its subjects in religious communities (*millets*) through which the subjects conducted their own affairs, headed by their own religious leaders.[5] Beginning in the mid-nineteenth century, Ottoman statesmen pursued a program of civil reform to create a modern state by restructuring the imperial administrative system. Although Bulgarians initially benefited from Ottoman reforms, some nationalists began to argue against Ottoman statesmen who promoted a homogenizing concept of Ottomanness (*Osmanlılık*) through reform of education, particularly women's education. In her embrace of domestic discourse, Kissimova went further than women in other female associations: she challenged the political power of the male civic leaders in her community as they struggled to adapt to the rapid changes occasioned by Ottoman civil reform (*Tanzımat*).[6] Her challenge was met with an opposition that exposed the limits of women's moral authority in Ottoman Bulgarian society.

A local perspective on the American Protestant–Bulgarian Orthodox encounter expands the debate about cultural imperialism and contributes to the endeavor to reconceptualize the extension of American culture abroad. Recent scholarship suggests that researchers need to take a closer look at missionary projects from the perspective of the host culture and within a larger, global context.[7] From this angle, events reveal complex dynamics that transcend a dichotomous discussion of imperialism and resistance to illuminate an environment in which different cultures met, competing ideas contended for authority, and members of local communities embraced new ideas, recrafted them to further their own ends, and in some cases used them to promote radical causes. By bringing new ideas to Ottoman Christians in their local languages, missionaries supported the use of those languages as vehicles for the introduction of new ideas.[8] They could not, however, control the ways in which Ottoman Christians might use new ideas to advance their own objectives.

Bulgarian sources lead to unexploited materials for the study of American Protestant missionaries in the Ottoman empire—reports of Bulgarian women's organizing activities in the Bulgarian press, the Bulgarian-language Protestant mission magazine *Zornitsa* (*Day Star*, 1864–71), and the translated writings of the American missionary Martha Jane Riggs. Riggs's writings underscore the malleability of domestic discourse in a context of extensive social transformation. Riggs and Kissimova never met, but their connection, through *Zornitsa*, divulges a pattern of cultural transfer that showcases the appeal of American ideas about women's domestic responsibilities, female education, and national progress. That tenuous connection also throws into relief the gendered constraints within which American women missionaries and Bulgarian women operated in their respective projects to assert female moral authority as an essential element of nation building.

A local perspective through a gendered lens also challenges historiographical interpretations that overlook the centrality of women to social change in late Ottoman Bulgarian society.[9] A focus on women and gender reveals a broader narrative of cultural transfer by exploring a series of overlapping partnerships among Americans and Bulgarians in the European heartland of the Ottoman Empire. It begins with Martha Jane and Elias Riggs, missionaries with the American Board of Commissioners for Foreign Missions (ABCFM, or American Board), who set sail initially for Greece in September 1832. Martha Jane wrote *Letters to Mothers*, an advice manual for women, which Elias published, initially for a Greek audience, in Izmir in 1842. Two decades later, the translation partnership of Elias Riggs and the Methodist Episcopal Church missionary Albert Long assured the Bulgarian publication of *Letters to Mothers* in *Zornitsa*, which Long edited. Martha Jane's *Letters* reached a female Bulgarian audience thanks to Long's friendship with Kissimova, who became a subscription agent for *Zornitsa* and a prominent public speaker on behalf of female education. Kissimova's partnership with her brother, Pandeli, encouraged her to undermine the financial and political authority of the Turnovo town council. Finally, the speeches of Kissimova and other Bulgarian women attracted the attention of male journalists, who adopted domestic discourse to shape the project of Bulgarian nationalism writ large. Bulgarians refashioned domestic discourse as an anticolonial tool with which to undermine Ottoman imperial reform.

TRANSLATING DOMESTICITY: MARTHA JANE
RIGGS WRITES *LETTERS TO MOTHERS*

Martha Jane Riggs does not appear in official mission history. She has left no correspondence in the missionary archive. Details of her life can be garnered through her obituary and the letters of her husband. Born to Presbyterian Scots-Irish parents in New Vernon, New Jersey, on July 3, 1810, Martha Jane Dalzel attended a female seminary at Elizabeth, New

Jersey, and taught briefly before her marriage on September 18, 1832.[10] One month later, the Riggses embarked from Boston as missionaries of the American Board. They joined an evangelical Protestant endeavor to "regenerate" newly independent Greece and reform the Greek Orthodox Church. After the Greek War of Independence against the Ottoman Empire, evangelical Christians in the United States expected to see independent Greece become a beacon of Christian republicanism in the East.[11] The American Board planned nothing less than a Protestant reformation of the Greek Orthodox Church, expecting reform to spread among the Christians of the Ottoman Empire in Europe and western Asia. Female education was a key element of their strategy, and women were vital to the plan. According to Senior Secretary Rufus Anderson, "Nowhere can the wives of missionaries, if they are properly qualified, be more useful than they may now be in Greece, through this medium."[12] Martha Jane Riggs expected to be useful as a teacher to Orthodox girls and women.

When the Riggses arrived in Greece, several British and American missionaries already operated schools for Greek girls.[13] The Riggses settled in Argos, where they opened the first American Board school on the Greek mainland. They began with an elementary school in 1834; within three years, they added a secondary level (common school), organized a teacher-training course, and appointed a Greek female assistant from among their pupils; by 1838, more than one hundred students attended the school.[14] American Board missionaries were initially welcomed in independent Greece and in Greek communities throughout the Ottoman Empire. Their girls' schools were well attended, and their schoolbooks were well received. Government support, lack of Greek schools, and changing attitudes about the desirability of female education all contributed to the acceptance of mission aid, but government and mission policy changed in 1838.

Increasing Greek resistance to Protestant teachings, decreasing mission budgets after the Panic of 1837, and a lack of Greek converts compelled Anderson to reconsider policy.[15] He closed the Argos school. Disappointed, the Riggses urged the mayor of Argos to continue their work, impressing upon him "the great importance of *female education*" and "the influence, good or bad, of mothers."[16] In a major shift of mission policy, however, Anderson declared formal preaching to be the focus of mission work, to which all other missionary activities were subservient. Because preaching was an area of work restricted to ordained missionaries, Anderson now attached less value to women's work. He reassigned the Riggses to Izmir (Smyrna), a major seaport south of Istanbul (Constantinople) that was the center of missionary publishing in the Ottoman Empire. Elias was to supervise the mission's printing operations in the Greek language. Martha Jane's duties remained unspecified.

The Riggses' move to Izmir in 1838 coincided with changes in their family: five of their children were born there, and Martha Jane turned her attention to domestic arrangements. She also began to write. Her personal library included several American mothers' manuals. Among them were Thomas Gallaudet's *The Child's Book on the Soul* and *The Mother's Primer, to Teach Her Child Its Letters and How to Read*, John Abbott's *The Mother at Home*, and Lydia Sigourney's *Letters to Mothers*.[17] These popular antebellum readings that celebrated the power of maternal influence within the home and society shaped the format and content of Martha Jane Riggs's writings. Having access to the mission's printing press, the Riggses took advantage of a new medium through which to advocate for female education and advance the ideal of maternal influence. Elias arranged to publish Martha Jane's writings, a series of letters that she titled *Letters to Mothers*, in a print run of five hundred copies, which sold out within months in 1842. A second edition appeared in 1844.[18]

The American domestic discourse expounded by Martha Jane Riggs found its way into the publications of Greek and Bulgarian Orthodox Christians who were associated with the American Protestant mission in Izmir in the 1840s.[19] It also appeared sporadically in the nascent Bulgarian press in Istanbul in the 1850s. But it was not until the 1860s that it gained visibility and relevance as Riggs's writings reached Bulgarian women. *Letters to Mothers* found a receptive audience among a small number of literate women who were critical of the lack of progress in female education and sought to establish their own moral authority in urban Ottoman Bulgarian society.

PROMOTING DOMESTICITY: MARTHA JANE RIGGS
CONTRIBUTES *LETTERS TO MOTHERS*
TO *ZORNITSA*

Following another shift in American Board policy after the Crimean War (1853–56), Martha Jane and Elias Riggs moved with the mission press from Izmir to Istanbul, where Elias eventually assumed responsibility for supervising the translation of the Bible into modern Bulgarian. In that endeavor, he was joined by Long and the Bulgarian journalist Petko Rachev Slaveykov, among others. Together, they made up the editorial team for *Zornitsa*. Through their contacts with Bulgarian teachers and journalists, Riggs and Long learned about the ethnic Bulgarian movement to establish Bulgarian-language schools, develop a Bulgarian press and literature, and urge reforms (including demands for Bulgarian-speaking clergy and a Bulgarian-language liturgy) within the Greek Orthodox Church to which they belonged within the Ottoman administrative system. A national movement based on educational and religious reform was congenial to American missionaries, who saw it as an opportunity to promote Protestant teachings. Bulgarians needed reading materials, and Long planned to put "the lessons of a Gospel literature" into the hands of Bulgarian children.[20] *Zornitsa* became the medium through which he introduced evangelical Protestant morality into Bulgarian society.

The monthly magazine was itself something new and modern. As a staple of the fledgling Bulgarian press it contributed to the development of Bulgarian reading communities throughout the Ottoman Empire.[21] It was the first Bulgarian-language magazine to be illustrated, the first to target the family as a reading unit, and the first to publish articles for women and children who, according to Long, were growing up "a reading generation" in a nation of adults who were largely illiterate.[22] *Zornitsa* always included articles for women and children. Martha Jane Riggs's *Letters* began to appear in its first issue.

Martha Jane Riggs offered a manual on Christian motherhood for Orthodox mothers. She presented American Protestant views on child rearing, emphasizing three themes. First, educated Christian women contribute to the progress and prosperity of nations by shaping the character of future generations. Second, educated Christian women understand that they are responsible for the physical nurture of their infants. Third,

Martha Jane Riggs and Elias Riggs in
Istanbul (Constantinople), ca. 1864.
By permission of Helen Sarah Riggs Rice,
great-granddaughter of Martha Jane
and Elias Riggs.

mothers shape the early education of their children and their intellectual,
moral, and religious development. The pedagogical content of Riggs's
writings may have accounted for their popularity. In his memoirs, the
prominent Bulgarian educator Atanas Iliev remarked that until he went to
Prague to study pedagogy (in 1869) the only material he had read in
Bulgarian on childhood instruction was Riggs's *Letters to Mothers*.[23] What
more likely appealed to Bulgarian women in a period of deepening Bulgarian nationalism was the model of the educated Christian mother and
the elevated status she enjoyed in society by virtue of her contribution to
national progress. By correlating the status of women with national progress and prosperity, Riggs argued that women's domestic responsibilities
took on national significance.

Riggs insisted that mothers had a duty to their nation and to God to
raise "useful members of society" and assured her readers that only educated Christians could successfully meet this challenge.[24] She extolled the

virtues of the educated Christian wife and mother, whose intellectual abilities and moral superiority brought harmony to the household and guided the character of her children, instructing them in their civic responsibilities in this life and assuring their spiritual preparation for the next. According to Riggs, the most useful contribution a woman could make to society was to "exercise the office of maternal teacher."[25] She encouraged Bulgarian women to rethink their relationships with their children, arguing that mothers should take charge of the moral guidance of their sons and prepare their daughters for the responsibilities of marriage and motherhood.[26] Daughters in particular should be taught to appreciate the spiritual and intellectual elements of life more than ornamental talents and personal wealth.

The civilizing discourse of evangelical Protestants expounded by Martha Jane Riggs asserted that women owed their elevated status in American society to Protestant Christianity, which had raised women from the degradation of ignorance, superstition, and heathenism.[27] In this view, national progress was positively correlated with the status of women in society: Christian nations prospered because women were educated and respected; non-Christian nations failed to prosper because women were degraded and benighted. Antebellum American evangelical periodicals, above all children's magazines, regularly published graphic illustrations of supposed heathen practices that served to demonstrate the superiority of Christian womanhood: Indian mothers who practiced female infanticide, Chinese mothers who bound the feet of their daughters, and Muslim women who languished in harems were stock stereotypes in the arsenal of the missionaries. They contributed to shaping the national identity of evangelical women and legitimized the work of women missionaries.[28]

Being subject to the Ottoman censor, *Zornitsa* could not directly criticize the status of Muslim women, but missionary stereotypes from other non-Christian societies found their way into Riggs's letters and into the magazine. One article described the practice of foot binding and the negligence of girls' education in China.[29] Its message was that ignorance and superstition were the causes of women's low status in China, which in turn was the reason for China's failure to prosper. Another article was accompanied by a graphic illustration that showed a sari-clad woman standing on the banks of a river preparing to throw her baby daughter into the water. Lurking in the water was a large, wide-jawed crocodile. Here the message was that the mother planned to send her daughter to an early death to save her from a life of misery in a society that devalued women.[30]

Riggs and Long attempted to draw parallels between Bulgarian societies and non-Christian societies. Even among Bulgarians, they noted, parents planned different birth celebrations based on the child's gender: the birth of a boy gave greater cause for joy. The implications were clear: Bulgaria as a nation would not prosper because daughters were not appreciated and Bulgarian women were neither respected nor educated. As Christian women, they had an advantage. If they were educated, they could more easily differentiate themselves from non-Christian women in the Ottoman Empire. Articles in *Zornitsa* encouraged Bulgarian women to reflect on images of non-Christian women in India and China and then ponder the treatment of women in their own society. Pressing the message home, one article claimed that Bulgaria needed mothers, "not just girls in their ornaments and finery, but mothers; sober-minded, God-fearing, educated mothers." Indeed, the future of the Bulgarian nation depended "more on the current generation of Bulgarian women, and not so much on their men" because mothers were "a nation's teachers and leaders."[31]

Riggs advised women to begin a process of preparation for their leadership roles within women's organizations. She encouraged her readers to organize regular meetings at which they could discuss reading materials and educate each other.[32] Here again she offered Bulgarian women an American model of the maternal association that missionary women transported to the Ottoman Empire in the 1830s. The women met regularly to pray and discuss articles from American women's magazines. The women of Turnovo were among the first to organize, founding their association in 1869.[33] Their association is important because it establishes connections among women's organizing activities, *Zornitsa*, and the rearticulation of American domestic discourse through the Bulgarian-language secular press. Evgeniya Kissimova is at the center of these connections.

ENCOUNTERING DOMESTICITY: EVGENIYA KISSIMOVA SUBSCRIBES TO *ZORNITSA*

Zornitsa appealed to women like Evgeniya Kissimova because it was the only Bulgarian-language periodical that printed articles for, by, and about women. Domestic discourse resonated with them because it established a new form of authority for a small number of literate women in an emerging urban middling class. Traditional Bulgarian family structure recognized the authority of mothers, particularly mothers of sons, and their importance as conduits of culture. What was new in Martha Jane Riggs's message was the positive, optimistic emphasis on women as leaders and on motherhood as a productive contribution to society and national prosperity at a time of extensive social change and growing Bulgarian nationalism.

Only one or two generations removed from preindustrial society, a small but influential number of literate women lived in towns where significant change took place in the mid-nineteenth century.[34] In small towns and large villages, men were absent for several months of the year, traveling long distances to trade or work in the Ottoman capital. As a result, women managed households alone and developed trading skills.[35] Urban and rural women alike engaged in entrepreneurial activities, running inns, renting workshops, loaning money, and selling food to passing travelers. Their work contributed to the family economy. Women who were obliged to work outside the family economy hired themselves out for pay as servants, harvesters, and textile workers in fledgling rural proto-industrial workshops.[36] Beyond this economic activity, Christian women of the expanding urban middling classes had no organizational structure outside the home.

Women lacked a public forum through which to extend their sphere of influence. Wives of well-to-do merchants and artisans attended church with their families and went on pilgrimages to local holy sites. The church and the bathhouse were their only gathering places, offering them their only opportunity to exchange information; reading rooms and coffeehouses were for men only. Within Christianity and Islam, charitable donations fulfilled an important social function, but few women had the wealth to exert much influence. By the 1860s, some urban Bulgarian women had become accustomed to subscribing to periodicals and contributing modest amounts of money to support book publications.[37] Building on the traditions of charitable giving, and using neighborhood churches as their gathering sites, Bulgarian women began to organize publicly in 1869 to assert their moral authority as Christian mothers and improve educational opportunities for their daughters.

Kissimova was in the vanguard of women's organizing activities. Born in 1831 into an artisan-merchant family that traded in woolen cloth, she later married a local merchant. Her family's prominence was assured by her father's status as a Christian who had made a pilgrimage to Jerusalem.[38] Kissimova attended a cell school in her neighborhood, a small, one-room school attached to a local church where she was taught by a nun. A historian of Turnovo described her education as being quite inadequate, but Kissimova was remarkable in that she was a literate woman at a time when Bulgarian literacy has been estimated at only 3 percent.[39] Her father was not literate, but in 1850 her brother Pandeli became a subscription agent for *Tsarigradski vestnik* (1848–62), the only Bulgarian-language newspaper then published in the Ottoman Empire. Kissimova later became a subscription agent for *Zornitsa*. She befriended Albert Long after her brother introduced him to the family in 1859. She was appreciative of Long's efforts on behalf of women's education, and he was grateful for her work as a subscription agent for *Zornitsa*.[40]

In 1869 Kissimova informed Long that Bulgarian women were beginning to organize. He reported this development to the Methodist Episcopal Church missionary society in New York, remarking enthusiastically that "a very wide field of usefulness" was opening up for the missionaries.[41] Women's organizers read *Zornitsa*, mission tracts, and *Letters to Mothers*. Here was confirmation that the missionaries had an appreciative audience and that their efforts to reach Bulgarian women were successful. Yet despite the success of Riggs's *Letters*, Bulgarian women like Kissimova were not about to convert to Protestantism. The message of domestic discourse was a platform from which they could advocate for female education and thereby enter the public sphere. But Kissimova took the idea of women's moral authority to more radical lengths. She also challenged the moral and political authority of the men on the Turnovo town council, whom she believed had not met their responsibility to provide a basic education for the girls of the town.

REARTICULATING DOMESTICITY: KISSIMOVA CHALLENGES THE TURNOVO TOWN COUNCIL

Kissimova was determined to raise educational standards for Bulgarian Orthodox women. Although individual Bulgarians had made efforts to provide basic instruction in reading for girls in the 1850s, few schools

for girls existed in the 1860s.[42] In her first public speech at the inaugural meeting of the Turnovo women's association on September 8, 1869,
Kissimova commended the townswomen of Turnovo for organizing. "Our
half" had recognized the need for education, she said. It was time to stop
spending money on trinkets and invest instead in their daughters' educations so that women would be worthy of the name of mother and earn the
respect of their menfolk.[43] Kissimova encouraged all women who attended
the inaugural meeting to sign their names in a register and list their
donations, thereby making public their actions and declaring that they
meant business.

To persuade her audience of the power of education, Kissimova offered
an example of the ideal mother who understood that her chief responsibility was to educate her daughter in stark contrast to a description of
uneducated Indian mothers who drowned their baby daughters. Kissimova's use of the missionary stereotype is conspicuous, coming as it did
only three months after *Zornitsa* published an article accompanied by an
image of an Indian woman casting her baby into a river where a crocodile
lay in wait.[44] Kissimova implied that Bulgarian women did not wish to be
counted among the uneducated, non-Christian women of the world. Be-
moaning the poor social status of Bulgarian women and their lack of
educational opportunities, she insinuated that Bulgaria would fail to prosper as a nation unless Bulgarian women were respected and their daughters educated.

Kissimova's speech indicated that she was aware of some form of racial
hierarchy. She aspired to be counted among Europeans, not Asians. She
deplored Bulgarian women's "shameful level of education" compared to
the education of European women and lamented the fact that Bulgarian
men were being educated at home and in Europe, while "our poor sex"
remained "mired in ignorance."[45] Kissimova commended her members for
beginning a good work and implored them to continue to raise education
for Bulgarian women to the level of that in Europe. In the Ottoman
Empire, at a crossroads between Europe and Asia, she looked west to
Europe for comparisons, not east or south to Orthodox Greece.

While attempting to establish comparisons with Europe, Kissimova
also sought to distinguish Bulgarian women from other Ottoman women,
particularly Greek women, but she was careful not to criticize the Ottoman government. Referring to a long history of Greek cultural expansion

in Ottoman Europe, Kissimova blamed the Greeks for forcing a Greek liturgy and Greek schools on Bulgarians but praised the Ottoman head of state for reforms that had extended freedom of religion to Bulgarians. She advanced the idea of female education in the service of the Bulgarian nation and the Ottoman Empire. The purpose of the women's association, she announced, was to educate Bulgarian girls to be worthy mothers because "only worthy mothers can nurture worthy sons who are useful to the fatherland and to the sultan."[46] Kissimova's expression of dual loyalty indicates that she recognized Ottoman reforms that encouraged ethnic and religious minorities to develop their communities in harmony with their allegiance to the sultan.

Kissimova was committed to change. In her view, Bulgarian women owed it to themselves and their daughters to act decisively. If they faltered, they would be held in disdain. Reiterating a message that had earlier found expression in *Zornitsa*, she reminded them that "our dear Bulgaria has no greater need than for worthy, educated mothers." She hinted that the women's activities were not well received in all quarters. Some members of the Bulgarian community had expressed an opinion that women were meddling in business that did not concern them. Kissimova urged her audience to ignore the "unpleasant voices" that scoffed at their activities.[47] She implored them not to be discouraged.

Women were frequently disparaged for their organizing activities. When the women of Karlovo went to their town council with the initial capital to build a girls' school, the town council turned them away on the pretext that the town barely had funds to pay for a boys' school, let alone a girls' school. Forced back on their own resources, the women warned the councilmen "not to meddle in our affairs" as they continued to collect their own funds and succeeded in raising the entire capital for the construction of a girls' school.[48] At the inaugural gathering of the women's association in Braila in 1870 (the first Bulgarian women's association outside the Ottoman empire) Marin Drinov, founder of the Bulgarian Literary Society, warned the women present that people would sneer at their initiative but that they should not despair. He reminded them of the example of American women educators. "America progresses," he noted, "because the education of the American nation is entirely in the hands of American women," where female teachers outnumbered male teachers two to one.[49] Drinov lent his support to the cause in Braila.

In Turnovo, Kissimova was joined by the first generation of young Bulgarian female teachers, the wives of prominent Bulgarian community leaders, and the wives of priests. They organized in the one public space to which they had regular access, their neighborhood churches, and always invited priests to bless their gatherings. Emphasizing the importance of their religion, the women celebrated the founding of their organization, the Women's Council, on the feast day of the birth of the Virgin Mary and the opening of their first girls' school on the Day of the Annunciation. They easily reconfigured the American Protestant ideal of educated Christian womanhood to serve educated Orthodox womanhood.

The Turnovo women printed a brochure to publicize their association and list their objectives: they planned to open a treasury to collect voluntary donations, fund a girls' school in the town, and pay the salary of a female teacher.[50] If funds permitted, they intended to found girls' schools in the surrounding villages and provide for needy girls in town. In this way, they would impose a new urban understanding of women's responsibilities and exert control over expanding educational opportunities for rural women and impoverished urban women. The organizational structure of the association included a president, a treasurer, a secretary, and representatives from each neighborhood church who reported to interested women in the neighborhood. A priest acted as the women's spiritual leader but also had a responsibility to report their activities to the town council. Kissimova organized with the support of the leading townswomen, under the social and religious protection of the Orthodox Church, and with the knowledge of prominent townsmen, but she could not protect the women's association from the intervention of the all-male town council.

Pandeli Kissimov advised his sister to avoid antagonizing the men on the town council. He suggested that the women visit their neighbors in groups of two or three to collect money for their association. His advice about fundraising and investments included a recommendation that they leave the principal to grow and use only the interest for the girls' schools. He also advised Kissimova to talk to all elderly women and property-owning women in their neighborhoods and invite them to bequeath their wealth to the cause of female education. He urged her to do so "particularly secretly, and not to inform the men."[51] Kissimov expected opposition from the leading men on the town council who were troubled by the women's newfound independence of action.

Tensions subsequently arose between Kissimova and the town council, which tried to bring the Women's Council under male control. The town council attempted to impose a male president on the women's association, suggested that the women's activities be subsumed under the men's reading room, and demanded to manage the women's funds.[52] Kissimova accused the town council of making "unfounded accusations and inconceivable threats" against the women, as a result of which the women unanimously agreed to break off relations with the town council.[53] The men were incensed by the name the women had chosen for their organization. They urged the women to change it to a more neutral option, such as "women's association" (*zhensko druzhestvo*).[54] The name Women's Council (*zhenska obshtina*) was patterned on the town council (*gradska obshtina*) and suggested a political challenge.

In Turnovo, Kissimova insisted on retaining the name Women's Council, refused to subsume the women's association within the men's reading room, continued to manage the women's association funds, and raised enough money to build a school and fund a teacher's salary. She lost the battle for control of the Women's Council, however, when the town council accused her of mismanaging the funds. In response, she published a detailed statement of the association's accounts from September 1869 through March 1872 and signed it "the former president of the 'Women's Association.'"[55] Kissimova's accounts were accompanied by the commentary that criticized Kissimova for her poor emulation of Protestant missionaries. The article declared that the women in Turnovo had elected a new board of officers and changed their name from Women's Council to Women's Benevolent Association "Joy." The opposition of the men of Turnovo was defused when some women in the town opted for a profile that reflected a less political ambition.

Kissimova stepped down from the presidency of the Turnovo Women's Council in March 1872. In her three years as president, she used Protestant tactics to organize Bulgarian women and rearticulated an American domestic discourse to establish her own moral authority. Her goal was to improve educational opportunities for Bulgarian girls and advance the idea of women's contributions to Bulgarian Ottoman society. Her success attracted the attention of the local town council and prominent Bulgarian newspapermen. Emboldened by her new status, she insisted that the women of Turnovo name their own organization and control their own finances. In this she encountered the gendered constraints of Ottoman Bulgarian society and forfeited the progress she made between 1869 and 1872. By then, however, the Bulgarian press had adopted the refrains of domestic discourse.

NATIONALIZING DOMESTICITY:
BULGARIAN JOURNALISTS ADOPT
DOMESTIC DISCOURSE TO ADVANCE
BULGARIAN NATIONALISM AND SUBVERT
IMPERIAL OTTOMAN REFORMS

Bulgarian women spearheaded a movement for women's education in 1869 and had a significant influence on national discourse about the value of education for women. Articles about education, enlightenment, and national progress had been staples of the Bulgarian press in Istanbul since its inception in 1848, but articles about women's education appeared infrequently before 1869. Women's education featured prominently as a topic of discussion in the Bulgarian press only after women began organizing and made "educated motherhood" a public issue.[56] Petko Slaveykov, who worked on the editorial team for *Zornitsa*, was one prominent newspaperman who increasingly turned his attention to the issue.[57] As late as 1867, Slaveykov recommended that priests should teach children their faith and language.[58] By 1869, however, he no longer considered priests qualified for this work. Instead, he insisted that women should teach children. He argued that educating women was more important to the future of the nation because women, as mothers and teachers, would raise future generations of Orthodox Bulgarians. According to Slaveykov, the educating of women would demonstrate the progress of the Bulgarian nation.[59] Slaveykov devoted increasing amounts of column space to promote women's education. He argued that church funds should be set aside to provide for schools of higher education to train girls to be teachers who would prepare better mothers for future generations.[60] Ultimately, he came to promote a view that American evangelicals found entirely acceptable: only when Bulgarian women were educated and earned the respect of their menfolk could Bulgarians count on progress and enjoy "the true civilization of the gospel."[61]

Why did domestic discourse become so prominent in 1869? The answer is found in the larger Ottoman context in which Americans and Bulgarians operated. As part of their reform program, Ottoman statesmen drafted requirements for a comprehensive Ottoman educational system. Bulgarians followed debates on the drafts in the press in the 1860s. One series of articles in particular countered the centralized Ottoman model by recommending the American model of local community control of education and strong support for female teachers.[62] In 1869, the Ottoman Public Education Law called for empirewide, government-controlled, postelementary education in Turkish.[63] For the first time, Ottoman law provided for compulsory elementary education for girls and the establishment of a teacher-training institute for women. Ottoman proposals were disconcerting to Bulgarian nationalists, who feared Bulgarians would lose their religious and ethnic identity in Ottoman state schools. The new law galvanized the Bulgarian community, women and men alike, to advocate more adamantly for female education. American domestic discourse promoted by Protestant missionaries served the Bulgarian nationalist cause writ large as Bulgarian nation building entered a new phase to oppose the Ottoman Public Education Law.

CONCLUSION

By adopting a local and gendered perspective to the study of American missionaries in Ottoman Europe, I have sought to discover what happens to American domestic discourse when it travels abroad and to explain its attraction in a distant environment. The same ideals that encouraged many antebellum American women to work on behalf of the expanding American nation and gave them a political stake in the outcome of the nation appealed to an emerging middling urban class of Bulgarian women during a period of broad social change. Maternal influence and educated Christian womanhood were empowering concepts for women like Martha Jane Riggs and Evgeniya Kissimova, who were able to justify their public work on the platform of educated motherhood. Both women ultimately confronted the limits of their authority as they encountered the gendered constraints of their environments. Riggs was obliged to relinquish her teaching when Rufus Anderson forced a shift in mission policy that deemphasized women's contribution to mission; but her partnership with her supportive husband ensured the continuation of her work through the medium of the press. Kissimova was forced to yield the presidency of the Turnovo women's association in the face of strong male (and some female) opposition to the emergence of female independence as the men of the Turnovo town council thwarted her radical challenge to their authority. In her case, lack of local male support (her brother Pandeli published in Bucharest) reduced her ability to counter opposition.

Yet the work Riggs and Kissimova did to promote female education shows that the nationalizing and colonizing potential of domestic discourse was sufficiently malleable to serve nationalist—and even anti-colonial—ends in a different context. In the late Ottoman Empire, where they faced the colonizing projects of Greeks and Turks, some elite urban Bulgarian Orthodox Christians welcomed an American discourse they could rearticulate to shape an emerging sense of Bulgarian national identity and purpose. A small literate group of Bulgarian women used Protestant gender ideology to subvert American and Ottoman reform projects while they challenged the gender restrictions they faced daily. Their meetings to celebrate maternal influence and promote female education became opportunities to observe Orthodoxy and contribute to a Bulgarian movement for national recognition within the empire while promoting their own demands. Ultimately they worked to advance their own anti-imperialist objectives on several fronts. As a nationalist discourse that emphasized difference and ethnic superiority, the message of educated Christian womanhood was well suited to the nationalist goals of a small group of prominent Bulgarians as they worked to shape a Bulgarian consciousness and preserve ethnic and religious difference within the constraints of Ottoman reform.

As an example of the ways in which American cultural ideals were transmitted, reconfigured, and internalized to promote social change in a new environment, the case study encourages scholars to move beyond the concept of cultural imperialism to explain the cultural interactions of American missionaries and the people among whom they worked. It is precisely because women did much of the cultural work of nation and empire that historians need to look at their contributions to American expansionism in the first half of the nineteenth century, when the missionary impulse was a leading commitment to the extension of American ideals abroad.

NOTES

1 *Pravo*, May 29, 1872, 2. All translations from Bulgarian language sources are mine.

2 Anne L. Kuhn, *The Mother's Role in Childhood Education: New England Concepts, 1830–1860* (New Haven: Yale University Press, 1947); Mary P. Ryan, *The Empire of the Mother: American Writing about Domesticity 1830–1860* (New York: Haworth Press, 1982); Kathryn Kish Sklar, *Catharine Beecher: A Study in American Domesticity* (New York: W. W. Norton, 1973).

3 On the simultaneous development of the American discourse of domesticity with the ideology of manifest destiny, see Amy Kaplan, "Manifest Domesticity," *American Literature* 70, no. 3 (1998), 581–606. On the ways in which domestic discourse shaped the experiences and practices of American women missionaries in the nineteenth century, see Patricia Grimshaw, *Paths of Duty: American Missionary Wives in Nineteenth-Century Hawaii* (Honolulu: University of Hawaii Press, 1989); Jane Hunter, *The Gospel of Gentility: American Women Missionaries in Turn-of-the-Century China* (New Haven: Yale University Press, 1984); Amanda Porterfield, *Mary Lyon and the Mount Holyoke Missionaries* (New York: Oxford University Press, 1997); Dana Robert, *American Women in Mission: A Social History of Their Thought and Practice* (Macon, Ga.: Mercer University Press, 1996); Mary Zwiep, *Pilgrim Path: The First Company of Women Missionaries to Hawaii* (Madison: University of Wisconsin Press, 1991).

4 James A. Field Jr., "Near East Notes and Far East Queries," *The Missionary Enterprise in China and America*, ed. John K. Fairbank, 23–55 (Cambridge, Mass.: Harvard University Press, 1974).

5 Benjamin Braude and Bernard Lewis, eds., *Christians and Jews in the Ottoman Empire: The Functioning of a Plural Society* (New York: Holmes and Meier, 1982).

6 The literatures on the Bulgarian National Revival and Ottoman reform are extensive. For recent syntheses, see Roumen Daskalov, *Kak se misli Bulgarskoto vuzrazhdane* (Sofia: Lik, 2002); Roderic H. Davison, *Essays in Ottoman and Turkish History, 1774–1923: The Impact of the West* (Austin: University of Texas Press, 1990); Roderic H. Davison, *Reform in the Ottoman Empire, 1856–1876* (New York: Gordian Press, 1973); Nikolay Genchev, *Bulgarskoto vuzrazhdane*, 4th ed. (Sofia: Ivan Vazov Press, 1995); Fatma Müge Göçek, *Rise of the Bourgeoisie, Demise of Empire: Ottoman Westernization and Social Change* (New York: Oxford University Press, 1996); Donald Quataert, "The Age of Reforms, 1812–1914," *An Economic and Social History of the Ottoman Empire, 1300–1914*, ed. Halil İnalcık and Donald Quataert, 759–94 (Cambridge: Cambridge University Press, 1994).

7 Ryan Dunch, "Beyond Cultural Imperialism: Cultural Theory, Christian Missions, and Global Modernity," *History and Theory* 41 (2002), 301–25; Jessica C. E. Gienow-Hecht, "Shame on US? Academics, Cultural Transfer, and the Cold War—A Critical Review," *Diplomatic History* 24, no. 3 (2000), 465–94; Rob Kroes, "American Empire and Cultural Imperialism: A View from the Receiving

End," *Rethinking American History in a Global Age*, ed. Thomas Bender, 295–313 (Berkeley: University of California Press, 2002).

8 Lamin Sanneh, *Translating the Message: The Missionary Impact on Culture* (Maryknoll, N.Y.: Orbis Books, 1989).

9 In the historiography of American missions among the Bulgarians, early works tended to the hagiographical, celebrating the lives of male missionaries who translated the scriptures, contributed to a national Bulgarian literature, and transported the New England spirit to the Balkans. Subsequently, Bulgarian Marxist historians acknowledged the contributions of missionaries to higher education for boys while accusing them of laying the groundwork for future economic imperialism. Women missionaries are invisible in this earlier scholarship. See, for example, James F. Clarke, *Bible Societies, American Missionaries and the National Revival of Bulgaria* (New York: Arno Press, 1971); William Webster Hall Jr., *Puritans in the Balkans: The American Board Mission in Bulgaria, 1878–1918, A Study in Purpose and Procedure* (Sofia: Kultura, 1938); Ivan Ilchev, "Robert Kolezh i formiraneto na bulgarska inteligentsiya, 1863–1878g," *Istoricheski pregled* 1, no. 1 (1981), 50–62; Tatyana Nestorova, *American Missionaries Among the Bulgarians (1858–1912)* (Boulder: East European Monographs, 1987); Andrey Pantev, *Istoricheski pregled kum bulgaristika v Angliya i SASHT, 1856–1919* (Sofia: Nauka i izkustvo, 1986); Petko Petkov, "Amerikanski misioneri v bulgarskite zemi, XIX do nachaloto na XX v," *Istoricheski pregled* 46, no. 5 (1990), 18–32.

10 Elias Riggs, "A Missionary for Fifty-Five Years," *Missionary Herald* 84, no. 2 (February 1888), 59–62.

11 On American philanthropic aid for the Greeks, see Angelo Repousis, " 'The Cause of the Greeks:' Philadelphia and the Greek War for Independence, 1821–1828," *Pennsylvania Magazine of History and Biography* 123, no. 4 (1999), 333–63. On the perspectives of evangelical Americans on the war and the progress of Protestantism, see the first chapter of Clifton Jackson Phillips, *Protestant America and the Pagan World: The First Half Century of the American Board of Commissioner of Foreign Missions, 1810–1860* (Cambridge: East Asian Research Center, Harvard University, 1969).

12 Rufus Anderson, *Observations upon the Peloponnesus and Greek Islands, Made in 1829* (Boston: Crocker and Brewster, 1830), 330.

13 Constantia Kiskira, " 'Evangelising' the Orient: New England Womanhood in the Ottoman Empire, 1830–1930," *Archivum Ottomanicum* 16 (1998), 279–94; Angelo Repousis, "*The Trojan Women*: Emma Hart Willard and the Troy Society for the Advancement of Female Education in Greece," *Journal of the Early Republic* 24, no. 3 (2004), 445–76.

14 Extracts from American Board 26th annual report, *Missionary Herald* 32 (January 1836), 1; extracts from Elias Riggs's journal, *Missionary Herald* 32 (February 1836), 56–57; 33 (January 1837), 7, and (February 1837), 70; Elias Riggs, "A Missionary for Fifty-five Years."

15 On Greek nationalism, see Paschalis M. Kitromilides, " 'Imagined Communities'

and the Origins of the National Question in the Balkans," *European History Quarterly* 19, no. 2 (1989), 149–92.; on the shift of mission policy, see Paul William Harris, *Nothing but Christ: Rufus Anderson and the Ideology of Protestant Foreign Missions* (New York: Oxford University Press, 1999).

16 Letter, Elias Riggs to Rufus Anderson, November 27, 1838, ABC:16.7.1, vol. 6, item 97. Papers of the American Board of Commissioners for Foreign Missions (ABC), Houghton Library, Harvard University, Cambridge. Source material from the ABCFM archives is used with permission of Wider Church Ministries of the United Church of Christ.

17 Elias Riggs to Rufus Anderson, February 20, 1839, ABC:16.7.1, vol. 6, item 98; *List of Books and Tracts Published by Protestant Missionaries in Malta, Corfu, Greece, Turkey, and Syria* (Izmir: ABCFM, 1839).

18 *The Mother's Manual, or Letters to a Sister about the Instruction of Children* (in Greek), 2d ed. (1842; Smyrna: G. Griffith, 1844); Letters, Elias Riggs to Rufus Anderson, September 22, 1842, and January 24, 1843, ABC:16.7.1., vol. 6, items 119 and 123.

19 Scholars have traced the influence of mission publications in Greek- and Bulgarian-language periodicals printed in Izmir but have not appreciated the introduction of American evangelical ideas about women. See James F. Clarke, "Konstantin Fotinov, *Liuboslovie* and the Smyrna Bulgarian Press," *The Pen and the Sword: Studies in Bulgarian History by James F. Clarke*, ed. Dennis P. Hupchick, 321–27 (Boulder: East European Monographs, 1988); Nadya Danova, *Konstantin Georgiev Fotinov v kulturnoto i ideyno-politicheskoto razvitie na Balkanite prez XIX vek* (Sofia: BAN, 1994).

20 Letter, Albert Long to John P. Durbin, October 10, 1862, United Methodist Church Archive-General Commission on Archives and History (hereafter UMCA-GCAH), Madison, New Jersey.

21 On literature, the press, and reading in Ottoman domains, see Elizabeth Brown Frierson, "Unimagined Communities: State, Press, and Gender in the Hamidian Era" (Ph.D. diss., Princeton University, 1996); Johann Strauss, "Who Read What in the Ottoman Empire (19th–20th Centuries)," *Arabic Middle Eastern Literatures* 6, no. 1 (2003), 39–76.

22 Letter, Albert Long to John P. Durbin, October 10, 1862, UMCA-GCAH. On literacy among Bulgarians, see Krassimira Daskalova, *Gramotnost, Knizhnina, Chitateli, Chetene* (Sofia: Lik, 1999).

23 Atanas Iliev, *Spomeni* (Sofia: BAN, 1926), 116.

24 "Pisma za mayki: Purvo pismo. Maychini chuvstva i maychini dluzhnosti," *Zornitsa*, January 1864, 3–5.

25 "Pismo treto. Vliyanie na khristiyanstvoto v sustoyanieto na zhenite.—Primeri na maychinoto vliyanie," *Zornitsa*, March 1864, 21–23.

26 "Pismo 20. Bogatstvo—gordost—prostota," *Zornitsa*, July 1867, 54–55.

27 "Pismo treto. Vliyanie na khristiyanstvoto v sustoyanieto na zhenite.—Primeri na maychinoto vliyanie," *Zornitsa*, March 1864, 21–23.

28 David Morgan, *Protestants and Pictures: Religion, Visual Culture, and the Age of American Mass Production* (New York: Oxford University Press, 1999), 227–29; Lisa Joy Pruitt, *A Looking-Glass for Ladies: American Protestant Women and the Orient in the Nineteenth Century* (Macon, Ga.: Mercer University Press, 2005).

29 "Sustoyanieto na zhenite v Kitay," *Zornitsa*, May 1864, 33–34.

30 "Indiyska mayka," *Zornitsa*, June 1867, 42, and June 1869, 46–47.

31 "Za maykite. Bulgarskite mayki," *Zornitsa*, January 1866, 4.

32 "Pismo vtoro, Nuzhnite na maykite preimushtestva," *Zornitsa*, February 1864, 13–13.

33 Margarita Cholakova, *Bulgarsko zhensko dvizhenie prez Vuzrazhdaneto, 1857–1878* (Sofia: Albo, 1994); Barbara Reeves-Ellington, "Gender, Conversion, and Social Transformation: The American Discourse of Domesticity and the Origins of the Bulgarian Women's Movement, 1864–1876," *Converting Cultures: Religion, Ideology and Transformations of Modernity*, ed. Dennis Washburn and A. Kevin Reinhart, 115–40 (Leiden: E. J. Brill, 2007).

34 Raina Gavrilova, *Bulgarian Urban Culture in the Eighteenth and Nineteenth Centuries* (Selinsgrove, Pa.: Susquehanna University Press, 1999).

35 Michael Pailaret, *The Balkan Economies c. 1800–1914: Evolution without Development* (Cambridge: Cambridge University Press, 1997), 161; Olga Todorova, "Bulgarkata-Khristiyanka ot XV do XVIII vek," *Istoricheski pregled* 4 (1992), 3–28.

36 Pailaret, *The Balkan Economies*; Todorova, "Bulgarkata," 3–28.

37 Anna Ilieva, "Subscription Lists and the Development of Education for Girls in the 1840s and 1850s." Paper presented at the International University Seminar on Balkan Studies, Ninth International Round Table Bansko, Bulgaria, February 27–29, 2000.

38 Pandeli Kissimov, *Istoricheski raboti: Moite spomeni*, vol. 1 (Plovdiv: Edinstvo, 1897); Yordan Kuleliev, *Devicheskoto obrazovanie v V. Turnovo predi Osvobozhdenieto, 1822–1877* (Veliko Turnovo: Zhensko druzhestvo Radost, 1936).

39 Daskalova, *Literaturnost*.

40 Letters, Long to Kissimova, 14 April 1866 and 28 December 1869. Papers of Evgeniya Kissimova, items 5740 and 5727, Bulgarian Historical Archive (hereafter BHA), Sofia.

41 Missionary Society of the Methodist Episcopal Church, 51st Annual Report (1870), 131–36.

42 Angel Dimitrov, *Uchilishteto, progresut i natsionalnata revolyutsiya: Bulgarskoto uchilishte prez Vuzrazhdaneto* (Sofia: BAN, 1987); Virdzhiniya Paskaleva, *Bulgarkata prez vuzrazhdaneto* (Sofia: Otechestven front, 1984).

43 *Pravo*, September 27, 1869, 122.

44 "Indiyka mayka," *Zornitsa*, June 1869, 46–47.

45 *Makedoniya*, November 8, 1869, 199.

46 Ibid.

47 Ibid.

48 *Pravo*, March 1, 1871, 1.

49 *Chitalishte*, 1870, 109–14.

50 Papers of Evgeniya Kissimova, BHA, IIA6744.

51 Letter, Pandeli Kissimov to Evgeniya Kissimova, December 3, 1869, Papers of Evgeniya Kissimova, BHA, IIA5726,

52 Letter, D. Ivanov to Evgeniya Kissimova, 2/14 January 1870, Papers of Evgeniya Kissimova, BHA, IIA5738; Document, Turnovo Town Council, April 2, 1872, BHA, II.A3463; *Pravo*, 29 May 1872, 2.

53 Woman's Council to the Turnovo Town Council, November 28, 1871, BHA II.A.5763.

54 Document, Turnovo Town Council, April 2, 1872, BHA, IIA3463

55 *Pravo*, May 29, 1872, 2.

56 "Za obrazovanieto na zhenskiya pol," *Pravo*, December 20, 1869 and March 28 to April 27, 1870; "Za obrazovanieto na detsata," *Pravo*, July 20, 1870; "Za obrazovanieto na zhenata" *Pravo*, March 6, 1872.

57 Bulgarian historiography recognizes Slaveykov as a major advocate of female education in the 1860s, but the changing trajectory of his writings about women has not been adequately studied. See Cholakova, *Bulgarskoto Zhensko dvizhenie*; Krassimira Daskalova, *Ot syankata na istoriyata: Zhenite v bulgarskoto obshtestvo i kultura* (Sofia: Bulgarskata grupa za istoricheskoto izsledvane na zheni i pol, 1998); Paskaleva, *Bulgarkata*.

58 "Zhenite, uchitelite i dukhovenstvo," *Gayda*, August 15, 1866, 261; "Obshtestvenoto obrazovanie," *Makedoniya*, May 20, 1867, 101, and "Uchilishtniya vupros" *Makedoniya*, November 11, 1867, 201.

59 "Zhenata: Vazhnostta i v krugut na obshtestvoto i neynoto vuzpitanie v Bulgaria," *Makedoniya*, July 26, 1869, 137.

60 "Raboti za predstaviteli," *Makedoniya*, July 31, 1870, 251.

61 "V zashtita na zhenite," *Makedoniya*, November 9, 1871, 179.

62 "Obshtenarodno obuchenie v amerikanskite uchilishta," *Vremya*, March 5, 1866 to June 4, 1866, reprinted from the *Revue des Deux Mondes*.

63 Ottoman proposals were published in the Bulgarian press. See *Pravo*, August through October 1869; for Ottoman educational and citizenship reform, see Benjamin C. Fortna, *Imperial Classroom: Islam, the State, and Education in the Late Ottoman Empire* (Oxford: Oxford University Press, 2002); Kemal Karpat, "Millets and Nationality: The Roots of the Incongruity of Nation and State in the Post-Ottoman Era," *Christians and Jews in the Ottoman Empire: The Functioning of a Plural Society*, ed. Benjamin Braude and Bernard Lewis, 141–69 (New York: Holmes and Meier, 1982); Selcuk Aksin Somel, *The Modernization of Public Education in the Ottoman Empire, 1839–1908: Islamization, Autocracy and Discipline* (Leiden: Brill, 2001).

Women, Empire, and the Home Mission Project
in Late Nineteenth-Century America

Derek Chang

Joanna Moore abandoned her dream of becoming a foreign missionary in 1855. Just three years earlier, Moore, a twenty-year-old unmarried schoolteacher from Pennsylvania, had experienced a conversion to Christianity and joined a local Baptist church. Inspired by a returned missionary's stirring sermon, Moore soon set her sights on overseas evangelical work, but her responsibilities of caring for an ailing mother dashed her hopes of ministering to the so-called heathen in India. Moore's missionary zeal was rekindled in 1863 as she listened to the testimony of a man who had recently visited an encampment of former slaves in the U.S. South. Moved by the plight of these refugees of the Civil War, Moore dedicated herself to domestic missionary labors among African Americans, thus embarking on a lifelong vocation. In her memoir, she acknowledged a connection between her early desires and her eventual life's work. "I gave up preparation for the Foreign Field in 1855, because my parents very much needed me," she observed. "And yet in one sense I have been a foreign missionary ever since."[1]

Moore quickly came to see a connection between her efforts in the South and Christian missions in Africa. Her memoir lists numerous instances of raising money for African missions, linking the fate of Christian freedpeople in the United States to the conversion of Africans.[2] She undoubtedly also found the war-torn South and its African American inhabitants to be unfamiliar, even alien. Moore had been inspired by exotic images of former slaves that must have mapped easily onto common understandings of Asian heathen: "There passed before my imagination a panorama of bondmen, tied down with cords of ignorance, superstition, and oppression."[3] Her odyssey first to Island No. 10 on the Mississippi River and then throughout the South confirmed this sense of foreignness.

Almost twenty-five years later another female missionary began her labors in another domestic field. On May 15, 1888, Sarah ("Sallie") Elizabeth Stein became a teacher at the Baptist Chinese Mission School in Fresno, California. Like Moore, Stein had joined a Baptist church as a young woman, worked as a schoolteacher, heard the call of foreign missions, and attended college to prepare for her calling. And, like Moore, Stein understood her efforts in the United States to be closely connected to foreign evangelical labors. Her posting in California was a continuation of the religious work that had taken her to Canton (Guangzhou), China, for eight years before her arrival in Fresno, and her observations about her domestic mission invariably drew upon comparisons with her endeavors abroad. She glumly observed that crossing the Pacific and entering the United States did not cause Chinese residents of Fresno to disavow their "hearts . . . of superstition and idolatry." Stein ministered to a population that seemed to be somehow alien and that endowed her domestic evangelical work in Fresno with a sense of the foreign.[4]

The missionary lives of Joanna Moore and Sallie Stein illustrate two critical aspects of late nineteenth-century domestic evangelizing and suggest a third. First, they illuminate the connections between home and foreign missions that underscore the comprehensive ambitions and far-reaching practices of American evangelicals. They also frame a process of defining racial difference that depended on the identification of peoples and territories that lay outside the literal and metaphorical boundaries of the nation. Second, the increased attention to blacks and Chinese coincided with the expansion of formal evangelical labors by women and the growing rhetorical importance of gender in home missions. The confluence of these trends helped to racially mark blacks and Chinese through gendered discourses of domestic respectability and belonging. Finally, Stein's frustration hints at a broader characteristic of home missions: their negotiated nature. African American and Chinese clients contested evangelicals' notions of difference by advancing alternative models, ideas, and institutions.

By examining these connections, confluences, and contests, I argue in this essay that female evangelicals played a central role in Baptist home missions well beyond their stated aim of spiritually converting African Americans and Chinese immigrants. Home mission women participated in a project that sought to create a Christian nation. The emancipation of four million African American slaves and the arrival of tens of thousands of Chinese made the goal of providing an assimilative conduit for inclusion of these populations more important than ever. Yet even as home missionaries worked to transform the spiritual lives of blacks and Chinese and render them acceptable for national inclusion, their rhetoric and methods reinforced cultural distinctions between themselves and the objects of their proselytizing.

The historian Peggy Pascoe has argued that the emphasis on culture not only distinguished home mission women from the growing number of intellectuals who attributed racial and ethnic difference to biology, but also constituted a basis upon which "to challenge biological determinism as it applied to ethnic minority women." In Pascoe's assessment female evangelicals were, therefore, "antiracists who anticipated the distinction between biologically determined race and socially constructed culture."[5] To be sure, missionary assessments of difference often stood in stark contrast to the scientific racism of the late-nineteenth century. And ostensibly the identification of cultural and religious difference was meant to be only the first step in a proselytizing process that would assimilate blacks and Chinese into the national polity.

Nevertheless, as they evaluated religious and cultural disparities to determine membership in the nation, home mission women contributed to and deployed a cultural racial discourse. Although it was perhaps an unintended consequence, they nonetheless helped to identify aliens within the borders of the nation and reinforced domestic boundaries by marking internal others. The escalation of anxiety about racial threat and disorder, exemplified by the crescendo of rhetoric about the Negro Problem and the Chinese Question, constrained ascendant conceptions of national belonging, limiting the space for the kind of difference identified by missionaries. An examination of home missions to blacks and Chinese thus exposes a form of racial marking that seems decidedly at odds with traditional histories of late nineteenth-century racialism. Yet the cultural racism of these home missionaries illuminates the power of a racial discourse linked not to biology but to culture, gender, and the nation.[6]

CONNECTIONS

Joanna Moore and Sallie Stein represented a fundamental element of home missions that connected their endeavors in the United States to the work of American evangelicals abroad. In the rhetoric of advocates, in missionary practice, and in the depiction of the objects of proselytizing as cultural and racial others, home missionaries saw their national project as part of a broader, worldwide mission. This multilayered linking of the domestic and foreign components of evangelicalism mirrored the dialectical relationship between U.S. nationalism and imperial ambition during the last third of the nineteenth century. More important, the process by which missionaries identified the objects of their domestic project with foreign populations marked Chinese immigrants and African Americans as aliens even within the territorial boundaries of the United States. In short, evangelicals played a key role in representing Chinese and blacks as racial and national others.

Baptist home mission ideology was well suited to the broader social, political, and economic developments of the late nineteenth century. It was also part of a remarkably ecumenical home mission movement that had grown out of overlapping sacred and civic concerns, born of spiritual fervor and social and political uncertainty. At the heart of this movement lay an ideology of evangelical nationalism—the religious and secular faith in a nation spiritually and materially transformed by evangelical Christianity and fueled by a desire for territorial and demographic expansion. As Americans faced the challenges of North–South reunion, African American emancipation, the closing of the frontier West, and increased immigration, evangelicals would deploy this rhetoric of national mission and Christian empire with renewed vigor.[7]

The belief in the connection between America's spiritual and civic fates was not unique to Baptists. However, Baptists represent an illuminating case. The energy with which denominational organizations like the American Baptist Home Mission Society (ABHMS) pursued institution building among freedpeople in the South was rivaled only by that of the American Missionary Association, and the Baptist commitment to missions to Chinese on the Pacific coast (as well as in China) had few equals. Baptists believed their denomination to be the most fundamentally democratic, emphasizing local autonomy and congregational authority, eschewing ecclesiastical hierarchy, and ultimately accentuating the tensions at the heart of home mission ideology and practice. At the forefront of the dilemmas facing missionaries was the question of when proselyte communities would be deemed self-sufficient enough to be independent of missionary supervision and guidance. This question underscored the uneven power relations between missionaries and proselytes and confounded straightforward notions of congregational authority and democratic practice.

Home mission advocates aggressively made connections between domestic and foreign ambitions. In 1878, for example, the ABHMS Executive Board proclaimed, "Whenever Home Missions succeed, there manifests itself not the spirit of Home Missions only, but Foreign likewise. . . . He who wishes well the world's evangelization, will take care that the spirit of Home Missions is nourished, and that the basis of all evangelical influence is broadened by their successes."[8] The previous year, the Women's Baptist Home Mission Society (WBHMS) had made its domestic mandate clear: "To carry forward the work of Christian women for the evangelization of the heathen and semi-heathen people and homes in our country."[9] However, the group's male-run counterpart, the ABHMS, reminded supporters that home and foreign missions were equal parts of a comprehensive project. The WBHMS would play a crucial role in attempts by American evangelicals to bring Christianity to "the uttermost parts of the earth." Significantly, home missionaries would "begin at Jerusalem," an allusion to the central position of America as the wellspring of a worldwide Christian empire.[10]

The links between overseas evangelical expansion and domestic missions were more than merely rhetorical. Dozens of missionaries joined Stein's transpacific travels. In fact, during her posting in Canton, she worked with at least two missionaries who had ministered to Chinese in the United States. They were merely reversing a pattern established by the first Baptist missionary among Chinese in California, J. L. Shuck, who had been one of the earliest American missionaries to China before returning to the United States to minister in Sacramento.[11]

Perhaps no family better exemplified this trend than the Hartwells. Jesse, the family's patriarch, crisscrossed the Pacific Ocean during a missionary career that spanned more than half a century. He traveled to China for the first time shortly after receiving a commission from the Foreign Mission Board of the Southern Baptist Convention (FMB SBC) in

1858. Hartwell returned to the United States in 1878 after the death of his second wife, and he persuaded the Home Mission Board (HMB) of the SBC to allow him to try to revive its Chinese mission in San Francisco. By 1884, the HMB could no longer afford to support Hartwell and the mission, and the ABHMS took over sponsorship of Baptist labors in the city. He later would be named the superintendent of Chinese missions on the Pacific coast.[12]

In California, Jesse worked alongside his daughters, Nellie and Anna. Born in China, Nellie and Anna both held positions as teachers in the San Francisco Chinese Mission School. By the spring of 1888, when the twenty-five-year-old Nellie set sail for southern China under an FMB SBC commission, she had spent enough time at the school to form close relationships with Chinese who attended classes. Her younger sister, Anna, would soon follow Nellie overseas after graduating from the Baptist Missionary Training School in Chicago in 1891 and spending a year as her father's assistant in San Francisco.[13]

Whereas the Hartwells, Stein, and others traversed the Pacific, Baptist missionaries at work in the postemancipation South, despite Joanna Moore's musings about Africa and African Americans, rarely crossed the Atlantic. Nevertheless, as Moore's fundraising efforts indicate, Baptist home missionaries understood their work among southern blacks to be intimately connected to the efforts to evangelize Africa. In 1882, the mission official H. L. Morehouse insisted upon this close relationship between African Americans and the conversion of Africa, arguing that the endeavors of missions in the South were vitally important because it was within these institutions that "the missionary spirit for the evangelization of Africa is fostered . . . and the sympathies, the prayers and the contributions of the freedmen are being evoked for their pagan kin across the sea."[14]

Morehouse reproduced a common assumption. ABHMS officials and missionaries asserted rather than demonstrated the link between black southerners and Africa. In fact, Morehouse's use of "pagan kin" as the operative connection is an informative turn of phrase. It suggests both a cultural evaluation of Africans' religious state and a link based on lineage or blood. The affinity between black Americans and Africans, in this sense, was based not just on common non-Christian cultural origins but also on biology. Direct comparisons between the spiritual and social condition of African Americans and Africans reinforced these assessments. One official, for instance, asserted that black women "realize, all too bitterly, from the depths of their own sad experiences that Africa lies all bout them, and that the ignorance and superstitions of their own homes must be done away with first of all."[15] When Moore claimed to be a kind of foreign missionary, she was contributing to a discourse that moved blacks beyond the spatial boundaries of the nation and marked them as aliens.

This alienating process was even more evident in Chinese home missions, where the idea of foreign objects of missions was explicitly linked to a discourse of exclusion. White evangelicals also believed that Chinese who resided in the United States would play a special role in the conversion of China. In part, this belief was based on the observation of high rates of return migration.[16] This fact gained salience as missionaries found their efforts stymied by the anti-Chinese movement of the 1870s and 1880s, which made proselytizing and institution building difficult and seemed to encourage return to China. In 1875, for example, a Baptist committee noted, "The great majority of Chinese emigrants have a fixed purpose of returning to their native land. . . . A convert won to Christ, from among the Chinese in America, is a native helper won for China."[17] Return migration made domestic missions even more important; they were crucial to the evangelization of China—the *primus inter pares* of nations for American missionaries.[18]

A closer examination reveals that the idea of sojourning Chinese in America became a pivotal element of a racial representation. Certainly, rates of return migration reflected the desire of Chinese themselves. However, Europeans who journeyed to the United States often experienced comparable rates of return, but contemporary and scholarly accounts generally distinguished between European immigrants and Chinese sojourners. Sojourners were marked as outsiders, interested only in exploiting the economic opportunities of the United States before returning home to enjoy their riches. They were, therefore, undeserving of legal equality. This representation also linked them to images of contract and coolie labor that stood in striking contrast to the ideals espoused by the free labor rhetoric of the post–Civil War period. The sojourner representation was thus instrumental in paving the way for legal immigration restriction, and formal exclusion strengthened cultural notions that racially marked Chinese as aliens.[19]

Home missions became a central site for the formulation and elaboration of these mutually reinforcing ideas, and they reveal some of the implications of such a discourse. In the late 1870s, Baptist officials maintained that Chinese "are here but for temporary purposes" and thus settled on a strategy of *not* building "permanent institutions" like churches because there was no need "to mould [Chinese] society and civilization" in the U.S.[20] These evangelicals, to be sure, contributed to the cultural construction of a racist type. But they also demonstrated how such ideas could have material consequences, in this case the evaporation of support for institutional structures in America.

In the process of linking their domestic project to evangelical labors overseas, missionaries identified the objects of their missions as foreigners within the borders of the nation. Interestingly, the missionaries who ventured to China and the Pacific coast overwhelmingly hailed from the American South while those who worked among blacks all came from the North. In part, the missionaries' differing choices were a vestige of the antebellum split between northern antislavery Baptists and their slave-holding southern counterparts; white northern evangelicals' work in the South was a continuation of their antislavery legacy.[21] For white southerners, missions to the Chinese in the United States and in China were a way to minister to a population that was fundamentally more foreign (and perhaps seemingly safer) than all-too-familiar blacks.

No matter where the missionaries came from, that their missions culturally marked blacks and Chinese alike as aliens was no coincidence. African American emancipation and Chinese immigration directly challenged traditional notions of national identity, and Americans in the late nineteenth century agonized over the Negro Question and the Chinese Problem. By the end of the century, Jim Crow and exclusionist immigration policy became the legal framework for national belonging, and the cultural racial differences identified by home missionaries played directly into this reinvigorated whites only standard. As David W. Blight has argued, racial division, predicated on the delineation of difference, was a crucial component in the reconciliation of North and South in the decades after the Civil War.[22] And immigration exclusion, dependent upon sustaining notions of the Chinese as perpetually foreign, was a crucial element in the attempt of the Democratic Party to consolidate power.[23] If black citizenship and Chinese immigration were sacrificed on the altar of national reconciliation, consolidation, and progress, then home missionaries sharpened the sacrificial weapon by providing a language of essential difference that supported arguments for submission and separation.

But home missions were not solely about demarcating racial others. Ideally, they would serve as a conduit for creating Christian citizens of a Christian nation, and there lay within home mission ideology a radical possibility of inclusion. As Susan Yohn has observed of Presbyterian labors in the Southwest, evangelicals believed home missions "to be fundamental to the making of good American citizens."[24] During the late nineteenth century, as more women entered mission work, the tensions between national inclusion and racial exclusion pivoted increasingly on ideas of gender.

CONFLUENCE

Even as African American and Chinese populations attracted more attention from home missionaries, female evangelicals grew in importance both practically and rhetorically. Baptist women established two national organizations in 1877, the WBHMS, based in Chicago, and the Woman's American Baptist Home Mission Society (WABHMS) in Boston. In 1881, the WBHMS created the Baptist Missionary Training School for female evangelicals. Moore had anticipated the movement of women into formal missions when she entered the field in 1863, and she later received the first commission given by the WBHMS. By 1880, Moore would be one of thirty-two female missionaries, assistants, and teachers working in the South.[25] Likewise, when Stein arrived in Fresno in 1888 under a WABHMS commission she met her coworker, Mrs. Alanson D. Smith, at the mission school and joined seven other female Baptist missionaries ministering to Chinese in northern California.[26]

The institutionalization of female mission work was part of a larger movement of native-born, white, middle-class evangelical women whose activities reached beyond the traditional notions of the home. Like other Protestant women, Baptists relied on their standing as the moral centers of the home and the home's standing as the moral center of society to advance an expanded concept of the domestic realm, and for female missionaries the home was a unique site of access.[27] The Chicago-based women's society endeavored "to promote the Christianization of homes," and its sister organization in Boston asserted that "the elevation of . . .

women, and . . . the creation of truly Christian homes, where virtue and piety shall flourish, is emphatically the work of Christian women, and *only* theirs."[28]

Yet because home missions were paths that led not just to religious conversion but also to national inclusion, female evangelicals could be involved in secular matters. As domesticity occupied a more central position in this process, female missionaries became primary agents in defining who might be considered worthy of belonging to the nation.[29] This was what Moore had in mind when, as she explained the proper role of mission women, she declared, "The prosperity of our Nation depends upon our homes and home is what mother makes."[30]

The emphasis on domesticity meant also that the efforts of missions focused increasingly on female proselytes. Moore ministered to women and children almost immediately, visiting homes and creating Sunday and Bible schools. By the late 1870s, she was exploring the possibility of establishing "a training school for colored women," and, in 1885, she launched her "first real boarding school for women." Intended "for wives and mothers," the course of study trained female students in the domestic virtues of proper "housekeeping," "laws of health," and "social purity and temperance." To keep the goals of women's mission work explicit, Moore held regular "Mothers' and children's meetings, where all questions pertaining to the duties of wife and mother and child will be discussed and carried to God in prayer."[31]

Moore's work supplemented mission colleges and seminaries. By the time she established her first school, Baptist-affiliated institutions like the Wayland Seminary in Washington, D.C., and Shaw University in Raleigh, North Carolina, were already admitting women, and Sophia B. Packard and Harriet E. Giles had established the Atlanta Baptist Female Seminary. With the exception of the Atlanta school, these colleges and seminaries were originally concerned with training male leaders, especially ministers. Women's classes were added because male leaders could inhabit good Christian homes only if they had good Christian spouses. The emphasis at these schools was never entirely on domestic or industrial education, but this curriculum was seen as part of a broader educational spectrum, in which domestic skills complemented classical learning.[32]

On the Pacific coast, so-called rescue missions for prostitutes in San Francisco appear to have been the most common—or at least the most publicized—engagement between white female missionaries and Chinese women. Presbyterians, Congregationalists, and Methodists created mission homes for women who sought refuge from prostitution.[33] In these missions to "fallen" women, the interlinked ideals of domesticity, moral purity, and respectability took center stage.[34]

Baptists did not engage in formal rescue missions. The demographic particularities of the Chinese population in America complicated the ideal of women's work for women, for cultural practices and systematic exclusion severely limited female immigration.[35] Nevertheless, Baptist women did make an effort to reach Chinese homes, and, as a small, American-born generation of Chinese women developed, they even organized classes exclusively for young women and girls.[36] In 1885, for example, a fellow missionary in San Francisco reported that Janie Sanford made regular visits "among women and children."[37]

But Baptist devotion to domestic training also can be seen in female missionaries' tenacious desire to create schools for Chinese women. There is little extant evidence of what exactly occurred in these classes. However, the educational program probably consisted of training in the proper elements of middle-class womanhood. The curriculum most probably included prayer and Bible study for piety, supervision to ensure purity, and, to instill domesticity, lessons in cooking, housework, and child care.[38]

White female evangelicals on the Pacific coast also worked with male clients, but even in these endeavors gendered respectability remained at the center of training programs. Missionaries painted Chinese with the broad brush of heathen and all that religious designation's accompanying social ills, including the allegedly tyrannical treatment of women by Chinese men—a characteristic few evangelicals failed to note. Many complained that Chinese gender relations made the domestic education of women nearly impossible and thus prevented the creation of Christian families and homes. Such was the case in Portland, Oregon, in 1875, when exasperated Baptists explained that it was "not safe to undertake" a female training class, "owing to the prejudice of the Chinese to teaching women."[39]

In addition to catechism, then, missions to Chinese men would begin with instilling proper respect for women and would result in the "manly" acceptance of women's domestic education. As one missionary observed, after lamenting that Chinese women were prevented from such training, only "the teaching of Christian truth" could lead to "a noble and outspoken manhood in behalf of every good word and work."[40] If female rescue missions allowed allegedly degraded women to regain their moral purity, then missions to Chinese men instilled reverence for Christian womanhood, creating marriageable men for rescued women.[41]

Female missions in both fields offered unprecedented opportunities to their clients. In the South, the investment of missionaries in educational institutions would have a lasting effect, and mission officials understood this as a primary goal of their project. Black clients and white missionaries alike knew that teachers were community leaders, and Baptist-trained women emerged in leadership roles.[42] As Jim Crow strengthened its grip on the South, African Americans found refuge in missionary schools and churches. The message of hope that had pervaded these institutions during Reconstruction shifted to a more cautious strategy of community building and sustenance, but black schools especially would foster "an attitude of protest against Jim Crow," serving as a foundation for a greater assault on the system.[43] Chinese rescue missions most obviously gave women the chance to better their social condition by escaping exploitative sex work, and missions to Chinese men held the possibility of educational attainment and access to white sponsorship and resources.[44]

Moreover, beyond even the social possibilities they opened to clients and potential clients, home missions could foster sustained interracial, intercultural contact. Evelyn Brooks Higginbotham asserts that female missions could result in an "unlikely sisterhood" between white and black women, creating "structured avenues along which black and white women traveled together, heard each other's voices, and learned of each other's struggles and values."[45] Similarly, Pascoe has written convincingly of the emotional bonds that Chinese women and white female missionaries developed.[46] The links between missionaries and their clients also served a more practical purpose, most notably as the veil of oppression and restriction descended on the Jim Crow South and Exclusion Era America. The relationships forged in mission communities could provide blacks and Chinese access to limited resources and might offer protection from the worst abuses of white supremacy.

Yet the avenues that held such promise for mobility and interracial dialogue and communication traversed a white supremacist social landscape, and the power of missionaries as producers of cultural and racial knowledge should not be underestimated. Female missions produced a discourse of difference that marked blacks and Chinese as outsiders, complementing the elision of foreign and domestic fields. Neither the desire to convert nor the process itself afforded a neutral conduit for inclusion. Conversion hinged on identifying essential differences between mission women and their clients, and the evangelical goal of elevating target populations to respectability assumed their lesser condition.

Evangelicals typically defined difference through the depiction of client communities in letters and the religious press. They carefully catalogued religious practices, social relations, familial customs, material conditions, and behavior, reducing Chinese and African American religious life and social relations to a set of descriptions expressed in an evangelical nationalist vocabulary of progress and uplift. These writings constituted what Joan Jacobs Brumberg has referred to as "missionary ethnology."[47]

No other set of ideas and practices illustrates the limits of home mission contact better than the evangelical emphasis on gendered notions of respectability. On the Pacific coast, where the ideas of missionaries in China buttressed notions about heathen immigrants, the supposed paths to inclusion were articulated in a vocabulary that made it clear that clients would find it difficult to truly break the bonds of their cultural tendencies. Even rescue missions contributed to this discourse of difference. As Nayan Shah notes, as early as the mid-nineteenth century, "white politicians, missionaries, and physicians castigated Chinese female prostitution as a leading threat to the moral and social order."[48] Missionaries' focus on this dimension of sexuality and gender played a key role in racializing Chinese women. The "presumption that every Chinese woman is a prostitute"—an image developed in large part through missionary ethnologies—was a principal factor in the racial logic of immigration restriction even prior to the Exclusion Act of 1882.[49]

Missionaries also produced images of Chinese men in the United States that foreclosed any possibility of them attaining the characteristics of American manhood. The initial assessment of Chinese as patriarchal in the extreme gave rise to a discourse of manhood that emphasized the subordinated position of Chinese men to white women. In practice, it seemed, requiring Chinese men to submit to female missionaries as their social and moral betters was the most common method of instilling proper respect for female domestic purity and piety.

Gender disciplining appears vividly in a widely distributed WABHMS pamphlet in which a fictional home mission woman, Helen Dickinson, relates her triumphant conversion of Lee Jip and the tragedy of Lee Jip's accidental death. The relationship between Dickinson and Lee Jip (whom she calls Gypsy) is emotionally close, closer even than the intimacy required of evangelical conversion. In his "bright, winning face and soft, gentle eyes," Lee Jip is "more childlike than an American boy of half his age." Dickinson's language suggests that the relationship is more than one of missionary to proselyte: it is one of mother to son. She models a maternal relationship that reinforces a hierarchy, maintaining white female moral authority and the subordinate position of Chinese men.[50]

The parable also points to two ideas that place this depiction within a broader context of fixed national and cultural difference. Dickinson's nickname for Lee Jip, "Gypsy," is a direct allusion to the sojourner representation of the Chinese as unsettled, never intending to stay or become citizens. That Lee Jip perishes, even after accepting Christ, suggests that while evangelicals could be spiritually successful, the next step in home mission ideology, namely, inclusion in the Christian nation, remained unattainable. Chinese men were too autocratic, patriarchal, and heathen and yet not manly enough to be included in the nation. Female missionaries in the South participated in this double-edged process. Even as their work opened institutional support and possibilities for working alongside black women, it produced a vocabulary of difference pivoting on domestic respectability. Cleanliness and purity were at the center of Moore's catechism, and she went to great pains to educate black women about the "laws of health, including proper food, clothing, exercise, cleanliness, and care of the sick."[51]

Moore was not alone in her preoccupation. A flurry of reports from mission women in 1879 and 1880 underscores the central position of domestic cleanliness and its necessary corollary, filth-laden black clients, in evangelical literature. In these accounts, African American households needed "enlightening as to the efficacy of soap-suds."[52] The description of a former slave woman by a missionary in Tennessee illustrated the alleged problem: "I think I never saw a person so wretchedly dirty as one of these women was. Her filthy garments hung in tatters; her face was bedaubed with grease and coal-dust, her hands indescribable."[53] The repetition and dissemination of these images mapped onto a developing discourse that intertwined moral, cultural, hygienic, and physical difference as central to definitions of the black race.[54]

Female missionaries' emphasis on the essential and gendered differences of Chinese and blacks complemented the discourse that linked domestic and foreign evangelical efforts. These aspects of Baptist women's home missions illustrate what Amy Kaplan has referred to as two different but subtly linked notions of the term *domestic*. On one hand, female missionaries represented the growing number of trained women entering evangelical work, signaled the expansion of the domestic sphere, and exemplified domesticity and respectability as key signifiers for conversion. On the other hand, as they ministered to blacks and Chinese they played a central role in setting the standard of respectability that divided civilized from savage and defined the domestic against the foreign. They related Chinese immigrants and African Americans to populations beyond the territorial borders of the nation, marking those who resided in the United States as alien others. Although mission women tended to emphasize culture rather than biology, this demarcation of cultural difference, pivoting on who might be included in the nation, resulted in a culturally constructed racial discourse.[55]

CONTESTS

But if home missions were sites where missionaries' ideas about race were created and deployed, they were also sites where blacks and Chinese experienced, contested, and rearticulated race.[56] Mission records can be frustratingly silent when it comes to the thoughts, desires, and beliefs of clients. They can also be distorted by the missionaries' self-interested and culturally narrow perspectives, generally revealing more about their authors than about those to whom evangelicals minister.[57] However, they also might well serve as starting points for examining the lives of clients. A close reading of Baptist records and an understanding that clients' activities neither began nor ended in formal mission institutions are a foundation for reflecting upon how blacks and Chinese received the evangelical overture and how they countered the cultural racist discourses deployed by home missionaries.

Even as missionaries emphasized the foreignness of domestic client populations, black and Chinese clients rearticulated this discourse. African American Baptists, too, saw a direct link to Africa. The Baptist minister and antislavery activist L. A. Grimes, one of the few African American ABHMS officials, informed the society in 1866 that "the colored men have Africa on their minds. They wish to evangelize the land."[58] Two contradictory impulses drove this identification. To be sure, black evangelicals had imbibed racist depictions of Africa as a dark continent, and they endeavored to bring American Christian civilization to their ancestral homeland.[59] Nevertheless, they tempered the condescension of missionary uplift with what Sylvia Jacobs has identified as "a very genuine and fairly widespread sense of obligation for Africa."[60]

William W. Colley, a graduate of the Baptist-run Richmond Institute, took up this obligation in 1875 when he traveled to Liberia and Nigeria as an assistant to W. J. David, a white southerner. Colley soon became an ardent supporter of the increased involvement of black Baptists in Africa, chiefly through the creation of an African American foreign mission organization. As early as 1876, he declared, "I hope the colored brethren will begin their work in Africa this year, either by sending a man or supporting one. This is *their* field of labor."[61]

In large part, Colley's support for black evangelicals in Africa stemmed from his understanding that race linked African Americans and Africans. Yet his notion of race differed fundamentally from the biological foundations asserted by white missionaries. Colley saw more than a simple, essential commonality between Africans and his black American brethren.[62] His experience working with the white Mississippian David, who had no qualms about expounding on the superior qualities of whites, in addition to his experiences in Richmond in the 1870s undoubtedly shaped his belief that race was rooted in social conditions. If Sandy Martin's argument that the affinity black evangelicals felt with Africa constituted "a proto-pan-Africanism" is an overstatement, Colley's experience and perspective nonetheless informed how he understood racial difference.[63] Although they brought assumptions of a civilizationist discourse to their evangelical work, black advocates of African missions understood their racial obligation in social, historical, and political terms in which power was the central determinant. It was an identity forged of common experience more than of biology.

Chinese converts, too, actively crossed national borders to propagate Christianity, creating a transnational Baptist network that rearticulated the discourse of the sojourner. No one exemplified such border crossing better than Dong Gong. In 1872, Dong converted to Christianity in San Francisco, and by 1873 he had returned to Canton, where he attended a school run by the Baptist missionary R. H. Graves. By November 1874, Dong was on his way to Portland, Oregon, where he had been invited by the city's First Baptist Church to help establish a Chinese mission school. Dong remained in Portland to run the school until late 1880 or early 1881, when he returned to his wife and family in China. In ABHMS documents, Dong's arrival in Canton was signaled by his plea to his Chinese Christian brethren in Portland to contribute "several hundred dollars" for his mission project and chapel in China. Even after making his final return journey home, Dong's network extended back across the Pacific to the community of Chinese Christians in Oregon.[64]

Dong Gong was neither the first nor the only convert to preach the Gospel on both sides of the Pacific. Numerous others followed this transpacific path, and the vestiges of their movements can be found more in material form than in ABHMS records, for as they traveled they organized Bible studies, Sunday schools, religious meetings, mission schools, and churches.[65] They worked regionally throughout the Pacific coast in locations as far south as Los Angeles and in towns and hamlets like Astoria, Oregon. In China, they staffed American-run missions as "native helpers" and became pastors of their own congregations. They established institutions ranging from irregular religious meetings to full-fledged churches, and, even if it was never articulated, these autonomous and semiautonomous formations are evidence of a transnational network created by and for Chinese Christians.

Seen in light of the sojourner discourse, this network suggests that Chinese converts rearticulated a notion of belonging within a framework of American home and foreign missionary efforts. It was both as simple and as complex as making a virtue of a vice. Given the barriers to American national belonging thrust in front of them by the anti-Chinese movement and reinforced by missionary discourse, men like Dong Gong advanced another idea of belonging that transcended the nation as the primary form of social and political organization and made faith the sole marker of belonging.

Black and Chinese clients also rearticulated missionary ideas about domestic respectability. In fact, Higginbotham has found that black women "asserted their agency in the construction and representation of them-selves as new subjectivities" through a "politics of respectability." Through this oppositional politics, African American Baptist women attempted to combat racist structures and images by claiming the markers of respect-ability—education, manners, piety, purity—usually reserved for whites. In her study, Higginbotham is unsparing in her discussion of the class and status prejudices engendered by this black appropriation of missionary discourse. Nevertheless, she argues that "African Americans' claims to respectability invariably held subversive implications," above all in the shadow of the Jim Crow South. Higginbotham concludes, "The concept of respectability signified self-esteem, racial pride, and something more. It also signified the search for common ground . . . to be both black and American."[66]

This meant, for example, that women educated in mission schools could appropriate Baptist rhetoric about the importance of Christian wives and mothers and push the limits of national belonging through politics. A Baptist official claimed that "if we educate young men for the ministry, and leave them to make marriages with heathen women, we practically nullify all our efforts to elevate the race, by leaving young minds to be molded by ignorant, superstitious women." In making that claim he hoped to underscore the bounded domestic space over which Christian women were to preside.[67] But black women reinterpreted the meaning of Christian marriage to move beyond these circumscribed posi-tions. As Glenda Gilmore has observed, educated black women, such as those who attended Baptist schools, tended to see marriage as a "civil enterprise" in which "the ideal . . . was an 'industrious partnership.'" This partnership in the realm of formal politics took shape through a delegate-husband model in which "male voters often saw themselves as represent-ing their wives . . . as family delegates to the electoral sphere." When black men were stripped of the franchise, black women assumed greater political roles, relying on their connections to and experiences of interacting with white women to enhance their position as clients within Progressive Era states.[68]

On the Pacific coast, clients' appropriation of respectability also could be subversive. Women who entered rescue missions used the institutional support of evangelicals to insist upon less exploitative gender relations, including marriage, with Chinese men.[69] Moreover, much like black clients in the South, Chinese women who were rescued offered a compelling example of purity, piety, and self-respect that countered racist images. Chinese men, too, could offer models of educated, respectable manhood that served as counterexamples to anti-Chinese representations. Sam Song Bo, for example, demonstrated individual ambition, Christian morality, and evangelical zealousness that won him the financial support of many of Oregon's leading white residents and thus enabled him to pursue his education beyond the city's Baptist mission school.[70]

Yet more commonly and perhaps more interestingly, the mostly male world of Chinese in the United States—a world inhabited by Baptist home mission clients—offered up a daily alternative to missionary discourses of domestic respectability. Although judged to be uncivilized, illicit, and immoral by nineteenth-century evangelicals and subsequently deemed to be deviant by social scientists, homosocial domestic arrangements such as boardinghouses, mining camps, and the like were the everyday reality for Chinese men in the United States.[71]

Nevertheless, they themselves might have understood their domestic lives as something other than deviant. Split-household families, in which male migrants journeyed abroad for economic reasons, were not unusual, and Madeline Hsu has made a persuasive argument for understanding the homosocial world of Chinese men in America as a phenomenon that mirrored similar dynamics in China and that was bound together by secret societies and brotherhoods with long histories.[72] The experience of Chinese men in the United States might be seen not as abnormal but as merely an extension of traditional practices, and Chinese men's participation in mission networks suggests an adaptation of these practices.

African American and Chinese clients of missions contested the racialized ideas engendered by the home mission project. Significantly, blacks and Chinese countered these racist ideas through social and discursive practices that displaced the American nation as the primary engine of and model for evangelical belonging and subverted home missionaries' notions of domestic respectability. Because evangelicals' racialized notions of difference were deployed through nationalism and normative gender roles, African Americans and Chinese in the United States challenged those ideas on the very same terrain. In this sense, the antiracism of mission clients hinged quite necessarily upon the rearticulation of national and gender discourses and subjectivities as well.[73]

CONCLUSION

When Joanna Moore and Sallie Stein entered their respective home mission fields, they both were struck by a sense that they had embarked upon foreign missions even within the geographic space of the United States. For Moore in the post–Civil War South and for Stein in northern California, it was the people to whom they ministered that made these places most strange. "Some time in November, 1863, I landed on the desolate shore of Island No. 10," recalled Moore. "I cannot make you understand how it all seemed to me. I had scarcely ever seen a colored person, and had never spoken to but one till then."[74] Similarly, Stein's previous experience in Canton led her to conclude that the alien traits of the Chinese in Fresno were most reminiscent of those characteristics that had made her foreign labors so difficult. "Ancestral worship" continued to be the most significant barrier to conversion in California, and the observance of the Lunar New Year festival forced her to cancel mission school classes for a week.[75]

Moore and Stein stood at the center of the complex processes that marked blacks and Chinese, respectively, as alien others and underscored the centrality of gender and domestic respectability in defining the contours of the nation.[76] Their labors occurred within the borders of the United States; yet their rhetoric and programs linked these groups to populations beyond the spatial boundaries of the nation. At the same time, both women engaged in mission projects that upheld respectable domesticity as the standard for inclusion. That Moore, Stein, and other Baptist home mission women articulated racial difference through a language that, on one level, equated domestic with female and home and, on another level, understood domestic to be intimately related to foreign was no coincidence. They labored during a period when America was realizing the full scope of its continental empire, linking West to East and reuniting North and South, and when new groups sought inclusion into the nation's polity.

Yet this considerable power did not go unchallenged. Black and Chinese mission clients contested the contours and standards defined by white evangelicals. Their lives attest to attempts to imagine alternative visions of a Christian empire less concerned with narrow definitions of domestic respectability and racial difference and more capable of embracing a cosmopolitan conception of belonging based on shared social and historical experiences. For African Americans and Chinese immigrants, this creative feat of rearticulation held the possibility not only to resist and redefine race but also the very idea of proper gender roles and the nation itself.

NOTES

Many thanks to Connie Shemo, Daniel Walker Howe, Jeff Cowie, Aaron Sachs, Michael Smith, Michael Trotti, Rob Vanderlan, and two (anonymous) reviewers for their comments on drafts of this essay, to Peggy Pascoe for her generous encouragement and comments on a version of the essay I presented at the Berkshire Conference of Women Historians in 2005, and to the editors of this book and the participants of the Competing Kingdoms Conference of 2006 for such thought-provoking intellectual exchange.

1 Joanna P. Moore, *"In Christ's Stead": Autobiographical Sketches* (Chicago: Women's Baptist Home Mission Society, 1902), 19–20, 23, 45.

2 See esp. ibid., 55–56, 127, 128, 147, 152, 256, 262, 262, 266.

3 Ibid., 23.

4 EB of the American Baptist Home Mission Society (hereafter EB ABHMS), *Fifty-sixth Annual Report* (hereafter AR) (New York, 1889), 59, 128; Kathryn Choy-Wong, "Sallie Stein: Two Continents, Two Conventions, One Mission," *American Baptist Quarterly* 14, no. 4 (December 1995), 357, 358–61; *Home Mission Echo* (November 1888), 6. Quoted in Choy-Wong, "Sallie Stein," 361.

5 Peggy Pascoe, *Relations of Rescue: The Search for Female Moral Authority in the American West, 1874–1939* (New York: Oxford University Press, 1990), 143–44.

6 Paul Gilroy, *"There Ain't No Black in the Union Jack": The Cultural Politics of Race and Nation* (1987; repr. Chicago: University of Chicago Press, 1997), 43, 59–60. See also Ann Laura Stoler, "Sexual Affronts and Racial Frontiers: European Identities and the Cultural Politics of Exclusion in Colonial Southeast Asia," *Tensions of Empire: Colonial Cultures in a Bourgeois World*, ed. Frederick Cooper and Ann Laura Stoler, 203, 214 (Berkeley: University of California Press, 1997).

7 Laurie F. Maffly-Kipp, *Religion and Society in Frontier California* (New Haven: Yale University Press, 1994), 3. For more on my formulation of evangelical nationalism, see Derek Chang, "'Breaking the Shackles of Hierarchy': Race, Religion, and Evangelical Nationalism in American Baptist Home Missions, 1865–1900" (Ph.D. diss., Duke University, 2002).

8 EB ABHMS, *Forty-sixth AR* (New York, 1878), 33–34.

9 Quoted in Wendy J. Deichmann, "Domesticity with a Difference: Woman's Sphere, Women's Leadership, and the Founding of the Baptist Missionary Training School in Chicago, 1881," *American Baptist Quarterly* 9, no. 3 (September 1990), 145–46.

10 EB ABHMS, *Forty-fifth AR* (New York, 1877), 25.

11 Chang, "Breaking the Shackles of Hierarchy," 136–37. For an excellent article on Shuck's wife, Henrietta Hall Shuck, see also Louis G. Gimelli, " 'Borne Upon the Wings of Faith': The Chinese Odyssey of Henrietta Hall Shuck, 1835–1844," *Journal of the Early Republic* 14, no. 2 (summer 1994), 221–45.

12 Southern Baptist Convention Home Mission Board, *Minutes*, Southern Baptist Historical Library and Archives, Nashville (hereafter SBHLA). See entries for September 9, 1878, and December 3, 1878; EB ABHMS, *Fifty-second AR* (New York, 1884), 19. The SBC had been established in 1845, splitting from northern-dominated organizations, such as the ABHMS, over the commissioning of slave-holding missionaries.

13 Nellie Edwards Hartwell, San Francisco, to Henry A. Tupper, Richmond, November 2, 1887, in the hand of Nellie Edwards Hartwell, NEH Papers, SBHLA; EB ABHMS, *Sixtieth AR* (New York, 1892), 75.

14 Henry Lyman Morehouse, "Historical Sketch of the American Baptist Home Mission Society for Fifty Years," in *Baptist Home Missions in North America* (New York, 1883), 417.

15 Woman's American Baptist Home Mission Society (hereafter WABHMS), *Sixth Annual Report of the WABHMS, 1884* (Boston, Mass.: WABHMS, 1884), 10–12.

16 Between 1842 and 1882 rates of return among Chinese stood roughly at 47 percent.

17 EB, *Forty-third AR*, 11.

18 See, for example, "Importance of the China Mission," *Religious Herald*, January 15, 1846, 2, col. 3.

19 Lisa Lowe, *Immigrant Acts: On Asian American Cultural Politics* (Durham: Duke University Press, 1996), 10–12. See also Erika Lee, *At America's Gates: Chinese Immigration during the Exclusion Era, 1882–1943* (Chapel Hill: University of North Carolina Press, 2003); Claire Jean Kim, "The Racial Triangulation of Asian Americans," *Politics and Society* 37 (1999), 105–38.

20 "The Chinese—Will They Carry Back the Gospel?" *Baptist Home Mission Monthly* (hereafter BHMM) 1, no. 5 (November 1878), 71.

21 See James M. McPherson, *The Abolitionist Legacy: From Reconstruction to the NAACP* (Princeton: Princeton University Press, 1976).

22 David W. Blight, *Race and Reunion: The Civil War in American Memory* (Cambridge, Mass.: Harvard University Press, 2001).

23 Alexander Saxton, *The Indispensable Enemy: Labor and the Anti-Chinese Movement in California* (Berkeley: University of California Press, 1971).

24 Susan Yohn, *A Contest of Faiths: Missionary Women and Pluralism in the American Southwest* (Ithaca: Cornell University Press, 1995), 7.

25 EB, *Forty-eighth AR*, 50–51.

26 EB, *Fifty-sixth AR*, 128–29.

27 See esp. Pascoe, *Relations of Rescue*, xix, 33; Yohn, *A Contest of Faiths*, 36, 101. See also Patricia Hill, *The World Their Household: The American Woman's Foreign Mission Movement and Cultural Transformation, 1870–1920* (Ann Arbor: University of Michigan Press, 1985), 23–60.

28 Quoted in EB, *Forty-fifth AR*, 24; from the constitution of the WABHMS, reproduced in "Women's Work," *BHMM* 1, no. 1 (May 1875), 11.

29 Yohn, *A Contest of Faiths*, 7.

30 Moore, *"In Christ's Stead,"* 132.

31 Ibid., 60, 136, 150.

32 Evelyn Brooks Higginbotham, *Righteous Discontent: The Women's Movement in the Black Baptist Church, 1880–1920* (Cambridge, Mass.: Harvard University Press, 1993), 33. See also Chang, "Breaking the Shackles of Hierarchy," 275–76; James D. Anderson, *The Education of Blacks in the South, 1860–1935* (Chapel Hill: University of North Carolina Press, 1988).

33 See Pascoe, *Relations of Rescue*; Wesley S. Woo, "Protestant Work among the Chinese in the San Francisco Bay Area" (Ph.D. diss., Graduate Theological Union, 1984), 154–66.

34 Peggy Pascoe, "Gender Systems in Conflict: The Marriages of Mission-Educated Chinese American Women, 1874–1939," *Unequal Sisters: A Multicultural Reader in U.S. Women's History*, 2d ed., ed. Vicki L. Ruiz and Ellen Carol DuBois, 144 (New York: Routledge, 1994).

35 Between 1860 and 1900, women never exceeded 9 percent of the total Chinese population in the United States.

36 Martha J. Ames to Mary G. Burdette, October 1, 1898, Martha J. Ames Files, Archival Collection, Board of National Ministries, American Baptist Historical Society, Valley Forge, Pa. (hereafter cited as ABHS).

37 J. B. Hartwell, "Missions to the Chinese in America," *BHMM* 7, no. 4 (April 1885), 94.

38 See Pascoe, "Gender Systems in Conflict," 143–44.

39 Chinese Mission School Records, Portland, 1873–85, February 18, 1875, Baptist Church Records, MSS 1560, Oregon Historical Society, Portland.

40 *BHMM* 8, no. 3 (March 1886), 65.

41 Pascoe, "Gender Systems in Conflict," 144. See also Nayan Shah, *Contagious Divides: Epidemics and Race in San Francisco's Chinatown* (Berkeley: University of California Press, 2001), 79.

42 See Higginbotham, *Righteous Discontent*.

43 Raymond Gavins, "Fear, Hope, and Struggle: Recasting Black North Carolina in the Age of Jim Crow," *Democracy Betrayed: The Wilmington Race Riot of 1898 and Its Legacy*, ed. David S. Cecelski and Timothy B. Tyson, 201–2 (Chapel Hill: University of North Carolina Press, 1998).

44 Pascoe, *Relations of Rescue*, 157–65.

45 Higginbotham, *Righteous Discontent*, 102.

46 Pascoe, *Relations of Rescue*, 137–38.

47 Missionary literature functioned much like the European imperial travel writing analyzed by Mary Louise Pratt. See *Imperial Eyes: Travel Writing and Transculturation* (New York: Routledge, 1992), 64. Joan Jacobs Brumberg, "Zenanas

and Girlless Villages: The Ethnology of American Evangelical Women, 1870–1910," *Journal of American History* 69, no. 2 (September 1982), 341–71.

48 Shah, *Contagious Divides*, 79.

49 George Anthony Pfeffer, *If They Don't Bring Their Women Here: Chinese Female Immigration before Exclusion* (Urbana: University of Illinois Press, 1999), 86.

50 WABHMS, *One of His Jewels: A Story for Workers among the Chinese* (Boston: WABHMS, 1896), 4.

51 Moore, *"In Christ's Stead,"* 87, 153.

52 "Women's Work," BHMM 1, no. 8 (February 1879), 126. See also, "Women's Work," BHMM 1, no. 9 (March 1879), 142–43; "Women's Work," BHMM 1, no. 10 (April 1879), 158–59; "Women's Work," BHMM 1, no. 13 (July 1879), 206; "From the Field," BHMM 2, no. 1 (January 1880), 16.

53 "Women's Work," BHMM 1, no. 8 (February 1879), 126.

54 See esp. Tera W. Hunter's discussion of tuberculosis and race, *To 'Joy My Freedom: Southern Black Women's Lives and Labors after the Civil War* (Cambridge, Mass.: Harvard University Press, 1997), 187–218. A similar discourse of dirt, disease, and difference framed discussions of Chinese in San Francisco during the late nineteenth century. See Shah, *Contagious Divides*.

55 Amy Kaplan, "Manifest Domesticity," *American Literature* 70, no. 3 (September 1998), 582.

56 Michael Omi and Howard Winant define "racial formation" as "the sociohistorical process by which racial categories are created, inhabited, transformed, and destroyed," and racial rearticulation occurs when the established social order is rearticulated through a careful redefinition of racist discourse. This process "produces new subjectivity by making use of information and knowledge already present in the subject's mind" and can become a powerful antiracist tool. *Racial Formation in the United States: From the 1960s to the 1990s*, 2d ed. (New York: Routledge, 1994), 55, 99–101.

57 Vicki L. Ruiz, "Dead Ends or Gold Mines? Using Missionary Records in Mexican American Women's History," in *Unequal Sisters*, 312.

58 EB ABHMS, *Thirty-fourth AR* (New York, 1866), 34.

59 Donald F. Roth, "The 'Black Man's Burden': The Racial Background of Afro-American Missionaries and Africa," *Black Americans and the Missionary Movement in Africa*, ed. Sylvia M. Jacobs, 32 (Westport, Conn.: Greenwood Press, 1982). See also James T. Campbell, *Middle Passages: African American Journeys to Africa, 1787–2005* (New York: Penguin, 2006), 136–87; idem, *Songs of Zion: The African Methodist Episcopal Church in the United States and South Africa* (1995; repr. Chapel Hill: University of North Carolina Press, 1998).

60 Sylvia M. Jacobs, "The Historical Role of Afro-Americans in American Missionary Efforts in Africa," in *Black Americans*, 18.

61 Martin, *Black Baptists and African Missions*, 22, 49. Quote ibid., 49.

62 See esp. Campbell, *Songs of Zion*, xiii, 98.

63 Ibid., 1.

64 "The Portland Chinese Mission," BHMM 2, no. 1 (January 1880), 15; EB ABHMS, *Forty-first AR* (New York, 1873), 25; "Foreign Missions," *Home and Foreign Journal* 5, no. 11 (May 1873), 2, col. 1; "Brother E. Z. Simmons Proposes to go to California," *Home and Foreign Journal* 6, no. 9 (March 1874), 2, col. 4; First Baptist Church, Portland, *Manual and Directory of the First Baptist Church, The White Hall Temple, Portland, Oregon* (Portland: F. W. Baltes, 1906), 15–16; EB ABHMS, *Forty-ninth AR* (New York, 1881), 46; "From the Field," BHMM 3, no. 3 (March 1881), 60.

65 See "The Chinese—Will They Carry Back the Gospel?" 72; J. B. Hartwell to H. L. Morehouse, April 6, 1891, Morehouse Correspondence Files, Archival Collection, ABHS.

66 Higginbotham, *Righteous Discontent*, 186–88.

67 EB ABHMS, *Forty-second AR* (New York, 1874), 34.

68 Glenda Elizabeth Gilmore, *Gender and Jim Crow: Women and the Politics of White Supremacy in North Carolina, 1896–1920* (Chapel Hill: University of North Carolina Press, 1996), 18, 147–75.

69 Pascoe, *Relations of Rescue*, 161–65.

70 Chang, "Breaking the Shackles of Hierarchy," 338–39.

71 Missionaries and government officials viewed this "queer domesticity" as a danger to Christian morality and public health. Shah, *Contagious Divides*, 77–104.

72 Madeline Y. Hsu, *Dreaming of Gold, Dreaming of Home: Transnationalism and Migration Between the United States and South China, 1882–1943* (Stanford: Stanford University Press, 2000); idem, "Unwrapping Orientalist Constraints: Restoring Homosocial Normativity to Chinese American History," *Amerasia Journal* 29, no. 2 (2003), 229–53.

73 Omi and Winant, *Racial Formation in the United States*, 55.

74 Moore, *"In Christ's Stead,"* 26.

75 Choy-Wong, "Sallie Stein," 360, 361, 362.

76 Kaplan, "Manifest Domesticity," 582.

The Confluence of Race, Culture, Identity, and Nationality

Sylvia M. Jacobs

In the 1600s, Christianity could be found in Africa only in parts of Ethiopia, Egypt, North Africa, South Africa, and in the Portuguese colonies of Angola and Mozambique. It existed in regional pockets but was not widespread on the continent. Christian missionary efforts stalled during the seventeenth century and eighteenth, but the worldwide religious revival of the late eighteenth century and early nineteenth resulted in a surge of missionary fervor on the continent.[1] African American women contributed to the spread of evangelical Protestant Christianity in Africa.

White American churches were eager to send African Americans to Africa because of the high mortality rates among white missionaries on the continent. Some regions of Africa were known as the white man's grave. Church leaders mistakenly believed that black Americans, because of their African heritage, could better withstand the climate and high temperatures in Africa and had an immunity or greater resistance to African tropical diseases. They perpetuated the myth that black Americans were better suited than whites as missionaries in Africa. Ultimately, enough blacks survived to verify the idea that they had immunity to African fevers and were more adaptive than whites for mission work there. African American missionaries felt that their racial alliance with Africans and the legacy of the transatlantic slave trade made them more effective missionaries than whites, thereby creating a special niche for them in Africa.[2]

From 1820 to the early 1960s, when Africans assumed control of missionary work, 600 African American missionaries were appointed to Africa. Nearly half of them (260) served in sub-Saharan Africa during the European partition of the continent from 1880 to 1920. African American women represented almost half of the black missionaries stationed in Africa during the partition years. These women made their major contribution to African society in several areas. They established homes, orphanages, and schools for children; they developed agricultural and industrial schools; and they translated grammar books, dictionaries, hymns, proverbs, folk stories, and fairy tales into indigenous languages. They dedicated themselves to the task they believed would be most important: improving the lives and status of women and children in African society.[3]

Single and married women, black and white, attained only the status of assistant missionaries. Despite this restriction, foreign mission work offered American women of the nineteenth century and early twentieth new career options beyond the constraints of a "woman's proper sphere." Moreover, unlike "missionary wives," single women missionaries had some leeway in this profession because they did not have to juggle wifely duties, domestic responsibilities, and child rearing alongside mission work.[4]

The thinking of American mission boards emphasized direct evangelism and what were thought of as civilizing activities to convert peoples throughout the world to Christianity. Engaged in "woman's work for woman, wife to wife, sister to sister," women missionaries worked to transform the lives of women and children by promoting Western gender roles and functions. Along with Christianity, they transferred American culture and values and sought to reshape the identities of women in other societies. They taught female converts the Bible and prepared them to be proper wives for the newly converted male pastors. An extensive network of women missionary leaders took on an active role in church work and developed plans to carry out their work more effectively. American Christian church women collected thousands of dollars from mite boxes to support domestic and foreign programs and pay the salaries of single female workers at home and abroad.[5] The mite or alms boxes were used to collect small charitable contributions from church congregations to be given to the poor and promote a spirit of giving.

In this essay I focus on three prominent single African American women sent by the Women's Baptist Foreign Missionary Society to the Congo

Free State during the partition years. Louise (Lulu) Cecilia Fleming served there from 1887 to 1899, Nora A. Gordon from 1889 to 1893, and Clara Ann Howard from 1890 to 1895. The most important and lasting contribution of these women, as of all African American women missionaries in Africa, was the change they helped bring about in the lives of African women and children. As Margaret Crahan and Franklin Knight point out, women form the integral link in the process of socialization and cultural transmission among any people.[6] In all groups, women have the chief responsibility of rearing children. They pass on their society's history, traditions, customs, and culture. While working with Congolese girls and women, African American missionaries underwent a cultural transformation themselves, one which allowed them to identify with the culture in which they lived and empathize with the lives and plights of the women among whom they worked. They adapted their attitudes to at least a partial acceptance of the African way of life in order to be effective among them.[7] The essay examines their lives and work and explores the ways in which the women navigated racial and national identities in their encounters with Africans, white Americans, and Europeans against a background of exploitative European colonialism in the Congo and failed Reconstruction in the American South.

COLONIALISM, MISSIONS, AND THE AFRICAN NEXUS

When Lulu Fleming, Nora Gordon, and Clara Howard arrived in the Congo, it was a personal colony of King Leopold II of Belgium. Nothing in their previous lives in America could have prepared the three women for the conditions they found there. Not even the Jim Crow South had seen the level of abuse, exploitation, and violence that characterized the Congo Free State.

At the conclusion of the Berlin West African Conference of 1884–85, King Leopold II and his International Association of the Congo were recognized as sovereign in the Congo Independent State. This was the only instance in which an individual gained a colony in Africa. After 1891, Leopold deemed that all vacant land in the country would become the property of the state, which at the time essentially encompassed half of the territory there. He then moved to plunder the colony and extract the mineral resources of the land through concessionaire companies. Leopold, who viewed the Congo as his private property, had managed to convince the world for years that his presence in the colony was philanthropic. In reality, the Congo Free State government systematically slaughtered Africans who were conscripted to build a railroad, harvest rubber around the clock, and carry ivory out of the interior, all part of Leopold's grand scheme to plunder the country's natural wealth. A system of forced labor left methods of enforcement and punishment to local agents. Abuses became standard. Killings, mutilations, amputations, rapes, and other obscenities characterized the colonial regime. Numerous stories circulated of company soldiers returning from expeditions into the interior with baskets filled with amputated right hands or necklaces of ears. Tyranny often brutalized the lives of the Congolese in villages nearby the mission stations.[8]

Because of the similar circumstances of European domination and exploitation of Africans in Africa and the legalization of Jim Crow in the United States with the Supreme Court decision of 1896, which supported the principle of separate but equal, many educated, middle-class blacks argued for some kind of unity or Pan-Africanism among African peoples and the need to maintain the African nexus. Some members of the African American community in the period that Rayford Logan referred to as the nadir addressed themselves to the "scramble" for Africa.[9] This articulate group included journalists, religious and secular leaders, diplomats and politicians, travelers, and missionaries. Black American missionaries stationed in Africa were particularly outspoken, as they were able to observe more directly and intimately European activities there.

Two African Americans exposed the atrocities in the Congo. George Washington Williams, a soldier during the American Civil War and a writer, brought worldwide attention to the plight of Africans under European colonial rule, especially the conditions of the Congolese. Before traveling to the Congo, he met with Leopold to review the situation there. Although the monarch objected, Williams went ahead with his plans. After his fact-finding trip, Williams wrote a letter to Leopold on July 18, 1890, from Stanley Falls, Congo, detailing the extensive greed and cruelty he had observed. In "An Open Letter to His Serene Majesty Leopold II, King of the Belgians and Sovereign of the Independent State of Congo," Williams condemned the brutal, inhuman treatment the Congolese people suffered at the hands of the colonizers.[10]

William Henry Sheppard, a black Presbyterian missionary in the Congo from 1890 to 1910, served at the same time as Fleming, Gordon, and Howard. He also observed the abuses but initially was reluctant to publicize the terror he saw there. However, while on a lecture tour in the United States he spoke about a massacre he had seen. His report of atrocities began circulating. The international press picked up the story, catapulting Sheppard into the spotlight as a human rights crusader.[11] Awareness of the atrocities led to protests by missionaries and other observers, followed by investigations; the formation of the British Congo Reform Association and later the American Congo Reform Association; the condemnatory eyewitness report in 1904 of Robert Casement, the British consul to the Congo, on the brutal abuses there; and international criticism. Eventually, the Belgian government, which initially had wanted nothing to do with King Leopold's imperial dreams, reluctantly annexed the Congo Free State in November 1908.[12]

European and American missionaries assumed that Africans would be receptive to the new religions they brought because this was the fundamental belief of most evangelists. However, since Christianity and Christian missionaries failed to influence the racist attitudes of European colonialists in Africa, most Africans saw the two groups as allies in the mutual goal of the destruction of the African lifestyle and therefore surmised there was no difference between the two. This was true despite the fact that missionaries, for all practical purposes, represented the mission-sending societies that sent them out, not the governments of the countries where they originated.[13]

For Africans, Christianity perpetuated racial inequality, racial subjugation, and colonial domination. African Catholic and Protestant priests were relegated to inferior positions in their churches, African congregations were segregated from white ones, and white missionaries supervised African churches. Many Africans also believed that mission education was designed to indoctrinate them into a permanent state of subservience.[14]

The conflict of culture, ethnicity, identity, and worldview between the missionary and the potential convert was one of the major obstacles the Christian churches had to overcome in Africa. European and American missionaries, white and black, regarded the traditional African way of life and African values and customs with contempt. They attacked the foundations of African society and condemned traditional African religions, polygamy, and what they viewed as depravity in African life. Mission schools produced African children who were disrespectful of African traditions, denounced African religious practices, and held African culture in contempt. Therefore, the chief hostility of Africans to missionaries was that they tried to undermine the traditional African way of life. Missionaries hoped to destroy what they saw as barbaric and heathen among Africans. This attitude colored their proselytizing activities and explains the initial low conversion rates among Africans. Black American missionaries were well aware that in contemporaneous culture Africa was a symbol of depravity. Some reacted to this negative image by disavowing any significant links to Africa and Africans while for others Africa's glorious past was a source of pride and a rallying point for African American nationalism and uplift ideology. These views had less to do with the African way of life than with the low status of black Americans in American society.[15]

Part of the reason Africa and the rest of the non-Western world were seen in such a negative light by American black and white churches and for that matter by mission boards throughout the world had to do with the financial nature of the mission movement itself, which depended almost totally upon voluntary contributions. Missionaries had to prove the need for their work by emphasizing the "depraved, degraded, and debased" conditions in those areas where they labored. Pity increased contributions.[16]

Regardless of what their denominational affiliation or their location in Africa was or what colonial ruler had power in the colony where they were assigned, all missionaries used some of the same strategies to convert people. If one technique resulted in larger numbers of converts, it was used in that area among those people; if it did not increase church membership, it was abandoned. The founding of schools, particularly boarding schools, on mission posts proved to be the most successful method for increasing membership in mission churches.

Despite good conversion rates among children, missionaries had little success in winning converts in surrounding areas. They would invite people from nearby villages and towns to come to Sunday services on the mission stations. Or on Sunday afternoon, missionaries and evangelists would go to the villages, taking with them children from the stations. The clerics would preach while the others would sing. Although missionaries expected that this technique would result in more converts than on the mission stations, in reality fewer Africans converted in this way. Missionaries saw village visitation as the best strategy for expanding their work on a broader scale, but, the immediate focus of their work remained the mission school.[17]

There was a direct relationship between the establishment of mission boarding schools and the winning of converts, who were easier to find among children. Children lived year round in boarding schools, where missionaries had greater control over them. The children were encouraged to accept Western and Christian ideas and reject their old way of life. As their whole lives centered on the mission station, conversion for these children became more than a religious experience. It also resulted in a cultural and social metamorphosis. Given their training in the United States and the nature of women's work for women and children, Fleming, Gordon, and Howard participated as schoolteachers in just such transformations.[18]

The correspondence of Fleming, Gordon, and Howard shed light on the motivation, rewards, and experiences of African American women missionaries that were shaped by their interactions with Africans and Europeans in the Congo. The three women were graduates of prominent black seminaries in the South associated with the Baptist Church. Committed to the missionary cause in Africa, they dedicated their lives to it and ultimately lost their health to it. In reclaiming the lives of African American women for the historical record, one needs biographical sketches to establish their life trajectories, offer some explanation for the choices they made, and illuminate their experiences in the African nexus.

Lulu Fleming was the first black woman to be appointed and commissioned for career missionary service by the Women's Baptist Foreign Missionary Society of the West, an auxiliary of the American Baptist Missionary Union. Born a slave in Hibernia, Clay County, Florida, on January 28, 1862, Fleming converted in 1876 and was baptized on January 14, 1877, in Jacksonville, Florida. She attended Shaw University in Raleigh, North Carolina, graduating as class valedictorian on May 27, 1885, from the Estey Seminary Course. On March 17, 1887, Fleming set sail from the United States, reaching Palabala in the Congo, formerly the center of work for British Baptist missionaries, on May 16.

During her first term of service, Fleming was a matron for the girls at the station and a teacher of the primary and upper English classes in the day and Sunday schools. While on furlough for health reasons in 1891, she studied medicine, first entering Leonard Medical School at Shaw University and then in 1895 completing the full course at the Woman's Medical College of Philadelphia. She returned to Africa in 1895 as a medical missionary under the auspices of the Women's Baptist Foreign Missionary Society, supported by Grace Baptist Church in Philadelphia. She was posted initially at Irebu and subsequently at Bolengi in the Congo. In 1898 she married the Reverend "Tata" James. Nothing more is known about him. Before the end of her second term, however, Fleming was stricken with African sleeping sickness. She reluctantly returned to the United States for medical treatment and died in Philadelphia on June 20, 1899.[19]

Nora A. Gordon, born on August 25, 1866, to former slaves, graduated from Spelman Seminary (Spelman College, Atlanta, Georgia) in 1888 and became the first student from Spelman to go to Africa, departing in 1889. Her letters home describing her experiences in Africa convinced several Spelman students to volunteer for mission work on the continent. Under appointment to the Women's Baptist Foreign Missionary Society of the West, Gordon attended a missionary training institute in London conducted by two former missionaries in the Congo, before arriving at the mission station at Palabala. She worked with Lulu Fleming as a teacher in the mission school before transferring to the Lukunga mission station. There she was in charge of the afternoon school and supervisor of the printing office, where she set type for printing the first arithmetic textbook in the local language. In 1893, Gordon took a furlough in the United States. Two years later she married the Reverend S. C. Gardner of Jamaica and sailed with him to the Congo under appointment by British Baptists. Ill health forced her return to the United States in 1900. She died in Atlanta a year later, barely thirty-five years old.[20]

Clara Ann Howard, the second graduate of Spelman to go to Africa, was born on January 23, 1866, in Greenville, Georgia, and raised in Atlanta. One of the first students to enter Spelman Seminary when it was founded in 1881, she graduated valedictorian in 1887 as one of the school's first six graduates. After a short career as a teacher, which included a stint in Atlanta's public schools, Howard applied for a missionary assignment and was appointed to the Congo by the Women's Baptist Foreign Missionary Society. She sailed from Boston on May 3, 1890, arriving in the Congo the following month. Howard was stationed at Lukunga, where she worked alongside Gordon and took charge of the primary school, which eventually grew to one hundred pupils. She also had sole care of thirty home-less boys. After continuing bouts of malaria, poor health forced Howard to resign from the mission society on May 3, 1897. In 1899 she joined the faculty of Spelman Seminary and later worked as matron in the school's student boarding department. She died on May 3, 1935.[21]

The observations, activities, and attitudes of African American mis-sionaries stationed in Africa were discussed in the mail they sent home and recollections they wrote after they returned, including autobiogra-phies, biographies, and reminiscences. The content and nature of mission-ary correspondence varied, to some extent, depending on its intended audience—mission board or loved ones. The private letters missionaries sent to families and friends circulated widely, and excerpts appeared in mission and secular newspapers, magazines, and periodicals. Like their white counterparts, African American missionaries discussed two major items: personal matters and issues related to the functioning of the mis-sion station. Their writings reveal the preconceived notions black mission-aries held upon arriving in Africa, how they came to view the ancestral homeland and its inhabitants, and how their attitudes changed or did not change over time. Also recorded are their activities, their priorities, and their worries about whether or not they were able to balance the dilemma of their racial identification with that of the people they wished to convert. Whereas women missionaries in the Congo were concerned with educa-tional and cultural transformation, their male counterparts concentrated their efforts on religious conversion. In their reports home, these men discussed the establishment of mission stations and the number of con-verts. Since male missionaries were the ones that interacted directly with Belgian authorities in the Congo in regard to the successful administration of the mission stations, they were less likely to criticize colonial rule, least of all while they were still in Africa. As they assumed their place in the African diaspora, African American women missionaries used their corre-spondence to reflect on important aspects of their identity and expe-rience, which included race, culture, and the nature of their connection to Africa.[22]

In their writings, Fleming, Gordon, and Howard described African society and African people, including their homes, customs, traditions, dress, and religious practices. The three African American women missionaries discussed their experiences with African women and children since these were the people on whom they would concentrate their efforts and with whom they would spend their time while in the Congo. They also mentioned their relationship with white missionaries and their interactions with European colonial administrators. African American women missionaries were ever mindful that their writings home would be printed and reprinted in many publications in the United States and read by and to black and white audiences throughout the country. Therefore, although they enunciated some of the same stereotypes as white missionaries stationed in Africa, these women often tendered them with humorous or personal anecdotal stories.

DUTY TO THE ANCESTRAL HOMELAND

The motives of individual African American missionaries in Africa varied, but the overriding theme of duty to their ancestral homeland helps to explain why so many volunteered for mission work there. Undoubtedly, black American missionaries went to Africa as representatives of an American and Western culture. Like white Americans, most endorsed the Western image of Africa as a dark continent in need of the civilizing effects of Christianity. They supported mission work there, believing that by exposing Africans to Western religious, social, and cultural influences they would make the continent more acceptable to white America and to the wider world. White Americans made a point of constantly emphasizing the racial and historical link between African Americans and Africans. Because black Americans at this time felt that the negative images of Africa affected white attitudes toward them, they saw the evangelization of Africans as their special duty. As whites took up the putative white man's burden in Africa, black American missionary men and women volunteered to help in the civilizing mission there.

Fleming, Gordon, and Howard continually justified the need for the conversion of the Congolese to Christianity by describing them as dark and darkened people, an allusion not to their skin color but to their lifestyle. Fleming commented in a letter in 1887 on what in her eyes was the sad situation she found in the Congo: "Truly the people here . . . for centuries have been sitting in darkness."[23] In another letter early in 1891, she reported, "The work at Palabala has known its hardest trial this past year and also its greatest lesson. More people have been reached and some have turned from sin and darkness into light"—the light of Christianity, of course.[24] Howard referred to the Congo as a "dark land."[25] Gordon expressed a wish to "keep well and strong to work for the salvation of these poor people."[26]

Although they often went to Africa with the same negative images and stereotypes as whites about the continent and its people, as they worked among Congolese women and children, African American women came to identify personally with the people among whom they were working. They revealed that they relished the progress made by the people among whom they worked; some even admitted that they came to love them. It was not unusual in their letters for the women to refer to Africans as our people. Howard mentioned that she loved Africa and Africans and identified with them. She confessed that she had volunteered for mission work to help our "brothers and sisters in Africa."[27] After their return to the United States, African American women missionaries indicated that they had formed deep and lasting relationships with both women and men in the Congo.

Fleming, Gordon, and Howard faced some frustrations over the pace and progress of their work. They were disappointed that there never seemed to be enough resources for all mission programs, particularly those geared to women and girls. On a broader scale was their anxiety related to finances on the mission station and to the salaries of missionaries. These included the issues of limited staff, constant personnel shortages due to health problems and missionary furloughs, the need for reinforcements, inadequate supplies, the immensity of the work, insufficient financial support from the home church, and frustration with the rate of African conversion. On a more personal level, the missionaries were anxious about insufficient preparation and training for the field; lack of language instruction and difficulty surpassing language barriers; poor preparation for the new culture; adjustment to climate and temperature; constant health problems with prevalent typhoid fever, smallpox, and malaria along with their concomitant recurring attacks; isolation and loneliness; weariness; and a difficult adjustment to African customs and traditions. Most important, Fleming, Gordon, and Howard were apprehensive about what they considered to be the low status of women and girls in Congolese society.[28]

WOMEN'S WORK FOR WOMEN
IN THE CONGO: CONFLICTS OF CULTURE,
ETHNICITY, AND IDENTITY

As expected, Fleming, Gordon, and Howard focused their energies on African women and girls.[29] Fleming spoke about the importance of missionaries reaching African women. She lamented in an 1888 report, "All our converts thus far are men. Oh, how I long to see the women reached. The women must be reached in their homes, so must the children."[30] After some years in the Congo, Gordon insisted in a report home, "We very much need a girls' house. If we can save the women and girls and have intelligent Christian wives and mothers, the atmosphere of the community will be greatly changed."[31] Soon after her transfer to the Lukunga station, she expressed a hope of other women missionaries: "Indeed, our hearts have been made to rejoice because of these dear women who are coming to Jesus."[32] This was a common refrain repeated time and again by all women missionaries.

The three missionaries focused their attention on the one issue they believed would have the greatest impact on African society: getting the children and above all the girls from surrounding villages to attend the mission schools. They wanted to change dramatically and, by their standards, improve the lives of these girls by educating them. They hoped to alter African lifestyles through the uplift of African womanhood. Nonetheless, the missionaries often were frustrated that they were unable to "rescue" girls from conditions they viewed as inferior and demeaning. To them, African customs and traditions seemed to work against missionary efforts to improve the lives of girls and women; the missionaries feared they would be unable to improve the lot of the females.[33] Working to improve the status of women and children proved to be a daunting task.

To persuade children to attend the mission schools, many missionaries bribed the children with clothing or paid cash to their parents. Howard bragged that missionaries at her station did not pay a "dash" to the parents for letting their children come to school:

> The children are all free—that is, we do not believe in buying them as some do for the purpose of educating them, nor do we give their parents "dashes" or gifts for allowing them to remain. At first parents

would bring their children and say: "Here is my child, I want him to stay with you." They would wait around until he was dressed and then say: "Where is my gift?" Sometimes after trying to explain and tell them the object of the school, they would take the children back. I have not troubled myself about them, and have my first "dash" to give, and yet have all the time a large number of little noisy rompers. Now it is an understood thing and no one even mentions "dash."[34]

Missionaries questioned the practice of paying children to come to school; some wrote to mission secretaries in the United States to see if this was acceptable. As payment was frequently the only way to get students, missionaries had to resolve the conditions under which children (or their parents) would be paid to attend the mission schools. For African parents and children, clothing was the essential and minimal "dash."[35]

Clothing became an issue that consumed the energies of the missionary women. First, they had to find enough money in the mission budget to buy clothes for children to wear to school and for their upkeep on the station. Sometimes the missionaries even had to buy girls from their fathers who wanted to sell them or from husbands who had purchased them. At other times, the missionaries felt that some of the girls were converting just to get paid in some way or to please them. They often spoke of silently grieving because they were unsuccessful in getting girls. They regularly were saddened by the realities of these Congolese girls' lives and found that some of the things they demanded of them went against the tide of tradition, such as insisting that they wear certain clothing and requiring that they come to school regularly.

Recently, anthropologists have begun to reexamine the significance of clothing in various societies at different times. Missionaries tried to impose on converts their own concepts of decency and morality in terms of both thought and appearance. Obviously, clothes served as a way to hide the private areas of a person's body from the rest of the world. African American women missionaries were very sensitive to the nakedness of African girls and women. But people also wore clothing for functional and practical reasons, and it had specific cultural, social, political, economic, and religious meanings. Moreover, clothing was one of the ways to distinguish social class, wealth, gender, occupation, marital status, and ethnic affiliation. From the perspective of the colonial powers, clothing was a way to colonize the hearts and minds of the individuals residing in their newly conquered lands. Colonial powers utilized clothing to assert dominance. Whites were not inclined to see Africans as equals and used clothing as a means of maintaining inequality. Yet dress constituted a battleground on which Africans could assert their culture and build nationalism in their fight against external attacks on their way of life.[36]

Fleming, Gordon, and Howard believed that the girls emphasized the wrong things. They scolded them for wearing little clothing; but the girls wanted their bodies to be seen by African men. Missionaries deemed that the girls' only ambition was to be bought by some man for his wife; the girls wanted to get married and work in the fields for their husband so that he might be considered great by his large number of wives.[37] Possibly, the missionaries did not see that the lives of single African women were even more circumscribed than those of single African American women.

Howard asked churchwomen in America, "sisters in the civilized land" as she called them, to support financially the Congolese girls by sending dresses or cloth to make dresses. She emphasized that there was little difference between girls in the Congo and those in America: "Doubtless, many of you have formed a very strange picture of our Congo girls. Well don't do so again, for I have seen no difference. They are such as you daily meet and talk with, of all shades and colors. They do differ in one respect; that is they wear little or no clothing except a little piece of cloth or several rows of beads around their bodies. . . . [But] when they accept Christ, their eyes are opened and they began to want clothes, and especially dresses to cover their nakedness."[38] Missionaries considered the attire that African children wore to school improper. African children certainly did not dress for school in the same way American students did. Additionally, African parents were unable to afford the clothing or uniforms that were required. So the mission schools would have had to supply cloth or clothing for the students, anyway. Another critical issue that affected attendance was that the youngsters would not go to school if they were not dressed appropriately or like the other children.

Sometimes it was not just clothing that kept students from attending school. Missionaries bemoaned the progress of African children and blamed it on the customs and beliefs of the adults. A few African parents deemed that there were no advantages to having a Western education in African society. For that reason, Fleming was disappointed at losing a boy from her station in the Congo who she had hoped would be educated and baptized:

> One little boy in my school took a stand for Christ and began to grow bold [for] Christ. His master, a backslider, learning of this, took the dear little fellow out of school away to a distant town and compelled him to enter a temple and become a fetish boy. How my heart has followed this dear young [disciple?]. You can never know until you are bound in spirit with some poor soul who suffers persecution for the kingdom of God's sake. I have been with him in all of the bonds that bind him to that unholy temple with its unseeming images and suffered with him all the insults thrown into his face because of the hope he has in Christ. All this has been in soul but the suffering has been so real as has been his who suffers in body.[39]

But there may have been another reason the boy was taken out of school. Rural societies throughout the world value children as workers. Children are needed to help with farm work and to care for aged parents. A West African proverb that says, "Each extra mouth comes attached to two extra hands" speaks perfectly to the dilemma faced by African parents or guardians who had to give approval for their children to board at mission schools. On the one hand, they needed workers in the field, the more the better. On the other hand, there was the realization that their children probably should receive a Western education to prepare them for the new world they were entering.[40] In Africa, as elsewhere in the world throughout history, parents have had to make social trade-offs to benefit their children.[41]

The failure of missionaries to understand the gendered divisions of labor in the Congo and their experiences of labor in the American South also led to tensions between the missionaries and the women among whom they worked. Even when she did receive cloth from home, Howard was unable to get the women and girls to make dresses. She could not understand why they did not want to learn to sew until one Congolese woman explained it to her. As Howard tried to give the woman a needle and thread to restring broken beads, the woman exclaimed, "Am I a man? I don't want that needle to sew; that's man's work."[42] In Africa, men did the sewing.

In addition to their duties in the schools and on the station, missionaries' work on the attached farms was important to the maintenance of the stations. Missionaries grew crops and raised livestock for their food, but also to secure profits for the mission. Depending on their location in Africa, they cultivated a variety of foodstuffs, including rice, sugar cane, cassava, sweet potatoes, coffee, peanuts, pineapples, corn, bananas, and oranges. However, farming proved to be less profitable than the missionaries had hoped.[43] The issue of gardening and farming resulted in another culture clash between missionaries and Africans: in Africa these were jobs done by girls and women. African American women missionaries saw farming as demeaning: it reminded them of slavery, under which men, women, and children all labored in the fields. Besides, work in the gardens and fields kept the girls from attending school. In a letter, Howard compared the lives of girls in the Congo with those of girls in the United States:

> I have before me every day so many little boys and not many girls. I am very sorry not to have more girls; but let me tell you why the little African girls do not come to school. The little girls and women do all the garden work, and have to get food for their husbands and brothers. Little girls like you get up very early in the morning and with their little, short-handled hoes go to their gardens and dig away in the hot sun bare-headed and naked, with the exception of a loin-cloth, and seem happy. You would not be happy, I know, if you were obliged to live in this way. Would you? Thank God, dear girls, that you have a Christian papa and mama to care for you, and who like to give you food and clothes instead of having you do as the Congo girls do.[44]

Despite such comparisons, it was especially rewarding to black women missionaries when African women teachers went back to teach in their communities and nurses returned to the mission hospitals after being certified. The missionaries confessed their pride and satisfaction in seeing growth in women's work and district women's meetings, watching African women lead a worship service for the first time, and hearing of the neighboring schools in which classes were being taught by African teachers.[45]

Professional and personal fulfillment often went hand in hand. Howard related a story about how she and other missionaries prepared a Christmas dinner for boys on the station. The dining room table was set with a white tablecloth, glasses, silver-plated knives and forks, and dishes before the boys were called to eat. She reported, "Oh, if you could have seen their faces as they spied the table! It doubly paid for all the trouble." The missionaries served the boys and then cleaned the table afterward. Howard admitted that "it was such a pleasure to see them enjoy themselves and be so happy." She described the boys after the event: "Such a happy set! I love them very much."[46] In many of her letters, Howard talked about how much she loved the children.[47] She admitted in one note, "I love these children so much, and I think most of them care a great deal for me."[48] Isolated from their own family and friends, women missionaries found a sense of family with the children on whose behalf they worked.

RACE, CULTURE, AND IDENTITY IN COLONIAL RELATIONS

Some black Americans found that outside the United States they were able to live free of their homeland's constricting prejudice and racism. They experienced a shifting relationship with white Americans once they left the country. During the voyage to Africa, while in Europe, or after arrival in Africa, black women and men often had cordial and friendly encounters with whites that would have been unimaginable in the South. In this case, the racial norms in America were apparently suspended in favor of a shared nationality.[49]

Relations among blacks and whites were complicated by the colonial power structures in Africa. Before the establishment of colonial rule in Africa, European and American missionaries stationed on the continent depended on the goodwill of their African hosts: they had to adapt to the African chiefs and rulers. After partition, when all of Africa, except for Liberia and Ethiopia, came under the control of the European powers, missionaries operated independently only as long as the colonialists allowed it: they had to adjust to the new European colonial systems. In the Congo Free State, European colonizers controlled missionaries through the issuance of governmental decrees that required official authorization for mission activities.[50]

One dilemma missionaries in Africa faced after the partition was how to work effectively with European colonizers without jeopardizing their status as representatives of the various mission societies. After all, they were working toward their own goals of evangelization; they were not agents of the colonial powers. In this era of imperialism and racism, African American missionaries had to take care not to offend Europeans in Africa. They were sensitive about their presence because Europeans saw them not only as foreigners, Americans, but also as Africans or at least of African descent.

When Gordon arrived in the Congo in the late 1880s, soon after the Berlin Conference, she came face to face with hordes of European settlers in various regions of the continent. In a letter home, she denounced the large number of diverse groups around the mission station intent on exploiting the land and the people. In describing her neighbors, she mentioned that, "there are more than one hundred foreigners around the Pool, English, Scotch and American missionaries, Belgian officials and traders, and on the other side of the river there are French officials, traders, mostly Dutch, and Roman Catholic missionaries."[51] Black American missionaries were not only dealing with the large number of European administrators vying for control of territory on the continent, but also competing with foreign missionaries who, like them, were trying to win converts.

Howard criticized almost every colonial ruler in Africa. She condemned Belgian officials in the Congo for their indifference to the indigenous people: "The government authorities are pushing and extending their power into the interior with no thought of the moral and spiritual welfare of the people." She further excoriated the Portuguese for allowing foreign traders in their colonies to import rum and other distilled spirits she felt were destroying African bodies and souls. Inland, she accused British state officials of driving Africans from the towns by the cruelty of their state officials.[52]

Education was another area of tension between missionaries and colonial authorities. Colonialists wanted to counter the literacy and intellectual focus of mission schools. As would be expected in an era in which agricultural and mechanical schools were established as the proper type of education for African Americans, European colonial governments wanted mission societies and missionaries to organize the same types of institutions for Africans. Some denominations would eventually add agricultural, industrial, vocational, domestic science, and printing departments to their schools at the stations. Later, seminaries and hospitals were added.[53]

Race, culture, and identity were rendered more complicated for African Americans by the perceptions of the Africans among whom they worked.

Fleming told an interesting story about a trip she took through the Congo and the attitudes of the people she met. In one anecdote, she mentioned the reactions of a local king: "The King seemed overjoyed at our coming and wished us well in his land. He asked questions on the love and immortality of God and the resurrection of the dead and seemed downcast in soul to hear such astonishing truths. I then had the girl to tell him that I was one of his. My grandfather and his being [from] the same country. This he could or would not believe. "No, no," said he, "she is a white/black woman." Then all his town joined in saying it."[54] Africans often referred to African Americans as "white men and women in black skin," a reference not to their skin color but to their culture and nationality.

African American missionaries faced the dilemma of how to balance national allegiance with ethnic identity. They could not escape the fact that they were Americans. Even when they identified with Africans, they still valued their Americanism. Europeans viewed them as Americans of African descent. Africans saw them as Americans and as Westerners. Besides, in the final analysis, African American missionaries did not reject their American nationality. They were American citizens, maybe second-class citizens, but Americans first and foremost.

CONCLUSION

In the area of Christian foreign missionary work, conversion to Christianity implicitly meant the rejection of local religious and cultural practices and the acceptance of a Western religion and value system. Converts had to withdraw from indigenous ways and embrace Western behavior and customs. Mission ideology always assumed a negativism about the society in which missionaries worked and tended to imply that the positive image of an individual missionary toward African society and culture could not be separated from the work of societal transformation and religious conversion; in other words, they could respect African culture, society, and religion but still want to change them. In addition, there was a peculiar train of thought in missionizing that Africans could not be complimented at the same time that their way of life was being condemned.[55] Yet, even though they were, for the most part, ministering in non-Western and non-Christian areas, black American missionaries still did not necessarily denounce African society and religion outright. They confronted stereotypes about Africa by using detail and specificity to counter the monolithic, undifferentiated Africa that was the staple of Western thought.[56]

While ministering among Africans, women missionaries often underwent changes themselves that allowed them to identify with a foreign culture and relate to its people. Mostly, blacks understood that as missionaries in Africa their job was a religious, cultural, and educational transformation of Africans; in other words, a reinvention of what it meant to be African. At the same time, what also occurred was a reinterpretation of what it meant to be African American. Fleming, Gordon, and Howard came to see that although there were many differences between Congolese girls and women and African American girls and women, there were also some similarities, principally in the desire of each for advancement in their society.

The three women's thinking was transformed as they moved from broad generalizations about all Africans to the unique specificity and individuality of a particular group. Their initial pessimism about Africans and African society frequently turned into respect for the differences they observed in the Africans' ways of doing things. These missionaries came to understand that Africans did things in the way that was best for them in their environment and society. Additionally, because of their comparable experiences of oppression owing to their color and culture, African American missionaries came to believe they had a commonality with Africans and eventually gained insight into their lives.

The three African American women missionaries in the Congo had to wrestle with the frequent contradictions and conflicts between their allegiance, nationality, and culture as American citizens and their race, ethnicity, and identity as people of African descent. While they transferred American religion and culture to African peoples, they had to deal with the very hypocrisy of their own existence in a Jim Crow, segregated America. This was what W. E. B. Du Bois called the "double-consciousness" or "two-ness" of being black in white America: "It is a peculiar sensation, this double-consciousness, this sense of always looking at one's self through the eyes of others, of measuring one's soul by the tape of a world that looks on in amused contempt and pity. One ever feels his two-ness, an American, a Negro; two souls, two thoughts, two unreconciled strivings; two warring ideals in one dark body, whose dogged strength alone keeps it from being torn asunder."[57]

In the years Fleming, Gordon, and Howard pursued their calling in Africa, white American society denied blacks in the United States full equality and equitable justice. Fleming, Gordon, and Howard knew their job in the Congo Free State was the cultural, educational, and religious conversion of the Congolese people. But as they worked among them, they questioned whether their mission's rejection and substitution of African lifestyles with features of American society were a denial of themselves, their values and traditional identities. In the end, these three black American women missionaries in the Congo came to realize that admitting anything positive about the Congo, Congolese culture, and Congolese people and identifying with them did not exclude them from having a sense of loyalty, allegiance, and national identity as Americans.

NOTES

I am grateful to Jemetta Davis, my graduate assistant in the 2004–5 and 2005–6 academic years, for her assistance in preparing this chapter.

1 Joel E. Tishken, "Christianity in Colonial Africa," *Africa: Colonial Africa, 1885–1939*, vol. 3, ed. Toyin Falola, 157–59 (Durham: Carolina Academic Press, 2002).

2 Modupe Labode, "'A Native Knows A Native': African American Missionaries' Writings about Angola, 1919–1940," *The North Star: A Journal of African American Religious History* 4, no.1 (fall 2000), 1–14.

3 Sylvia M. Jacobs, ed., *Black Americans and the Missionary Movement in Africa* (Westport, Conn.: Greenwood Press, 1982).

4 Joyce M. Bowers, "Roles of Married Women Missionaries: A Case Study," *International Bulletin of Missionary Research* 8, no. 1 (January 1984), 4–8; Susan B. DeVries, "Wives: Homemakers or Mission Employees?," *Evangelical Missions Quarterly: The Journal for Understanding Missions* 22, no. 4 (October 1986): 402–10; Joanna B. Gillespie, "Mary Briscoe Baldwin (1811–1877), Single Woman Missionary and 'Very Much My Own Mistress,'" *Anglican and Episcopal History* 57, no. 1 (March 1988), 63–92; Sylvia M. Jacobs, "African Missionary Movement," *Black Women in America: An Historical Encyclopedia*, ed. Darlene Clark Hine, 14–16 (Brooklyn: Carlson Publishing, 1993); Ann White, "Counting the Cost of Faith: America's Early Female Missionaries," *Church History* 57, no. 1 (March 1988), 19–30.

5 Pierce R. Beaver, *All Loves Excelling: American Women in World Mission* (Grand Rapids: Eerdmans, 1968), and *American Protestant Women in World Mission: A History of the First Feminist Movement in North America* (Grand Rapids: Eerdmans, 1980); William J. Harvey, *Sacrifice and Dedication in a Century of Mission: A History of One Hundred Years of the Foreign Mission Board, National Baptist*

Convention, U.S.A., Inc., 1880–1980 (Philadelphia: Foreign Mission Board, National Baptist Convention, U.S.A., 1979); Evelyn Brooks Higginbotham, *Righteous Discontent: The Women's Movement in the Black Baptist Church, 1880–1920* (Cambridge, Mass.: Harvard University Press, 1993); Patricia R. Hill, *The World Their Household: The American Woman's Foreign Mission Movement and Cultural Transformation, 1870–1920* (Ann Arbor: University of Michigan Press, 1985); Othal Hawthorne Lakey and Betty Beene Stephens, *God in My Mama's House: The Women's Movement in the* CME *Church* (Memphis: CME Publishing House, 1994); Lawrence S. Little, *Disciples of Liberty: The African Methodist Episcopal Church in the Age of Imperialism, 1884–1916* (Knoxville: University of Tennessee Press, 2000); Sandy D. Martin, *Black Baptists and African Missions: The Origins of a Movement, 1880–1915* (Macon, Ga.: Mercer University Press, 1989).

6 Margaret E. Crahan and Franklin W. Knight, *Africa and the Caribbean: The Legacies of a Link* (Baltimore: Johns Hopkins University Press, 1979).

7 Delores C. Carpenter, "Black Women in Religious Institutions: A Historical Summary from Slavery to the 1960s," *Journal of Religious Thought* 46, no. 2 (winter–spring 1989–90), 7–27; Mary Eikenberry, "Women as Missionaries," *Brethren Life and Thought* 30, no. 1 (winter 1985), 47–49; Frederick J. Heuser, Jr., "Women's Work for Women: Belle Sherwood Hawkes and the East Persian Presbyterian Mission," *American Presbyterians: Journal of Presbyterian History* 65, no. 1 (spring 1987), 7–18; Sylvia M. Jacobs, "Afro-American Women Missionaries Confront the African Way of Life," *Women in Africa and the African Diaspora*, ed. Rosalyn Terborg-Penn, Sharon Harley, and Andrea Benton Rushing, 121–32 (Washington: Howard University Press, 1987), and id., "Give a Thought to Africa: Black Women Missionaries in Southern Africa," *"We Specialize in the Wholly Impossible": A Reader in Black Women's History*, Darlene Clark Hine, Wilma King, and Linda Reed, 103–23 (Brooklyn: Carlson Publishing, 1995); Ruth Tucker, "Female Mission Strategist: A Historical and Contemporary Perspective," *Missiology* 15, no. 1 (January 1987), 73–89; Barbara Welter, "'She Hath Done What She Could': Protestant Women's Missionary Careers in Nineteenth-Century America," *American Quarterly* 30, no. 5 (winter 1978), 624–38.

8 Adam Hochschild, *King Leopold's Ghost: A Story of Greed, Terror, and Heroism in Colonial Africa* (New York: Mariner Books, 1999); Robert July, *A History of the African People* (Prospect Heights, Ill.: Waveland Press, 1998), 295–96, 302, 425–28; Kalapo, "Central Africa," 343.

9 Sylvia M. Jacobs, *The African Nexus: Black American Perspectives on the European Partitioning of Africa, 1880–1920* (Westport, Conn.: Greenwood Press, 1981); Rayford W. Logan, *The Betrayal of the Negro, from Rutherford B. Hayes to Woodrow Wilson* (New York: Collier, 1972); Jacobs, ed., *Missionary Movement in Africa*.

10 John Hope Franklin, *George Washington Williams: A Biography* (Durham: Duke University Press, 1998).

11 Pagan Kennedy, *Black Livingstone: A True Tale of Adventure in the Nineteenth-*

Century Congo (New York: Viking Press, 2002); William E. Phipps, *William Sheppard: Congo's African American Livingstone* (Louisville: Geneva Press, 2002).

12 July, *African People*, 295–96, 302, 425–28; Kalapo, "Central Africa," 343.

13 Tishken, "Christianity in Colonial Africa," 157–59.

14 Andrew E. Barnes, "Western Education in Colonial Africa," in *Colonial Africa*, 146–48.

15 Barnes, "Western Education in Colonial Africa," 148; J. Mutero Chirenge, *Ethiopianism and Afro-Americans in Southern Africa, 1883–1916* (Baton Rouge: Louisiana State University Press, 1987), 44; Femi J. Kolapo, "Central Africa," in *Colonial Africa*, 356–57; Tishken, "Christianity in Colonial Africa," 170–72.

16 Sylvia M. Jacobs, "African Missions and the African American Christian Churches," *Encyclopedia of African American Religions*, ed. Larry G. Murphy, J. Gordon Milton, and Gary L. Ward, 10–23 (New York: Garland Publishing, 1993).

17 Labode, "African American Missionaries' Writings about Angola."

18 Jacobs, "African Missions," 10–23.

19 *Baptist Missionary Magazine* (1888, 1889, 1899); Jacobs, "Louise Cecilia Fleming," *Black Women in America*, 438–39; *Missionary Review of the World* (1888); *Woman's Baptist Foreign Missionary Society of the West* (1887–88, 1890–91). All biographical data on Lulu Fleming come from these sources.

20 *Baptist Missionary Magazine* (1890–91); Jacobs, "Nora Antonia Gordon," *Black Women in America*, 493–94; Florence Matilda Read, *The Story of Spelman College* (Atlanta, 1961); *Woman's Baptist Foreign Missionary Society of the West* (1890–91). All biographical data on Nora Gordon come from these sources.

21 Read, *Spelman College*; Clement Richardson, *The National Cyclopedia of the Colored Race*, vol. 1 (Montgomery: National Publishing, 1919); Jacqueline Jones Royster, "Clara A. Howard," *Black Women in America*, 586–87. All biographical data on Clara Howard come from these sources.

22 Jacobs, "Historical Role."

23 Fleming Letters, Letter no. 16, May 26, 1887, American Baptist Historical Society, Archives of the American Baptist Missionary Union, Rochester, New York.

24 Fleming Letters, Letter no. 1, September 10, 1887; no. 9, January 10, 1891.

25 Howard, *Spelman Messenger*, February 1892.

26 Gordon, *Baptist Missionary Magazine*, January 1890.

27 Howard, *Spelman Messenger*, April 1891.

28 Fleming Letters, Letter no. 9, January 10, 1891; Howard, *Spelman Messenger*, April 1891 and April 1892.

29 Fleming Letters, Letter no. 2, October 10, 1887; Gordon, *Baptist Missionary Magazine* (1890–91); Howard, *Spelman Messenger*, February 1892.

30 Fleming Letters, Letter no. 4, October 12, 1888.

31 Gordon, *Spelman Messenger*, May 1897.

32 Gordon, *Baptist Missionary Magazine* (1890–91).

33 Fleming Letters, Letter no. 2, October 10, 1887; Gordon, *Spelman Messenger*, May 1894; Howard, *Spelman Messenger*, February 1892.

34 Howard, *Spelman Messenger*, November 1894.

35 Ibid., January 1896.

36 Jean Allman, ed., *Fashioning Africa: Power and Politics of Dress* (Bloomington: Indiana University Press, 2004); Hildi Hendrickson, ed., *Clothing and Difference: Embodied Identities in Colonial and Post-Colonial Africa* (Durham: Duke University Press, 1996).

37 Fleming Letters, Letter no. 9, January 10, 1891.

38 Howard, *Spelman Messenger*, February 1892.

39 Fleming Letters, Letter no. 9, January 10, 1891.

40 Humanities Extension Publications Program, North Carolina State University, *Living in Our World: Africa, Asia, and the Pacific Realm* (Raleigh: North Carolina State University, 1998), 17.

41 Stephen O'Connor, *Orphan Trains: The Story of Charles Loring Brace and the Children He Saved and Failed* (Chicago: University of Chicago Press, 2001); Marilyn Irvin Holt, *The Orphan Trains: Placing Out America* (New York: Houghton Mifflin, 2001).

42 Fleming Letters, Letter no. 2, October 10, 1887; Howard, *Spelman Messenger*, February 1892.

43 Gordon discussed the farming of cotton on her mission station but concluded that it would not pay because of the heat, storms, dry season, and flood season. *Spelman Messenger*, May 1897.

44 Howard, *Spelman Messenger*, February 1894.

45 Gordon, *Baptist Missionary Magazine*, January 1890.

46 Howard, *Spelman Messenger*, December 1892 and December 1894.

47 For example, ibid.

48 Ibid., April 1891.

49 Gordon, *Spelman Messenger*, May 1897.

50 Michael Crowder, *West Africa Under Colonial Rule* (Evanston: Northwestern University Press, 1968), 363–65.

51 Gordon, *Spelman Messenger*, May 1897.

52 Howard, *Spelman Messenger*, November 1904.

53 Barnes, "Western Education in Colonial Africa," 150.

54 Fleming Letters, Letter no. 16, May 26, 1887.

55 Tishken "Christianity in Colonial Africa," 167–68.

56 Jacobs, "Historical Role."

57 W. E. B. Du Bois, *The Souls of Black Folk: Essays and Sketches* (New York: American Library, 1969), 16–17.

The Woman's Board of Missions
in the Philippines, 1902–1930

Laura R. Prieto

O f the twenty-eight missionaries sent to the Philippines by the American Board of Commissioners for Foreign Missions (ABCFM, or American Board) from 1902 to 1930, a decided majority of sixteen were women. For the first several years, the women were married to missionaries, but soon all concerned found that wives could not accomplish everything the American Board hoped. With increasing urgency, the board turned to the Woman's Board of Missions (Woman's Board), an association of women in New England founded in 1869 to cooperate with the American Board in "the Christianization, education and physical relief of women and children in foreign lands," mainly by shouldering the cost of dispatching single women missionaries.[1] The Woman's Board had been expansionist in the 1870s, dispatching and funding single women within American Board stations in nations from Turkey to China, India to Mexico. They espoused the nineteenth-century missiological concept of woman's work for woman, which linked Christianity to a higher status for women; by bringing Christianity to their sisters around the world, missionary women believed they were simultaneously breaking the bonds of women's secular (social and political) oppression. Though it had not taken on missionary work in any new locations in forty years, the Woman's Board responded with enthusiasm to the idea of elevating new American subjects in the Philippines as well.

The Philippines were not really a foreign mission, being a territorial possession of the United States since the end of the Spanish–American

War in 1898. Though the future of the Philippines remained uncertain—perhaps independence was in store at some undetermined date—its status as an American colony made it irresistible to evangelicals. The group of American Board women in Mindanao offers a valuable vantage point from which to analyze the crucial period of 1918–30, when mission work aimed most concertedly at Christianizing and Americanizing Filipina women and when the Philippines gradually transitioned from an imperial possession to self-government.

Most of the documentation that survives comes from the rich correspondence of three sisters with the Woman's Board that supported them. Isabel, Florence, and Evelyn Fox came from New Mexico, where they had been in close contact with home missionaries and with "Spanish speaking people." Their parents had recently died, forcing them to find their own way in the world. The middle sister, Isabel, was appointed by the American Board in 1918 and stayed in the Philippines until 1927. Florence, a trained nurse, followed in 1920 after a course of Bible study in New York, and she remained until 1932. Evelyn, the youngest, studied religious education at Boston University under the sponsorship of the Woman's Board and joined her sisters in the field in 1923, staying there until 1934.[2]

American Board officials, Woman's Board fundraisers, and missionaries in the field concurred that they needed women workers to spread the Gospel in the Philippines. The issue was especially crucial since, according to the common view, Filipinas exerted formidable influence over their husbands and children.[3] Americans, including the American Board missionaries, also associated the greatest potential of Filipinos with qualities that were largely gendered as feminine. That is, they noted the most promise for progress in Filipinos' musicality, their interest in spirituality, their warmth, sociability, and hospitality. Filipinos also seemed eager to learn, receptive both to biblical stories and to what Warwick Anderson calls the "gospel of hygiene": the acceptance of medical authority and institutions, concern for public health and sanitation, and "modern chemotherapeutics."[4]

In this context, what role did women missionaries play in the the early twentieth-century Philippines? In this essay I analyze the relationship the Woman's Board constructed between American women and Filipinas, whom they were "Christianizing, educating, and physically relieving" per the Woman's Board's Acts of Incorporation. A close consideration of gender in this enterprise reveals tensions within what might on the surface seem a cut-and-dried example of missionary imperialism. The Woman's Board was instrumental in creating institutions to empower Filipinas as women and Christians in their own image. Efforts to improve women's lives through clubs, medical care, and formal instruction culminated in the Woman's Bible Training School at Cagayan. The status to which American women hoped to elevate Filipinas incorporated a decidedly modern type of womanhood, including professionalized obstetrics and infant care, advanced education and professionalization, and athletics, all alongside Christianity.

This modern extension of woman's work for woman was ultimately incompatible with the political status of the Philippines as a colonial possession. The mission relied heavily on U.S. institutions in the Philippines and reflected or cooperated with American policies in its new territory. The American women missionaries could not "elevate" Filipinas to their own position because the state did not extend the same rights to Filipinas as to Americans. The position of American women as U.S. citizens was relatively tenuous to begin with, and recently won rights including woman suffrage did not extend to Filipinas.[5] The American missionaries' own cultural bias imposed limits as well; even those Filipinas identified as developing leaders remain almost invisible in the archival record. Furthermore, American women missionaries, including the Woman's Board, continued to prefer gender separatist strategies, even as a way to inculcate modern womanhood. These strategies became untenable by the end of the 1930s, leaving Filipinas to chart their own path toward the more powerful position that the Woman's Board missionaries initially imagined for them.

FOLLOWING THE FLAG

In the Philippines, women missionaries joined a diverse group of American colonial agents, including other missionaries, teachers, medical professionals, ethnographers, businesspeople, military troops, and bureaucrats. The singular nature of a missionary effort that followed the flag denoted a particular relationship with the state. A "deeply felt civilizing mission" was one of many factors guiding U.S. interest in the Philippines and a reason the United States took possession of the Philippines from Spain.[6] Though this "mission" was imagined primarily as secular, and though the state was often at pains to distinguish itself from the church (for example, in forbidding public school instructors to teach in Sunday schools), American civilization connoted Christianity, and Americanization paved the way for Protestant missionaries.

Whereas Protestantism was virtually unknown in the Philippines before and during Spanish rule, it explicitly accompanied U.S. conquest and occupation. U.S. Army chaplains, Young Men's Christian Association officers, and Bible societies hastened to the scene within months of the taking of Manila, soon followed by Protestant missionaries.[7] In the continued spirit of comity, several religious denominations agreed to a cooperative geographic division of the mission field.[8] The Methodist mission quickly grew to be the largest, followed by the first established mission, the Presbyterian.[9] Though stations and congregations varied in scale, Philippine missions possessed great symbolic importance in both imperialist and missiological terms. One influential text urged evangelical work in the Philippines as a singular chance to "confront" Catholicism in a globally significant field.[10]

The state and the mission shared the basic goal and method of "benevolent assimilation" through inculcation.[11] American imperialist rhetoric repeatedly referenced a protective role for the United States in the Philippines, imagining colonial rule as a period of tutelage during which Filipinos would become ready to rule themselves. Just as the missionaries hoped to Christianize and train native Filipinos who would then preach to their own people, so the United States devised municipal governments to grant Filipinos experience and practical education in "free self-government."[12] Formal education and participation in governance were important to both colonial projects. To this end, the U.S. government set up a public school system throughout the islands, dispatching over one thousand teachers to Manila beginning in January 1901; because this did not suffice to reach the entire Filipino population, mission schools played a companionate role. "Both the missionaries and government officials recognized that the type of instruction in the mission schools helped directly toward a trained citizenship and prepared for the day of Philippine independence," recalled the American Board historian Herbert Case.[13]

In 1902, just as Theodore Roosevelt declared an end to the Filipino insurrection against the United States, the American Board established its first mission in the new colony, at Davao on the island of Mindanao. Military and political unrest in the area meant there was a strong federal U.S. presence there. Christian (mostly Catholic) Filipinos in Luzon and the Visayas fought against U.S. colonial rule from 1899 to 1907; the Moros in Mindanao continued armed struggle against the Americans throughout the military occupation (1899–1903) until 1912, and rural unrest on the island persisted into the 1920s.[14] Simultaneously, the United States created the political unit of Moro province (1903–13), then reorganized the region as the Department of Mindanao and Sulu (1914), gradually and increasingly turning over authority to native (mostly Christian, both Catholic and Protestant) Filipinos by 1920.[15] The very religious diversity that made Mindanao so fascinating to some missionaries—the strong presence of Muslims and animists as well as Catholics—made the region seem overwhelmingly barbarous, even atypically Filipino to some American officials. Christian Filipino nationalists strategically disassociated themselves from the "uncivilized" Moros, Bagobos, Igorots, and Negritos.[16] Despite the tidy demarcations made by the Evangelical Union, which had assigned Mindanao to the Congregationalist American Board, the Visayas in the southern Philippines soon become the object of "Methodist designs" and a source of contention between the Presbyterians and Baptists who held formal title to the mission field there. Under internal and external criticism that it was neglecting its responsibility in this desirable region, the American Board opened a second station in Mindanao in 1915.[17]

The work for women in the Philippines was made distinct by the mission's relationship to the state. Americans were not vulnerable foreigners there, as they were in places like China, where American Board missionaries, including children, had been killed in the Boxer Rebellion. Rather they enjoyed the sanction and protection of the United States. While the exact relationship between the Philippines and the United States was being defined and challenged through the early twentieth century—most pointedly from the Insular cases through the Philippine Autonomy Act of 1916 and the Jones Act of 1917—domestic anti-imperialist agitation for Philippine independence had faded after 1900. Like Hawaii and Puerto Rico, the Philippines Islands belonged to the United States, so that any hope of autonomy could come only at the end of a long process of Americanization in the guise of preparing for democratic participation. This process often conflated political and religious identity. As Isabel Fox put it, "Only the knowledge of Christ will ever make them [the Moros] good citizens."[18] Protestantism was implicit in American culture and civilization, so the issue of Christianity was central in discussions of the Filipinos' capacity for self-government as well.

Americans generally perceived Filipinos as nominally Christian but in need of guidance and attention, especially to throw off Catholicism and superstition. Spanish culture and institutions cast a double-edged influence on the islands, in the missionaries' estimation. Evaluating the effects of Spanish colonization, the missionary Frank Laubach found that "Christianity [had already] raised womanhood to a higher position than it occupies in any other Oriental community." Catholicism staved off the encroachment of "Mohammedism" and prepared the Filipino people for the Protestant message.[19] Though there was no public dimension of domesticity for Spanish women, at least Filipinos valued and sheltered their daughters in the name of family honor, the missionaries observed: "A Filipina girl is a carefully guarded young person, and to be entrusted with the care of them is at once a privilege and a responsibility."[20] Americans did not oppose local practices like the use of chaperones because they readily perceived such protective measures as necessary in the eroticized, dangerous tropics. Missionaries evinced a concern with sexuality, nervously noting passionate romances among young Filipinos, incidences of elopements, and the frequency of serenades. Florence Fox was pointedly asked to deliver a lecture to the Young Women's Bible Conference at Baguio on sexual diseases, "what they were and ways to avoid them. . . . There was another trained nurse there, she spoke on the sacredness of our bodies."[21] If American missionaries championed greater freedom for Filipinas, there were nevertheless definite limits to the autonomy women should exercise.

While there was no consensus regarding future independence for the Philippines, missionary men's and women's comments consistently approved of the effect of American occupation. Even before her arrival Florence Fox expressed surprise that "the influence of the missionaries, and of the American occupation have worked wonders in most parts of these Islands." "Most of the people are much further advanced socially and educationally than I supposed they would be and it is surprising how ambitious [are] their ideas of the use and accumulation of money," although "their rather low and selfish ideas, and their low moral and spiritual standards, make one realize their need for the Gospel of Christ." Venturing into Moro-dominated territory for the first time, she confessed that "neither the houses, the place nor the people are as primitive as I thought they would be, and in a way I'm somewhat disappointed in that— but their civilization is mostly only what Roman Catholics give, and in these later years advanced somewhat by the influence of the United States and the Public Schools. Much remains to be done. Education has only begun."[22] Later comparing progress in the Philippines to the "gloomy" conditions in Japan, Florence Fox remarked, "I do think the American Occupation, together with the work of the Protestant Missionaries, has greatly lessened the gloom in the Philippines."[23]

Missionaries created kindergartens, Bible study, and networks of Sunday schools in order to prepare Filipinos for ministry. The second interdenominational conference held at Lake Lanao included one hundred Filipino delegates and sixty Americans.[24] Filipinos served as local pastors and as Bible women who taught religion and evangelized through the country. "With the very strong nationalistic feeling the only way to keep them loyal is by co-operation," observed Isabel Fox.[25]

The missionaries in Mindanao thus performed the usual, diverse range of mission work: Gertrude Black operated a kindergarten, Dr. Charles Sibley (and perhaps also Effa Seely Laubach, who was a trained nurse) practiced medicine, and all the missionaries tried to meet other community needs as well as participate in direct evangelizing. Beyond direct action, however, the Blacks, Sibleys, and Laubachs functioned as living exemplars of Christian families. The presence of spouses and children made these Americans seem more human, more comprehensible, and more worthy of trust. Though she described the Bukidnon "wild people" as being "timid and afraid," Effa Laubach found that "our little boy Charles always attracts their attention."[26] Single women too could exemplify Christian womanhood, providing an alternative model to that of a minister's wife.

Long past were the days when the American Board tagged missionaries' wives as assistant missionaries; now both halves of an appointed couple received the same title, and all missionaries, regardless of sex or marital status, were listed individually on the letterhead of the mission station. Perhaps in order to attract women, the board gave them a strong voice in mission affairs, including a full vote at mission meetings. This status contrasted sharply with governmental practice; when Governor Leonard

Wood visited the Cagayan station unexpectedly, he consulted only with the American men there about "the problem of the American Mestizo children here in the Islands," even though one of the conclusions reached was that the dormitory run by one of the women missionaries was an appropriate place for destitute mestiza girls.[27]

FILIPINAS AND AMERICANIZATION

If the goals of Christianizing, Americanizing, and modernizing were inseparable, nevertheless the first was the missionaries' organizing principle. Propagation of religious faith was, after all, the ultimate purpose of the mission; in Gertrude Granger Black's words, "Train us up a fine Christian body of young women and we will, with God's blessing, win the whole of Mindanao for His glory." Though native women evangelists, known as Bible women, would be essential, candidates for such work would emerge only gradually and would need training. In the meantime, organizations, Sunday schools, community activities (like Christmas programs), and volunteer opportunities (sewing for the hospital, for example) would lay the groundwork. Such methods could build from and cooperate with their secular counterparts, women's clubs, mother's associations, and public education. To this end, by 1930 the mission had gathered in "nearly 7000 in classes, including 600 women and girls."[28] Missionaries proselytized even the most commonplace American practices: they touted the health benefits of eating American corn rather than rice[29] and demonstrated popcorn making and typewriting in an effort to capture the interest of native peoples.[30]

Both Americans and Filipinos correlated modernity with Americanism and Protestant religion, not least when it came to womanhood and women's entrance into newly public roles. Thus secular parallels for inculcating Filipinas through women's groups and classes abounded outside the mission too. For example, the National Federation of Women's Clubs (NFWC), formed in 1920 under the influence of American clubwomen, shared similar concerns with infant care, child rearing, and home nursing. Being a modern Filipina in the 1910s and 1920s, explains the historian Mina Roces, "meant speaking English, getting an education, and taking up new roles in the public sphere."[31] The club movement's embrace of women in public roles did not at first address political emancipation, however. Filipinas turned to feminism only gradually, and again only after American influence, including Carrie Chapman Catt's tour in 1912. Before the mid-1920s even groups calling themselves Feminista devoted themselves to woman-centered social work rather than to feminist politics and woman suffrage. Two American governor-generals, Francis Burton Harrison and Leonard Wood, endorsed woman suffrage before the NFWC did in 1923.[32] At the mission as well, clubs led women to claim public authority and leadership but only incrementally, as when members of the various Dorcas societies formed a Woman's Association in order to take more responsibility for church matters.[33]

More than emancipating Filipinas politically, women's groups helped disseminate American gender ideology, particularly as refracted by consumer culture. Missionaries used American magazines to stay current on "civilized" styles. Isabel Fox subscribed not only to the *Christian Herald* and *Biblical Review* but also to the fashion-oriented *Delineator* and the *Woman's Home Companion*.[34] In a letter to the home office, Effa Laubach praised a recently baptized Filipina, "one of our stars," for "reading my Ladies Home Journal and know[ing] what the girls in America are doing."[35] U.S. consumer culture set the standards of beauty against which Filipinas were measured. As the historian Kristin Hoganson observes, "U.S. fashion writing presented the spread of European fashion as an index of civilization in Asia and the Middle East." Too much constriction or concealment (as with veils) and too much exposure of the body both "clearly called for Western sartorial intervention."[36]

Missionary women associated modern American aesthetics in dress with comfort, practicality, and simplicity. Isabel Fox praised Moro women's "sorong" as "very modest" but added, "One longs to do something to their hair. It does look so untidy and uncomfortable."[37] Her sister Florence judged that "Filipino clothes are not very practicable, and they are not used to wraps."[38] In this, as in other aspects of daily life, Americanization was a sign of progress as well as modern femininity: "My girls are sensible children and prefer simple American clothes as a rule," wrote Isabel, even though they "look like grown up ladies," older than they are.[39] Class evidently played a part in who adopted the preferred style. Isabel observed that although most little Filipinas wear bobbed hair with bangs, "little high class girls dress in dainty dresses with all the frilly underwear very like her little American cousin. . . . Little girls that play about the thatch houses and in the market wear a single colored slip."[40]

Hospital work bound modern womanhood and Christianity together with a more immediate practical application: relief of suffering. The hospital building itself offered a permanent structure, unlike the transient clubs or Sunday schools. But the superiority of modern medicine was not self-evident. Florence Fox, a trained nurse, felt herself engaged in a concerted struggle against local midwives. "Many people yet depend on their own old and dirty, untrained midwives," she complained with exasperation. "We [at the hospital] have had very few cases of confinement. We cannot seem to win the confidence of the people to accept our help at this time. They seem to be prejudiced both by ignorance and their poverty, and I think both their religion and superstition have something to do with their reticence at this time."[41] For Fox, childbearing was not about the sanctity of motherhood but about the superiority and authority of scientific discourse; modern maternity called for professional medicine. Being a single woman with no personal experience of childbirth, Florence had to demonstrate the superiority and value of her training to Filipinas. Only after helping to heal the skin affliction of her mission colleagues' child, David Woodward, did she feel a breakthrough. "What I did for the Woodward baby has been a good advertisement, and has given me a fruitful topic of conversation with native mothers. What I have told them about infant feeding and infant care has had much more weight and they have not been so afraid to try my advice."[42] In her view, the health and civilization of Filipinas were both at stake; thus she blamed the "dirty work" of midwives for infant deaths and ridiculed folk practices.

The Woman's Board spent most of its energies in the Philippines on enabling and enriching Filipina girls' education. Isabel Fox initiated a practical institution in relation to the public school system: a dormitory that would enable girls to attend the provincial high school in Cagayan. The United States ran an entire system of public education in the Philippines, encompassing primary schools, intermediate industrial schools focusing on practical education, and one high school per province. According to the educator and bureaucrat David Barrows, the high schools "are actually colleges or institutes and have ample grounds, numerous buildings, shops, and dormitories. The high schools are the real intellectual and social centers for each province."[43] Schools functioned as an important tool to prepare both civil servants and a professionalized middle class, that is, a government bureaucracy run by Filipinos and a modernized, Americanized society in the Philippines.[44] Higher education played a role in this as well; an act of the legislature established the University of the Philippines in 1908, with colleges in agriculture, arts, engineering, fine arts, law, medicine, and veterinary science. U.S. policies opened education, law, medicine, journalism, and other professions to Filipinas for the first time.[45] Filipino teachers greatly outnumbered Americans. Though American teachers were more likely to be female than male, in Cagayan's province of Misamis a lone American man taught school amid 155 Filipino and 119 Filipina teachers.[46]

The missionaries found an audience ready for instruction in language and manners. Helen Dority, an American girl in Mrs. Robert Black's kindergarten, modeled the shaking of hands to her ethnically diverse classmates; a photograph of the moment also captures how the attentive pupils are already assimilated in terms of dress and self-presentation.[47] Though missionaries recognized the necessity of learning the Visayan language, each new arrival dedicating herself to that task, it was a point of pride for Effa Laubach to declare, "My Sunday school class is composed of young girls who speak English fluently. Indeed it is hard for them to speak extemporaneously in Visayan. They say they think in English and prefer to use English."[48]

Though American educations offered certain advantages—not least of which was a route for upward economic mobility—some Filipino families (Moros in particular) were reluctant to send their daughters to school with boys.[49] Additionally, in the missionaries' eyes a secular education was ultimately insufficient; as Marian Wells Woodward commented, "Although the public schools have done much to enlighten the present generation, nevertheless this progress is hindered by conditions in the homes."[50] A girls' dormitory appealed to Filipino parents as a protected space to board their daughters, and as a Christian home to inculcate certain moral and religious values in young Filipinas—a place where, for example, prayers would be said morning and night, and Bible verses and hymns learned. "Aside from giving these girls . . . a good home and proper care and chaperonage, we have striven to give them a true home ideal, an idea of sanitation . . . and to build up a Christian character," reported Evelyn Fox.[51]

Gertrude Granger Black's kindergarten class, Mindanao, ca. 1911. By permission of the Houghton Library, Harvard University (ABC78, box 4, folder "Black"), and Wider Church Ministries, United Church of Christ.

In appealing for funds to support the enterprise, the Woman's Board periodical *Life and Light* emphasized the "proper protection" and "personal care" that Isabel Fox would take of the girls and noted that the dormitory represented an "enlarge[ment] of the borders of her home."[52] The magazine subsequently captioned a photo as "Miss Fox and Her Family of Girls"; the metaphor was not entirely misplaced since Isabel referred to residents as "a family of my own."[53]

The dormitory was not strictly a spiritual corrective for the secular Americanization obtainable through public education. While the mission did not directly organize girls' athletics, for example, it supported and celebrated this modern dimension of femininity through the dormitory work. Along with teachers attending intensive programs at the normal school, the dormitory hosted visiting athletic teams, especially girls' baseball teams. "In December, during the provincial meet, we borrowed cots and filled the Bible Class room," reported Isabel Fox in 1923. "This made a great deal of confusion but we think it paid and made us more friends."[54] Like the dormitory work in general, it was a means of serving a community need and simultaneously gathering young Filipinas where they might be influenced. Athletic teams were organized by schools at the local level, organized into associations by the director of education, and brought to the capital, Manila, for competitions. The first women from Mindanao whom Effa Laubach met were on a girls' baseball team from Oroquieta, competing at the carnival in Manila; the more she spoke with them and watched them play, the more she admired them. "I admit that I am prejudiced, but I do not think that in all the United States there is a team that could beat the Oroquieta girls as they played that afternoon," she effused. "They were just healthy and strong, and had practiced very, very faithfully, and had never injured their health with too many sweets." Laubach appears to have approved of the way they celebrated their victory —"screaming with joy" on carnival rides, "eating American candy and Filipino peanuts," and attending the movies for the first time. Their dormitory's chapel service the next morning enthralled them just as much as the public amusements the night before; as aspects of Americanization these were, it would seem, entirely compatible.[55] Baseball, basketball, and other sports were unknown to Filipinas prior to the American occupation.[56] The enthusiasm for girls' baseball matched the contemporary celebration of physical vitality and recreational sports among American women. It even reflected postings of mission vacancies that enumerated the pleasures of sea bathing and tennis for women who might take up the work. For Filipinas and Americans alike, athletics denoted a modern womanhood.

The dormitory proved a successful venture; Isabel Fox herself found it a surprisingly easy and "splendid opportunity for doing personal work."[57] Yet Isabel intended for the dormitory to be more than an end unto itself. She hoped to make it a setting for her "greatest joy": a Bible school to train native women. "The Bible work is the heart and soul of the Women's work," she wrote. "The dormitory could go on without it, but—oh, the other is so vastly more important, and the two work in so well together."[58] She seems to have developed, if not derived, her idea for a Bible Women's School from her stopovers in Japan on her journey from the United States; on her way to the Philippines she found "inspiration and courage" at various such schools at Yokohama and Kobe.[59] Special training schools for Bible women had developed quickly in established mission fields; by 1900, over three thousand women studied in such schools, including forty institutions in China and more than thirty in India.[60] Higher education for women was a significant, prestigious cooperative venture for the ecumenical World's Missionary Committee of Christian Women; the establishment of several "union colleges" for women in India and China energized projects

Anna Isabel Fox, unnamed Bible students, and Florence Fox, ca. 1921.
By permission of the Houghton Library, Harvard University (ABC78, box 15, folder "Fox, Florence"), and
Wider Church Ministries, United Church of Christ.

for denominational women's colleges as well.[61] Yet in 1925, the Woman's Board supported only one other training school for Bible women (among twenty-nine girls' boarding schools, three hundred day schools, and twenty kindergartens).[62] The Woman's Board embraced Fox's vision with an exceptionally large disbursal of thirteen thousand dollars in 1923 from the estate of Ellen Carruth, an older member of the board.[63] Carruth's legacy enabled the construction of a building to serve both as an enlarged girls' dormitory and Bible Training School in Cagayan.

Bible scholars would set the tone for other girls in the house and naturally become leaders within the community, attracting dormitory girls to the school; meanwhile, the dormitory would help support the school financially. Though in its few years of operation the school had a small enrollment, the Bible school students and alumnae extended the mission's reach into the community. Its outlines vividly demonstrate the Woman's Board's commitment to the gradual transfer of mission work into indigenous hands, a development the board saw as progressive. "Certainly it is in the spirit of the times in our most advanced mission fields to give over responsibility to native leaders as fast as they are able to assume it," wrote Secretary Mabel Emerson of the Woman's Board as she increased appropriations to cover a greater number of native assistants in 1927.[64] As ever, there was an implicit connection to the role of the state in uplifting the Philippines: "What is the special opportunity of the Mission school? To send out Bible women as well trained as the Government teachers."[65] Thorough training for such a corps was essential. "The Bible Training School fits young women to become religious leaders, as wives of teachers and pastors, and as Bible women," an advertisement for an additional teacher noted.[66]

As was true of the women missionaries' work more broadly, religion provided the framework of the Bible school curriculum but did not comprise its totality. Even before the school was established, the women imagined that a "modern education" would include "new ideas of sanitation and hygiene" along with "the ideal of a strong, pure, Christian girlhood" to lay the groundwork for "Christian motherhood" and a strong church. Such an education would "transform the home, and best of all, transform the life."[67] Consequently, Christian study of Scripture shared space on the curriculum with practical education and liberal arts and sciences. "A practical course of home nursing" for all Bible women would enable them to "help in the homes they enter," wrote Isabel Fox, incorporating an idea already in place at the Methodist Deaconess Training School in Manila.[68] The "practical" centered on medical knowledge, from nursing to "ventilation and sanitation"[69] but also domestic science and gardening.[70] In addition, students would study health sciences (including obstetrics), sociology, music, English, and history in conjunction with the Bible. Composition, reading, psychology, and pedagogy would ideally round out a course of study "to develop . . . independence of thought and action."[71] Potential students saw an advantage to such diverse instruction as well.[72]

Upon completing the three-year curriculum, the Bible women would constitute a vanguard to spread the Gospel among their people. "There are many strong points to recommend the growing use of the Bible woman in all the mission fields," Helen Montgomery wrote.[73] Indeed, missionaries increasingly relied upon them. According to the initial organization of "native female helpers" by the Woman's Board from 1869, "Each Bible-woman is under the superintendence of a female missionary, whose aim is to make this largely a work of love";[74] but by the twentieth century, the so-called native helpers also received salaried support from the Woman's Board for their work as teachers and evangelists. "We do need Biblewomen [*sic*] in all our towns, to reach the women in their homes," explained Isabel Fox to the readers of *Life and Light*.[75] This necessity was partly pragmatic; the work of Bible women did not flounder against the same linguistic and cultural differences faced by Americans who came to visit or lead prayer. But their contribution was not strictly functional. Even after she gained fluency in Visayan, Isabel continued to tour with "our woman evangelist" (perhaps a reference to Elisea Eguia); in 1922, for example, the pair went on a long trip to recruit dormitory and Bible school students.[76] "There is so much that native women can do, if they have the training they need, that we missionaries cannot do," Isabel Fox commented candidly. "They go into the homes, and meet the people on a common ground. . . . I suppose the racial barrier exists in all lands. But in some cases at least, the question of Philippine independence makes it seem unusually strong here. Still they are friendly and lovable though proud, and it needs infinite tact. Our hope is in trained Filipina leaders."[77]

Though direct documentation is sparse, a number of Bible women appear in the records of the Woman's Board, some by name. Miss Chacon was the first Bible woman in Mindanao; she worked as Frank Laubach's secretary and later served as Isabel's "companion and assistant," leading evening prayers at the girls' dormitory. Isabel Maandig taught first-year classes, including Christian doctrine, for the Women's Bible School beginning in 1924. She also conducted the Visayan Woman's Bible class, the majority of whom became church members.[78] The Woman's Board employed Maandig from 1924, when she graduated from the Bible school, through 1927, raising her annual salary from $180 to $210 during that time. Evelyn Fox hoped eventually to pass on charge of the dormitory to Maandig. All the Bible scholars taught Sunday schools, some leading multiple classes. They also organized women's meetings, and they traveled to other towns to evangelize and recruit dormitory residents, which implicitly promoted American public education.[79] Often the American women would initiate a woman's class and then hand it over to the "older girls." "Some people may think of our students as absorbers only during their training," noted Evelyn Fox. "But the fact is, that during training they have done

Grace Evelyn Fox, Isabel Maandig, and dormitory pets, 1928. By permission of the Houghton Library, Harvard University (ABC78, box 15, folder "Fox, Grace"), and Wider Church Ministries, United Church of Christ.

important work in a center which is regarded as the most strategic on the North Coast. And without them the work could not have been carried on."[80] Miss Lumasag shepherded the "substantial congregation" at Buenavista, which was without a regular pastor.[81]

Julia Sotto de Yapsutco epitomized the American women's vision of the modern, Christian Filipina. Yapsutco was well educated and ardent in her faith, inspired her husband's conversion, published a religious periodical in Visayan, started a women's club, taught the Bible, and became a preacher after her husband's death. She became, like the Woman's Board of Mission workers, a woman with other women's concerns at heart but not limited to the domestic circle. She also used her position as a Bible woman authoritatively, demanding that the United States live up to the promises of benevolent assimilation. "The Christians in America are helping the widows and the fatherless children of other nations, and will they not also help the hungry souls in the Philippines?" Yapsutco exhorted in a letter to Frank Laubach. "If the Philippines will become a corrupted nation, who is to blame? Is not her stepmother, America? We are blaming Spain for not teaching us the right path, and will we also blame America for not teaching us the Word of God when she had the chance to do it?" Laubach published the letter in *Life and Light* to rouse interest in the mission.[82]

Becoming a Bible woman may have offered a form of upward mobility to Filipinas. The position was salaried; in fact, public schools could be competition for employment. Isabel Fox returned from a tour to find all five of the girls she had lined up for evangelical work "scattered" to teaching positions elsewhere.[83] Bible students could hope to have sponsorship for further studies in the United States, as was proposed for Yapsutco. Though ad hoc, such actions by the Woman's Board paralleled the *pensionado* scholarship program, by which colonial government paid the transportation costs to the United States for students seeking higher education. American universities were asked to waive tuition for this select group of Filipino students; in return, pensionados were to serve the Philippine government after completing their education.[84]

Just as the Bible school became established, however, a controversy erupted over women's training for missions. The controversy partly concerned whether programs to prepare Bible women to evangelize in their own right should be separate from programs to prepare wives for ministers. The controversy also concerned the powerful ecumenical movement. The Silliman Institute in Dumaguete, a great cooperative enterprise to educate native pastors, had already brought together Congregationalists and Presbyterians and had sporadically accepted women students, usually the wives of male students. Irving and Mary Channon, American Board missionaries who taught at Silliman, proposed to close Isabel Fox's newly minted Woman's Bible School, while a faction at the Cagayan station countered that Silliman should not admit women because that policy undermined the efforts of the Woman's Board. "In the effort to conciliate the several groups in this mission, some of our missionaries have taken the stand of approving both schools. This will eventually mean the death of the women's work at Mindanao, for the Bible school that is part of the larger educational institution will gradually win out," predicted Isabel Fox.[85]

While the Bible Training School became the focal point in a struggle over the autonomy of women's mission work, the Woman's Board itself was being absorbed by the American Board. In 1922 *Life and Light* became a section of the American Board's *Missionary Herald*. The editors of *Life and Light* explained the change with a domestic analogy, that the Woman's

Board was simply moving "from the old and dearly-loved family home into a new domicile[.] We miss the beloved, though perhaps shabby nooks, the old garden where the children have played, the thousand and one dear associations, but the new rooms are more spacious, they are fresh and beautiful with harmonious decorations and the windows have a wider outlook upon God's world."[86]

Then in 1926 the Woman's Board itself, along with its sister organizations in the Midwest and on the Pacific coast, ceased independent existence. Other women's missionary societies were also forced to abdicate their autonomy as church hierarchies absorbed them. Integration of women's boards into denominational boards peaked in the 1920s. In 1922, for example, the Presbyterian General Assembly voted to merge the Woman's Board of Foreign Missions with its denominational Board of Foreign Missions.[87] In absorbing its women's boards and branches, the American Board was thus following a broader trend among Protestant denominations and indeed an even wider cultural decline in gender-separatist strategies. As the historian Francesca Morgan recently observed, woman-centered institutions tended to subsume their interests to the leadership of men in this era.[88] Anticipating the merger as inevitable, the Committee on Missionary Organization expressed misgivings about the losses in giving, in enthusiasm, and in women's defined responsibility for mission work that they feared would ensue. As of 1925, the Woman's Board for Missions supported 138 missionaries and assistants in the field and 250 Bible women, 29 boarding schools for girls, 300 day schools, 20 kindergartens, 5 training schools (2 specifically for the Bible women), and 3 hospitals and dispensaries.[89] Yet in 1926 separate work by all three regional Congregationalist Woman's Boards abruptly ceased. While the American Board appointed women to its steering committee and even to the post of vice president, women's representation among the leadership still fell decidedly short of the requirements set out in the plan of merger.[90]

The trend was coincidentally reflected in a personal development when Isabel Fox married a fellow missionary, the recently widowed Dr. Floyd Smith, in 1925. The parties themselves noted the parallel with humor that was perhaps a bit forced. "Dr Smith says to tell you that the Woman's Board and the American Board were to unite anyway," wrote Isabel Fox, "we simply do it a little earlier."[91] Her insistence that the marriage was not planned and her apologies for changing her position so soon after her furlough reflect an understanding of how serious a concern this was for the Woman's Board. Yet, as it did with regard to the merger, the Woman's Board sought a silver lining in the news: "I hardly need to tell you that our disappointment in losing you from our own ranks is more than balanced by our sense of joy in your new found happiness. We certainly do give you our blessing and shall continue to count you as part of our family and when it comes to that, two years hence with all the foreign boards united there will be no mine and thine, but ours."[92]

Though she continued to teach for the remainder of the school year, Isabel gave up the directorship of the institution she had created. Her sister Evelyn replaced her ably in that post but the question of coeducation overshadowed the difficult transition. Isabel and Floyd Smith left the mission shortly thereafter. In 1929 the American Board shifted the two most experienced couples (the Laubachs and the Woodwards) out of Cagayan to establish a fourth Philippines mission at Dansalan (Lake Lanao), where they would have more direct contact with Muslim Filipinos— as well as a more receptive audience of Americans and mestizo families. The Woman's Bible Training School at Cagayan "discontinued" in 1930– 31, to reopen as part of the coeducational, interdenominational Silliman Institute.[93]

In practice, then, the transfer of the missions into Filipino hands meant the end of separatist woman's work for woman. Budget reductions ended the American Board's affiliations with Florence Fox and Evelyn Fox in 1932 and 1934, respectively. Meanwhile, the number of Filipino nationals employed increased to ten times the number of American missionaries by 1941.[94] It seems a minority of these nationals were Filipinas. Male pastors, not Bible women, would become the vanguard of Protestant Christianity in the Philippines.

CONCLUSION

American imperialism galvanized the Woman's Board of Missions into action. By sending its emissaries into new overseas territory, the board claimed a place for Protestant Christianity *and* for women as essential to the spread of American civilization. Officers and fieldworkers alike showed vibrant ambition and a steady faith in the advantages that their religion and their government would bring to the islands. U.S. institutions and values would help roll back the oppression of women, in particular; education, a scientific approach to childbearing, and a recognized place in the public sphere would improve women's daily lives and maximize the contribution they could make to their families and communities. Missionaries, like other New Women, measured social progress partly through the expansion of women's freedom and naturally expected that women elsewhere would want to follow their lead.[95]

But the independence American missionaries actually brought to Filipinas was limited. First, in Americans' eyes, there would need to be a period of tutelage, not only in the Bible but in government. This transitional era did not have a clear end point; Florence Fox was not alone in declaring, "I would not like to see the Philippines given their independence now nor for a long time to come, for gloom would soon settle again, and conditions fall backward, I think."[96] And if Philippine men seemed to need American protection and guidance, evidently Philippine women required political chaperonage even longer. Though local opposition to women in politics was minor, it was not until 1937 that Filipinas gained suffrage or were allowed to run for office.[97] Even Spain embraced this most modern aspect of modern womanhood before the United States permitted it in the Philippines. As the Manila-based *Woman's Home Journal* reported pointedly in May 1932, "Today the Spanish woman is on complete equality with the men politically. And the plans are to revise the civil code to modify those provisions relating to woman's civil status so that they conform to the modern conceptions of her rights and privileges under the new order of things." The success of woman suffrage in Spain highlighted the comparatively lower status of women in the Philippines, where despite the "coming of the Americans," the old Spanish code of laws "remains in force . . . after more than three generations."[98] By this logic, Filipinas would have been better off under the continued colonial control of Spain than under the benevolent assimilation of the enlightened, democratic United States.

NOTES

I would like to thank Hanna Clutterbuck, who provided indefatigable research assistance, Richard Canedo for his sharp editorial eye, and the attentive librarians at Houghton Library, Harvard College.

1 Fiftieth Annual Meeting of the Woman's Board of Missions (Boston, 1918), 6. American Board of Commissioners for Foreign Missions, Houghton Library, Harvard University, Cambridge (hereafter ABC) 91.6.

2 "Service of Commission for Evelyn Fox" (1923) and "We and the Foxes: A Ten-Minute Program" (n.d.), folder 22:44, box 25, ABC 77.1.

3 Kenton J. Clymer, *Protestant Missionaries in the Philippines, 1898–1916: An Inquiry into the American Colonial Mentality* (Urbana: University of Illinois Press, 1986), 81.

4 Warwick Anderson, "States of Hygiene: Race 'Improvement' and Biomedical Citizenship in Australia and the Colonial Philippines," *Haunted by Empire: Geographies of Intimacy in North American History,* ed. Ann Laura Stoler, 98–99 (Durham: Duke University Press, 2006).

5 On Filipina suffrage, see Mina C. Roces, "Women in Philippine Politics and Society," *Mixed Blessing: The Impact of the American Colonial Experience on Politics and Society in the Philippines,* ed. Hazel M. McFerson, 159–89 (Westport, Conn.: Greenwood Press, 2002); Antoinette Raquiza, "Philippine Feminist Politics: Disunity in Diversity?" *Civil Society Making Civil Society,* ed. Miriam Colonel Ferrer, 171–87 (Quezon City: Third World Studies Center, 1997).

6 M. Adas, "Improving on the Civilizing Mission?" *Itinerario* 23, no. 4 (1999), 44–66.

7 Clymer, *Protestant Missionaries in the Philippines,* 5.

8 William Strong, *Story of the American Board* (Boston: Pilgrim Press 1910), 454; Rev. James B. Rodgers, *The Evangelist* (June 20, 1901).

9 Clymer, *Protestant Missionaries in the Philippines,* 5–6.

10 John Marvin Dean, *The Cross of Christ in Bolo-land* (Chicago: Revell, 1902), 7.

11 President William McKinley articulated the policy of "benevolent assimilation" on December 21, 1898.

12 On political education and colonial state builders, see Julian Go, "The Chains of Empire: State Building and 'Political Education' in Puerto Rico and the Philippines," *The American Colonial State in the Philippines: Global Perspectives,* ed. Julian Go and Anne L. Foster, 182–216 (Durham: Duke University Press, 2003); O. Garfield Jones, "Teaching Citizenship to the Filipinos by Local Self-Government," *American Political Science Review* 28 (1924), 285–95.

13 H. E. B. Case, "The Philippine Islands" (typescript), 5. ABC 88.

14 For example, see the Colorum rebellion of 1923 in northeastern Mindanao; Vince Boudreau, "Methods of Domination and Modes of Resistance: The U.S. Colonial State and Philippine Mobilization in Comparative Perspective," in *The American Colonial State,* ed. Go and Foster, 261–63.

15 Raul Pertierra and Eduardo F. Ugarte, "American Rule in the Muslim South and the Philippine Hinterlands," *Mixed Blessing,* ed. McFerson, 197.

16 Paul Kramer, *The Blood of Government: Race, Empire, the United States, and the Philippines* (Chapel Hill: University of North Carolina Press, 2006), 340–41.

Kramer cites serious proposals in 1905 and 1909 to cordon off the Muslim-dominated south from the Christianized rest of the Philippines in order to give the United States the direct control necessary for progress and assimilation.

17 On the complicated contest over jurisdiction in the Visayas, see Clymer, *Protestant Missionaries in the Philippines*, 39–50.

18 Isabel Fox Smith (AIF) to Mabel Emerson, May 25, 1926, ABC 17.9.2.

19 Frank Laubach, *People of the Philippines* (New York: George H. Doran, 1925), 81.

20 "Field Correspondents: Miss Anna Isabel Fox writes from Cagayan Station, P.I." *Life and Light* (hereafter LL) 50, no. 2 (February 1920), 73.

21 FF to KL, February 25, 1921, ABC 17.9.2.

22 Ibid.

23 Ibid.

24 Case, "The Philippine Islands," 12.

25 AIF to Mabel Emerson, May 25, 1926, ABC 17.9.2.

26 Mrs. F. C. Laubach, "Our New Philippine Task," LL 48, no. 6 (June 1918), 251.

27 Anna Isabel Fox, "Summer Work at Cagayan," LL 52, no. 9 (September 1922), 323.

28 Case, "The Philippine Islands," 9.

29 Marian Wells Woodward, "Conditions among the Filipina Women," LL 48, no. 5 (May 1918), 211.

30 "Mrs. F. C. Laubach writes from the Philippine Islands," LL 48, no. 9 (September 1918), 374.

31 In the eyes of Spanish-identified critics, this sort of woman was a *sajonista*, or "Saxonist." Roces, "Women in Philippine Politics," 161, 181.

32 Ibid., 173–75.

33 Case, "The Philippine Islands," 12.

34 AIF to KL, February 2, 1920, ABC 17.9.2.

35 Effa Laubach to Kate Lamson, May 28, 1918, ABC 17.9.2.

36 Kristin Hoganson, "The Fashionable World: Imagined Communities of Dress," *After the Imperial Turn: Thinking with and through the Nation*, ed. Antoinette Burton, 268, 273 (Durham: Duke University Press, 2003). Also see Roces, "Women in Philippine Politics," 171.

37 Anna I[sabel] Fox, "A Vacation among the Moros," LL 49, no. 11 (November 1919), 496.

38 FF to KL, May 5, 1921.

39 Anna Isabel Fox, "My Philippine Girls," LL 51, no. 1 (January 1921), 22.

40 AIF to KL, June 7, 1920, ABC 17.9.2.

41 FF to KL, December 27, 1922, ABC 17.9.2.

42 FF to KL, March 5, 1922, ABC 17.9.2.

43 David P. Barrows, *History of the Philippines*, rev. ed. (Yonkers-on-Hudson, N.Y.: World Book, 1924), 354.

44 Boudreau, "Methods of Domination," 266.

45 Roces, "Women in Philippine Politics," 179.

46 *Census of the Philippine Islands 1918*, vol. 4, part 2 (Manila: Bureau of Printing, 1921), 200.

47 "Black, Rev & Mrs Robert T.," box 4, ABC 78.1.

48 Mrs. F. C. Laubach, "Our New Philippine Task," LL 48, no. 6 (June 1918), 251.

49 Effa Laubach to KL (Foreign Secretary of the Woman's Board), May 28, 1918, ABC 17.9.2. Also see Effa Laubach, LL 48, no. 9 (September 1918), 347.

50 Marian Wells Woodward, "Conditions among the Filipina Women," LL 48, no. 5 (May 1918), 211.

51 Report of Fourth Year of Girls' Dormitory [1923], Documents and Reports, ABC 17.9.2.

52 Kate G. Lamson, "Editorials: Another Open Door," LL. 49, no. 8 (September 1919), 306.

53 "Field Correspondents: Miss Anna Isabel Fox writes from Cagayan Station, P.I.," LL 50, no. 2 (February 1920), 73.

54 Report of Fourth Year of Girls' Dormitory, ABC 17.9.2.

55 Effa L. Laubach, "Junior Department / Girl Champions of the Philippines," LL 50, no. 10 (October 1920), 463.

56 Janice A. Beran, "Americans in the Philippines: Imperialism or Progress through Sport?" *International Journal of the History of Sport* 6, no. 1 (1989), 62–87.

57 "Field Correspondents: Miss Anna Isabel Fox writes from Cagayan Station, P.I." LL 50, no. 2 (February 1920), 72.

58 AIF to KL, July 1, 1923, ABC 17.9.1.

59 "Miss Anna Isabel Fox, our new missionary to the Philippines, writes from Cagayan," LL 49, no. 1 (January 1919), 35.

60 R. Pierce Beaver, *American Protestant Women in World Mission* (Grand Rapids: Eerdmans, 1980), 121.

61 Ibid., 166, 168.

62 Kate G. Lamson, "History of the Woman's Board for Missions" (typescript, 1927–28), 85. ABC 88.

63 KL to Evelyn Fox, October 8, 1923, ABC 17.9.2; Woman's Board for Missions, *29th Annual Report* (1896). Ellen Carruth was an officer of the WBM for twenty-three years, first as assistant treasurer, then treasurer.

64 Mabel Emerson to Evelyn Fox, December 1, 1926, ABC 17.9.1.

65 Untitled, November 19, 1925, folder 1:9, box 1, ABC 9.5.1.

66 "WANTED: Teacher of Religious Education and Music," folder 1:9, box 1, ABC 9.5.1.

67 Marian Wells Woodward, "Conditions among the Filipina Women," LL 48, no. 5 (May 1918), 211.

68 Anna Isabel Fox, "Summer Work at Cagayan," LL 52, no. 9 (September 1922), 323.

69 FF to KL, May 5, 1921, ABC 17.9.2.

70 Mrs. F. C. Laubach, "Our New Philippine Task," LL 48, no. 6 (June 1918), 251.

71 Evelyn Fox to KL, November 4, 1923, ABC 17.9.1.

72 "Field Correspondents / Miss Florence Fox writes from Cagayan, Philippine Islands," LL 52, no. 10 (October 1922), 369.

73 Helen Barrett Montgomery, *Western Women in Eastern Lands: An Outline Study of Fifty Years of Woman's Work in Foreign Missions* (New York: Macmillan, 1911), 117.

74 Mrs. Miron Winslow, "Our Bible-Women," in Third Annual Report, Woman's Board of Missions (Boston: Rand, Aver and Frye, 1871). ABC 91.6.

75 "Field Correspondents / Miss Anna Isabel Fox of Cagayan, Philippine Islands, writes," LL 52, no. 5 (May 1922), 197.

76 LL 52, no. 10 (October 1922), 365.

77 Anna Isabel Fox, "Summer Work at Cagayan," LL 52, no. 9 (September 1922), 323.

78 G. Evelyn Fox, Fourth Annual Report of the Woman's Bible Training School, ABC 17.9.2.

79 See AIF to KL, October 19, 1922, ABC 17.9.2.

80 "The Cagayan Women's Bible Training School," typescript [1924?], ABC 17.9.2.

81 "Field Work September 15 to October 27, East Coast" typescript, folder 65:19, ABC 77.1.

82 Letter to Frank Laubach; published as Julia de Yapsutoo [*sic*], "Field Correspondents" LL 51, no. 6 (June 1921), 234.

83 AIF to KL, June 7, 1920, ABC 17.9.2.

84 One pensionado from Cagayan was allocated in 1903–4. Alexander A. Calata, "The Role of Education in Americanizing Filipinos," in *Mixed Blessing*, ed. McFerson, 92.

85 AIF to KL, March 9, 1924, ABC 17.9.2.

86 "Editorials: A Word of Farewell," LL 52, no. 12 (December 1922), 423.

87 Beaver, *American Protestant Women*, 200, 185; Dana Lee Robert, *American Women in Missions: A Social History of Their Thought and Practice* (Mercer, Ga.: Mercer University Press, 1996) 302–7; and Patricia R. Hill, *The World Their Household: The American Women's Foreign Mission Movement and Cultural Transformation, 1870–1920* (Ann Arbor: University of Michigan Press, 1985), 167.

88 Francesca Morgan, *Women and Patriotism in Jim Crow America* (Chapel Hill: University of North Carolina Press, 2005).

89 Lamson, "History Woman's Board," 85.

90 "Plan of Proposed Merger of the American Board and the Three Woman's Boards," March 10, 1925, folder 7:5 "Special Papers," box 7, ABC 9.5.1; folders 1:1 "Officers and Staff," 1:2 "Prudential Committee, 1810–1949," ABC 77.1.

91 AIF to Miss Lee, September 25, 1925, ABC 17.9.2.

92 Unsigned (Lee?) to AIF, November 19, 1925, ABC 17.9.2.

93 See folder 22:44, box 25, ABC 77.1

94 Case, "The Philippine Islands," 16, cites 4 missionaries and 6 nationals under the ABCFM in the Philippines in 1910 versus 12 missionaries and 122 nationals in 1941.

95 Laura Wexler, "The Fair Ensemble: Kate Chopin in St. Louis in 1904," *Haunted by Empire*, ed. Stoler, 281.

96 FF to KL, May 5, 1921, ABC 17.9.2.

97 Roces, "Women in Philippine Politics," 177.

98 "Emancipating the Spanish Woman," *Woman's Home Journal* [Manila], Year 7, no. 1 (May 1932), 1.

Religion, Race, and Empire in the U.S. Protestant Women's Missionary Enterprise, 1812–1960

Mary A. Renda

In 1810, when the recently evangelized Harriet Newell learned of a friend's decision to "quit her native land to endure the sufferings of a Christian among heathen nations," she cast herself on a path toward action that would be followed by generations of U.S. Protestant women. "Is she willing to do all this for God; and shall I refuse to lend my little aid [?]," she wrote. Within two years, as Mary Kupiec Cayton tells us, the young Harriet had married Samuel Newell and set out for the Asian subcontinent to pursue a life of mission work. Nearly ninety years later, the Anabaptist H. Frances Davidson echoed Newell's self-authorizing invocation of God's purposes, even as she reflected on the educational and professional bona fides that might, in another context, have seemed to authorize her missionary leadership near Bulawayo in what is now Zimbabwe. Wendy Urban-Mead points out that Davidson justified her mastery and use of the isiNdebele language with the same rhetorical flourish: "I feel that the Lord has given me the opportunity [of an education] for some purpose of his own, and shall I neglect to improve the talents He has given me[?]"

In the years between Newell's and Davidson's declarations, white U.S. Protestant women crafted the ways and means for action from a theology of submission to God's purposes. Catharine Beecher resisted the terms of conversion urged upon her by her father, the prominent Calvinist Lyman Beecher, but in time crafted a more democratic version of evangelical Christianity, one that might empower women in all their daily labors as servants of the Lord and agents in the knitting together of an increasingly vast nation.[1] Mary Lyon, founder in 1837 of Mount Holyoke Female Seminary, worked to expand the scope of U.S. women's action beyond the borders of the nation. Her tombstone bears the mark of her commitment: "There is nothing in the universe that I fear but that I shall not know all my duty, or shall fail to do it."[2] By the 1890s, the scope of Christian women's action had widened so as to leave nothing, apparently, beyond its reach. "Do everything," was by then the motto of the Women's Christian Temperance Union, the Protestant women's independent, interdenominational, and international vehicle for action, then headed in the United States by Frances Willard. Inspired by the example of Harriet Newell, as we learn from Mary Cayton, and by the work of Beecher, Lyon, and Willard, generations of women followed their ambition—and their faith—into the mission field.

Doing everything was for U.S. Protestant women both deeply personal and productive of far-reaching social and political consequences. Women missionaries wrestled with their own subordination to men, the rigors of their faith, the demands of their education, the dangers of travel, the disorientation of finding themselves in unrecognizable cultures, the meanings of race for themselves and for those they encountered, the challenges put to them by those they wished to convert, and at times the inconsistencies of their own beliefs. They were intensely motivated; not lightly did a woman decide to marry a stranger and set sail for an isolated archipelago, challenge her mission board by adopting a child born of another culture, or take on the challenge of opening an orphanage without the support of any mission board at all. But they were also encouraged and enabled by the fact that their work was useful to others—to husbands, ministers, publishers, the sick and the orphaned, women and men marginalized within their societies, local elites, and European imperial overlords, among others. Their work and their disposition to action in the name of God filled a variety of needs opened up by the specific material and political contexts into which missionary women ventured at home and abroad.

What was the nature of their impact? How did it relate to the histories of nationalism and empire with which this phase of missionary activity was coterminous? The essays in this book do not answer in one voice. But taken together they suggest that all that doing did not accrue to the same ends. U.S. women's missionary work both fed and undermined empires,

Mary Lyon's gravestone at Mount Holyoke College, 1885.
By permission of Mount Holyoke College Archives and Special Collections.

national states, and the free rein of capitalist markets. It reinforced racism and exclusion in "imperial encounters at home," as Derek Chang argues, and offered assistance to Cecil Rhodes's imperial theft in southern Africa according to Wendy Urban Mead. But it also served to strengthen anticolonial nationalisms and even to trouble missionary women's own racism. How shall we understand such seeming contradictions in the history of U.S. Protestant women's missionary work?

Drawing often on multiple archives and highlighting the role of local actors in the history of missionary projects, these essays show that for all of U.S. Protestant women's emphasis on taking action to remake the world, the changes wrought by their mission work were not simply of their own doing. Collaboration required negotiation and compromise. Even where an imperious disposition inclined a missionary leader like Lillian Trasher, the founder of an Egyptian orphanage, to keep a firm grasp on leadership, Beth Baron argues that political change required adaptation and adjustment in the mission program. In other cases, missionary objectives were more thoroughly routed, as in Bulgaria, where, Barbara Reeves-Ellington tells us, feminists eagerly accepted domesticity and female education in the name of nationalism but rejected Protestantism; or in Japan, where educators valued the resources missionaries contributed to women's colleges but rejected, as we learn from Rui Kohiyama, the domestic education championed by U.S. missionary women. Anti-imperialist forces could also curtail missionary work, as in China and Egypt.

But the impact of the missionary enterprise also depended on how U.S. women pursued mission work, and these essays contribute much to our understanding of the ways they negotiated the material and political contexts that supported and troubled their hopes, their visions, and their efforts. Building on this dimension of the scholarship collected here, I will turn now to some of the broad patterns of their circumstances and their work, including the gendered forms of agency they devised, how these forms embedded the fabric of empire in the institutions they crafted to carry forward their work, and how the pattern of imperial perspectives played out in missionaries' interactions with those they encountered in the mission field. I will take up the question, raised here by Jane Hunter, Susan Haskell Khan, Connie Shemo, and others, of antiracism in mission work and consider the evolution of missionary efforts in relation to the agendas and programs of those they encountered in the mission field.

"THE LIMITS, WHICH A SENSE OF PROPRIETY HAS IMPOSED ON FEMALE EXERTION"

This book takes its readers through vastly different phases in the history of U.S. Protestant women's missionary work as well as through a wide range of denominational efforts, and this diversity alone would guarantee that the stories told here of women's ability to claim spaces for action and influence must vary widely. Differences in class position are also important. Helen Montgomery, leader of the ecumenical women's foreign mission movement and the main attraction as a lecturer at the Jubilee celebration of the movement in 1911, reflected on the changing fortunes of the women who supported missionary work, from the cent societies of the early republic to "the era of women with check books as well as . . . small change."[3] Her friend and the main organizer of the Jubilee celebration, Lucy Peabody, who with Montgomery is featured in Rui Kohiyama's essay in this book, was the widow of Henry Wayland Peabody and inherited the wealth he gained as a merchant with offices stretching from the British metropolitan center to South Africa, Yucatan, the Philippines, and New

South Wales.[4] Lucy Peabody not only had her own checkbook, she had the power to persuade Laura Spelman Rockefeller to use hers to make a million-dollar contribution toward the building of women's colleges in Asia, and the political contacts necessary to arrange a White House reception for the celebration. Hattie Bailey, thirty-six years old and single, with her seven years of grammar school, her twelve years working in a dry goods store, and her Moody Bible Institute training for mission work, had, to say the least, rather different prospects as she departed in 1918 for Shanghai, where she would spend the next several decades working with the China Inland Mission's Door of Hope homes, as we learn from Sue Gronewold.

For both the wealthy widow and the single woman with little education and relatively few prospects, the second decade of the twentieth century offered paths to action unavailable to the Harriet Newells and Catharine Beechers of the nineteenth, but the gender norms and paradigms worked out in the earlier period—the master narratives, so to speak, of white American women's power—continued to hold possibility and sway as subsequent generations of women and men, both within and beyond the borders of the United States, put those narratives to their own uses. As early as 1800, the Boston Female Society for Missionary Purposes, founded by Mary Webb, turned the attention of Baptist and Congregational women toward mission work in North America and overseas over a decade before the advent of men's coordinated efforts in the American Board of Commissioners of Foreign Missions.[5] In the decades to come, a woman's obligation to comport herself in compliance with class- and gender-appropriate behavior, what the men of the American Board called in 1813 "the limits, which a sense of propriety has imposed on female exertion," ironically, constituted an opening for as well as a bar to action. This was not merely a matter of acceding to the limits placed upon them, out of deference to male authority in the home and the church, though obedience to husbands was an important aspect of their propriety. Protestant women seized the gendered structure of obligation—the injunction to live out a tightly prescribed model of womanhood, one in which religious piety, maternal care, and domestic industry defined the main contours of acceptable female behavior—to authorize and enlarge their scope of action, from fundraising efforts to work as missionaries and educators to temperance and moral reform activism. For Catharine Beecher this was

Daguerreotype of Mary Lyon, 1845.
By permission of Mount Holyoke College Archives
and Special Collections.

Catharine Beecher, ca. 1870.
By permission of the Harriet Beecher Stowe Center,
Hartford, Conn.

explicit: every woman's proper labors contributed to the building of a "glorious temple."[6] For Mary Lyon, correct feminine deportment was consistent with the management of self, time, money, and intellect that would underwrite women's agency.[7] As is clear in Barbara Reeves-Ellington's account of Martha Riggs's *Letters to Mothers*, the resulting embrace of female duties could be seen to position women as national leaders.

By midcentury, U.S. Protestant women had begun to proffer public gestures of refusal and defiance rather than deference to male authority, a shift that prefigured the profound changes in gender ideology in the century to come. Thus the response of one member of the New York Female Moral Reform Society to the charge that prostitution was too indelicate a matter to lay within the proper domain of female action: "Go on, ladies," she exhorted her compatriots, "go on in the strength of the Lord."[8] The shift was also stunningly evident in the temperance movement of the 1860s, as Ohio women entered saloons, broke open kegs, and let beer and liquor run into the streets. Such scenes made abundantly clear that deference to male authority (or to men's wishes) was inconsistent with women's own obligations to God and conscience. In missions, too, women defied men and asserted their refusal of second-class citizenship.

Thus in China in the 1880s, as Connie Shemo explains, Gertrude Howe consulted her own conscience when she decided to prepare her adopted Chinese daughter, Kang Cheng, along with a small group of other Chinese girls, for medical education despite male missionaries' opposition to her undertaking.[9] And in the spirit of a newly dawning feminism, in 1911 Helen Montgomery declared that the "Christian woman . . . will not consent to stay behind closed doors and be treated like a child."[10] By the 1920s, a younger generation of missionary women came to reject the language of "woman's work" and sought, in Susan Haskell Khan's words, "to transcend familial responsibilities." Women's power could be *embodied* in new ways, as well, with the advent of athleticism for women. Laura Prieto offers the image of Isabel Fox, missionary to the Philippines, exultant over the shrieks of joy let out by a victorious Filipina softball team—quite a contrast to the twinned emphasis in Mary Lyon's day on "physical culture" alongside the cultivation of a gentle and measured feminine voice.[11]

Yet many U.S. Protestant missionary women continued to teach the values associated with "true womanhood" in an earlier era—even as they personally set aside normative domesticity to live out public careers in religious and social service. Sue Gronewold indicates that evangelical women missionaries unsuccessfully contested their exclusion from decision-making bodies at the China Inland Mission (CIM) in the 1920s. But from 1900 to the 1930s, CIM missionary women at the Door of Hope rescue home in Shanghai sought to convey to their charges the primacy of marriage in the female life course and the crucial role of the Christian wife as "helpmate constructing a wholesome Christian home." As Gronewold persuasively argues, the young, working-class women residents of the home painstakingly constructed dolls designed to teach their makers deeply conservative lessons about "the proper ordering of society," lessons that appealed both to U.S. evangelicals and to Chinese nationalists. And in Asyut, Egypt, as we learn from Beth Baron, Lillian Trasher presided over an orphanage from 1911 until her death in 1961, with strict segregation of boys and girls and a similarly conservative pedagogy. Yet, like Hattie Bailey at the Door of Hope, Trasher embodied an alternative model of womanhood as she challenged gender norms, traveling, for example, through Egyptian villages and towns to raise funds and gather resources for her orphanage.

Across time and differences of class, denomination, and political persuasion, two themes persist in U.S. Protestant women missionaries' embrace of what I have called the master narratives of white American women's power.[12] One is the language of domesticity and female responsibility that framed missionary women's agency. Amy Kaplan's "Manifest Domesticity," much cited in this book, provides a compelling account of the cultural power associated with domesticity in the mid-nineteenth century; and the continued importance of the theme is signaled in the title of Patricia Hill's history of the women's missionary movement after 1870: *The World Their Household*.[13] The essays collected here extend our understanding of the operation of this trope in specific mission contexts. The other persistent theme, which bears further scrutiny, is the racial dimension of women's missionary work among women. The two themes are linked, as Kaplan emphasizes, showing that by the 1840s "the capacity for domesticity" came to be seen as "an innate defining characteristic of the Anglo-Saxon race" and "America [came to be] seen as manifesting the universal progress of women."[14] Kaplan's account of the process of racialization through gender, that is, through a particular narrative of women and domesticity, serves as a point of departure for the debates staged here.[15] Barbara Reeves-Ellington, Derek Chang, Sue Gronewold, Susan Haskell Khan, and others highlight the pattern, from stories about the degraded status of women in China and India that appeared in the Bulgarian-language mission newspaper *Zornitsa* to the struggles of New Women missionaries in the 1920s to transform their own gendered racism and to deal with the racial legacy of the earlier women missionaries in whose steps they walked.

The persistent appeal of the conceit that white-dominated Christianity, with its culturally specific notions of decorum, had something uniquely liberating to offer women around the world helps us understand how U.S. Protestant women's efforts were sutured into the logics of empire, even as individual missionary women resisted racism and criticized the policies of imperial states. Missionary work did lead some women and men to oppose racism and imperialism. Yet imperial logics shaped the missionary endeavor through culturally inherited patterns of motivation and agency (linked to notions of bondage and liberation) and through social patterns of institutionalization, including those embedded in the building of independent women's missionary organizations. To consider this process more fully, I turn back to Cayton's account of the proliferation of Harriet Newells in New England and the New England diaspora between 1800 and 1840.

"A SCENE OF ACTION"

In 1813, when the men of the American Board of Commissioners of Foreign Missions called attention to the "limits, which a sense of propriety has imposed on female exertion," they did so in order to praise New England women for having found, in their fundraising work for foreign missions, "a scene of action" that did not exceed those limits. Yet, the "scene of action" afforded by mission projects in need of funding and would-be missionary ministers in need of wives gave way in time to more expansive platforms for female action and opinion. Cayton's account of women's role in the evolution of the Evangelical press and the construction of a benevolent public enables us to appreciate the specific material and social context that conditioned early missionary women's agency and amplified their voices in a polity initially premised on their public silence. Evangelical magazines, Cayton points out, hitched their success to a female readership by aligning themselves with evangelical organizations and by addressing women directly. As women responded, shifts in magazine content—at first, ministers merely relied more on the actual words of deceased women in funeral sermons—began to make room for women, as teachers, missionary wives, and financial supporters of missionary endeavors, to shape public discourse in terms of compassion and self-sacrifice. Eventually, women found their way to authorship—even, at times, putting forward their critiques of male (and presumably ministerial) editorial decisions. The result, Cayton argues, was the emergence of an alternative public sphere and a new "social imaginary" that supported women's action. Cayton traces the wide embrace of this social imaginary through naming practices, as accounts of the "martyred" Harriet Newell led to the proliferation of Harriet Newells throughout the New England diaspora.

In this way, Cayton shows the genesis of imperial attitudes in the material as well as spiritual and cultural circumstances of white women in the early U.S. republic. The impulse to empire rested, for these women, in an attitude of horror at the wretchedness of "heathen women," an attitude cultivated by a newly emerging evangelical enterprise.[16]

In order to assess the patterns of female missionary benevolence and human concern that emerge in these essays, and especially how these patterns did and did not lead white women to oppose racism, we must take account of the attitude of horror that benevolence called forth. For long before *Godey's Lady's Book* and the U.S. war with Mexico, examined by Amy Kaplan; long before the period of Reconstruction considered by Derek Chang; long before the advent of missionary ethnologies analyzed by Joan Jacobs Brumberg, here, in the earliest Protestant women's overseas missionary endeavors, was the spirit of racism that would animate more than a century of what Methodists, among others, later called "woman's work for woman."[17]

The attitude of horror that moved such women speaks to the racial contexts that shaped their affective lives, bringing to mind Raymond Williams's delineation of "structures of feeling." Williams called attention to "meanings and values as they [were] actively lived . . . characteristic elements of impulse, restraint, and tone . . . affective elements of consciousness and relationships . . . thought as felt and feeling as thought.[18] It is not merely that missionary thought constructed a certain representation of women around the world as the denigrated antithesis of an exalted Christian womanhood. More than that, the figure of the denigrated heathen woman was integral to the mobilization of women missionaries and missionary supporters in the context of women's oppression in the United States. It moved women to act and constituted the racial (and racist) structure of motivation in which concern for other human beings existed, "interlocking and in tension," to use Williams's phrase, with both the conviction of their own advantage and superiority and the experience of their circumscribed sphere of action.[19]

The examples with which I began suggest some of the ways white Protestant women imagined themselves as powerful and carved for themselves a space for action while faced with their own exclusion from full citizenship. For white New England women in the early years covered by this book, the experience of that exclusion was mediated by the conquest of Native American lands to the south and west, the advent of new racial meanings in the context of slavery's entrenchment, and the growth of trade contacts with peoples of Asia and the Pacific islands. Insofar as these contexts defined God's purposes, the social values and racial meanings of U.S. society came to be layered into deeply felt experience, and specifically into the structure of motivation that animated missionary women's work. The rhetorical and practical moves by which these women claimed the capacity and authority to act—to take on grand schemes for changing both the world and the circumstances of their lives—helped to set the terms in which racism and imperialism would come to be embedded in their work and the movement to which it later gave rise.

If the racial, national, and colonial contexts of the early republic established the initial forms of Protestant women's agency in the United States, those forms were carried forward in and by a constellation of evolving institutions, including churches (in which women congregants predominated), evangelical publications, seminaries, mission boards, and missionary societies, with their particular pedagogical programs, fundraising mechanisms, and connections to churches and other denominational structures. These institutions served to reproduce and elaborate the racial dimension of white Protestant women's agency in relation to changing historical contexts. Indeed, this was the process by which racism was institutionalized. Individual Protestant women, white and black, native-born and immigrant, Chinese and Mexican, would go on to challenge and transform the racial structures of Protestant women's mission work, but as they did so they would have to contend with the weight of institutional racism they inherited. Jane Hunter describes the successful campaign to change the title of the periodical known until the 1890s as the *Heathen Woman's Friend*, but the conceit of superiority continued in its pages under the new heading, *Woman's Missionary Friend*. Gertrude Howe breached the boundaries of racial propriety in China and raised the threat of contamination for a mission board committed to a more distanced form of proselytizing, incurring "censure and rejection" in the process, as Connie Shemo demonstrates. We learn here, too, that U.S. women missionaries in the Congo Free State, China, and India all found themselves at odds with racist fundraising appeals at home, limited by the fact that pity paid. And as Susan Haskell Khan shows, in the 1920s editors at home framed missionary attempts at antiracism within enduring frames of racial reference. In these and other ways, the need for institutional support put brakes on challenges to racism.

The figure of the oppressed heathen woman and the structure of racist motivation of which it was a part were thus passed down to subsequent generations, reproduced with variations in successive phases of women's

Mount Holyoke Female Seminary, ca. 1845 (Currier & Ives).
By permission of Mount Holyoke College Archives and Special Collections.

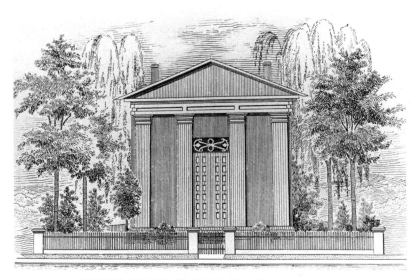

Hartford Female Seminary, ca. 1856.
By permission of the Harriet Beecher Stowe Center, Hartford, Conn.

missionary work and activism, down to the present day—despite the fact that white U.S. Protestant women invoked their obligation to the Lord, at times, in opposition to racism.[20] For successive generations of white missionaries and missionary supporters, institutional structures helped to perpetuate an intimate, deeply felt link between the claim to an active life of service and a racialized fantasy of rescue.[21] Dana Robert captures this connection when she defines *civilization* as "the nineteenth-century term for liberation."[22] And Laura Prieto captures a moment in which a white missionary revealed her attachment to the racial differences that underlay the fantasy of rescue through her disappointment that Filipinos of the southern Moro region were not "as primitive" as she thought they would be. To do the work of the Lord was, for white women, implicitly to affirm their own position and superiority.

African American Protestant women also invoked Christianity as an authorizing discourse as they worked to carve out a space for their own action in U.S. society, and their experiences offer crucial perspectives on the processes by which missionary work reproduced racism even as some missionaries fought against it. "I am but a feeble instrument," wrote Maria Stewart in 1831, in an exhortation to the "daughters of Africa" to embrace action, "ambition," and "force" and to answer the "scorn" of nations by claiming education for themselves and their daughters.[23] Writing and preaching for but a few years in the early 1830s (she was the first woman known to have addressed a mixed audience in the United States), Stewart set African American women apart from the nation, referring to white women as "American ladies," from whom women of African heritage might learn how to seize institution-building power.[24] Stewart emphasized the importance of crafting institutions to carry forward their demands, values, and priorities for action. Such institution building was indeed an important feature of free black society in the antebellum period, with the establishment of independent black churches, antislavery societies, mutual benefit organizations, newspapers, and educational endeavors. But free African Americans had limited resources and black women an even more uphill battle for support in their claims to religious leadership.

As African American women pursued their institutional goals, they made use of the resources they found in the missionary offerings of white Protestants. During Reconstruction, white home missionary societies set about the work of evangelizing the freed people, sending white women as

RELIGION

AND THE

PURE PRINCIPLES OF MORALITY

THE SURE FOUNDATION ON WHICH WE MUST BUILD.

PRODUCTIONS FROM THE PEN OF

MRS. MARIA W. STEWARD,

WIDOW OF THE LATE JAMES W. STEWARD, OF BOSTON.

INTRODUCTION.

FEELING a deep solemnity of soul, in view of our wretched and degraded situation, and sensible of the gross ignorance that prevails amongst us, I have thought proper thus publicly to express my sentiments before you. I hope my friends will not scrutinize these pages with too severe an eye, as I have not calculated to display either elegance or taste in their composition, but have merely written the meditations of my heart as far as my imagination led ; and have presented them before you, in order to arouse you to exertion, and to enforce upon your minds the great necessity of turning your attention to knowledge and improvement.

I was born in Hartford, Connecticut, in 1803 ; was left an orphan at five years of age ; was bound out in a clergyman's family ; had the seeds of piety and virtue early sown in my mind ; but was deprived of the advantages of education, though my soul thirsted for knowledge. Left them at 15 years of age ; attended Sabbath Schools until I was 20 ; in 1826, was married to James W. Steward ; was left a widow in 1829 ; was, as I humbly hope and trust, brought to the knowledge of the truth, as it is in Jesus, in 1830 ; in 1831, made a public profession of my faith in Christ.

From the moment I experienced the change, I felt a strong desire, with the help and assistance of God, to devote the remainder of my days to piety and virtue, and now possess that spirit of independence, that, were I called upon, I would willingly sacrifice my life for the cause of God and my brethren. All the nations of the earth are crying out for Liberty and Equality. Away, away with tyranny and oppression ! And

1

Pamphlet written by Maria W. Stewart (misspelled here as Steward) published in Boston, 1831. Courtesy of the Trustees of the Boston Public Library / Rare Books.

well as men into the South to teach and to spread their faith. The conceit of racial as well as class superiority shaped this mission work, with the imperative to spread a version of Christianity that could counter the supposedly primitive, overly expressive, and emotional religiosity of the southern African Americans.[25] Spelman College, founded in 1881, shared with some earlier missionary institutions a residential approach to shaping character, as it sought to mold African American women leaders who could, it was hoped, in turn help to civilize the mass of southern African Americans. As Derek Chang argues, Baptist missionaries figured African Americans, as well as Chinese immigrants on the West Coast, as foreigners within the nation's boundaries through discourses of domesticity and gendered respectability. At the same time, Chang also emphasizes that Baptist missions provided crucial alliances and institutional resources, which were then taken up by African Americans and, on the West Coast, by Chinese immigrants.

Spelman Seminary, 1884. Courtesy of Spelman College Archives.

These considerations help to situate the scene of action for African American women missionaries as they set off for African mission fields in the late nineteenth century. Sylvia Jacobs highlights the sense of "duty to their ancestral homeland" that motivated such women as Nora Gordon, Clara Howard, and Lulu Fleming, two graduates of Spelman and one of Shaw University, to take up mission work in the Congo Free State. U.S. racism shaped their perceptions of Africa, as they viewed Congolese women's agricultural work through the lens of African American experiences with slavery, and the onslaught of European colonial settlement with their own experiences of Jim Crow in mind. Clara Howard served up a healthy portion of criticism for European colonialism, and Jacobs points out that "although they often went to Africa with the same negative images and stereotypes as whites about the continent and its people, as they worked among Congolese women and children, African American women came to identify personally with the people among whom they were working." Still, Jacobs emphasizes the essential accuracy of African perceptions of U.S. missionaries as fundamentally allied with European colonialism in their common desire to destroy African ways of life. Ironically, it was in service to the goal of challenging racism at home, Jacobs points out, that such women "endorsed the Western image of Africa as a dark continent in need of the civilizing effects of Christianity."

Where missions operated in conjunction with the U.S. government, whether with Native Americans within U.S. borders or overseas, the institutional apparatus of the colonial state was integral to the unfolding of women's public agency, even as distinct cultural patterns also shaped their relation to racism. Betty Ann Bergland's account of Norwegian Lutheran women in the early twentieth-century Bethany Indian Mission, operated by the Bureau of Indian Affairs from 1900 to 1917, offers us a picture of sisterhood as a goal of women's missionary work that served diverse institutional ends in the context of sectarian conflict and collaboration with Washington. Projecting a maternalist presence, the women of the Bethany Indian Mission cast Indians as children, as they knitted themselves together across organizational divisions. This process culminated, it seems, in 1917, when the three North American Lutheran synods united and reassumed control of the mission from the federal government. In that same moment, women established a new level of collective power by taking responsibility for the mission's work.[26] While distinct cultural streams shaped the Bethany Indian Mission—for example, the Norwegian Lutheran notion of an obligation incurred by settlers, who understood themselves as receiving the gift of land from Native American peoples—Bergland shows that these immigrants embraced their new national identity and culture in part by taking on some of the main patterns of U.S. racism.

In the Philippines under U.S. occupation, white Protestant women sought to press forward their program to liberate women through Christianity, borrowing, as it were, the agency of the imperial state. Laura Prieto argues that missionary women sought to elevate and empower Filipinas "as women and Christians in their own image" as part of the imperial project of the U.S. colonial state, but that the structural context as well as "missionaries' own cultural bias" undermined their efforts. U.S. Protestant women leaned on the power of the state even as they sought to reform that state, as Ian Tyrrell explains.[27] Tyrrell argues that, in part through their collaboration with powerful men, women of the WCTU not only challenged colonial state policies with regard to alcohol and prostitution in the Philippines, but also laid the political groundwork for their eventual success in promoting prohibition at home. His point that Alfred Thayer Mahan, one of the architects of U.S. empire, sat on the Board of Missions underlines the affinity between women's missionary work and the work of empire, with their common emphasis on American moral righteousness and superiority. Tyrrell further suggests that the transnational moral crusading of the World's WCTU, "boring" as it did into the strongholds of the

British empire, established a model for deterritorialized forms of empire that the United States would come to embrace in the twentieth century.

I have emphasized the persistence of racism in patterns of subjective experience and agency and in the institutional forms that carried women's missionary programs forward as well as some of the ways in which such persistence arose out of a diverse array of circumstances.[28] At once paths to female empowerment and tools of oppression, these patterns served the ends of empire and exploitation. Yet as these essays demonstrate, deeply rooted social and cultural patterns came to be refracted through diverse encounters on the mission field. New contexts both challenged and reinforced the established mechanisms of U.S. cultural power and the ingrained forms of missionary endeavor, leading to a wide array of outcomes.

ENCOUNTERS ON THE MISSION FIELD

For U.S. Protestant women who ventured into mission fields, the scene of action inevitably shifted from the circumstances that enabled their choice to venture forth to encounters that would recast their perspectives and even their emotional investment in mission work. The essays presented here offer numerous examples of the ways in which racism and imperial convictions about the superiority of the United States could yield to more respectful attitudes and even loving relationships as missions "foster[ed] sustained interracial, intercultural contact," in Derek Chang's words. They show, too, that mission work could be co-opted irrespective of missionaries' attitudes and perspectives and that the already imperial contexts in which U.S. women labored could reinforce their racism.

At times, missionaries would be made to confront contradictions in their own beliefs. In the case of the Brethren in Christ mission in southern Africa, led by H. Frances Davidson in the years surrounding the beginning of the twentieth century, we learn from Wendy Urban-Mead that fictive kin language shared by missionaries and their Ndebele proselytes created a cultural bridge and that the ritual practice of the holy kiss led white missionaries to override a racially prescribed social distance from Africans, even as Davidson praised Cecil Rhodes's bravery, generosity, and enlightened imperial leadership. For a time, Davidson cultivated unusually close and respectful working relationships with a few Ndebele men and upheld the egalitarianism of the interracial holy kiss, until the formalization of colonial bureaucracy introduced modern, medical logics that articulated the danger of "contamination" by "racially different" bodies. And in the 1920s, U.S. Protestant women's "gestures of friendship with the New Woman of India were equivocal," Susan Haskell Khan points out, "and often contradictory" but critical nonetheless, particularly in light of their long-term role in "the emerging Protestant ecumenical movement," which helped to shape both U.S. influence abroad and "the early civil and human rights movements" in the United States. Yet they did not generate a language of friendship on their own; Indian nationalists pried them from notions of redemption and drove them to it.

In addition, the international and intercultural contexts of the mission field challenged missionary agendas and changed their outcomes even as missionary women persisted in their views. Nitobe Inazo and Yasui Tetsu in Japan; widowed Egyptian mothers of Lillian Trasher's orphans as well as heads of state in Egypt; Pandita Ramabai, Muthulakshmi Reddy as well as the poor and lower castes of Indian society; Evgeniya Kissimova in Bulgaria; Julia Sotto de Yapsutco in the Philippines, with her demands; poor women, nationalist leaders, and aspiring female doctors in China; Chinese men in Seattle; Pearl Archiquette in Wisconsin; and African Americans in the Baptist mission fields of the U.S. South all claimed the missionary enterprise for their own purposes, and the imprint of their perspectives and agendas at times succeeded in overriding missionary intentions.[29] Thus missionary women's very usefulness to others meant that their efforts were at times derailed, made to serve purposes other than their own or God's—as they imagined them.

The impact of the mission field on U.S. Protestant women's relation to racism and empire, whether they came to new perspectives through personal relationships or were pushed by members of their host societies to do so, suggests we might revisit an idea proposed by Emily Rosenberg. In "Rescuing Women and Children," Rosenberg identifies two traditions of international women's activism, two "historical imaginaries" that have been important in feminist international organizing. One involves stories of rescue that have, as we have seen, a long genealogy. The other arises out of twentieth-century traditions of transnational feminism. Yet this book suggests that their genealogies may be entwined. In the essays collected here, we can trace some of the forces that made possible the more respectful transnational coalitions to which Rosenberg refers as well as the deeply embedded fantasies of rescue that fueled the master narratives of American women's power and agency—and U.S. imperial fantasies more generally. In the possibility that these distinct approaches to international women's activism may have common origins, moreover, we can see a cautionary tale. For the line between the two approaches to the possibilities of women's liberation traces a narrow and treacherous path in a world shaped by racism and empire.

What, then, to make of all that doing? U.S. Protestant women's missionary action has trailed along with it a harsh history of imperial implication. Indeed, the very notion of industry, of doing, was and continues to be part of a colonial cast of mind. The role of industry as a personal value, as a tenet of faith, and as an aspect of U.S. nationalism offers an example of the way women's missionary endeavors could underwrite U.S. empire building. Industry was and continues to be a central and culturally specific value linked to the history of Protestant women. They elaborated the importance of this value, led in many ways by Catharine Beecher, through their focus on domesticity as the special realm of women's industriousness. In *Aloha Betrayed*, Noenoe Silva turns our attention to one of the first scenes of U.S. missionary women's endeavor and points out that the imposition of this value prepared the way for the transformation of the Hawaiian economy and the production of Hawaiian men as workers for sugar plantations. In Hawaii and elsewhere, moreover, missionaries cast nonwaged work as a form of slavery, the answer to which was the liberation available through not only Christianity but also waged labor.[30] Similarly, Derek Chang tells us that Baptists praised Chinese industriousness —perhaps not surprising given industrialists' interest in supporting Chinese immigration as a means to undermine what they perceived as the unreasonable and unruly demands of European American workers.[31] In both examples, inculcating the value of industry served to cultivate habits of mind and structures of feeling conducive to capitalist economic relations. Protestant missionary women worked to instill these values and to have them reinforced in domestic settings. At the same time, they carried their own commitment to industry as a badge of superiority. Women's industriousness was part and parcel of the culture of U.S. imperialism— part of a structure of meanings and feeling that served to underwrite the fitness of U.S. Americans (and sometimes specifically missionaries) to rule.

But neither the imperial origins of a disposition to act nor the damage it has wrought can account for its significance. For that, we must look also to the ways it has been broadly useful and to the challenges to imperial relations that it has made possible. In his forthcoming book, Derek Chang tells the story of Henry Martin Tupper, a white Baptist missionary whose dogged determination to act on behalf of African Americans in Raleigh, North Carolina, was rooted in his sense of himself as a white man as well as a Christian leader.[32] But faced with the opposition of entrenched white power in a region diving headlong into what Rayford Logan called the nadir of African American experience, Tupper held fast to his sense of his commitment to God. What one observer said of the minister holds as well for some of the U.S. Protestant women featured in this book: he was "a most forbidding New England type," for whom duty was primary, but, the observer went on, "the truth is that a less . . . determined people would be badgered almost to death and driven away."[33] The women featured here did not all hail from New England, but they inherited, in different ways, elements of the culture of sacrifice and benevolence cultivated in the New England diaspora of the Harriet Newells. They molded themselves in relation to a culturally particular and specifically gendered version of a dogged determination to act on behalf of others and in the name of God.[34] The essays here help us to appreciate the force and complexity of their determination and of the worlds that both molded and challenged it.

My concluding essay has traced some of the cultural and political patterns limned by the essays in this volume and by the literature to which it adds a crucial new chapter, patterns that illuminate the paths missionary women traveled on their way to championing the kingdom of God and the ways in which their actions came to bear fruit. These essays help us to grasp the interaction of personal faith with political circumstance and of intimate lives with the production of new spheres of public action that both animated and troubled the cultures of empire from the missionary dreams of the early U.S. republic to the challenges of international alliance and friendship in the interwar years of the twentieth century and beyond.

NOTES

1 Kathryn Kish Sklar, *Catharine Beecher: A Study in American Domesticity* (New York: Norton, 1973), 31–33, 38, 40.

2 Mary Lyon's grave is located on the campus of Mount Holyoke College in South Hadley, Massachusetts.

3 Patricia R. Hill, *The World Their Household: The American Woman's Foreign Mission Movement and Cultural Transformation, 1870–1920* (Ann Arbor: University of Michigan, 1985), 165–66.

4 Hill, *The World Their Household*, 161–62.

5 Dana Robert, *American Women in Mission: A Social History of Their Thought and Practice* (Macon, Ga.: Mercer University Press, 1997), 5. This was prompted, Robert explains, by the British Baptist missionary William Carey heading to India.

6 Catharine Beecher, *A Treatise on Domestic Economy* (Boston: Marsh, Capen, Lyon, and Webb, 1841), 144; Amy Kaplan, "Manifest Domesticity," *The Anarchy of Empire in the Making of U.S. Culture* (Cambridge, Mass.: Harvard University Press, 2002), 30.

7 Helen Lefkowitz Horowitz, *Alma Mater: Design and Experience in the Women's Colleges from their Nineteenth-Century Beginnings to the 1930s* (Boston: Beacon Press, 1984), 12; Robert, *American Women in Mission*, 100–101.

8 Quoted in Michael Goldberg, "Breaking New Ground, 1800–1848," *No Small Courage: A History of Women in the United States*, ed. Nancy Cott (New York: Oxford University Press, 2000), 216.

9 Robert, *American Women in Mission*, 185. Denominational differences as well as variation within denominations (and other factors) may have made more and less room for such refusals: Frances Davidson's extensive leadership role in the Brethren in Christ mission was supported by one male missionary leader but later cut short by another, as Wendy Urban-Mead discusses.

10 Hill, *The World Their Household*, 162.

11 Dana Robert, *American Women in Mission*, 112.

12 Regional differences in the United States, racial and cultural differences among the missionaries, and the political and cultural differences of host societies are also important.

13 Kaplan, *Anarchy of Empire*, 39–40; Hill, *The World Their Household*. The language of domesticity was widely deployed and not limited to those with conservative leanings.

14 Kaplan, *Anarchy of Empire*, 39–40. These quotations are from Kaplan's discussion of Sarah Josepha Hale, the author and editor of *Godey's Lady's Book*.

15 See also Laura Wexler, *Tender Violence: Domestic Visions in an Age of U.S. Imperialism* (Chapel Hill: University of North Carolina Press, 2000).

16 On this point, see also Lisa Joy Pruitt, *A Looking-Glass for Ladies: American Protestant Women and the Orient in the Nineteenth Century* (Macon, Ga.: Mercer University Press, 2005).

17 On "woman's work for woman," see Robert, *American Women in Mission*, 123, 130–88. See also Joan Jacobs Brumberg, "'Zenanas and Girlless Villages: The

Ethnology of American Evangelical Women, 1870–1910," *Journal of American History* 69, no. 2 (September 1982), 347–71.

18 Raymond Williams, *Marxism and Literature* (New York: Oxford University Press, 1977), 132.

19 Ibid., 132.

20 In this connection, see Nancy Marie Robertson, *Christian Sisterhood, Race Relations, and the YWCA, 1906–46* (Urbana: University of Illinois Press, 2007).

21 See Emily Rosenberg, "Rescuing Women and Children," *Journal of American History* 89, no. 2 (2002), 456–65, reprinted in *History and September 11th*, ed. Joanne Meyerowitz, 81–93 (Philadelphia: Temple University Press, 2003).

22 Robert, *American Women in Mission*, 130.

23 Maria Miller Stewart, "Religion and the Pure Principles of Morality, the Sure Foundation on Which We Must Build," *Words of Fire: An Anthology of African American Feminist Thought*, ed. Beverly Guy-Sheftall, 28–29 (New York: New Press, 1995).

24 Ibid., 28.

25 Evelyn Brooks Higginbotham, *Righteous Discontent: The Women's Movement in the Black Baptist Church, 1880–1920* (Cambridge, Mass.: Harvard University Press, 1993), 34.

26 While Bergland emphasizes the women's subordination, there is a suggestion of something else in the women's decision to marshal male power behind their own will.

27 See also Ian Tyrrell, *Woman's World, Woman's Empire: The Woman's Christian Temperance Union in International Perspective, 1880–1930* (Chapel Hill: University of North Carolina Press, 1991), 147.

28 I have necessarily glossed over many other circumstances, which sometimes pulled in different directions. For example, a growing cosmopolitanism combined with a reform agenda in the late nineteenth century and early twentieth to shape a less nationalist perspective than that which characterized earlier missionary views. In this spirit, notwithstanding her investment in racist hierarchies, Helen Montgomery indicated in 1912 that there was as yet no Christian nation on the face of the earth, a view she shared with Frances Willard. See Hill, *The World Their Household*, 137; Tyrrell, *Woman's World*, 13. See also Kristin L. Hoganson, *Consumer's Imperium: The Global Production of American Domesticity, 1865–1920* (Chapel Hill: University of North Carolina Press, 2007).

29 The examples cited here are drawn from essays in this volume by the following authors, in order: Kohiyama, Baron, Tyrrell, Haskell Khan, Reeves-Ellington, Prieto, Gronewold, Shemo, Chang, Bergland.

30 Noenoe Silva, *Aloha Betrayed: Native Hawaiian Resistance to American Colonialism* (Durham: Duke University Press, 2004), 49–54.

31 Derek Chang, *Converting Race, Transforming the Nation: Evangelical Christianity and the Problem of Difference in Late-Nineteenth Century America* (Philadelphia: University of Pennsylvania Press, forthcoming), Introduction.

32 Ibid., chap. 5.

33 Quoted ibid.

34 The culture of sacrifice and benevolence rewarded nineteenth-century U.S. women missionaries with an expanded scope of knowledge, experience, and action, as we have seen, and, at times, reinforced women's subordination to men. As the social and political character of women's lives changed over the course of that century and into the next, sacrifice persisted as a powerfully gendered trope that entailed both rewards and dangers for U.S. Protestant women.

Anagol, Padma. "Indian Christian Women and Indigenous Feminism, c. 1850–c. 1920." *Gender and Imperialism*, ed. Clare Midgely, 79–103. Manchester: Manchester University Press, 1998.

Barlow, Tani, ed. *Gender Politics in Modern China*. Durham: Duke University Press, 1993.

Baron, Beth. "Women's Voluntary Social Welfare Organizations in Egypt." *Gender, Religion and Change in the Middle East: Two Hundred Years of History*, ed. Inger Marie Okkenhaug and Ingvild Flaskerud, 85–102. New York: Berg, 2005.

Bays, Daniel H., and Grant Wacker. *The Foreign Missionary Enterprise at Home: Explorations in North American Cultural History*. Tuscaloosa: University of Alabama Press, 2003.

Beaver, Pierce R. *All Loves Excelling: American Women in World Mission*. Grand Rapids: Eerdmans, 1968.

———. *American Protestant Women in World Mission: A History of the First Feminist Movement in North America*. Grand Rapids: Eerdmans, 1980.

Bederman, Gail. *Manliness and Civilization: A Cultural History of Gender and Race in the United States, 1880–1917*. Chicago: University of Chicago Press, 1995.

Bender, Thomas, ed. *Rethinking American History in a Global Age*. Berkeley: University of California Press, 2002.

Bowie, Fiona, Deborah Kirkwood, and Shirley Ardener, eds. *Women and Missions, Past and Present: Historical and Anthropological Perspectives*. Oxford: Oxford University Press, 1993.

Brouwer, Ruth Compton. *Modern Women, Modernizing Men: The Changing Missions of Three Professional Women in Asia and Africa, 1902–69*. Vancouver: UBC Press, 2002.

Brumberg, Joan Jacobs. *Mission for Life: The Judson Family and American Evangelical Culture.* New York: New York University Press, 1984.

——. " 'Zenanas and Girlless Villages': The Ethnology of American Evangelical Women, 1870–1910." *Journal of American History* 69, no. 2 (September 1982), 347–71.

Burton, Antoinette. *At the Heart of the Empire:Indians and the Colonial Encounter in Late-Victorian Britain.* New Delhi:University of California Press, 1998.

——. *Burdens of History: British Feminists, Indian Women, and Imperial Culture, 1865–1915.* Chapel Hill: University of North Carolina Press, 1994.

Campbell, James T. *Songs of Zion: The African Methodist Episcopal Church in the United States and South Africa.* Chapel Hill: University of North Carolina Press, 1998.

Carpenter, Joel, ed. *Earthen Vessels: American Evangelicals and Foreign Missions 1880–1980.* Grand Rapids: Eerdmans, 1990.

Chin, Carol. "Beneficent Imperialists: American Women Missionaries in China at the Turn of the Twentieth Century." *Diplomatic History* 27, no. 3 (2003), 327–52.

Clymer, Kenton J. *Protestant Missionaries in the Philippines, 1898–1916: An Inquiry into the American Colonial Mentality.* Urbana: University of Illinois Press, 1986.

Comaroff, Jean, and John Comaroff. *Of Revelation and Revolution: Christianity, Colonialism, and Consciousness in South Africa.* Chicago: University of Chicago Press, 1991.

Cooper, Frederick, and Ann Laura Stoler, eds. *Tensions of Empire: Colonial Cultures in a Bourgeois World.* Berkeley: University of California Press, 1997.

Cox, Jeffrey. *Imperial Fault Lines: Christianity and Colonial Power in India, 1818–1940.* Stanford: Stanford University Press, 2002.

Deichmann, Wendy J. "Domesticity with a Difference: Woman's Sphere, Women's Leadership, and the Founding of the Baptist Missionary Training School in Chicago, 1881." *American Baptist Quarterly* 9, no. 3 (1990), 141–57.

Dunch, Ryan. "Beyond Cultural Imperialism: Cultural Theory, Christian Missions, and Global Modernity." *History and Theory* 41 (2002), 301–25.

Flemming, Leslie A. "New Models, New Roles: U.S. Presbyterian Women Missionaries and Social Change in North India, 1870–1910." *Women's Work for Women: Missionaries and Social Change in Asia,* ed. Leslie A. Flemming, 35–57. Boulder: Westview Press, 1989.

Freedman, Estelle. "Separatism as Strategy: Female Institution Building and American Feminism, 1870–1930." *Feminist Studies* 5, no. 3 (1979), 512–29.

Gilmore, Glenda Elizabeth. *Gender and Jim Crow: Women and the Politics of White Supremacy in North Carolina, 1896–1920.* Chapel Hill: University of North Carolina Press, 1996.

Gilroy, Paul. *"There Ain't No Black in the Union Jack": The Cultural Politics of Race and Nation.* Chicago: University of Chicago Press, 1997.

Go, Julian, and Anne L. Foster. *The American Colonial State in the Philippines: Global Perspectives.* Durham: Duke University Press, 2003.

Grimshaw, Patricia. "Faith, Missionary Life, and the Family." *Gender and Empire*, ed. Philippa Levine, 260–80. Oxford: Oxford University Press, 2004.

——. *Paths of Duty: American Missionary Wives in Nineteenth-Century Hawaii.* Honolulu: University of Hawaii Press, 1989.

Haggis, Jane. "White Women and Colonialism: Towards a Non-Recuperative History." *Gender and Imperialism*, ed. Clare Midgely, 45–75. Manchester: Manchester University Press, 1998.

Hall, Catherine. *Civilizing Subjects: Metropole and Colony in the English Imagination, 1830–1867.* Chicago: University of Chicago Press, 2002.

Hardt, Michael, and Antonio Negri. *Empire.* Cambridge, Mass.: Harvard University Press, 2000.

Harris, Paul. *Nothing But Christ: Rufus Anderson and the Ideology of Protestant Foreign Missions.* New York: Oxford University Press, 1999.

——. "Cultural Imperialism and American Protestant Missionaries: Collaboration and Dependency in Mid-Nineteenth Century China." *Pacific Historical Review* 40, no. 3 (1991), 309–38.

Hawley, John, ed. *Fundamentalism and Gender.* New York: Oxford Press, 1994.

Hietala, Thomas R. *Manifest Design: American Exceptionalism and Empire.* Rev. ed. Ithaca: Cornell University Press, 1985.

Higginbotham, Evelyn Brooks. *Righteous Discontent: The Women's Movement in the Black Baptist Church, 1880–1920.* Cambridge, Mass.: Harvard University Press, 1993.

Hill, Patricia. *The World Their Household: The American Woman's Foreign Mission Movement and Cultural Transformation, 1870–1920.* Ann Arbor: University of Michigan Press, 1985.

Hoganson, Kristin L. *Consumer's Imperium: The Global Production of American Domesticity, 1865–1920.* Chapel Hill: University of North Carolina Press, 2007.

——. *Fighting for American Manhood: How Gender Politics Provoked the Spanish–American and Philippine–American Wars.* New Haven: Yale University Press, 1998.

Horowitz, Helen Lefkowitz. *Alma Mater: Design and Experience in the Women's Colleges from Their Nineteenth-Century Beginnings to the 1930s.* Boston: Beacon Press, 1984.

Hsu, Madeline Y. *Dreaming of Gold, Dreaming of Home: Transnationalism and Migration between the United States and South China, 1882–1943.* Stanford: Stanford University Press, 2000.

Huber, Mary Taylor, and Nancy C. Lutkehaus, eds. *Gendered Missions: Women and Men in Missionary Discourse and Practice.* Ann Arbor: University of Michigan Press, 1999.

Hunter, Jane. *The Gospel of Gentility: American Women Missionaries in Turn-of-the-Century China.* New Haven: Yale University Press, 1984.

Hutchison, William R. *Errand to the World: American Protestant Thought and Foreign Missions.* Chicago: University of Chicago Press, 1987.

Jacobs, Sylvia M, ed. *Black Americans and the Missionary Movement in Africa.* Westport, Conn.: Greenwood Press, 1982.

Jacobson, Matthew Frye. *Barbarian Virtues: The United States Encounters Foreign Peoples at Home and Abroad, 1876–1917.* New York: Hill and Wang, 2000.

Jayawardena, Kumari. *The Other White Woman's Burden: Western Women and South Asia During British Colonial Rule.* New York: Routledge, 1995.

Kaplan, Amy. "Manifest Domesticity." *American Literature* 70, no. 3 (1998), 581–606.

———. *The Anarchy of Empire in the Making of U.S. Culture.* Cambridge, Mass.: Harvard University Press, 2002.

Kohiyama, Rui. *Amerika Fujin Senkyoshi.* Tokyo: University of Tokyo Press, 1992.

Kramer, Paul. "Empires and Exceptions: Race and Rule between the British and United States Empires, 1880–1910." *Journal of American History* 88 (March 2002), 1314–53.

———. *The Blood of Government: Race, Empire, the United States, and the Philippines.* Chapel Hill: University of North Carolina Press, 2006.

Kwok, Pui-lan. *Chinese Women and Christianity, 1860–1927.* Atlanta: Scholars Press, 1992.

Lian, Xi. *The Conversion of Missionaries: Liberalism in American Protestant Missions in China, 1907–1932.* University Park: Pennsylvania State University Press, 1997.

Little, Lawrence S. *Disciples of Liberty: The African Methodist Episcopal Church in the Age of Imperialism, 1884–1916.* Knoxville: University of Tennessee Press, 2000.

Lodwick, Kathleen. *Educating the Women of Hainan: The Career of Margaret Moninger in China, 1915–1942.* Lexington: University of Kentucky Press, 1995.

Love, Eric. *Race Over Empire: Racism and U.S. Imperialism, 1865–1900.* Chapel Hill: University of North Carolina Press, 2004.

Mani, Lata. *Contentious Traditions: The Debate on Sati in Colonial India.* Berkeley: University of California Press, 1998.

Martin, Sandy D. *Black Baptists and African Missions: The Origins of a Movement, 1880–1915.* Macon, Ga.: Mercer University Press, 1989.

McClintock, Anne. *Imperial Leather: Race, Gender and Sexuality in the Colonial Contest.* New York: Routledge, 1995.

Morgan, Francesca. *Women and Patriotism in Jim Crow America.* Chapel Hill: University of North Carolina Press, 2005.

Pascoe, Peggy. "Gender Systems in Conflict: The Marriages of Mission-Educated Chinese American Women, 1874–1939." *Unequal Sisters: A Multicultural Reader in U.S. Women's History,* ed. Vicki L. Ruiz and Ellen Carol DuBois, 139–56. New York: Routledge, 1994.

———. *Relations of Rescue: The Search for Female Moral Authority in the American West, 1874–1939.* New York: Oxford University Press, 1990.

Porterfield, Amanda. *Mary Lyon and the Mount Holyoke Missionaries.* New York: Oxford University Press, 1997.

Pratt, Mary Louise. *Imperial Eyes: Travel Writing and Transculturation.* New York: Routledge, 1992.

Pruitt, Lisa Joy. *A Looking-Glass for Ladies: American Protestant Women and the Orient in the Nineteenth Century*. Macon, Ga.: Mercer University Press, 2005.

Reeves-Ellington, Barbara. "A Vision of Mount Holyoke in the Ottoman Balkans: American Cultural Transfer, Bulgarian Nation-Building and Women's Educational Reform, 1858–1870." *Gender and History* 16, no. 1 (2004), 146–71.

Robert, Dana Lee. *American Women in Mission: A Social History of Their Thought and Practice, The Modern Mission Era, 1792–1992*. Macon, Ga.: Mercer University Press, 1996.

Robertson, Nancy Marie. *Christian Sisterhood, Race Relations, and the YWCA, 1906–46*. Urbana: University of Illinois Press, 2007.

Roediger, David R. *Colored White: Transcending the Racial Past*. Berkeley: University of California Press, 2002.

Rosenberg, Emily. "Rescuing Women and Children." *History and September 11th*, ed. Joanne Meyerowitz, 81–93. Philadelphia: Temple University Press, 2003.

——. "Gender." *Journal of American History* 77, no. 1 (1990), 116–24.

——. *Spreading the American Dream: American Economic and Cultural Expansion, 1890–1945*. New York: Hill and Wang, 1982.

Ruiz, Vicki L. "Dead Ends or Gold Mines? Using Missionary Records in Mexican American Women's History." *Unequal Sisters: A Multicultural Reader in U.S. Women's History*, ed. Vicki L. Ruiz and Ellen Carol DuBois, 298–315. New York: Routledge, 1994.

Schlesinger, Arthur Jr. "The Missionary Enterprise and Theories of Imperialism." *The Missionary Enterprise in China and America*, ed. John Fairbank, 366–73. Cambridge, Mass.: Harvard University Press, 1974.

Seat, Karen. *"Providence Has Freed Our Hands": Women's Missions and the American Encounter with Japan*. Syracuse: Syracuse University Press, 2008.

Semple, Rhonda Anne. *Missionary Women: Gender, Professionalism and the Victorian Idea of Christian Mission*. Suffolk, UK: Boydell Press, 2003.

Sharkey, Heather J. *American Evangelicals in Egypt: Presbyterian Missionaries and Muslim–Christian Encounters in an Age of Empire*. Princeton: Princeton University Press, 2008.

Silva, Noenoe. *Aloha Betrayed: Native Hawaiian Resistance to American Colonialism*. Durham: Duke University Press, 2004.

Singh, Maina Chawla. *Gender, Religion, and "Heathen Lands": American Missionary Women in South Asia, 1860s–1940s*. New York: Garland, 2000.

Sinha, Mrinalini. "Gender in the Critiques of Colonialism and Nationalism: Locating the 'Indian Woman.'" *Feminism and History*, ed. Joan Wallach Scott, 477–503. New York: Oxford University Press, 1996.

——. *Specters of Mother India: The Global Restructuring of an Empire*. Durham: Duke University Press, 2006.

Sklar, Kathryn Kish. *Catharine Beecher: A Study in American Domesticity*. New York: W. W. Norton, 1971.

Snow, Jennifer. *Protestant Missionaries, Asian Immigrants, and Ideologies of Race in America*. New York: Routledge, 2007.

Stoler, Ann Laura. *Carnal Knowledge and Imperial Power: Race and the Intimate in Colonial Rule*. Berkeley: University of California Press, 2002.

——, ed. *Haunted by Empire: Geographies of Intimacy in North American History*. Durham: Duke University Press, 2006.

Tomlinson, John. *Cultural Imperialism: A Critical Introduction*. Baltimore: Johns Hopkins University Press, 1991.

Tyrrell, Ian R. "Making Nations/Making States: American Historians in the Context of Empire." *Journal of American History* 86, no. 3 (1999), 1015–44.

——. *Woman's World/Woman's Empire: The Woman's Christian Temperance Union in International Perspective, 1800–1930*. Chapel Hill: University of North Carolina Press, 1991.

Urban-Mead, Wendy. "Girls of the Gate: Questions of Purity and Piety at Mtshabezi Girls' Primary Boarding School, 1908–1940." *Le Fait Missionaire*, no. 11 (September 2001), 75–99.

Van der Veer, Peter. *Conversion to Modernities: The Globalization of Christianity*. New York: Routledge, 1996.

Westerkamp, Marilyn J. *Women and Religion in Early America, 1600–1850: The Puritan and Evangelical Traditions*. New York: Routledge, 1999.

Wexler, Laura. *Tender Violence: Domestic Visions in an Age of U.S. Imperialism*. Chapel Hill: University of North Carolina Press, 2000.

Williams, Walter. *Black Americans and the Evangelization of Africa, 1877–1900*. Madison: University of Wisconsin Press, 1982.

Yohn, Susan. *A Contest of Faiths: Missionary Women and Pluralism in the American Southwest*. Ithaca: Cornell University Press, 1995.

Zaccarini, Cristina. *The Sino-American Friendship as Tradition and Challenge: Dr. Ailie Gale in China, 1908–1950*. Bethlehem, Pa.: Lehigh University Press, 2001.

Zwiep, Mary. *Pilgrim Path: The First Company of Women Missionaries to Hawaii*. Madison: University of Wisconsin Press, 1991.

CONTRIBUTORS

BETH BARON is a professor of Middle Eastern history at the City College and Graduate Center, City University of New York. She is a co-editor of *Women in Middle Eastern History: Shifting Boundaries in Sex and Gender* (1991), the author of *The Women's Awakening in Egypt: Culture, Society, and the Press* (1994) and *Egypt as a Woman: Nationalism, Gender, and Politics* (2005), and cofounder and current editor of the *International Journal of Middle East Studies*.

BETTY ANN BERGLAND is a professor of U.S. history in the History and Philosophy Department at the University of Wisconsin, River Falls.Her publications on gender, ethnicity, immigration, and race in American culture and history appear in various journals, edited volumes, and encyclopedias. She is completing a book that examines relations between immigrants and indigenous peoples in the Upper Midwest during the nineteenth century and twentieth. She is the co-editor of a forthcoming book, *Gendering Norwegian American History*.

MARY KUPIEC CAYTON is a professor of history and American studies at Miami University in Ohio. She is the author of *Emerson's Emergence: Self and Society in the Transformation of New England, 1800–1845* (1989) and a co-editor of two prize-winning reference works, *The Encyclopedia of American Social History* (1993) and *The Encyclopedia of American Cultural and Intellectual History* (2001).

DEREK CHANG is an associate professor of history and Asian American studies at Cornell University. He is the author of " 'Marked in Body, Mind, and Spirit': Home Missionaries and the Remaking of Race and Nation," in *Race, Nation, and Religion in the Americas* (2004), edited by Henry Goldschmidt and Elizabeth McAlister. His book *Citizens of a Christian Nation: Evangelical Missions and the Problem of Race in Nineteenth-Century America* will be published in 2010 by the University of Pennsylvania Press.

SUE GRONEWOLD is an associate professor and the chair of the History Department at Kean University, Union, N.J. She is the author of *Beautiful Merchandise: Prostitution in China 1860–1937* (1982) and "Exile and Identity: The Door of Hope in Taiwan, 1955–75," in *Women in Modern Taiwan*, edited by Murray Rubinstein (2003). She is completing a book entitled "Encountering Hope: The Door of Hope Mission in Shanghai and Taipei."

JANE H. HUNTER is a professor of history and an associate dean of the College at Lewis and Clark College, Portland, Oregon. She is the author of *The Gospel of Gentility: American Women Missionaries in Turn-of-the-Century China* (1984) and *How Young Ladies Became Girls: The Victorian Origins of Girlhood in the United States* (2002).

SYLVIA M. JACOBS is a professor of history at North Carolina Central University. She is the author of *The African Nexus: Black American Perspectives on the European Partitioning of Africa, 1880–1920* (1981), the editor of *Black Americans and the Missionary Movement in Africa* (1982), and a co-editor of *The Encyclopedia of African-American Education* (1986).

SUSAN HASKELL KHAN recently received a doctor of philosophy degree in history from the University of California, Berkeley. She is currently working on a book on the history of American Protestant missionaries in India.

RUI KOHIYAMA is a professor of American and gender studies at Tokyo Woman's Christian University in Japan. She is the author of *As Our God Alone Will Lead Us: The Nineteenth-Century American Women's Foreign Missionary Enterprise and Its Encounter with Meiji Japan* (1992). She is completing a book on the decline of the American women's missionary enterprise in the twentieth century within the context of increasing tensions arising from modernity and international conflicts.

LAURA R. PRIETO is an associate professor of history and of women's and gender studies at Simmons College, Boston. She is the author of *At Home in the Studio: The Professionalization of Women Artists in America* (2001). She is completing a survey entitled *Women in America: Issues and Controversies* for Facts on File as well as a book on American womanhood and imperialism during the era of the Spanish-American War.

BARBARA REEVES-ELLINGTON is an associate professor of U.S. history at Siena College, Loudonville, New York. She is the author of "A Vision of Mount Holyoke in the Ottoman Balkans" (*Gender and History*, 2004) and "Gender, Conversion, and

Social Transformation," in *Converting Cultures: Religion, Ideology, and Transformations of Identity* (2007), edited by Kevin Reinhart and Dennis Washburn.

MARY A. RENDA is an associate professor of history and chair of the Department of Gender Studies at Mount Holyoke College. She is the award-winning author of *Taking Haiti: Military Occupation and the Culture of U.S. Imperialism, 1915–1940* (2001). Her work tracks the imprint of racism and gender in the history of U.S. imperialism and anti-imperialism, and her essay "Practical Sovereignty: The Caribbean Region and the Rise of U.S. Empire" appears in *The Blackwell Companion to Latin American History*, edited by Thomas Holloway (2007).

CONNIE A. SHEMO is an assistant professor of history at the State University of New York, Plattsburgh. She is the author of " 'How Better Could She Serve Her Country?': Cultural Translators, U.S. Women's History, and Kang Cheng's Amazons in Cathay," *Journal of Women's History* (winter 2009) and " 'To Develop Native Powers': Shi Meiyu and the Danforth Memorial Hospital Nursing School, 1903–1920," *Gender and Christianity, Early Chinese Christian Women*, edited by Jessie Lutz (forthcoming). She is completing a book entitled "An Army of Women: The Medical Ministries of Kang Cheng and Shi Meiyu, 1896–1937."

KATHRYN KISH SKLAR is Distinguished Professor of History at the State University of New York, Binghamton. She is the author of *Catharine Beecher: A Study in American Domesticity* (1973) and *Florence Kelley and the Nation's Work: The Rise of Women's Political Culture, 1830–1900* (1995), the co-author of *Social Justice Feminists in the United States and Germany: A Dialogue in Documents, 1885–1933* (1998), and the author of other books and articles on women and social movements. She co-directs the Website and online journal *Women and Social Movements in the U.S., 1600–2000*.

IAN TYRRELL is Scientia Professor, School of History and Philosophy, University of New South Wales, Sydney, Australia. He is the author of seven books, including *Sobering Up: From Temperance to Prohibition in Antebellum America, 1800–1860* (1979); *Woman's World / Woman's Empire: The Woman's Christian Temperance Union in International Perspective* (1991); and *Transnational Nation: United States History in Global Perspective since 1789* (2007); and is a former editor of the *Australasian Journal of American Studies*.

WENDY URBAN-MEAD is a member of the faculty in the Master of Arts in Teaching Program at Bard College. She is a co-editor of *Social Sciences and Missions* (Brill) and the author of "Dynastic Daughters," in *Women in African Colonial Histories* (2002), edited by Jean Allman, Susan Geiger, and Nakanyike Musisi.

BARBARA REEVES-ELLINGTON is an associate professor of U.S. history at Siena College, Loudonville, New York.

KATHRYN KISH SKLAR is Distinguished Professor of History at the State University of New York, Binghamton.

CONNIE A. SHEMO is an assistant professor of history at the State University of New York, Plattsburgh.

Library of Congress Cataloging-in-Publication Data

Competing kingdoms : women, mission, nation,
and the American Protestant empire, 1812–1960 /
edited by Barbara Reeves-Ellington, Kathryn Kish Sklar,
and Connie A. Shemo.
p. cm. — (American encounters/global interactions)
Includes bibliographical references and index.
ISBN 978-0-8223-4658-6 (cloth : alk. paper)
ISBN 978-0-8223-4650-0 (pbk. : alk. paper)
1. Women in missionary work—United States—History—19th century.
2. Women in missionary work—United States—History—20th century.
3. Protestant churches—Missions—History—19th century.
4. Protestant churches—Missions—History—20th century.
5. Protestant churches—United States—History—19th century.
6. Protestant churches—United States—History—20th century.
7. United States—Foreign relations—19th century.
8. United States—Foreign relations—20th century.
I. Reeves-Ellington, Barbara.
II. Sklar, Kathryn Kish.
III. Shemo, Connie Anne.
IV. Series: American encounters/global interactions.
BV2610.C665 2010   266'.023730082—dc22
2009041171

WN ÷ 30 = .85